Classroom Companion: Business

The Classroom Companion series in Business features foundational and introductory books aimed at students to learn the core concepts, fundamental methods, theories and tools of the subject. The books offer a firm foundation for students preparing to move towards advanced learning. Each book follows a clear didactic structure and presents easy adoption opportunities for lecturers.

More information about this series at http://www.springer.com/series/16374

Harald Øverby · Jan Arild Audestad

Introduction to Digital Economics

Foundations, Business Models and Case Studies

Second Edition

Harald Øverby
Norwegian University of Science
and Technology
Gjøvik
Norway

Jan Arild Audestad
Norwegian University of Science
and Technology
Gjøvik
Norway

Originally published by Create Space Independent, Scotts Valley, CA, USA, in 2018 with ISBN 978-1986751391

ISSN 2662-2866   ISSN 2662-2874 (electronic)
Classroom Companion: Business
ISBN 978-3-030-78236-8   ISBN 978-3-030-78237-5 (eBook)
https://doi.org/10.1007/978-3-030-78237-5

© The Editor(s) (if applicable) and The Author(s), under exclusive license to Springer Nature Switzerland AG 2021

This work is subject to copyright. All rights are solely and exclusively licensed by the Publisher, whether the whole or part of the material is concerned, specifically the rights of translation, reprinting, reuse of illustrations, recitation, broadcasting, reproduction on microfilms or in any other physical way, and transmission or information storage and retrieval, electronic adaptation, computer software, or by similar or dissimilar methodology now known or hereafter developed.

The use of general descriptive names, registered names, trademarks, service marks, etc. in this publication does not imply, even in the absence of a specific statement, that such names are exempt from the relevant protective laws and regulations and therefore free for general use.

The publisher, the authors, and the editors are safe to assume that the advice and information in this book are believed to be true and accurate at the date of publication. Neither the publisher nor the authors or the editors give a warranty, expressed or implied, with respect to the material contained herein or for any errors or omissions that may have been made. The publisher remains neutral with regard to jurisdictional claims in published maps and institutional affiliations.

This Springer imprint is published by the registered company Springer Nature Switzerland AG
The registered company address is: Gewerbestrasse 11, 6330 Cham, Switzerland

To Janny and Synnøve

Foreword

It is my great pleasure to introduce this important book. While the impacts of digital technologies are growing with far-reaching magnitudes, the academic field of digital economics is still in its inception and definition phases, with even fewer textbooks. This book fills an important void by bringing together theories from economics, management science, system dynamics, and business modelling to provide overview and structure to this emerging field. The book will be useful both for graduate and under-graduate courses, and for researchers who wish to have a salient overview and introduction.

The book has a clear pedagogical structure and flow, where each chapter features abstract, learning objectives, definitions, logical partition with sub-headings, theory presentations, cases, boxes, and concluding set of Q&A. With this lay-out, the book is immediately appealing for parsing and selection of chapters that seem more interesting. The order between chapters is also clear, one building upon each other, starting with the technologies, and moving step by step into more and more sophisticated topics. Toward the end, there are chapters with quite advanced mathematical modelling, together with some specific application areas such as big data and network neutrality. The final chapter provides an overview of digital regulation, as a final integrating chapter that brings to bear many of the economic analysis tools presented earlier.

While organizing and summarizing theories of relevance for the topic, the book also has some important intellectual contributions and perspectives. Among others, the book emphasizes the integration of Porter's strategy framework with the value network perspective which serves to integrate both traditional strategy analysis with new theories relating to value creation in digital networks. Moreover, the integration of the multi-sided platform theories with the value network theory and network effects is an important way forward to operationalize the multi-sided platform theory further. The authors have developed a set of excellent illustrations to further illustrate the importance of the various relations between multi-sided platforms with other theories and constructs. The book also provides a helpful historical context by referring the readers to origins and authors of important concepts, such as ecosystems and path dependencies, and by so doing providing teasers for further reading.

In summary, the book provides an integrated overview of a field of increasing importance and has done so in a very pedagogical fashion. The book should be a welcome contribution for courses in strategy, business, and digital economics. The book is suitable for both undergraduate and graduate level engineering students, taking advantage of the advanced mathematical modelling.

I give this book my heartfelt recommendation and invite the reader to enjoy this tour of digital economics, in the company of two experts and enthusiastic guides!

Erik Bohlin
Editor-in-Chief, Telecommunications Policy
Professor in Technology Assessment
Department of Technology Management & Economics
Chalmers University of Technology
Göteborg, Sweden
April 14, 2021

Preface

This book is an introduction to digital economics. It is highly cross-disciplinary and draws upon knowledge from several academic disciplines such as telecommunications, computer science, management science, business modeling, economics, and mathematics to explain the digital economy. To fully comprehend digital economics, it is important to understand how the information and communication technology (ICT) is underpinning all digital businesses.

The six biggest companies by capitalization (by 2021) are all major stakeholders in the digital economy. The digital economy can no longer be ignored as an oddity in economy theory. On the contrary, the economics of digital goods and services has become a key element in the understanding of how the world economy works.

Several topics covered by this book are included in the curricula taught at several business and economics schools around the world. This book is unique as it approaches topics in digital economics from a technology point of view. We believe that this is essential since digital economics is a result of the evolution of information and communications technologies, and not vice versa.

The field of digital economics is complex and cannot be fully understood using theories from traditional micro-economics alone. It is necessary to adopt existing theories using knowledge from system dynamics, management science, and business modelling.

We wrote this book to support the growing community of students and practitioners with textbook material that links the theoretical foundations of digital economics with practical examples and case studies.

Harald Øverby
Gjøvik, Norway

Jan A. Audestad
Gjøvik, Norway
May 2021

About this Book

This book is about *digital economics*—the branch of economics studying digital goods and services. Innovations and developments in information and communication technology (ICT) have laid the foundations for this branch of the economy. This includes technologies such as social media, apps, cloud computing, mass storage, data mining, cryptocurrencies, and sharing services. These services have already made deep imprints on today's business landscape. Both private businesses and the public sector embrace ICT to achieve cost benefits, efficiency, and competitive advantages. However, what we are witnessing is just the beginning of an economic revolution as the full potential of the digital economy is about to be harvested.

The major goal of this book is to provide a theoretical basis for digital economics and to show how these theories can be applied to the study of real-world economics and business phenomena. The book is cross-disciplinary, explaining how the interaction between markets and important innovations in telecommunications and information technology has shaped the digital economy. The field of digital economics is characterized by transient market behavior, feedback mechanisms, global markets, many stakeholders, and technology dependencies never seen in any markets before. The book highlights this complex ecosystem.

The book is written for advanced undergraduate courses in digital economy for students in computer science, economics, and management. To get the full benefits from the book, a student needs first courses in computer science, calculus, and economics. The book may also be of interest to a broad range of professionals, including economists, business consultants, managers, and computer scientists since it studies the impact several technological, social, and economic disciplines have on the evolution of the digital economy.

Each chapter may contain, in addition to the main body of the chapter, elements such as:
- *Learning goals are* at the beginning of the chapter.
- *Case studies* are real-world examples of digital products and markets.
- *Examples* are used to show concrete applications of the theoretical material not associated with a particular real-world case.
- *Boxes* contain supplementary material. In particular, mathematical derivations are contained in boxes to make the text more accessible.
- *Questions and answers* are included at the end of each chapter. The questions are not direct repetition of elements in the text but may require search for information in other sources, e.g., the web.
- *Further reading.* Some chapters contain references to books or articles providing deeper insight into the material presented in that chapter.

The book consists of 22 chapters. These chapters can be grouped into several themes:

- ▶ Chapter 1 is an introduction where the basic concepts of the digital economy is defined.
- The *technological evolution* of digital networks, goods, and services is the topic of ▶ Chaps. 2, 3, and 20. ▶ Chapter 2 shows the timeline of major inventions in the information and communication technology leading to the digital marketplace we see today. ▶ Chapter 3 shows how the communication network converges into a single network based on the Internet technology and, thus, replacing dedicated networks such as the telephone network. ▶ Chapter 20 contains supplementary material on the impact of the big data technology on the digital economy – big data is a core technology for several of the biggest companies in the digital economy. Technology is a side issue in almost all chapters since almost all aspects of the digital economy are intimately connected to the technology.
- *Key characteristics of the market* are identified in ▶ Chaps. 4, 5, 6, 7 and 18. ▶ Chapter 4 describes the ecosystem of digital markets, including the various stakeholders that shape the business landscape. This chapter also shows that the protocol structure of the Internet divides the digital businesses into two separate business categories: Internet service providers and application and content providers. This division is the key element behind the enormous innovation of digital applications since 2000. ▶ Chapter 6 is one of the most important chapters in the book since it defines the basic characteristics of digital goods and services and what makes them different from physical goods. The most important characteristic is that the marginal cost of digital products is zero, allowing companies to offer digital services free of charge and thereby generating a tremendous market for them. Combined with big data technology, these companies may then exploit the data they collect about their users to generate revenues from advertisements and other products. ▶ Chapter 5 describes how the telecommunications market evolved from de facto monopolies to full competition, and ▶ Chap. 7 outlines new production models for digital services enabled by the technological evolution. ▶ Chapter 18 contains supplementary mathematical models describing how these markets evolve as a function of time.
- Various *strategic issues* are contained in ▶ Chaps. 8, 9, 10, 11, 12, 13, 14, 15, and 16. ▶ Chapter 8 discusses how value is created in different businesses: chains producing physical goods, shops solving problems for clients, and networks acting as mediators between groups of clients. One particularly important strategic element is network effects, or positive feedback from the market. This is explained in ▶ Chap. 9. ▶ Chapter 10 about multisided platforms is an application of the theories of ▶ Chaps. 8 and 9. The other chapters in this groups are concerned with other strategic issues such as path dependence (11), lock-in (12), formation of monopolies and oligopolies (13), acquisitions and mergers (14), development of technical standards (15), and the long tail (16).
- ▶ Chapters 17 and 19 are about *business modeling*. ▶ Chapter 17 characterizes the digital markets as e-commerce markets, network access markets, and information services markets. ▶ Chapter 19 demonstrates, using several real-life

examples, the use of the business model canvas and the stakeholder relationship model as powerful tools for business planning and analysis.
- *Regulations* are the subject matter of ▶ Chaps. 21 and 22. ▶ Chapter 21 is about the complex political issue of net neutrality. Net neutrality implies non-discriminate access to and use of the Internet. In some countries, this is an obligatory regulation while not in other countries. ▶ Chapter 22 is about other types of regulations concerning provision and use of the communications infrastructure.

Contents

1	The Digital Economy	1
2	Information and Communication Technologies	17
3	Convergence of Technologies and Services	33
4	Digital Economy Ecosystem	45
5	Digital Market Evolution	61
6	Digital Goods and Services	73
7	Production Models	91
8	Value Creation Models and Competitive Strategy	103
9	Network Effects	123
10	Multisided Platforms	149
11	Path Dependence	165
12	Lock-In and Switching Costs	177
13	Digital Monopolies and Oligopolies	193
14	Mergers and Acquisitions	207
15	Standards	217
16	The Long Tail	231
17	Digital Markets	243
18	Digital Market Modeling	259
19	Digital Business Models	281

20	**Big Data Economics**	305
21	**Net Neutrality**	323
22	**Digital Regulation**	335
	Service Part	
	Index	349

About the Authors

Harald Øverby
(born 1979) is a professor at the Norwegian University of Science and Technology (NTNU). He received his M.Sc. in computer science in 2002, a B.Sc. in economics in 2003, and a Ph.D. in information and communication technology in 2005. Øverby has also studied law at the University of Oslo in Norway. Øverby has published over 90 papers in international journals and conferences in the areas of communication technology, digital economics, business modeling, data coding, and optical networking. He has taught and developed university courses in the areas of digital economics, business, and law since 2010. He was the Head of Department of Telematics (NTNU) from 2013 through 2016. Øverby is a 1998 International Chemistry Olympiad bronze medalist.

Jan A. Audestad
(born 1942) is professor emeritus at the Norwegian University of Science and Technology (NTNU). He received his M. Sc. in theoretical physics in 1965. He has more than 50 years of experience in telecommunications both from academia and as researcher, research manager, and techno-economic adviser to the top management of Telenor. As adjunct professor of NTNU, he has taught courses in telecommunications networks, distributed processing, mobile communication, digital economics, and information security. He was one of the key scientists behind standardization of maritime satellite systems in the 1970s, GSM mobile communications in the 1980s, and intelligent networks and distributed processing in the 1990s. He was part of the team reorganizing Telenor to meet full competition in all sectors of telecommunications from 1995 to 2009.

Abbreviations

3G	Third Generation Mobile System
4G	Fourth Generation Mobile System
5G	Fifth Generation Mobile Systems
ADSL	Asymmetric Digital Subscriber Line
ARPU	Average Revenue per User
ASP	Application Service Provider
B2B	Business to Business
B2C	Business to Consumer
BMC	Business Model Canvas
BPQ	Buyer-Player-Quitter
C2B	Consumer to Business
C2C	Consumer to Consumer
CBPP	Commons-Based Peer Production
CP	Content Provider
CPU	Central Processing Unit
DAB	Digital Audio Broadcasting
EDGE	Enhanced Data rates for GSM Evolution
EEA	European Economic Area
FinTech	Financial Technologies
FTTH	Fiber to the Home
GPRS	General Packet Radio Service
GSM	Global System for Mobile Communications
HTML	Hypertext Markup Language
HTTP	Hypertext Transfer Protocol
IaaS	Infrastructure-as-a-Service
ICT	Information and Communication Technology
IoT	Internet of Things
IP	Internet Protocol
ISP	Internet Service Provider
ITS	Intelligent Transport Systems
ITU	International Telecommunication Union
LTE	Long Term Evolution
M&A	Mergers & Acquisitions
MC	Marginal Cost

MMOG	Massive Multiplayer Online Game
MMS	Multimedia Messaging Service
MOOC	Massive Open Online Course
MSP	Multi-sided Platform
MVNO	Mobile Virtual Network Operator
NFV	Network Function Virtualization
NMT	Nordic Mobile Telephone
NP	Network Provider
O-T	Odlyzko-Tilly
OTT	Over-the-Top Services
PaaS	Platform-as-a-Service
PC	Personal Computer
PDF	Portable Document Format
PSTN	Public Switched Telephone Network
SaaS	Software-as-a-Service
SCTP	Stream Control Transmission Protocol
SDN	Software Defined Networking
SIR	Susceptible-Infectious-Recovered
SLA	Service Level Agreement
SMS	Short Message Service
SOA	Service Oriented Architecture
SRM	Stakeholder Relationship Model
TCP	Transmission Control Protocol
UDP	User Datagram Protocol
URL	Uniform Resource Locator
VCR	Videocassette Recorder
VHS	Video Home System
VNO	Virtual Network Operator
VoIP	Voice over IP
VoLTE	Voice over LTE
WoW	*World of Warcraft*
WWW	Word Wide Web
XaaS	Anything as a Service

The Digital Economy

Contents

1.1 Introduction – 2

1.2 Definitions – 3

1.3 Digitization of the Economy – 8

1.4 Digital Economics – 11

1.5 Conclusions – 14

References – 15

© The Author(s), under exclusive license to Springer Nature Switzerland AG 2021
H. Øverby, J. A. Audestad, *Introduction to Digital Economics*, Classroom Companion: Business,
https://doi.org/10.1007/978-3-030-78237-5_1

Learning Objectives

After completing this chapter, you should be able to:
- Understand the size and versatility of the digital economy.
- Explain how the adoption of Internet access and mobile telephony has enabled the digital economy.
- Understand what is meant by digitization of the economy and how it is related to digitization of communication networks and production and storage of digital information.

1.1 Introduction

Information and communication technology (ICT) is everywhere around us—the Internet, smartphones, laptops, wireless networks, apps, and online video services such as Netflix and HBO. ICT has become ubiquitous, at least in the developed world. The pace of innovation in ICT is fast, and new technologies are emerging every year. Over the last few decades, ICT has changed how we work, how we spend and invest our money, and how we conduct our business. Telecommunications, finance, and media are industries in which ICT has significantly changed the business landscape.

Spotify and other providers of online music services have radically changed the business models of the music industry, particularly, reducing revenue streams from CD retail. Since an increasing amount of music is traded online, the need for physical stores selling CDs has almost vanished. Worldwide sales of recorded music have decreased by 45% from 1999 to 2014. The year 2014 also marked the first year in which online traded music matched sales from physical formats such as CDs (Reid, 2015).

E-banking has radically changed how we—as consumers—approach banks and other financial institutions. Most activities involving personal finance are now conducted over the Internet using smartphones or personal computers. For active e-banking users, there is no need to visit a physical bank to pay bills. Loans can be negotiated with the bank over the Internet. Cash is no longer needed to pay for bus or train tickets, car parking, or taxis.

At many airports, passengers check in automatically, put their baggage on the baggage drop belt, and pass through the gate to the airplane without the involvement of ground personnel. All passenger services are completely automatic, except for the security control.

It is the increased use of digital goods and services, often as a replacement for physical goods and non-digital services, which is responsible for this evolution. In fact, digital goods and services are the essential building blocks of the digital economy. Even though digital goods and services have gradually changed the business world for some time already, we are just now seeing the beginning of an economic revolution as the full potential of the digital economy is about to be harvested.

1.2 Definitions

Definition 1.1
The *digital economy* is an economy based on information and communication technology (ICT).

The digital economy is based on information and communication technologies such as the Internet, smartphones, mobile and wireless networks, optical networks, Internet of Things (IoT), cloud storage and cloud computing, sharing services, apps, and cryptocurrencies. The size and impact of the digital economy are driven by people's adoption of these technologies.

◘ Figure 1.1 shows the share of households with access to the Internet for the period 2005–2019 (ITU statistics, 2018). In 2005, only 20% had access to the Internet. Fourteen years later, in 2019, about 60% of the world's population has access to the Internet. Over the last decade, access to the Internet has increased in all parts of the world. However, there are significant differences—a digital divide—in Internet adoption between countries and within countries. While about 85% of households in the developed has access to the Internet, less than 50% of

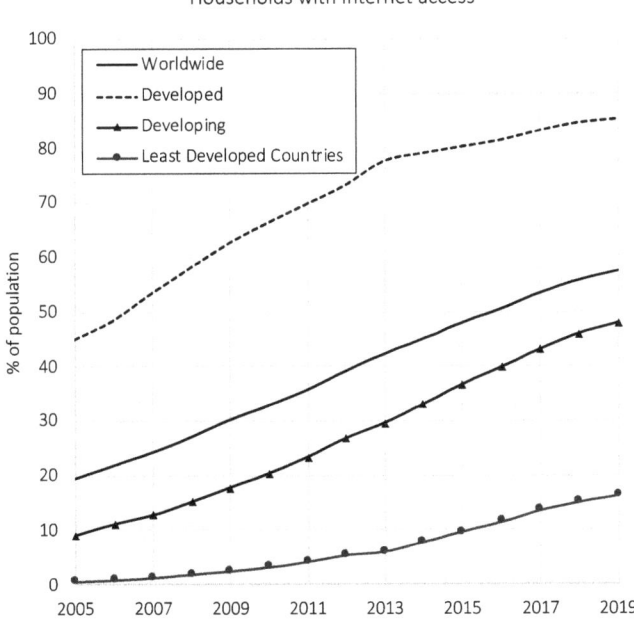

◘ **Fig. 1.1** Percentage of households with the Internet for the period 2005–2019. (Authors' own figure)

the households in the developing world has access to the Internet. A key question for the next decades is how to provide Internet access to the developing parts of the world.

An important evolution in the digital economy is the number of people using public narrowband and broadband mobile technologies. Cellular narrowband mobile systems (2G) offer global services such as telephony and SMS. Cellular broadband mobile systems (4G and 5G) support the use of smartphones to access the Internet. These technologies also support telephony and SMS, eventually phasing out the use of 2G and 3G systems. The number of users of public mobile networks has surpassed the number of people in the world—in 2020 there are 105 active mobile cellular subscriptions per 100 inhabitants in the world. The reasons for this are that many people have access to more than one device (e.g., one private smartphone and one for work) and that mobile phones are used as autonomous communication devices for connecting sensors and other devices on the Internet of Things (IoT) and the public infrastructures.

◘ Figure 1.2 shows the access to 4G/LTE mobile networks for the period 2015–2020. Observe that even in the least developed countries, about 40% of the population has access to 4G/LTE networks. For the same group of countries—i.e., the least developed countries—close to 90% of the population has access to mobile cellular networks, and about 75% of the populations has access to 3G networks. Hence, access to the mobile telephony is more widespread than access to the Internet.

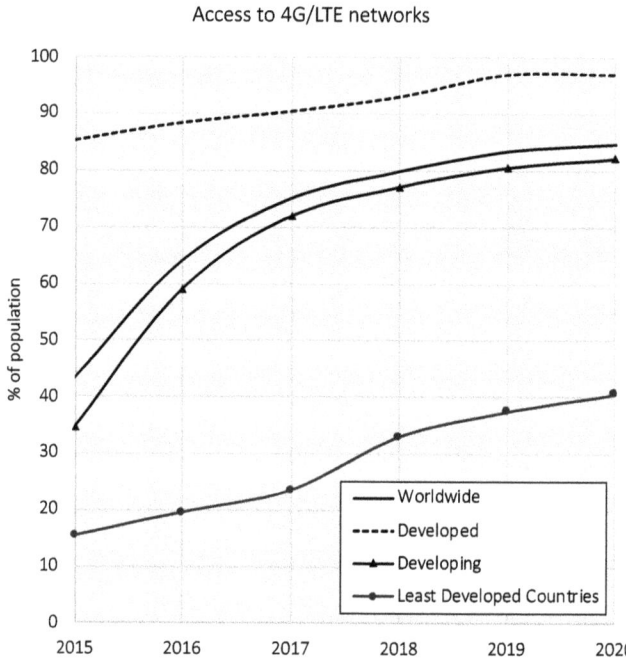

◘ **Fig. 1.2** Worldwide access 4G/LTE mobile networks. (Authors' own figure)

1.2 · Definitions

Access to the Internet has been proposed as a basic human right, and in 2016, the United Nations (UN) released a non-binding resolution condemning intentional disruption to such access by governments (Vincent, 2016). It is clear that access to the Internet has changed the lives of people and the way businesses operate and will increasingly do so as the other half of the world's population gets connected to the Internet.

> ▶ **Facets of the Digital Economy**
>
> Three representative examples of digital goods and services are presented to indicate the extent of the digital economy. Many more examples are provided throughout this book.
>
> **Facebook**: There are over three billion people worldwide using a social media service regularly. Facebook is the most popular of these services, with approximately 2.2 billion users. Facebook has had a significant impact on how people communicate and organize their social lives. The advertising industry has been dramatically changed because of the way social media advertisements can be tailored to match the attitudes and preferences of the users. Because of the company's global impact, Facebook founder, Mark Zuckerberg, was named "Person of the Year" by *Time Magazine* in 2010. However, Facebook is not without controversies, as witnessed by the Cambridge Analytica data scandal in 2018.
>
> **Airbnb**: Established in 2008, Airbnb has grown to become one of the biggest hospitality services worldwide. As of 2017, Airbnb has over 200 million users and offers over three million lodgings in 191 countries. Airbnb enables homeowners to rent out property to registered guests and is one of the best examples of the expanding sharing economy. Airbnb utilizes the concept of multisided platforms (▶ Chap. 10) and the long tail (▶ Chap. 16) in its business operations. Key enablers for Airbnb's success are the widespread adoption of Internet access, high-speed mobile networks, and smartphones. However, Airbnb has been blamed for reducing attractiveness in the neighborhoods in which it operates and has met resistance from authorities in, for example, Paris and New York.
>
> **Bitcoin**: Bitcoin (BTC) was established in 2009 by the still-unknown person or organization Satoshi Nakamoto. It has become the most valuable and well-known cryptocurrency. Bitcoin utilizes the blockchain technology to provide a distributed currency without any involved third parties. Bitcoin has the potential to become a true global currency. However, recent investigations have revealed several weaknesses with Bitcoin, including long transaction times and high energy usage. Other cryptocurrencies, such as Litecoin (LTC), Ethereum (ETH), and Ripple (XRP), may overcome these challenges and turn out to be the dominant cryptocurrencies of the future—if cryptocurrencies have any future at all. ◀

The size of the digital economy is hard to estimate. This is because ICT is an industry on its own (production of telecommunications networks, Internet equipment, mobile phones, applications, and software), but also because ICT is integrated into almost all other industries. ICT has enabled new business models, more efficient production methods, and new ways of interacting with consumers. One example is online trading (e-commerce) where people can buy almost any kind of merchan-

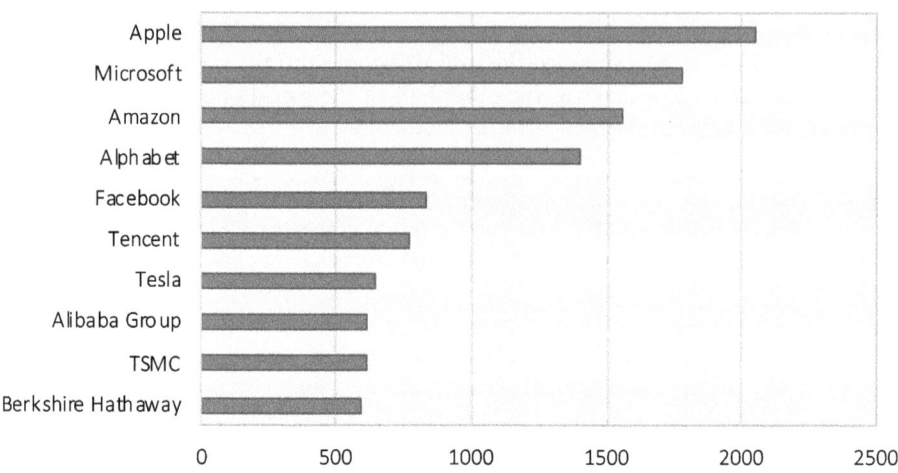

☐ **Fig. 1.3** Top ten corporations worldwide according to market cap. (Authors' own figure)

dise using the Internet. We are experiencing a transition from the industrial economy to the digital economy—from physical products to digital goods and services.

The world's six largest corporations by market capitalization as of the first quarter of 2021 (in descending order) are Apple, Microsoft, Amazon, Alphabet (Google), Facebook, and Tencent (Wikipedia, 2021). All of these companies produce digital goods and services and are major businesses in the digital economy. As of March 30, 2021, their combined market capitalization totals more than $8300 billion. ☐ Figure 1.3 illustrates the market cap of the top ten companies in the world.

These companies hold immense power in today's business world due to their size, span of operations, and international impact. They can be characterized as *digital conglomerates* as their business operations have expanded far beyond their original business idea (Tapscot et al., 2006). Google, for example, started out as a company delivering search engine services for Internet users. Today, Google offers, in addition to its search engine, e-mail (Gmail), instant messaging, learning platform (G Suit for Education), voice-over-IP (Google Hangouts), text editing (Google Docs), cloud storage (Google Drive), and several other platforms. Google has expanded its business operations into many sectors of the digital economy by acquiring competing companies and by horizontal and vertical integration.

The main asset of these companies is the network of consumers of the digital goods and services they offer. These users give rise to *network effects* (see ▶ Chap. 9) that generate huge value to these companies. Maybe the most striking fact is that these companies have only needed 20 years to gain their current market dominance. In 2008, the top five companies according to market capitalization included PetroChina, ExxonMobil, General Electric, China Mobile, and Industrial and Commercial Bank of China (ICBC). Of these companies, only China Mobile can be said to fully operate in the digital economy by offering Internet and mobile

1.2 · Definitions

access to consumers in China. As we saw above, the six top businesses in 2021 all belong to the digital economy, and one of them (Tencent) has become the biggest company in China. How do companies in the digital economy get so big? How is it possible for companies in the digital economy to accumulate so much value in such a brief time? These are some of the questions we will shed light on in this book.

Several *disruptive innovations* have contributed to the scope and size of the digital economy. A disruptive innovation is an innovation that creates a new market, often leading to a change in market leadership and the emergence of new companies which become the new market leaders (Christensen, 1997).

> ▶ **Failure to Accept Disruptive Technology**
> One of the most famous examples of disruptive innovations is the failure of the photography company Kodak. Kodak was one of the leading producers of chemical photography and camera films. Kodak failed to embrace digital photography in the 1990s and 2000s and lost the competition with Asian producers. Kodak filed for bankruptcy in 2012, and its patents were bought by a group of companies (including Google and Apple) for $525 million in 2013. Later that year, Kodak emerged from bankruptcy; however, with a vastly different market position compared to the market leader it once was in the 1990s. ◀

When ICT is at the core of a disruptive innovation, the market often changes from producing physical products to producing digital goods and services. Market sectors that have been significantly affected by ICT-based disruptive innovations are media, telecommunications, and finance (Grossman, 2016).

An important part of the digital economy is *e-commerce*. E-commerce is the online trading of physical and digital goods. Some of the largest companies in the digital economy (e.g., Amazon, Alibaba, and eBay) are in the business of e-commerce. We will come back to e-commerce in ▶ Chap. 17 and explore it in more detail there. One important aspect of e-commerce is user feedback and recommendations. Since e-commerce offers consumers the ability to touch, feel, and test the merchandise to only a limited degree, feedback and comments from other consumers may add trust to the shopping experience as explained in ▶ Box 1.1.

> **Box 1.1 Recommendations as Market Feedback**
> Recommendation and consumer feedback are key features in the digital economy. This often generates strong network effects resulting in more customers and more sales and may, sometimes, even lead to de facto monopoly business.
>
> Feedback from consumers can either be gathered directly from the consumer or indirectly by observing consumer behavior. One example of direct user feedback is when a consumer is asked to rate or comment on a product or service after purchase. This information, together with other information the retailer may gather about the consumer, can then be used to increase the sales by recommending other products to the consumer (see ◘ Fig. 1.4). Harvesting

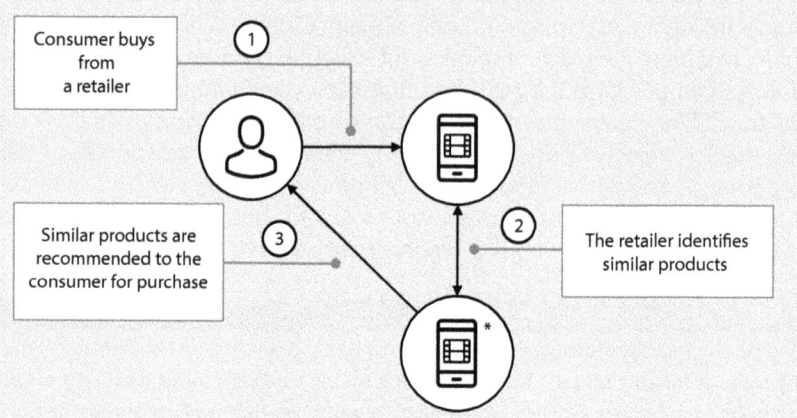

• Fig. 1.4 Recommendation system. (Authors' own figure)

information about the consumers, both directly and indirectly, is a core activity in the business model of many companies in the digital economy.

Reviews and feedback also serve another important role: they build trust in the shopping experience since the customer can read reviews and feedback from other customers. Such feedback helps remove information asymmetries in the digital economy. Encouraged by feedback and reviews from other customers, potential new customers will be better informed regarding the product they are about to buy.

An example of indirect user feedback is when Google is used for web browsing. Google may then use the search results to build up a user profile so that more and more accurate advertisements can be directed toward the user. This increases the value of Google as a provider of advertisements. The importance of indirect feedback is even more evident for Facebook where use of the "like" button, analysis of texts produced by the user, network of friends, and user activities are run through algorithms to build an accurate picture of the personality of the user. When you buy books from Amazon, they also recommend other books that may interest you. This is based on information stored about books you have previously bought or shown an interest in and on books bought by other customers with apparently similar interests.

1.3 Digitization of the Economy

The digital economy is triggered by three technological evolutions: digitization of data, development of digital ICT infrastructures, and digital processing and storage. The technological evolutions have experienced significant breakthroughs and growth in performance and user adoption in recent decades. • Figure 1.5 shows how these technological evolutions are related.

Data has historically been produced in analog formats such as books, letters, documents, photographs, tape recordings, and videos recordings. Today an increas-

1.3 · Digitization of the Economy

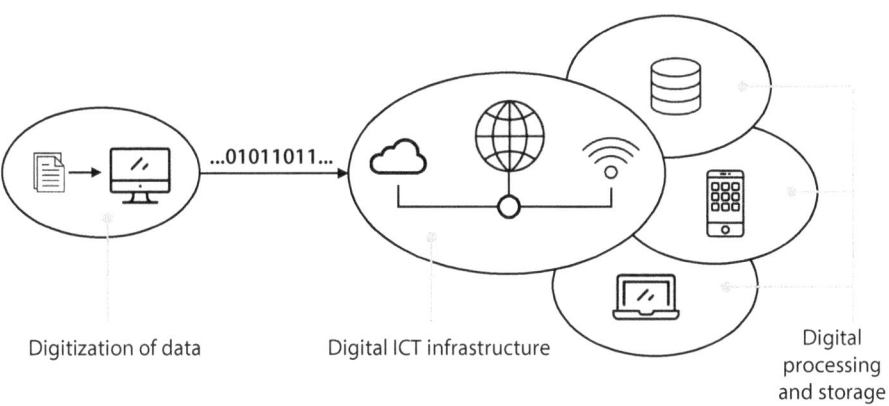

Fig. 1.5 Digitization of data, infrastructures, processing, and storage. (Authors' own figure)

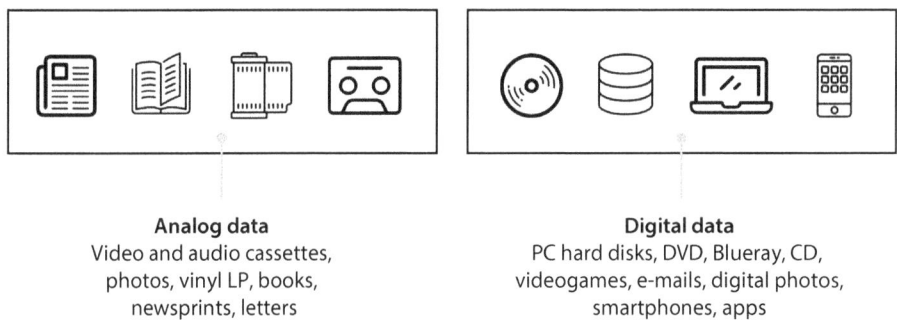

Fig. 1.6 Analog and digital data. (Authors' own figure)

ing amount of data is produced and stored digitally. Digitization of data means that the data is encoded as a sequence of bits ("0" or "1"). Examples of digital data are music stored as files on a computer, books downloaded on a personal computer or a tablet, bank account information in an e-bank application, e-mails, movies and music streamed from the Internet, apps installed on smartphones, and instant messaging services. Examples of analog and digital data are shown in Fig. 1.6. Most telephone services are also digitally encoded; that is, the voice signal is encoded as a sequence of digital bits before these bits are transported over a digital ICT infrastructure to the receiver where the bit sequence is again transformed into an analog voice signal. Cable television, and, to some extent, radio (e.g., DAB), is also digitally coded and transported over digital communication networks.

Fifty years ago, all data was stored in analog formats, and digitization of voice and video signals and experiments with transmission of digital data had just begun. As Fig. 1.7 shows, the amount of data stored digitally worldwide has grown from about 1% in 1986 to about 94% in 2007 and that the digitization of the telecommunication networks has increased from about 20% to 99% over the same period of time (Hilbert & López, 2011). The evolution from an analog to a digital society has then taken place over just one generation.

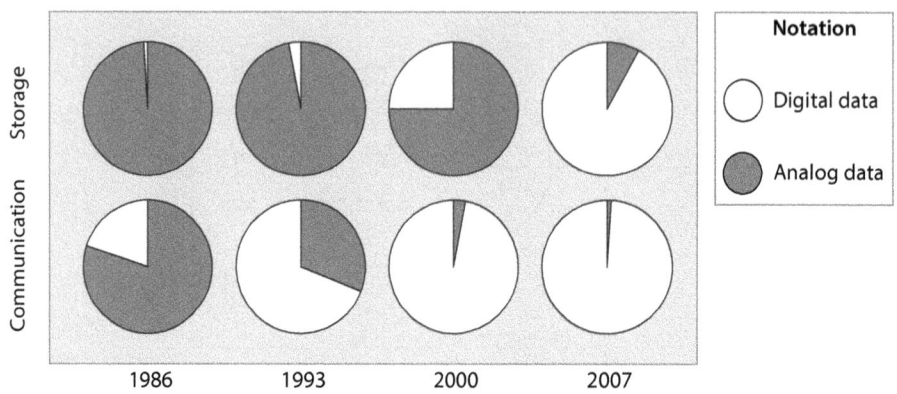

■ Fig. 1.7 Evolution of digital data storage and communication. (Authors' own figure)

Today, an enormous amount of digital data is generated (Data is giving rise to a new economy, 2017). In 2017, for every minute that passed, 400 hours of video were uploaded on YouTube, 15 million text messages were sent between mobile users, three million search queries were handled by Google, 510,000 comments were posted on Facebook, and over 45,000 pictures were posted on Instagram. For every second that passed, more than 10,000 photos were shared on Snapchat (Schultz, 2019). And this is just a small fraction of the total data generated today. Data is generated directly not only by users but also by sensor devices connected to the Internet (e.g., weather sensors, wearable devices, and smart watches). These devices contain processing and data storage units and are becoming gradually cheaper and smaller and are rapidly finding new applications producing more data. In addition, huge amounts of historical analog data—letters, books, films, television shows, pictures, church registers, and other documents—are converted into digital data.

This amount of data vastly surpasses what any human mind can process. Data has become abundant, whereas the human capability to process this data is a scarce resource. Since all this data is in a digital format, the data can be transmitted, processed, and stored extremely efficiently and at low costs, producing a collective knowledge base most people will have access to. Companies and governments apply big data techniques and artificial intelligence to analyze these data for various purposes.

Since the 1980s, there has been an extensive rollout of a worldwide digital ICT infrastructure. In 2020, the core element of this infrastructure is the Internet and consists of components such as local wireless networks, digital subscriber lines, public mobile networks, satellite networks, optical core networks, submarine optical cables, and dedicated networks for distress communications, air traffic control, and broadcast. The digital infrastructure has enabled worldwide communication of digital data with high capacity, low latency, and high reliability. The historical evolution of the most important of these technologies is examined in ▶ Chap. 2.

It is the combination of digitized data, fast communication networks, and mass storage that empowers the digitization of the economy. The business plan of, for example, Facebook requires that all data (text, images, and video) exist in digital format, that there is a worldwide digital communication network attaching the users to the platform, and that there is enough mass storage capacities to store all user data.

The advances in microprocessors and mass storage of digital data have resulted in the evolution of digital devices with fast processing and cheap storage capabilities. Today's smartphones have the same processing power as supercomputers had 20 years ago. While 20 megabytes was the standard storage capacity of home computers in 1995, the storage capacity of smartphones 20 years later is more than 100 gigabytes, that is, 5000 times bigger. The cost of storage has shown similar trends. The cost of one gigabyte of storage in 1995 was about $1000. Twenty years later, in 2015, the same amount of storage cost $0.02. This evolution is a result of the packing density of transistors on microchips which has doubled every 2 years since the early 1970s (Moore's law). The quality and inflation-adjusted price of information technology equipment has decreased on average by 16% per year from 1959 to 2009 (Nambiar & Poess, 2011). Moreover, network capacity increases and cost of optical fibers decreases following similar laws.

Currently, there is no end to the increase of data produced, stored, communicated, and processed. The most significant increase is expected to arise from IoT applications. By 2020, it is estimated that there will be more than 50 billion IoT devices connected to the Internet—more than four times as many as in 2017 (Nordrum, 2016).

1.4 Digital Economics

Digital economics is the branch of economics studying digital goods and services. Hereafter, the term "digital goods" is used when collectively referring to both "digital goods and services." This is because there is seldom a need to make the distinction between "digital goods" and "digital services." The full term is used when this distinction is necessary.

Digital goods comprise everything that is digital: data produced by users, digital applications and services provided over the Internet, and the storage and processing of such data. A digital good can be:
- Any kind of software
- Any type of file stored digitally
- A smartphone app and associated services
- Any type of digital information
- Content of a website
- Any communication session
- Any application supported by the Internet
- Trade and bank transactions

> **▶ Automation**
>
> Automation is the use of technology to execute a process without human intervention. Information and communication technologies provide significant opportunities for automation, primarily due to the massive increase in computation, storage capacities, and communication bandwidth. This has further led to many digital innovations such as cloud computing, machine learning, big data, and Internet of Things (IoT). Automation seeks to reduce costs and increase revenues, competitiveness, and customer satisfaction. It is a part of the ongoing digitization of the economy and society at large. ICT-based automation projects can be found in almost every business sector replacing human workforce by automated digital services, robots, and algorithms. A big concern for politicians and policy makers is whether this wave of automation will destroy more jobs than it creates.
>
> — *Financial Technologies* (FinTech) is the use of new and emerging technologies to replace traditional financial services. Examples include mobile payment services, cryptocurrencies, blockchain methods, crowdfunding, and smart contracts. A major challenge associated with FinTech is data security.
> — *Robotic Process Automation* (RPA) is a form of business process automation based on using software robots as workers instead of humans. These robots can perform repetitive tasks such as updating websites, answering questions from customer, and sending standardized e-mails. More advanced robots, based on cognitive automation, are being developed.
> — In the manufacturing industry, automation is collectively referred to as *Industry 4.0*. This implies the use of ICT to create smart factories based on industrial robots. 3D printing is an example of an Industry 4.0 technology. Here, industrial products are created on demand at customer premises outside the traditional manufacturing plants.
> — *Intelligent Transport Systems* (ITS) is the use of ICT to automate the road and transportation sector. Examples of ITS applications include smart traffic signs and self-driving cars; both contribute to lower costs of transportation and increased traffic safety. ◄

The complement to digital goods and services is physical goods and non-digital services, comprising goods that can be touched and felt and have a physical presence (e.g., cars, books, computers, and furniture) and services that are not digital in nature (e.g., hairdressing, carpentry, and teaching).

> **Definition 1.2**
> *Digital economics* is the branch of economics studying digital services and goods.

The academic field of digital economics overlaps and relates to other fields of economics. Digital economics is also known under different designations, each designation having a slightly different focus and scope. Some of these are:

— **Network economy** focuses on businesses in which much of the economic value is generated by network effects (see ▶ Chap. 9). Network effects are abundant in the digital economy and explain how value is generated in several, but not all, digital businesses.

- **Platform economy** focuses on businesses that act as platforms. The primary business idea is to connect two or more user groups (two-sided or multisided markets). Platform economy is closely related to network economies since network effects are also important drivers for platform businesses. However, not all network economies are platform economies and vice versa. Multisided platforms are described in ▶ Chap. 10.
- **Information economy** focuses on information products and how they are produced and traded. The information economy is part of the digital economy, but the latter is broader in scope since it also includes more than pure information goods.
- **Data economy** focuses on the business of harvesting and analyzing data. Data is gathered from users or the environment and stored in large databases. Big Data techniques and artificial intelligence are applied to analyze the data, where the purpose is to extract information of value to businesses or governments. Such data may also be traded on the market, for example, as input to statistics or as the basis for producing targeted advertisements.
- **Virtual economy** is the economy of virtual worlds, e.g., *World of Warcraft* and *Second Life*. To some extent, virtual economies reflect the real economy regarding the supply and demand of goods, trading, and network feedback. Virtual economies are mostly disconnected from the real economy. However, there are examples of virtual economies that can generate trade in the real economy (e.g., gold farming in *World of Warcraft*).
- **Internet economy** comprises the economics of Internet goods and services. Since most of the economic activity within the context of digital economics is performed over the Internet, Internet economy is close in scope to digital economics. One important digital market that is excluded in the Internet economy is the economics of telecommunications, that is, the market for broadcast, Internet, and mobile and fixed network services.
- **Attention economy** is related to the value created by people's attention. User attention is an important element in many digital business models. The basis for the attention economy is that data has become abundant, while people's attention-span remains a scarce resource. There are business models that exploit people's attention-span to generate revenue; the most well-known are those based on advertisements.
- **Sharing economy** is the economy in which people or organizations share goods and services such as Airbnb and Uber. The sharing economy has also been termed **access economy**, **peer-economy**, **collaborative economy,** and **crowdsourcing capitalism**.
- **Abundance economy** is the economy of goods and services that are abundant; that is, they are close to unlimited in supply. Many digital services exhibit abundance features, since they can be copied with zero marginal cost. This challenges one of the most fundamental assumptions in neo-classical economics, namely, that resources are scarce. In several digital economies they are not!
- **Digital economics**, as defined in this book, encompasses all or parts of the terms explained above. It is important to point out that digital economics is a young academic field of study. New terms appears, and definitions of existing terms are revised as researchers gain increased understanding of the field and as new technologies expand the boundaries of the digital economy and enable new business opportunities.

1.5 Conclusions

In 2020, seven of the ten largest corporations by market capitalization are in the digital economy business. Moreover, Apple is now about four times bigger than the corporation that is number eight in the list. Ten years ago, there were only two companies in the digital economy among the ten largest corporations (Apple and Microsoft).

The evolution in favor of businesses in the digital economy is a result of the digitization of society: by 2020, almost all communication infrastructure worldwide is digital, and almost all data is available in digital formats.

The companies in the digital economy comprise several industrial sectors, for example:
- Information and content producers and providers (e.g., newspapers, television channels, bloggers, YouTube, Netflix)
- Social media providers (e.g., Facebook, LinkedIn, Twitter)
- Manufacturers of devices and software (Microsoft, Apple)
- Operators of fixed and mobile network infrastructure (Internet and mobile network providers, Starlink)
- Electronic payment services and banking (PayPal, Bitcoin minters)
- E-commerce (eBay, Amazon)
- Sharing service providers (Uber, Airbnb)
- Cloud computing
- Multiplayer interactive game providers

The digital economy has created new business opportunities that did not exist before as is evident from the list.

Questions
1. Name the ten largest companies in the world by market capitalization. Which of them are in the digital economy?
2. How large share of the world population has access to the Internet?
3. Does everyone in the world have access to mobile telephony?
4. How will digitization of the economy impact the country you live in? Search the web for news articles (two or three articles are sufficient), and discuss how digitization influences the economy, the public sector, and business domains.

Answers
1. Apple, Microsoft, Amazon, Alphabet, Facebook, Tencent, Tesla, Alibaba Group, TSMC, and Berkshire Hathaway. All of them are businesses in the digital economy except Tesla, TSMC, and Berkshire Hathaway.
2. About 50%.
3. No, many people in poor parts of the world do not have access to mobile telephony.
4. The answer to this question depends on where you live. However, there are a few general observations such as access to the internet and mobile services, access to vast amounts of information, automation of industrial production, automated access to societal functions, and so on.

References

Christensen, C. (1997). *The innovators dilemma: When new technologies cause great firms to fail.* Harvard Business School Press.

Data is giving rise to a new economy. (2017, May 6). *The Economist.*

Grossman, R. (2016, March 21). The industries that are being disrupted the most by digital. *Harvard Business Review.*

Hilbert, M., & López, P. (2011, April). The world's technological capacity to store, communicate, and compute information. *Science, 332.*

ITU statistics, 2018.

Nambiar, M., & Poess, M. (2011). Transaction performance vs. Moore's Law: A trend. In *Performance evaluation, measurements and characterization of complex systems (TPCTC 2010)* (Lecture Notes in Computer Science) (Vol. 6417). Springer.

Nordrum, A. (2016, August 18). Popular internet of things forecast of 50 billion devices by 2020 is outdated. *IEEE Spectrum.*

Reid, P. (2015, October 27). IFPI Digital Music Report 2015: Global digital revenues match physical for first time. *The Music Network.*

Schultz, J. (2019, August 6). How much data is created on the internet every day. *Micro Focus Blog.*

Tapscot, D., Ticoll, D., & Herman, D. (2006). *Digital conglomerates: Setting the agenda for enterprise 2.0.* New Paradigm Learning Corporation.

Vincent, J. (2016, July 4). UN condemns Internet access disruption as human rights violation. *The Verge.*

Wikipedia. (2021) *List of public corporations by market capitalization.* (Wikipedia website visited April 12, 2021)

Further Reading

Brian Arthur, W. (2015). *Complexity and the economy.* Oxford University Press.

McAfee, A., & Brynjolfsson, E. (2017). *Machine, platform, crowd.* W. W. Norton & Company.

Shapiro, C., & Varian, H. R. (1999). *Information rules: A strategic guide to network economy.* Harvard Business School Press.

Information and Communication Technologies

Contents

2.1 Introduction – 18

2.2 Timeline for the ICT Evolution – 19

2.3 Factors Constraining Evolution – 24

2.4 Internet of Things – 27

2.5 Conclusions – 30

References – 30

© The Author(s), under exclusive license to Springer Nature Switzerland AG 2021
H. Øverby, J. A. Audestad, *Introduction to Digital Economics*, Classroom Companion: Business,
https://doi.org/10.1007/978-3-030-78237-5_2

Learning Objectives

After completing this chapter, you should be able to:
- Explain how information and communication technology has evolved toward increasingly complex systems and applications.
- Understand that the ICT evolution has followed three intimately coupled lines of development: evolution of basic hardware technologies, evolution of fixed and mobile data networks, and evolution of application protocols, software, and services.
- Understand the impacts and potentials of the Internet of Things evolution.

2.1 Introduction

The evolution of information and communication technologies has followed three parallel timelines:
- The *innovation of technologies* from simple telephone and telegraph systems to the Internet supporting social media, sensor networks, apps, and many other digital services.
- The *convergence of services* in which the telephone and telegraph networks are replaced by the Internet (▶ Chap. 3).
- The *evolution of the telecommunications business* itself from monopoly to competitive markets (▶ Chap. 5).

In this chapter, we will look more closely at the technological evolution and postpone the other items to later chapters as indicated above.

The evolution that eventually led to today's digital economy started with the invention of the transistor in 1947 (see ▶ Box 2.1). This device could be more densely packed, was much cheaper, used less energy, was easier to handle, and was much more reliable than vacuum tubes. The transistor, and the miniaturization capabilities it eventually offered, led to a technical evolution at a speed the world never had seen before.

In 2019, approximately 23 billion devices containing microchip CPUs (central processing units) were connected to the Internet, making the global information and communications technology (ICT) infrastructure the largest machine ever built. Moreover, the number of connections increases by 10% per year, corresponding to a doubling time of 7 years. The forecast for 2025 is that more than 40 billion devices will be connected to the Internet (Cisco Visual Networking Index, 2019).

Box 2.1   The Transistor
The transistor is a semiconductor device used to switch and amplify electronic signals. It effectively replaced vacuum tube technology and enabled the production of cheap, low-power, and small electronic devices. It is the basis for almost all ICT devices such as microprocessors, personal computers, smartphones, and other electronic tools. It is the most important invention of

the twentieth century, perhaps the most important invention of all times.

Julius Edgar Lilienfeld had already filed a patent for the field effect transistor in 1925. However, because of the lack of high-quality semiconductor materials, it was impossible to build a working transistor at that time. The first practical implementation of the transistor was done at Bell Labs, USA, by John Bardeen, Walter Brattain, and William Shockley in 1947. What they invented was the first point-contact transistor which they patented the year after. They received the Nobel Prize in Physics in 1956 for their "research on semiconductors and their discovery of the transistor effect" (See ▶ https://www.nobelprize.org/prizes/physics/1956/summary/).

The transistor radio was the first commercial device designed using transistors (1954). In its early days, the transistor also found its use in pocket calculators, hearing aids, telecommunication switching equipment, and then, finally, the personal computer and the mobile phone. Today, transistors are mostly used as building blocks for integrated circuits which, in turn, are used to produce personal computers, smartphones, and other electronic devices. In 2014, more than 10^{18} transistors were produced. This is more than 100 million transistors for each human being on Earth. From 1960 to 2018, altogether 1.3×10^{22} transistors have been manufactured (Laws, 2018).

The size of a single transistor has continually gotten smaller since its inception in the 1950s, quite accurately following Moore's law. While the Intel 4004 microprocessor released in 1971 had 2300 transistors, each with a size of 10,000 nanometers, the 22-core Xeon Broadwell-E5 microprocessor released by Intel in 2016 has 7,200,000,000 transistors each with a size of 14 nanometers (Wikipedia, 2020). More transistors mean in general more computing power. Whether or not the size of transistors can be further reduced in the future according to Moore's law is an open issue. In the end, quantum effects, heating, and thermal noise may limit the minimum size of a transistor.

2.2 Timeline for the ICT Evolution

◘ Figure 2.1 shows the timeline for selected innovations that were essential for the development of the digital economy and the year they became commercially available or reached the mass market. The technologies listed in ◘ Fig. 2.1 are categorized as hardware, mobile/wireless, or software/services.

Prior to the commercialization of the World Wide Web in 1993, the telecommunications technology and the information technology were developed along two different paths.
1. Telecommunications is an old technology branch going back to the first electronic telegraph systems developed in the early nineteenth century. The predecessor of the International Telecommunications Union (ITU) was established in 1865 with the task to standardize the telegraph technology and encourage

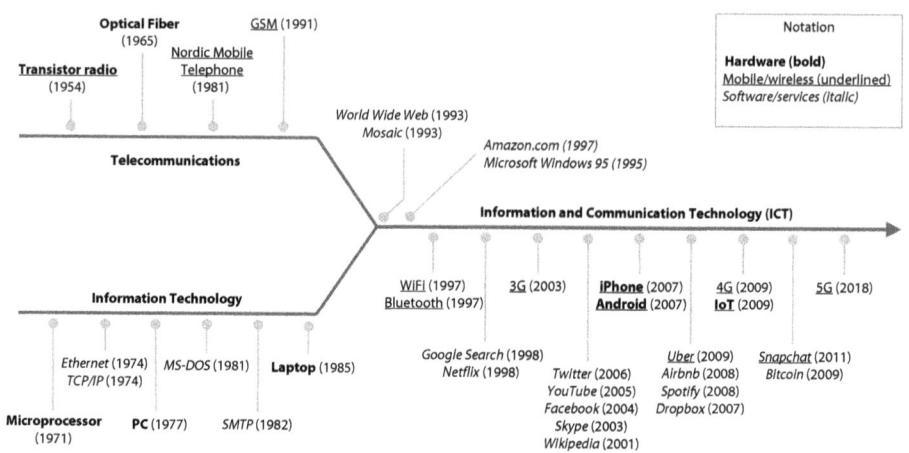

● Fig. 2.1 Timeline of ICT innovations. (Authors' own figure)

the establishment of a global telegraph network. Since then, specification and design of telecommunications networks and services have been done by the ITU and other standardization organization, the telecommunications industry, and international research programs in close cooperation. Until 1993, the development was primarily associated with digital transmission and switching of telephone services and simple data services.

2. Information technology is a much younger science with roots back to the 1950s when the first transistorized computers were designed. It has now become one of the world's largest and most influential industries. Basic information technologies such as computer architecture, processing platforms, data storage, algorithms, and programming were studied and developed at universities, by research organizations, and in the computer industry. In 1993, there were still only few applications of the information technology that required extensive support of communication technologies, the most important of which was e-mail on the Internet.

All this changed in 1993 when the two fields of information technology and telecommunications merged as a single technology now known as information and communication technology (ICT). The event that led to this transformation was commercialization of the World Wide Web in 1993, soon leading to a massive requirement for remote interactions between computers and for distributed processing of information. Since 1993, information technology cannot exist without telecommunications and vice versa.

The World Wide Web is enabled by the following technologies: Uniform Resource Locator (URL) for accurate addressing of information packages on the web, Hypertext Transfer Protocol (HTTP) for communication with web pages, and Hypertext Markup Language (HTML) for formatting and writing web pages. Together, these technologies allow users to post and access documents, images, videos, and other information across the Internet. Mosaic (1993) was the first graphical web browser which contributed to popularizing the WWW and, consequently, the Internet itself. Mosaic was later followed by Netscape, Internet Explorer, and Google Chrome.

The Internet is a global system for interconnected computer networks based on technologies and protocols such as Ethernet (1974) and TCP/IP (1974), allowing data to be transferred between two or more computers. The TCP/IP protocol suite was developed and tested as a part of the ARPANET project financed by the US Department of Defense but is now the worldwide open standard for data transmission on the Internet (see ▶ Box 2.2).

Box 2.2   The ARPANET

The ARPANET was a project with the major goal of building and demonstrating a data communication network based on packet switching. It was also the first communication network to implement the TCP/IP protocols. The ARPANET was funded by the US Department of Defense and launched in 1966. Packet switching was a novel technology at that time, challenging the established circuit switching technique used in telephone networks. The two key advantages of packet switching over circuit switching were efficient resource sharing and resilience against node and link failures. Some scientists and engineers doubted packet switching could be implemented due to its complexity.

In 1969, the ARPANET project built an experimental packet switched network connecting a few computer sites. In subsequent years, the ARPANET was refined and expanded to the network shown in ◘ Fig. 2.2. The first interna-

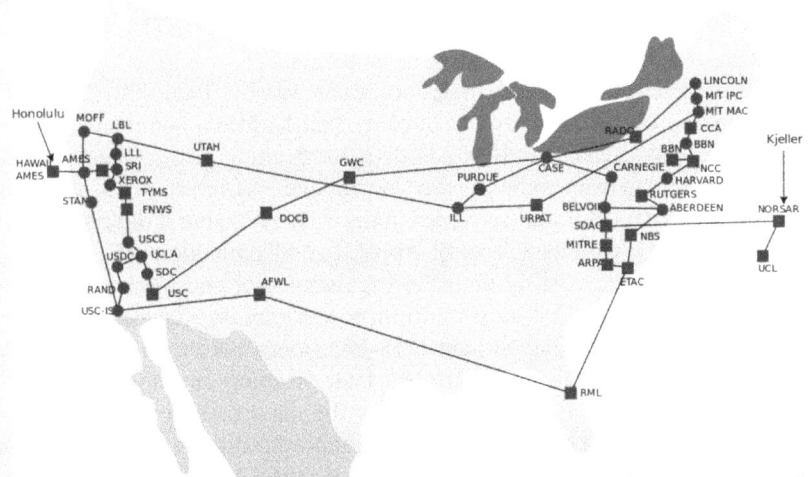

◘ Fig. 2.2   The ARPANET in 1974. Note that the first node outside the US was at Kjeller in Norway. (Public domain, source: ▶ https://commons.wikimedia.org/wiki/File:Arpanet_1974.svg)

> tional connection in the ARPANET was to Norway via a satellite link in 1973.
>
> ARPANET was the predecessor of the Internet where the key technologies in the current Internet were developed and tested. This includes packet switching, protocol layering, and the TCP/IP protocol suite. Many of the early services of the Internet, such as e-mail and file transfers, were also first developed and tested on the ARPANET. The ARPANET was decommissioned and replaced by NSFNET in 1990 and became the first part of the current Internet.
>
> The early Internet was mainly used at universities and research establishments. The network was hardly known outside these circles until the World Wide Web was commercialized and taken into use by several telecommunications carriers in 1993 and, thereby, becoming available to the public. The WWW technology had been invented by Tim Berners-Lee at CERN already in 1989, but since it was not invented by the telecommunications industry, it took a long time until they discovered the potential the new technology would have for the data communication market, a market the carriers had strived to build up for more than a decade without succeeding.

Optical fibers were invented in 1965 and, as the technology matured during the 1980s, eventually provided a high-speed global ICT infrastructure for the Internet. Most of the Internet backbone network is built using optical fibers. A single optical fiber, which is thinner than a human hair, can carry several hundred terabytes of data per second. An optical cable, consisting of several (sometimes hundreds of) optical fibers, can accommodate all traffic generated on the Internet today. With optical fiber technology, the Internet can be built with abundant capacity for decades to come.

One of the first "killer applications" of the Internet was e-mail which was standardized in 1982 with the Simple Mail Transfer Protocol (SMTP). E-mail soon became the key technology for exchange of messages.

The first commercially available microprocessor was the Intel 4004, released in 1971. It was based on the transistor technology that had been commercialized two decades earlier, enabling reliable and low-cost digital computing. Today, microprocessors are found in everything from computers to smartphones, refrigerators, cars, and toys. The personal computer (PC) was developed in the early 1970s, but it did not reach the mass market until 1977 with the release of Apple II and Commodore PET.

The PC disrupted the existing time-sharing mainframe and minicomputer systems by offering a dedicated low-cost multipurpose computing device for end users. The Microsoft Disk Operating System (MS-DOS) was released in 1981. It provided the technological basis for Microsoft's later products and dominance in the digital economy. The first laptop available for the mass market was the Toshiba T1100, released in 1985. The laptop is a PC combining display, keyboard, input-output devices, and storage in a miniaturized package. In 2018, more than 160 million laptops were sold (Shipment forecast of tablets, laptops and desktop PCs worldwide from 2010 to 2024. Statista, 2020). However, this number is small compared to the over 1.5 billion smartphones sold the same year (Number of smartphones sold worldwide from 2007 to 2021. Statista, 2020).

2.2 · Timeline for the ICT Evolution

The Nordic Mobile Telephone (NMT), released in 1981, was the world's first automatic cellular mobile telephony system. It introduced automatic roaming and handover but supported only voice communication. The Global System for Mobile Communications (GSM)—supporting voice, messaging, and data services—pioneered digital radio communication (1991). Initially, data communication was slow (less than 10 kilobits per second) and ineffective, but the data rate was later enhanced by technologies such as GPRS and EDGE. High-speed data, particularly on the link from base station to mobile terminal (usually referred to as the downlink), was introduced in 3G mobile systems (2003). The broadband technology was developed further in the 4G mobile systems launched in 2009. The latest mobile technology, 5G, was used at the 2018 Winter Olympics in South Korea and is now (2020) being rolled out on a large scale in Europe, Asia, and North America. 5G will support the Internet of Things (IoT). The family tree for mobile networks is contained in ▶ Box 2.3.

Box 2.3 Family Tree of Mobile Networks

Altogether five generations of mobile systems have been developed:

First generation (from 1981): NMT (Nordic countries), TACS (UK), Radiocom2000 (France), and C-Netz (Germany) offering only analogue telephony. These systems supported primitive roaming capabilities, though the method used in NMT became the basis for the more sophisticated roaming capabilities of GSM.

Second generation (1991): GSM offering digital telephony, data communication at speeds up to 10 kilobits per second (kbps), and short message service (SMS) over signaling channels. GSM was designed for automatic international roaming and non-disruptive handover.

Third generation (2001): 3G (or UMTS) is a dual system offering packet radio services at a 128 kbps (initially) for Interne services and GSM services for telephony and SMS. The architecture consists of two separate network architectures for data and telephony but using the same radio interface based on spread spectrum technologies. 3G is an extension of both the Internet and the telephone network.

Fourth generation (2009): 4G is an extension of the Internet offering only packet radio services including voice over IP (VoIP), narrowband data, broadband data, and streaming services over a dynamic mix of narrowband and wideband data channels. Interconnection with the fixed telephone network is via conversion units at the interface between the telephone network and the 4G network.

Fifth generation (2018): 5G is based on 4G but offers new features such as very high data rates, edge computing (cloud computing close to the mobile user, e.g., in the base station, to reduce latency), network slicing (allowing independent providers to operate simultaneously over the same infrastructure offering complex services to the same user), and connection of millions of remote sensors and other devices. 5G will be one of the basic technologies of the Internet of Things.

Intermediate technologies exist between the generations such as GPRS (General Packet Radio Service) offering packet radio with increased data rates over GSM and HSPA (high-speed data access) for increased data rates over 3G.

Bluetooth (1997) interconnects devices over very short distances, while Wi-Fi (1997) offers local network access using packet radio. Both technologies are widely employed today. Android (2007) and iPhone (2007) transformed smartphones into advanced computers also supporting the app ecosystems (Apple's App Store and Google Play). The smartphone apps are the main building blocks of the emerging location-based services such as Airbnb (2008) and Uber (2009), both being sharing services. Google (1998) enables users to search the World Wide Web for information. When Google was launched, there were several competing search engines; however, Google turned out to be technologically superior to its competitors and captured most of the market. The initial business of Netflix (1998) was DVD rental and sales by mail; now, Netflix provides online media streaming services to subscribers in over 190 countries. ▶ Amazon.com (1997) launched a successful e-commerce website.

When home computers and laptops became ubiquitous in the developed world, Internet services such as Wikipedia (2001), Skype (2003), Facebook (2004), YouTube (2005), Twitter (2006), Dropbox (2007), and Spotify (2008) emerged. These services, satisfying different user needs, were not the first in their respective service category. However, with a combination of technological superiority, smart design, and luck, they managed to become the dominating services. Every year new innovations emerge in different markets and fields. Bitcoin (2009) emerged with the idea of disrupting the banking system by offering a cryptocurrency that enabled trade and money transfers without third-party involvement. Likewise, Snapchat (2011) sought to fill gaps in the social media market by enabling private sharing of pictures and videos on mobile devices.

2.3 Factors Constraining Evolution

Digital services cannot exist without ICT. Innovations in computer networking and wireless technologies give rise to new services which, in turn, have major impacts on the digital economy at large. Note that some of the basic information and communication technologies still in use, including TCP/IP, HTTP (World Wide Web), Ethernet, and GSM, are now more than 25 years old. Several of these technologies have been expanded and improved several times during their lifetime. For example, IP exists in two versions (IPv4 and IPv6). GSM has generated a whole new family of mobile communication systems—3G, 4G, and 5G—all of them built on the basic principles first outlined in the GSM project. On the other hand, the basic connection-oriented protocol on the Internet—TCP—has been unchanged since 1974.

Despite all these improvements, the original technologies are still widely used. For example, IPv4 (42 years old) and GSM (30 years old) are still important Internet and mobile network technologies, respectively. Now, 4G and 5G technologies are rapidly replacing GSM but, still, mobile networks support GSM to back global roaming services. Any efforts to shut down GSM have, so far, failed except in a few countries (e.g., Australia, USA, and Singapore).

Communication technologies are evolving slowly. The most important reason for the slow adaptation of some of the new technologies is the huge investments required for implementing them. Even a small improvement of a technology is expensive to install, simply because of the vast volume of existing equipment designed to the old standard. Therefore, it may sometimes take more than 10 years before the technology is taken into use after it is specified and ready for the market. For example, it took more than 10 years from the HTTPS specification (encrypted web access) was finalized until it was taken into use. IPv6 was ready for implementation in 1996. Nevertheless, in 2016, more than 95% of the Internet traffic was still carried on IPv4 networks. This is because Network Address Translation (NAT) has increased the available address space for IPv4 and, hence, postponed the introduction of IPv6. Because 4G and 5G mobile networks only support IPv6 and IPv6 is implemented on almost all input/output devices of computers, this is now (2020) about to change. It is assumed that IPv6 will soon replace most of IPv4 worldwide.

On the other hand, both the development time and adaptation time for many app-based digital services (such as Airbnb and Uber) are very short. The reason is that many of them are simple software packages—easy to develop, install, and use. The rapid evolution of apps took place after iPhones and Android phones were marketed in 2008.

One important requirement for introducing a new technology is backward compatibility; that is, the new technology should support equipment or software designed to the old standard. One compatibility requirement is that new equipment should be capable of operating in the old environment. This objective is fulfilled for public mobile communication; a smartphone designed for 5G must also support 4G, 3G, and GSM so that it can be used everywhere. This implies that the smartphone must support the radio interface for all mobile standards so long as these standards are in use. In addition, it must support Wi-Fi and Bluetooth. This backward compatibility ensures that new families of mobile systems can be introduced smoothly without rebuilding the network completely.

The reliability of the infrastructure is also a concern that may influence the rate by which new technologies are implemented. ICT and electric power production are the two most critical infrastructures of society. If any of these infrastructures stops, society will soon grind to a halt since all other infrastructures depend critically on them. All activities of modern society involve computation, sharing, and storage of data. Therefore, these activities are vulnerable to cyberattacks where the purpose is to destroy, disable, or gain illegal access to computer resources and infrastructures. Events have also shown that most ICT systems are taken out of service either at the same time a power outage occurs or shortly afterward if devices or networks are equipped with standby power such as batteries or diesel aggregates (which most of them are not) (Northeast blackout of 2003, 2020).

Innovations in ICT will continue to have impact on the digital economy in the future. Technologies such as machine learning, robotics, smart factories, smart cities, and 3D printing all show great potential for disrupting existing business sectors and providing the foundations for upcoming digital services. Machine learning techniques are already utilized in several digital services. One example is algorithms used to recommend products to consumers based on previous customer habits. Another example is voice recognition systems such as Apple's Siri. This evolution is considered further in ▶ Chap. 20.

Box 2.4 Cryptocurrencies

Cryptocurrency is a type of digital currency that uses cryptography to secure transactions and generate new units. Transactions in cryptocurrencies are performed without any centralized authority. Cryptocurrency uses the blockchain technology employing a public and decentralized database of encrypted records. Blockchain is a versatile technology that can be used to design smart contracts as well as cryptocurrencies. A general advantage of cryptocurrencies is their ability to support secure transactions of money without a third-party stakeholder involved, potentially with reduced cost and lower transaction delay.

Bitcoin (2009) was the first decentralized cryptocurrency and the first practical implementation of the blockchain. Bitcoin involves many distributed miners that confirm transactions between two parties. Transactions are recorded as a chain of blocks (thereby the name "blockchain") on a decentralized and distributed public ledger.

Bitcoin has the potential to become a true global digital currency. It can be traded on international digital currency exchanges. However, the price of Bitcoin has been extremely volatile compared to other currencies such as US dollar and euro (see ◘ Fig. 2.3). The current value of 1 Bitcoin is about 60,000 USD (April 2021), rising from about 7000 USD in April 2020. Because of this, the use of Bitcoin in the trading of goods and services has been limited. The popularity of Bitcoin has also spurred the creation of many other cryptocurrencies such as Ethereum, Litecoin, Ripple, and IOTA. There are currently more than 3400 different cryptocurrencies in various stages of development.

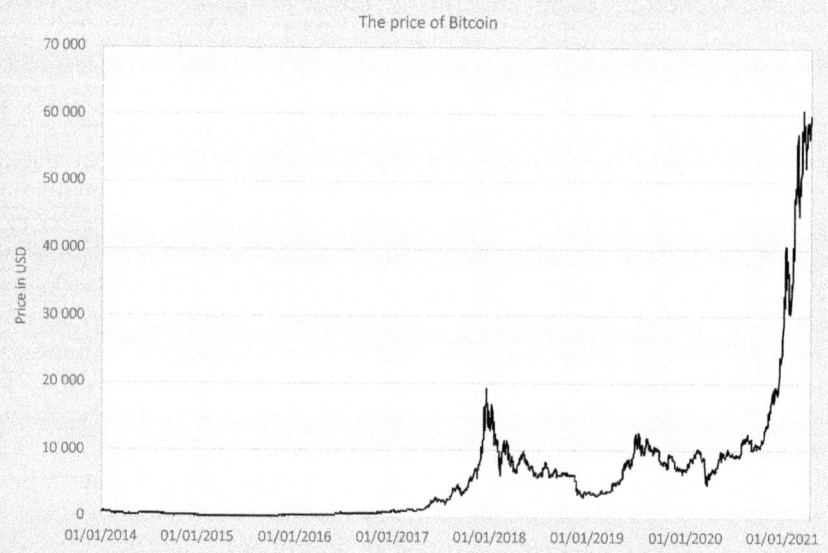

◘ **Fig. 2.3** The price of one BTC in US dollars from January 2014 to April 2021. (Authors' own figure)

> Cryptocurrencies, in particular Bitcoin, have met much criticism and have been compared to economic bubbles such as the Tulip Mania in 1637 and the South Sea Bubble in 1720. Cryptocurrencies have also been used in money laundering and in funding of criminal activities.

2.4 Internet of Things

Interactions between humans (e.g., speech and e-mail) and between humans and machines (e.g., downloading of films and payment services) are traditionally the core elements in the evolution of telecommunications technology comprising network architecture, network management, communication protocols, and services. Most telecommunications statistics is still concerned with the number of individuals connected to the Internet and mobile networks, the amount of traffic they generate, and the revenues this traffic creates for the telecommunication operators. This simple picture of telecommunications is now changing. During the last decennium, autonomous communication between machines not involving humans has become increasingly important. This includes remote sensing and control, grid computing, driverless cars, smart homes, smart cities, smart grids, infrastructure management, and several other applications. IoT devices may report to and receive commands from centralized platforms, for example, automatic reading of power and freshwater consumption, or interchange message with one another without involving a central processing platform, for example, vehicle-to-vehicle communication and vehicle-to-road infrastructure communication for autonomic driving.

Cisco has estimated that there will be almost 30 billion devices connected to the Internet by 2022. About 50% of these devices will be IoT devices and 25% will be smartphones (Cisco Annual Internet Report, 2020). The remainder will be TVs, PCs, and tablets. On the other hand, IoT devices will only generate 6% of the global Internet traffic. This is so because most IoT devices transmit few and short messages as compared to other users of the Internet. According to *Business Insider*, there are almost three times as many smart devices in people's homes as shown in Cisco's statistics; however, only a few of them are connected to the Internet. If these devices are also connected, then the increase in IoT devices will be dramatic, resulting in a tripling of the estimates of Cisco (Patel, 2018).

The applications of IoT devices are commonly divided into five categories: consumer, commercial, industrial, infrastructure, and military. Several applications exist already, but the number of applications is expected to escalate dramatically during the next few years. One consequence is that IP version 6 must be built out on a large scale to provide enough addressing space for the new applications. The 5G mobile network is already designed for this evolution, and it is assumed that 5G will play an important role in the evolution of IoT.

Consumer applications include smart home applications, elder care, and medical supervision managed by the users. Smart home applications may include wireless communication with light switches and appliances and remote control of air conditioning and security systems using smartphones. Assistance services includes voice-controlled devices (e.g., light switches and door openers), medical monitoring, activity monitoring, and other services making life easier for elderly and disabled people.

Commercial applications include smart health care, building and home automation, and smart transport systems. These applications are based on a mix of device-to-platform communication and autonomous communication between devices. Smart health care comprises technologies for monitoring of patients both at home and in hospitals. Examples are remote reading of measuring devices (e.g., blood pressure and heart rate monitors), monitoring and actuating implants such as pacemakers and insulin pumps, and supervising patients with chronic diseases and elderly people. Aruba estimates that IoT technology in health care will increase the workforce productivity and reduce the cost of health care by more than 50% (State of IoT Healthcare, 2019).

Building and home automation include safety alarms, energy saving, comfort, and occupancy monitoring (e.g., reducing heating if no one is at home).

Examples of smart transport systems are communication between vehicles, between vehicles and road infrastructure, smart parking, toll collection systems, fleet management, and road assistance (e.g., automatic accident alarm generated automatically by the vehicle). One application that has taken off at an unexpected rate is renting of electric kick scooters. The autonomous system combines services such as location management, payment, and status reporting.

Industrial applications facilitate the evolution of existing industrial automation using big data, AI, robotics, and autonomous interactions between devices, machines, control systems, and management systems at a much larger scale than today. Networked sensors and complex algorithms analyzing and acting upon real-time measurements will improve safety management, increase process efficiency, reduce waste of time and resources, and admit real-time plant optimization. This is often referred to as Industry 4.0 or the Fourth Industrial Revolution.

Infrastructure applications are management and control of infrastructures such as freshwater and sewage systems, railway tracks, roads, tunnels, bridges, energy production and delivery networks, and so on. The category also includes environmental monitoring of, for example, air pollution, freshwater quality, wildlife habitats, and soil conditions. IoT may also support smooth coordination between authorities (political, technical, and managerial) since the management of a particular infrastructures often involves several authorities.

Military applications include technologies for surveillance, reconnaissance, and battlefield operations.

Several technologies support IoT networking. These are short-range applications such as Bluetooth, Wi-Fi, Zigbee, and Z-Wave; medium range systems using 5G mobile networks; long range radio communication using ultralow bit rates (e.g., 300 bits per second); satellite networks, in particular, satellite terminals with small antennas (VSAT); and wired systems such as Ethernet, cable networks, and powerline communication. Several technologies may be connected in tandem, for example, a Wi-Fi network connecting several local sensors to a local processing platform connected to a 5G network.

There are several concerns regarding IoT, the most important of which are related to privacy, security, and safety. Efficient health-care applications generate enormous amounts of personal data. These data may be abused by the authorities for political manipulation and social control. Other abuses may be surveillance of people and recording of consumer behavior. In many IoT applications, sensitive information about people may be sent over multiple hops and stored and processed several times in different computers, severely increasing the probability that confidential information is compromised.

Security is the biggest concern related to IoT. The IoT will consist of billions of devices designed to different security standards (if any at all). Security concerns include weak authentication, weak or no access control protection, unencrypted messages, no firewall protection, and improper security updating. The result is a network with very many access points vulnerable to cyberattacks. In some applications, for example, autonomous driving and remote monitoring of medical devices, cyberattacks may result in accidents and loss of life. Poorly protected IoT devices may be captured and assimilated in large botnets to become formidable tools in distributed denial of service attacks. Internet of Things Security Foundation is a nonprofit international organization promoting security best practices and management.

Safety is an important issue in IoT systems, particularly, those used in complex systems where errors may lead to disasters. IoT systems may, as all software systems, contain bugs, flaws, and unintended interactions. One characteristic of complex systems is that they may contain pathways into hidden states causing deadlock or other errors. These states may be legitimate operational states in some applications but may cause problems in other cases. The existence of such conditions is difficult to identify using standard software production and checking tools. Systems controlling hardware are particularly vulnerable to errors leading to unsafe physical states because of the damage they may instigate, for example, power grids, sluices regulating river flows, pacemakers, or traffic safety systems for autonomous driving.

The term Internet of Things was coined by Kevin Ashton at Procter & Gamble in 1999 (Ashton, 2009). At that time, a few simple logistics applications existed such as routing of luggage in airports, tagging of containers and goods for simple identification and sorting, and locating objects and animals (e.g., tagging of cattle and pets). Between 2008 and 2009, the number of objects connected to the Internet surpassed the number of people connected to the network. According to Cisco, the ratio of connected objects to connected people was only 0.08 in 2003, while in 2010 this number had increased to 1.84 (Evans, 2011).

There are several obstacles slowing the evolution of IoT: lack of killer applications; unclear business propositions and usability; lack of standards and interoperability; security, safety, and privacy concerns; and, perhaps the most important, IoT not fitting easily into traditional public or industrial governance structures.

2.5 Conclusions

The evolution of the digital economy is intimately connected to several technological innovations.
- The evolution started by the invention of the transistor in 1947. The evolution ever since is intimately linked to how densely transistors can be packed on microchips and how fast microelectronic circuits can operate.
- The Internet offered a simple, cheap, and effective communications platform for data communication (especially since the early 1980s). The Internet allowed computers to be interconnected in a dynamic, flexible, and effective way.
- The World Wide Web created the real killer applications (commercialized in 1993) enabling social media, high-speed streaming services, and sharing services. It is the World Wide Web that created the digital economy as we know it today.
- The evolution of data communication over digital mobile cellular networks started with GSM in 1991 and gained speed when the 3G technology was introduced 10 years later. Cellular mobile systems make communications ubiquitous in a new way by making it independent of place and time.

These events have led to the convergence of networks and services as explained in ▶ Chap. 3. With the Internet of Things, ICT has entered new and enormous fields of applications.

Questions
1. Give examples of both new and old information and communication technologies that are still in use today.
2. What are the major challenges that may hamper the evolution of IoT?
3. Why are mobile systems (public or local) so important in IoT?

Answers
1. Old technologies include TCP, IP, and SMTP. New technologies include smartphones, Bitcoin, and 5G.
2. Privacy concerns, safety and reliability of operation, prone to cyberattacks, lack of standards, does not fit well with traditional governance standards.
3. Because very many applications require wireless access (health care, autonomous driving, smart transport, environmental surveillance, etc.); easier and faster to install.

References

Ashton, K. (2009, June 22). That "Internet of Things" Thing. *RFID Journal*.
Cisco Annual Internet Report (2018–2023). (2020, March 9). White Paper. *Cisco*.
Cisco Visual Networking Index: Forecasts and Trends 2017–2022. (2019). White paper. *Cisco public*.
Evans, D. (2011). The Internet of Things. How the Next Evolution of the Internet is Changing Everything. *CISCO White Paper*.

References

Laws, D. (2018, April 02). 13 sexillions & counting: The long & winding road to the most frequently manufactured artefact in history. *Computer History Museum*.
Northeast blackout of 2003. (2020, December 17). *Wikipedia*.
Patel, H. (2018). How IoT & smart home automation will change the way we live. *Tristate Technology*.
State of IoT Healthcare. (2019). *Aruba* (Hewlett Packard Enterprise).
Wikipedia. (2020, December 17). *Transistor count*.

Further Reading

Abbate, J. (1999). *Inventing the internet*. The MIT Press.
Brynjolfsson, E., & Saunders, A. (2013). *Wired for innovation*. The MIT Press.

Convergence of Technologies and Services

Contents

3.1 Dedicated Networks – 34

3.2 Early Attempts of Service Integration – 35

3.3 Service Integration over the Internet – 37

3.4 Toward Next-Generation Network – 40

3.5 Conclusions – 42

References – 43

© The Author(s), under exclusive license to Springer Nature Switzerland AG 2021
H. Øverby, J. A. Audestad, *Introduction to Digital Economics*, Classroom Companion: Business,
https://doi.org/10.1007/978-3-030-78237-5_3

Learning Objectives

After completing this chapter, you should be able to:
- Explain how the evolution from dedicated networks for telephony, data communications, and broadcast to an integrated network supporting all types of technologies has taken place.
- Appreciate the roles of the Internet and mobile networks as generators of this process.
- Understand how the convergence has changed the technological landscape.

3.1 Dedicated Networks

Historically, separate and dedicated communication networks were designed for carrying different telecommunication services. This means that a separate and dedicated physical infrastructure was constructed for each digital service offered. Hence, the provision of a new service (e.g., TV or radio) demanded the building of a completely new physical infrastructure, in which most cases had huge up-front costs. Examples of such dedicated network include:
- Public switched telephone network (PSTN) for telephone services. This network also supports the facsimile service and several value added services, for example, premium rate calls, free-phone, televoting, and particular call handling services such as time-dependent call routing.
- Public mobile networks for voice, data, and messaging services (SMS and MMS).
- Wireless one-way networks for audio and television broadcasting.
- Cable and satellite networks for audio and television broadcasting.
- Telex network for low-speed text transmission.
- Satellite access networks for communication with ships, aircraft, land mobile terminals, and remote areas (e.g., Inmarsat, Skyphone, and Iridium).
- Dedicated data networks for various digital data services, for example, the X.25 network and the Internet.
- Dedicated networks for search, rescue, and distress communications.
- Fixed and wireless telegraphy networks using the International Morse Code, for example, used for distress communications with ships and for railway signaling.

All these networks, except the telegraphy networks, the telex network, and some early data networks (X.25), are still in operation today. Telegraphy based on the International Morse Code was standardized for continental Europe in 1851. Other countries, e.g., the UK and USA, used other incompatible methods. In 1865, the International Telegraph Union—now the International Telecommunications Union (ITU)—was established for the purpose of technical, operational, and commercial standardization of a single international telegraphy service to be used in all parts of the world. The service was mandatory for commercial ships for distress communications until 2000 when the International Maritime Organization (a specialized UN organization) decided that telegraphy was no longer needed since satellites offered a more reliable service. The world's oldest telecommunications service was terminated after about 150 years of operation. However, the technology is still used by radio amateurs. The services offered by the telex network has been replaced by email, and the public X.25 packet switched data network has been replaced by the Internet.

Audio broadcasts have been sent as analog signals over wireless networks since the 1920s (also denoted "over the air audio broadcasting"). From 1993, digitized audio broadcasts have also been offered over the Internet (Internet radio, web radio, or webcasting). Over the air radio broadcasting is now also shifting from analog to digital technology (e.g., digital audio broadcast (DAB)) and are also offered as real-time services over the Internet (Internet radio) as well as over wireless networks. Television programs have, in addition to over the air transmission, been broadcasted over dedicated cable networks since the 1950s and over satellites since 1976. From the early 2000s, television programs have also been available over the Internet. Some television broadcasters, such as the BBC, offer their television programs on web pages in addition to delivering them over cable or satellite networks. The Internet allows listening to or viewing broadcast services at any time independently of when the program was transmitted over wireless or other media. There are also several pay-per-view Internet services such as Netflix and HBO offering movies, series, and other video content. Some television companies only offer their programs over the Internet.

3.2 Early Attempts of Service Integration

Attempts to design one integrated network supporting services carried by the PSTN and dedicated data networks started in the late 1970s resulting in the Integrated Services Digital Network (ISDN) standard in 1988. The failure of ISDN was that it did not amalgamate the telephone network and the packet data network into a common network except at the subscriber line. The transport network for telephony and data still existed as two separate networks. The next attempt was to merge the telephone network and packet data network into a single transport network using the Asynchronous Transfer Mode (ATM) technology. This attempt failed because the technology was ready for implementation at the same time as the Internet expanded into a worldwide platform open for access for everyone. At the same time, cellular mobile communications grew rapidly offering location-independent services on a global scale.

To appreciate the challenges associated with service integration, some basic technological concepts must be understood: *circuit switching, packet switching, connection-oriented transfer of data, and connectionless transfer of data.*

Definition 3.1
Circuit switching implies that a physical two-way (duplex) connection between the users exists so long as the communication session lasts.

The telephone network is a circuit switched network where a two-way physical connection is established over several telephone exchanges for the duration of the call. A circuit switched connection can be used for only one communication session at a time.

> **Definition 3.2**
>
> *Packet switching* implies that chunks of data (e.g., speech or video samples, emails, web pages, and so on) are sent as independent packets of data.

At the switching devices in the network (the routers), the packets are queued before they are forwarded to the next router or to the recipient. Moreover, packets belonging to different communication sessions are arbitrarily mixed when they are sent over the communication links between routers and between routers and terminals. For this reason, packet switched networks offer better utilization of the communication infrastructure than circuit switched networks: for voice communication, each direction of a telephone circuit is on average busy only 40% of the time so that 60% of the transmission capacity is wasted. For the transfer of pictures and documents over the telephone network (telephoto or facsimile), both directions of communication are used, but only one is occupied by transfer of information.

> **Definition 3.3**
>
> *Connection-oriented transfer* means that an association is established between the users before information is transferred between them. The association is retained until all information has been transferred.

> **Definition 3.4**
>
> *Connectionless transfer* means that no such association is established, and data is transferred in independent packages.

A circuit switched connection is always connection oriented, while a data connection may either be connection oriented or connectionless. Connection-oriented packet switched connections are also referred to as *virtual circuits*. Note that the Internet protocol (IP) itself is connectionless. Connection-oriented data transfer is achieved by imbedding a connection-oriented protocol in the IP packets. The most used connection-oriented protocol on the Internet is the Transmission Control Protocol (TCP) (the TCP/IP protocol suit).

The idea behind the *Integrated Services Digital Network* (ISDN) was to provide both telephone services and packet switched data transmission over the infrastructure of the telephone network. It turns out that it is impossible to incorporate packet switching in a circuit switched environment. The ISDN, therefore, consists of two parallel transport networks: the telephone network and the—now obsolete—X.25 packet switched data network. Therefore, the ISDN never became a common network for circuit switched and packet switched services. On the other hand, data services and telephone services can easily be integrated on the copper lines connecting the user to the network by simple multiplexing methods. The ISDN signaling protocol and the multiplexing on the subscriber line also allows the ISDN user to connect to several other users at the same time.

The two most important advantages of ISDN are that new subscriber lines need not be deployed for data transmission and that several simultaneous communication sessions can be established on each subscriber line. However, ADSL and related subscriber line technologies provide similar and simpler solutions to provide broadband data combined with telephony over subscriber lines. ISDN are also nicknamed as "Innovations Subscribers Don't Need" or "It Still Does Nothing" since the technology does not offer much more than was already available on the PSTN and dedicated data networks.

Asynchronous Transfer Mode (ATM) was developed for supporting both telephony and broadband data over a common packet switched high-speed optical network (140 megabits per second). The development of ATM took place during the 1990s coinciding with the commercialization of the Internet. Data and speech samples are sent in small data packets containing only 48 bytes of information. Short packets (or cells as they are called) sent at high speed makes it easy to avoid that the voice and video signals are destroyed by timing fluctuations. Because of the particular routing algorithm chosen for packet transfer, all data is sent in a connection-oriented mode; that is, a complete connection must be established between the users before data is sent. This applies independently of the amount of data being sent—even the transfer of less than 48 bytes fitting into a single cell requires the establishment and release of a connection.

At the time when the ATM specification had been finalized, the Internet had been commercialized and had already replaced most of the X.25 networks. Internet is a simple and cheap network, and, initially, users were not urging for integrating voice and data communication. Because of the popularity of the Internet and the rapid increase in mobile communication, ATM was never realized in large scale, and the ATM Forum promoting the technology became the Broadband Forum in 2005 concerned with broadband network technologies in general.

3.3 Service Integration over the Internet

The success of providing voice communications over the Internet is related to the development of voice coding standards referred to as voice over IP (VoIP). Development of these standards begun in 1995 by Microsoft and Intel and in 1996 by ITU. During the early 2000s, VoIP providers proliferated. The largest application of VoIP two decades later is over 4G and 5G mobile networks. 4G and 5G mobile networks offer only packet switched Internet connections for all services, and circuit switched applications are no longer offered in the latest generations of mobile networks.

It also turns out that the Internet is an excellent network for providing many different types of services. The TCP/IP protocol stack enables the offering of different services with different requirements to quality-of-service. The flexible addressing scheme of the Internet also enables worldwide transfer of data. The open nature of the Internet enables a wide range of services that use the Internet as a communication platform, including web browsing, voice and video communication, messaging, gaming, banking, and information retrieval. Hence, the Internet is technical capable of offering most—if not all—services that have previously been transported over different dedicated networks.

In 2021, it is evident that the traditional telecommunications infrastructure is soon to be replaced by only two networks: a cellular mobile Internet and a fixed Internet, both offering the same services. The difference between them is the way in which the users are connected to the network. In the cellular mobile Internet, the users are connected via 4G or 5G land mobile networks or via low Earth orbit (LEO) satellite systems (see the example in ▶ Sect. 3.4). In the fixed Internet, the users are connected via cables or optical fibers. The major difference between these networks is the bandwidth: it is simpler to offer wideband data via optical fibers than over wireless connections. ◘ Figure 3.1 illustrates how this convergence has gradually taken place during the last 30 years. The conversion process is illustrated by the arrows from the fixed telephone service and broadcast service to the mobile and fixed Internet services. The arrows are plotted against technological evolutions either triggering or enhancing the process.

Since GSM was put into operation in 1991, the fixed-telephone service has gradually been replaced by the mobile telephone service. While the number of subscriptions of mobile cellular services has tripled between 2005 and 2018 globally,

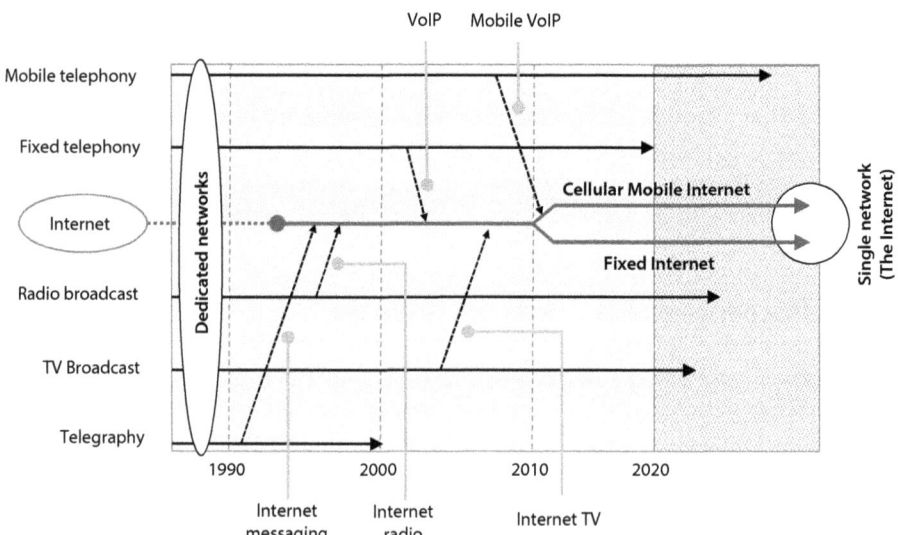

◘ Fig. 3.1 The evolution from many dedicated networks to a single network—the Internet constituting a fixed and a mobile part. Over time, services previously only available on dedicated networks move over to the Internet. Finally—when the Internet contains all service functionality available on dedicated networks—the dedicated network is shut down. (Authors' own figure)

3.3 · Service Integration over the Internet

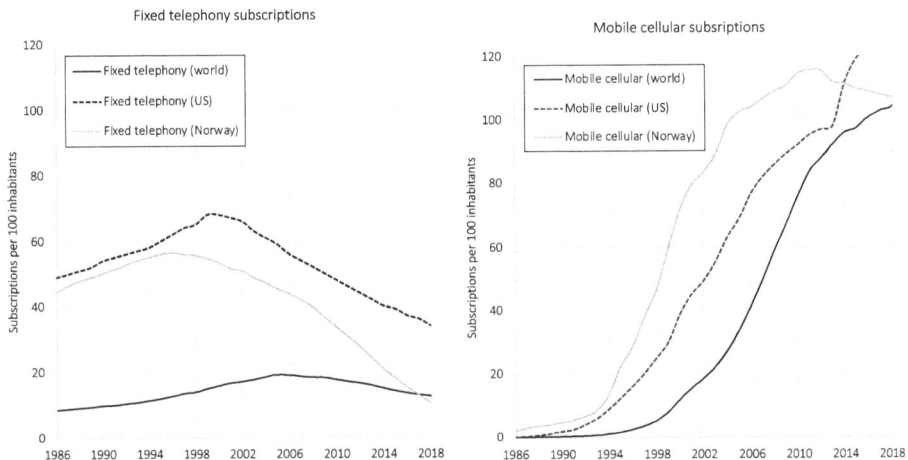

■ **Fig. 3.2** Evolution of fixed telephony and mobile cellular subscriptions. (Authors' own figure, data extracted from (The World Bank Open Data. ► https://data.worldbank.org/))

the number of fixed-telephone subscriptions is reduced by about 30% in the same period (see ■ Fig. 3.2 (The World Bank Open Data. ► https://data.worldbank.org/)). The situation in the Nordic countries is even more dramatic: the number of fixed-telephone subscriptions is halved from 2013 to 2018, giving a halftime of only 5 years (Telecommunications services in the Nordic and Baltic countries in 2018, 2019). The smartphone market in the Nordic countries has been saturated during the same period, indicating that most individuals in these countries are now only using their smartphones as their only telephone services. The same smartphone is also most often used for both private and business purposes, also reducing the need for the fixed-telephone service in industry and public and private organizations. Part of the fixed telephone traffic has also been replaced by voice over IP (VoIP) and related technologies (Skype, Google Hangouts, and WhatsApp). However, this replacement of the fixed telephone service was slow until 4G was put into operation around 2010. This triggered the rapid reduction in fixed telephones we see today. By the end of 2020, the telephone network was terminated in Norway, and the service has been replaced by 4G and 5G mobile networks.

The mobile Internet service is the component of the general mobile service carrying packet data over IP. The service was introduced when the GPRS (General Packet Radio Service) functionality was added to the GSM system in 2000. GPRS was developed further in the 3G standard, and until 4G was released, the cellular mobile communications networks were designed as dual networks, where one part offered circuit switched telephone services and the other part offered packet switched data services over a common radio interface. 4G, opened in the early 2010s, is a pure Internet system only offering packet switching based on IP version 6 technologies called IP Multimedia System (IMS) and VoLTE. VoLTE (Voice over Long-Term Evolution) is a more bandwidth efficient and flexible technology than the ordinary VoIP technologies used on the Internet. The general international trend is (as in Norway) that 4G and 5G mobile network technologies will replace the telephone network. Interworking units between the mobile Internet and the PSTN will connect regions where the PSTN still exists.

Most audio broadcast and television services are now also available as real-time streaming services over the Internet. This is often referred to as webcasting. Webcasting does not require a separate network of radio transmitters, cables, or satellites to reach the audience. It only requires broadband access to the internet, and shows may be produced using cameras on smartphone or personal computers or standalone webcams. The technology is cheap, and anyone may afford to produce real-time video programs and send them over the internet—or become a webcaster. However, there may be certain restrictions associated with webcasting; for example, if the program contains copyrighted material (e.g., music), the producer may have a license from the authorities to broadcast it as a commercial product. Examples of webcasting are real-time audiovisual dissemination of lectures, meetings, concerts, weddings (nicknamed wedcast), and funeral ceremonies. Certain webcasts may be viewed for free, while some are paid for per view, and still others require prepaid subscription fees.

One type of broadcasting service is the podcast. The term was originally used for radio programs made available as audio files that could be downloaded to iPods. Podcast is now more generally used for episodic series of audio or video shows that can be downloaded to MP3 players, other media players, smartphones, or computers as webpages. Some podcasters offer subscription services where the episodes are downloaded automatically to the user equipment.

Even though most television and radio broadcasts are available on the Internet as webcasts and podcasts, there will still be a need for broadcasting services over cables, satellites, and radio transmitters for a long time to come.

3.4 Toward Next-Generation Network

We have just seen that the fixed telephone network is about to disappear and be replaced by "all-IP" high-speed core and broadband access networks supporting a mixture of simultaneous voice, messaging, video, broadcast, and data services. This network is then the first network satisfying the definition of the next-generation network (NGN). In 2004, Study Group 13 of ITU-T defined NGN as follows (The quote paragraph is found on the link: ► https://www.itu.int/ITU-T/studygroups/com13/ngn2004/working_definition.html):

"A next-generation network (NGN) is a packet-based network which can provide services including Telecommunication Services and is able to make use of multiple broadband, Quality of Service-enabled transport technologies and in which service-related functions are independent from underlying transport-related technologies. It offers unrestricted access by users to different service providers. It supports generalized mobility which will allow consistent and ubiquitous provision of services to users."

The evolution toward the NGN has taken a long time but has recently gained speed mainly because of the rapid rollout of 4G networks in many countries. The reasons for the slow start were both technological and commercial. Technological

3.4 · Toward Next-Generation Network

reasons were, for example, related to low data rates in mobile systems, insufficient capacity in transport networks resulting in large fluctuations in the delay of data packets making them unsuitable for broadband streaming services, slow computer hardware, and simply because it takes time to develop and implement new technologies. The most important commercial reason is that it is expensive to build a new network.

One approach toward new network configurations is the use of low Earth orbit satellites. Some of these projects are reviewed in the case study.

IP in the Sky

The feasibility of offering satellite services directly to the users of maritime and aeronautical applications using geostationary satellites was confirmed by several studies in the late 1960s. This led to the establishment of the Inmarsat organization in 1981, primarily offering satellite communications to ships and later also to aircraft. These systems are using geostationary satellites at a height of 36,000 kilometers above the Equator. These systems require big and expensive satellites and are not feasible for cheap broadband communications with handheld terminals. For this purpose, several systems using lightweight satellites in low Earth orbits (LEO) (less than 2000 kilometers above the Earth) have been put into operation or are planned. For more details, see the homepages for the projects listed below.

Iridium is a system consisting of 66 satellites in polar orbits at a height of 780 kilometers above the Earth. The original concept included 77 satellites, and the system was named after the element with atomic number 77 in the periodic table, iridium, since the system looked like an atomic nucleus surrounded by 77 electrons. The Iridium system was downscaled to 66 satellites. Element number 66 is dysprosium, a less appealing name, so that the original name was kept.

Iridium commenced operation in 1998 after severe initial financial problems, offering telephone services to handheld terminals. Since 2018, the system also offers data communications with data rates from 128 kilobits per second to 8 megabits per second to fixed and mobile terminals.

Globalstar is an American company offering telephone services and low-speed data communications (9.6 kilobits per second) to portable telephone and data terminals. The system consists of 24 satellites at a height of 1400 kilometers in orbits with an inclination of 52 degrees.

ORBCOMM offers Internet of Things (IoT) connections using both cellular and satellite networks. The company has more than two million subscribers in more than 130 countries. The satellite network consists of 31 lightweight satellites in various low Earth orbits offering low-speed data communications to IoT devices. The company has offered satellite communications since 1990.

Teledesic was founded in 1990 to build a global satellite network for broadband Internet communications. The system should consist of 840 satellites in low Earth orbits. It was soon downscaled to 288 satellites. The project was abandoned in 2002

(Godwin, 2002). Bill Gates was one of the founders of the company. Even though the system was never built, it is interesting because the idea behind the project lived on and may now be realized as OneWeb and Starlink commence operation.

OneWeb is a UK-based company that launched the first satellites in February 27, 2019. The constellation will eventually consist of 650 LEO satellites offering Internet services globally.

Starlink is a satellite system established by SpaceX, a company founded by Elon Musk. The system will consist of thousands of small LEO satellites offering global broadband Internet access for everyone. By the end of 2020, more than 1000 satellites have been placed in orbit.

There are several other planned projects, for example, by Facebook and Amazon.

3.5 Conclusions

Since the early 1970s, the telecommunications industry has been striving to specify techniques by which the telephone services and the data services can be supported by a single network. This led first to the development of the ISDN and thereafter to ATM. Both attempts failed: ISDN since, except for the subscriber line, it did not really integrate the PSTN and the data network and ATM because the technology was too late and was replaced by the much cheaper and more flexible Internet just when it was ready for implementation.

All types of services can be adapted to the Internet technology. In this respect, the Internet is a true integrated network. However, it took several years before the Internet became an important carrier of voice services so that the service integration process could really commence. This had to wait until the 4G mobile network was put into operation in 2010.

GSM was put into operation in 1991 offering mobile telephone services. The foremost advantage of mobile communication is flexibility: mobile networks allow people to make and receive telephone calls and other services anytime and anywhere. During the next two decades, the mobile networks were developed into a mobile Internet supporting all services—voice, data, and broadcast—by a single technology (4G). This evolution finally resulted in a fully integrated network, and the convergence of all services could eventually commence. In 2020, there is technically no need for a separate telephone network. In Norway, the telephone network was terminated in 2020.

However, there may still be a need for dedicated networks because the Internet may not be reliable enough to support critical infrastructures such as distress services, energy production, and finance.

Questions
1. What are the major benefits and challenges of a fully converged ICT infrastructure?
2. How will the cost of operating and managing ICT infrastructures change due to convergence?

3. Is it possible for the Internet to accommodate all kinds of services offered on current dedicated networks?
4. How will Starlink alter the competition in the telecommunications market?

Answers
1. The major benefit is that there will be fewer networks to build, maintain, and operate. The network will offer many new services and combine them in new ways that will support new applications. The major challenge is competition since it will be easier to build new networks.
2. Managing and operation of the network will probably be cheaper and more efficient.
3. The Internet offers best-effort services. This makes it difficult to guaranty quality-of-service objectives related to resilience, latency, timing accuracy and jitter, loss of information, and priority. Therefore, it may not be possible to support certain applications (e.g., distress operations) in a proper way, hence requiring dedicated networks.
4. Starlink will, because of global coverage, compete with all other telecommunications operators worldwide. They will also offer communications to areas which are not accessible to other telecommunications operators.

Exercise
List some of the new benefits 5G systems will offer. Search the Internet (e.g., Wikipedia) to find out more about 5G systems.

Answers
This is some of the benefits:
- Offer wide-band wireless services in the range of 400 megabits per second to 2 or more gigabits per second (depending on cell size and frequencies).
- Better utilization of the frequency spectrum (less overhead and more efficient access technologies).
- Better mix of radio cell sizes (from a few meters to several kilometers).
- Offer edge computing, thereby reducing the latency for certain applications, e.g., for applications on the Internet of Things. Edge computing means that software and storage are brought close to the user, e.g., located in the base station.
- New methods for orchestrating services consisting of multiple applications (network slicing).
- Capable of connecting millions of devices to the same base station (e.g., sensor networks).
- Convergence of cellular mobile networks and Wi-Fi and other local area network technologies.

References

Godwin, R.. (2002, October 3). Teledesic backs away from satellite. *ZD Net*.
Telecommunications services in the Nordic and Baltic countries in 2018. (2019, December 14). *Report received from NKOM (Norwegian Communications Authority)*.

Digital Economy Ecosystem

Contents

4.1 Ecosystem Metaphor – 46

4.2 Ecosystem Components – 48

4.3 The Layered Internet as Ecosystem Component – 51

4.4 Computer Infrastructure and Platforms as Ecosystem Components – 54

4.5 Applications and Content as Ecosystem Component – 56

4.6 Consumers as Ecosystem Component – 56

4.7 Authorities as Ecosystem Components – 57

4.8 Conclusions – 58

References – 59

© The Author(s), under exclusive license to Springer Nature Switzerland AG 2021
H. Øverby, J. A. Audestad, *Introduction to Digital Economics*, Classroom Companion: Business,
https://doi.org/10.1007/978-3-030-78237-5_4

Learning Objectives

After completing this chapter, you should be able to:
- Identify both direct and indirect the stakeholders in the ecosystem of a company in the digital market.
- Analyze the impact each stakeholder has on the market performance.
- Identify the interactions, critical relationships, and dependencies between the stakeholders.

4.1 Ecosystem Metaphor

The concept of business ecosystems was first proposed by James F. Moore in 1993 in a *Harvard Business Review* article (Moore, 1993):

"To extend a systematic approach to strategy, I suggest that a company be viewed not as a member of a single industry but as part of a *business ecosystem* that crosses a variety of industries. In a business ecosystem, companies coevolve capabilities around a new innovation: they work cooperatively and competitively to support new products, satisfy customer needs, and eventually incorporate the next round of innovations."

Since then, the concept has been used regularly as a tool to analyze business strategies; in particular, the complex businesses arising in the digital economy.

The concept is a biological metaphor since many of the new digital businesses are imbedded in a complex community of other cooperating and competing businesses and customers much like the coevolving ecosystems in biology. Removing one stakeholder from this community may have severe repercussion on the businesses of the remaining stakeholders in the same way as the removal of one species in a biological ecosystem may sometimes alter the whole ecosystem system in a negative way or even destroy it. ▶ Box 4.1 illustrates the vulnerability of a biological ecosystem where the removal of a single species destroys the whole ecosystem. Industry may be equally vulnerable to apparently small alterations in the business environment, for example, change in regulations, customer habits, discovery of new raw materials, and better production methods.

Box 4.1   Illustration of the Vulnerability of a Biological Ecosystem

The vulnerability of a biological ecosystem is illustrated by a small but well-documented ecosystem in the salt marches in Southern California (Lafferty & Morris, 1996). The ecosystem consists primarily of four species: the parasite *Euhaplorchis californiensis*, horn snails, killifish, and seabirds. The horn snail and the killifish are intermediate hosts for the parasite. The bird is the final host in which the parasite matures sexually and produces eggs

4.1 · Ecosystem Metaphor

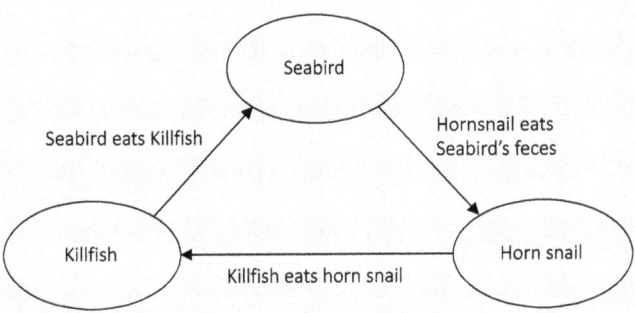

Fig. 4.1 Biological ecosystem. (Authors' own figure)

that are spread by the bird's feces that are eaten by the snails. This completes the life cycle of the parasite as shown in **Fig. 4.1**.

The parasite alters the behavior of the intermediate hosts: the snails search for water where they are eaten by the killifish; the infected fish is no longer afraid of birds and becomes an easy prey. In one area, the authorities decided to remove the parasite to make the beach healthier. This caused a complete collapse of the ecosystem: the snails no longer searched for water, the killifish disappeared since there was no more easily accessible food close to the shore, and so did the birds because easy prey was no longer available.

The biological metaphor is a fruitful analogy since the complexity and unpredictability of the evolution of the information technology is a result of visible and hidden as well as planned and unplanned interactions within a business ecosystem consisting of entrepreneurs, researchers and developers, software and hardware platform providers, system integrators, network providers, government authorities, and communities of individuals participating directly or indirectly in the evolution (Muegge, 2013). Examples of systems resulting from such complex and unpredictable interactions are the Internet itself and the smartphone technology consisting of an intricate hierarchy of devices, services, and applications. Peer-production, crowdsourcing, and the use of free and open software make the ecosystem even more multifaceted and unpredictably complex (see ► Chap. 7).

The digital economy depends intimately on the information and communication technology (ICT) and consists of elements such as the Internet, smartphones, data storage, and processing. Put differently, digital services require ICT to manage and propagate its value proposition to the consumers. The interplay between digital services, information and communication technologies, providers of digital services, competitors, digital marketplaces, consumers, and society at large is the core feature shaping the digital economy. This interplay is called the *digital economy ecosystem*.

> **Definition 4.1**
> The *digital economy ecosystem* describes the relations and dependencies between digital services, ICT infrastructures, digital markets, and authorities in a socioeconomic context.

4.2 Ecosystem Components

The only way to appreciate the complexity of the business ecosystem of digital services is to identify the basic technologies and building blocks it contains.

◘ Figure 4.2 illustrates the digital economy ecosystem and some basic technologies and stakeholders on which it depends. The global ICT infrastructure—owned by the Internet service providers (ISPs) and the network providers (NP)—is the carrier of digital services, including applications and content. This ICT infrastructure consists of interconnected networks of networks including the Internet, mobile networks, wireless networks, local area networks, fiber networks, and satellite networks. It also includes storage of data and computing facilities. The ICT infrastructure is accessed by various types of user equipment—devices—including mobile phones, smartphones, PCs, laptops, and other terminals. Such user equipment is manufactured and offered by device providers (DP). Application service providers (ASPs) offer applications to the consumers by trading them in the digital marketplace. Applications run on devices and may feature content offered by content providers (CP). An example of this is YouTube—an ASP—offering video content to users, in which the producers of content are CPs. Consumers and pro-

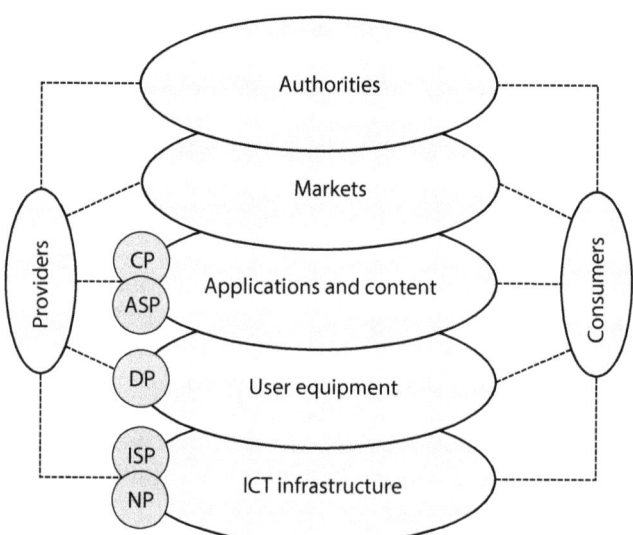

◘ **Fig. 4.2** The digital economy ecosystem. (Authors' own figure)

4.2 · Ecosystem Components

viders interact with authorities adapting legal frameworks and satisfying societal demands. To understand this complex environment, it is necessary to investigate how the different elements of the digital ecosystem interact with one another.

A digital service usually depends on other digital services to provide value to consumers. Existing digital services are also the basis for the development of new digital services. For example, the business of Amazon depends on digital payment services to offer e-commerce, and Spotify depends on access to digitized music to provide streaming services to consumers. These services may, in turn, depend on various functionalities offered by several ICT providers and other providers of hardware and software support functions. Together, these dependencies make up the digital economy ecosystem for the particular business. It may be impossible to identify all dependencies merely because of complexity and transient relationships that may arise and vanish during the production of the good. The complexity of the ecosystem is exemplified in ◘ Fig. 4.3 where a digital Service A depends on two other digital services (B and C) as well as two technologies (cloud storage and wireless access). Furthermore, Service E depends on Service A, while Service D and Service A depend on each other. ◘ Figure 4.3 also suggests a simple method by which the ecosystem can be modeled to analyze the impact each dependency has on the primary business. This analysis may also uncover critical dependencies, unexpected vulnerabilities, structural weaknesses, and other problems.

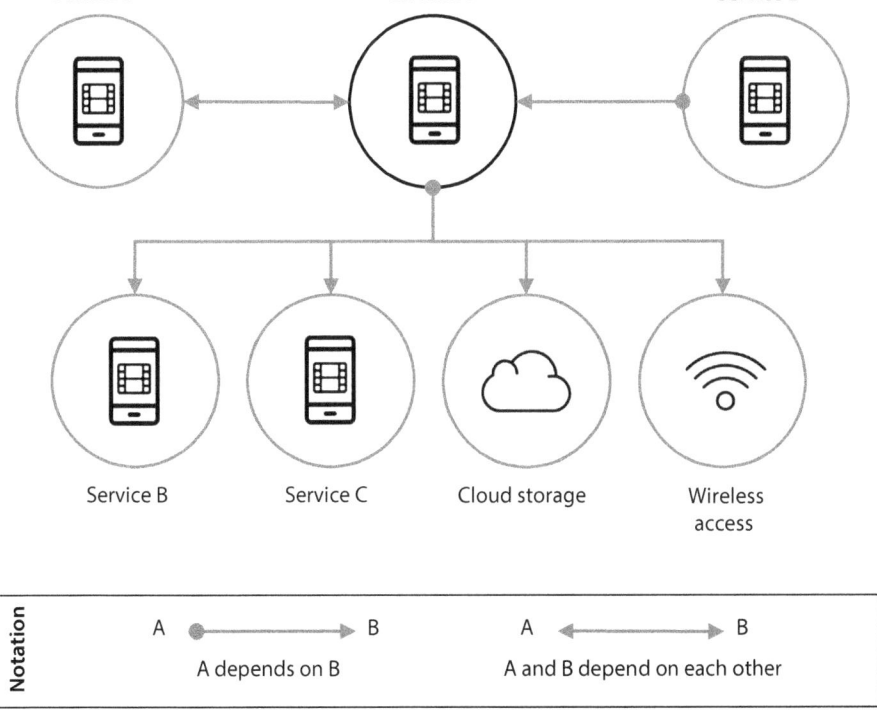

◘ **Fig. 4.3** Dependencies in the digital economy ecosystem. (Authors' own figure)

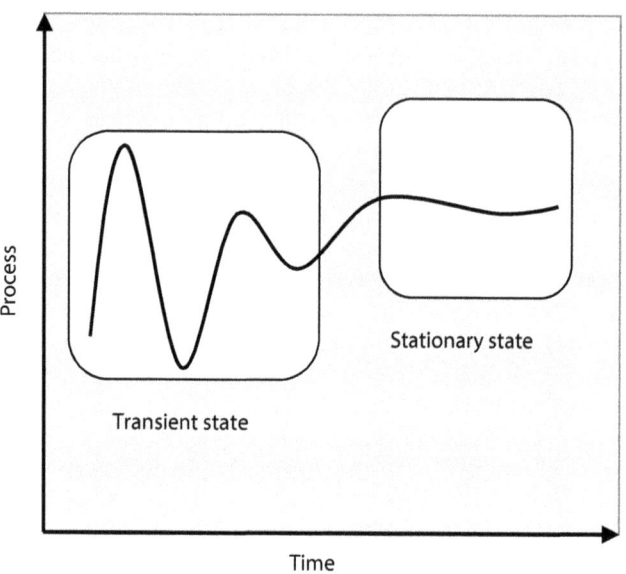

Fig. 4.4 Transient and stationary states. (Authors' own figure)

The complexities and dependencies in the digital economy ecosystem result in a market that is never the same from one day to the next. Changes such as new stakeholders entering the market, development of new technologies, variations in consumer adoption, altered competition arenas, new legislation and market regulations, and fluctuating dependencies among the stakeholders, all contribute to a market state that is more transient in nature than stationary. ◘ Figure 4.4 illustrates the difference between transient and stationary states. The transient view of the digital economy is consistent with the teachings in *complexity economics* (Durlauf, 1998). In complexity economics, the basic argument is that the economy is ever-changing and will never reach a stationary state. The reasons for this are rooted in the *digital economy ecosystem* and the rate of *technological innovation*.

For a stationary market to exist, most of the market aspects mentioned above must be stable and unchanging. In the digital economy, new technologies are, in contrast to stationary markets, developed and adopted at a rapid rate. A good example is digital mobile communication which has changed from supporting simple telephone and messaging services (GSM in 1990) to offer a mix of telephone services, messaging services, data services, broadband streaming services, and IoT (5G in 2020) by adding new service capabilities, upgrading the network architecture, and implementing new access technologies every few years.

New technologies often lead to new business models, thereby causing changes in the digital economy ecosystem. In mobile communications, this has been an evolution from simple services offered by a single telephone services provider to services offered by an amalgamation of almost all kinds of application service providers (ASPs). All this contributes to the transient nature of the digital economy.
► Chapter 18 presents quantitative models for analyzing the transient nature of the digital economy.

4.3 The Layered Internet as Ecosystem Component

One of the most important events in the evolution of digital markets was the commercialization of the World Wide Web (WWW) in 1993. Before 1993, network operation and service provision were integrated industries, and consumers could not freely choose network access independently of service. The WWW led to a restructuring of the ICT business in which network operation and service provision became independent industries. This was possible because of the layered technological architecture of the Internet.

◘ Figure 4.5 shows the layered Internet model in which the Internet is divided into three parallel planes: networks, user equipment, and applications. The

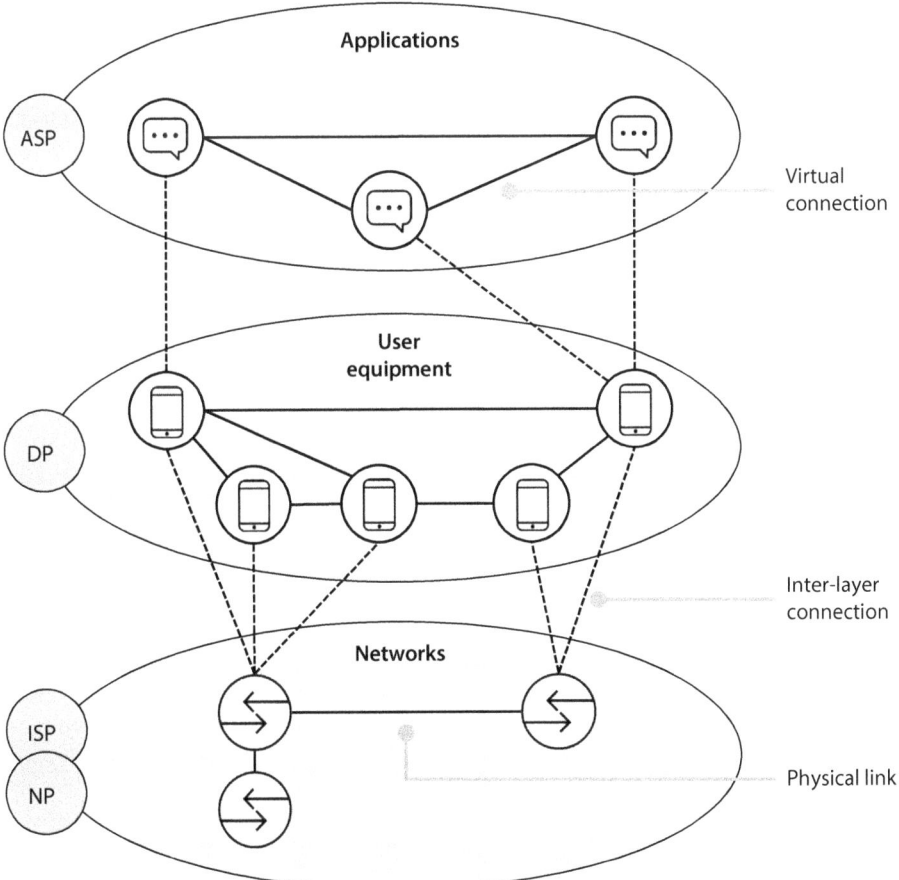

◘ Fig. 4.5 The layered Internet model. (Authors' own figure)

three planes correspond to three independent business areas: (1) networks; (2) the development, production, and sale of user equipment; and (3) the provision of services, information, system management, and remote sensing and control (Audestad, 2007).

The *networks plane* shows the physical communication network as a graph in which communication links (physical links) interconnect the routers using the Internet protocol (IP). This graph then symbolizes the physical network supporting the businesses of the network providers (NPs) and the Internet service providers (ISPs). This is, strictly speaking, what is defined as the Internet.

The *user equipment plane* consists of a graph in which the hosts (e.g., computers, servers, and databases) are nodes, and a connection between two hosts indicates that the hosts are taking part in a common computation. This is the transport layer, and TCP/UDP/SCTP[1] connections exist between hosts. The user equipment plane is the business domain of the device providers (DPs).

The *application plane* is a graph in which software objects (applications) are nodes. A connection between two nodes (often referred to as virtual connection) indicates that the corresponding software objects take part in a common computation. A smartphone and downloaded apps are nodes in such a graph. This graph is dynamic and may alter configurations in milliseconds. This may then include complex configurations such as cloud computing, software-defined networking (SDN), virtualization (NFV), and service-oriented architecture (SOA). The application plane is the business arena of the application service providers (ASPs) and the content providers (CPs).

Since software runs on computers and computers are connected to the Internet, there also exist vertical interactions (inter-layer connections) between the layers as shown by dotted lines. Note that the structures of the graphs on each layer are independent of one another except that there must be a path in the network plane connecting two hosts in order for a TCP/UDP/SCTP connection to exist between them. A TCP/UDP/SCTP link must exist between two software objects running on different hosts to take part in a common computation.

Note also that competition takes place between stakeholders on the same layer of this model. There is no competition between operators on different layers. The user equipment layer can then be regarded as the demarcation line between the business segments of the ISPs in the network plane and the ASPs in the application plane. The important point is that the ISP cannot perceive what kind of services is carried by the network since this is obscured by the protocol on the transport layer (TCP/UDP/SCTP) itself and the Transport Layer Security (TLS) encryption protocol in particular. This has a severe impact on pricing regimes available to the ISP: since the ISP cannot identify the type of service, the ISP cannot levy differentiated charges. The ISP is then forced to apply service-independent

---

1 TCP = Transmission Control Protocol for connection-oriented data transfer, UDP = User Datagram Protocol for sending of uncorrelated data packets in the connectionless mode, SCTP = Stream Control Transmission Protocol for supporting both connection-oriented and connectionless services in the same data transfer session

4.3 · The Layered Internet as Ecosystem Component

charging. This separation of services and networks is also one of the core premises of net neutrality (see ▶ Chap. 21)—the ISP cannot discriminate between different uses of the network and, therefore, cannot levy charges reflecting the value of the service offered by the ASP.

The businesses of the ISP and the ASP are independent in the sense just described. The businesses of the ISP and the ASP are also complementary in the sense that each needs the other to conduct its own business. The ASP cannot offer services without the assistance of ISPs, and the ISP does not create value for the consumers beyond that of transferring bits and providing basic communication services. Hence, the ISP needs the ASP to make the network attractive and useful for consumers, and the ASP need the ISP to deliver the services to the consumers.

One particular consequence of this decoupling of ASP and ISP functionality is over-the-top (OTT) media services in which the ASP offers services that traditionally were supported by dedicated networks—such as the telephone network and cable television networks—without any involvement by the ISP other than sending the information in unspecified IP packets to the consumers. See ▶ Box 4.2 for Skype as a typical over-the-top telephone service. Note that voice over IP (VoIP) may not always be an over-the-top service since several VoIP applications require particular protocol support from the ISP, for example, using the Session Initiation Protocol (SIP) for establishing and deleting the call and supporting quality of service management. In this case, the ISP can distinguish VoIP from other Internet services and levy charges based on this knowledge. The telephone service in 4G and 5G mobile systems is a VoIP service of this type, but competition from Skype has limited the opportunities of mobile operators to levy differentiated telephone charges based on call duration and distance.

Box 4.2 Skype and Over-the-Top Services

Skype is a digital service providing chat, voice, and video communication for Internet users. Skype was launched in 2003 as a desktop service. It was bought by eBay in 2005 for $2.6 billion and by Microsoft in 2011 for $8.5 billion. In 2013, Skype had almost 40% of the international voice and video market (Gara, 2014).

Skype is a contributor to the ongoing convergence of digital services along with other providers of voice-over-IP services such as Google Hangouts and appear.in. These are examples of over-the-top (OTT) services. They provide free voice, video, and messaging over the Internet, thereby competing with the traditional telephone and video services. The introduction of Skype and other voice-over-IP services has had a significant impact on the digital economy in which the main outcome is a dramatic decrease in prices for telephone calls both nationally and internationally. Mobile network operators offer free telephone services in their subscription schemes to meet the competition from Skype and other similar OTT services.

At the time Skype was launched, the users of traditional telephone services had to pay for the volume, duration, and distance of the calls they made. Skype undermined these payment methods by offering free calls between Skype users anywhere in the world. It is no wonder why people abandoned the expensive traditional telephony services and adopted Skype, especially as a replacement for long-distance calls. Skype is a typical value network, mediating communication between users. The company has high fixed costs (e.g., software development and infrastructure costs) and low or close to zero marginal costs. The value of Skype corresponds to the size of the network; that is, the number of users.

All web services, including Skype, use either http or https (encrypted http access) as carrier protocols. It is, therefore, not possible to distinguish between different services from the type of protocol only. Moreover, the web services include most of the services on the Internet. The internet service provider cannot levy time and volume-dependent charges for web services (e.g., a fixed price per byte) because then some services would be too expensive (e.g., video streaming services), while other services would cost almost nothing (e.g., email). This is net neutrality in practice: the ISP cannot discriminate data on the Internet based on type of content. For this reason, the ISP can only take fixed access charges, often based on the amount of data that can be downloaded per month as prescribed in the subscription contract plus additional charges if the user downloads more than the contractually agreed amount of data. On the other hand, the ASP may levy differentiated fees for apps, films, and music.

OTT services in general drives the convergence of digital services by providing the traditional teleservices at a lower cost over the Internet.

4.4 Computer Infrastructure and Platforms as Ecosystem Components

The software modules required to produce a digital service run on computer platforms. The platform is made up of the equipment in the equipment plane of ◘ Fig. 4.5 and is the mediator between the network infrastructure and the application software. The platform may consist of a single computer or be a distributed system of interconnected computers, possibly owned by different organizations or people. The overall platform architecture may, therefore, be very complex and involve several stakeholders who must cooperate to provide the service offered to the consumers. Google maps showing the GPS location of the user is an example of a service requiring at least two independent providers of partial information.

The most common platform is *cloud computing* offering services ranging from pure infrastructure support to complete software packages and any combination thereof. In the cloud computing business model, the provider of the digital service or good does not own all the production facilities but rent some of them from other stakeholders (the cloud providers). The service provider then reduces the need for investments in ICT infrastructure and can focus entirely on the core business. Other advantages are that the provider can reduce the time to develop the product considerably, meet challenges associated with fluctuating market size, eliminate the need for expert knowledge of processing and storage technologies, and reduce the need for system management and maintenance.

The key concept in cloud computing is "Everything as a Service" with acronyms EaaS or XaaS. There are three main categories of services:

- **Infrastructure as a Service (IaaS)**

In this case, the client rent access to the IT infrastructure of the cloud provider (computers, databases, servers, communication interfaces, and network). The IaaS provider offers a virtual machine architecture supporting a number of simultaneous and functionally separated clients. Each client will then view the cloud as an individual computer where the client may develop and run arbitrary software, also including own operating systems and security protection if required. The client has no control over the underlying infrastructure but may have control over operating systems, storage, use of software libraries, and security settings.

A related concept is *network virtualization* where the user is not aware of the fact that the processing activities are distributed over several computers. This implies that the user perceives the system as a single computer over which the user has exclusive control.

- **Platform as a Service (PaaS)**

In this case, the cloud provider offers a software development environment for the clients. The PaaS platform may contain programming tool kits, software libraries, as well as operating systems, compilers, and databases. App Engine is a PaaS platform offered by Google for development of web applications.

- **Software as a Service (SaaS)**

In this case, users are given licenses to use application software and database functions. All processing is then managed by the cloud provider. Examples of SaaS are access to office software, maps, Geographic Positioning System (GPS), Geographic Information System (GIS), human resource management, gamification, collaboration, learning, and many other applications.

Grid computing is the interconnection of many heterogeneous computers to perform particularly large computational tasks. The grid is different from the cloud in the sense that the computers involved are lightly connected, and each of them performs a dedicated and invariant task. The grid may then be viewed as a vast distributed supercomputer. The number of active computers in the grid involved in the same task at any instant is also varying since the computers are usually used by the grid only when they are not busy with computations initiated by the owner of the computer. Typically, the grid consists of computer facilities at universities and research institutions.

Tasks using grid computing are computationally hard problems such as studying protein folding processes, simulating climate models, searching for large primes, and analyzing particle collisions at CERN. There are several active international grids.

4.5 Applications and Content as Ecosystem Component

The number of applications available to customers is enormous, in particular, after the smartphone entered the market in 2012. The number of available apps in Google Play Store and Apple's App Store were about 3.0 million and 3.4 million, respectively, by the end of 2020 (Number of available apps in the Apple App Store from December 2020. Statista. December 10, 2020; Number of available applications in the Google Play Store from December 2009 to September 2020. Statista, December 10, 2020).

Some digital products are produced and sold by a single ASP only involving the ISPs for transporting the information to the customers. The biggest companies in the digital business, e.g., Facebook, Twitter, YouTube, and Google, are conglomerates consisting of several subsidiaries providing most of the content associated with the company. They also run their own computer platform, and some of them even offer ISP services and cloud computing.

Services may also be complex, involving not only an ASP but also several content providers and platform providers. One example is newspapers. A newspaper may buy or receive free information from other newspapers or magazines and engage freelance journalists or photographers. The newspaper is also member of a web of text and video content providers, news agencies, and stock photography agencies.

4.6 Consumers as Ecosystem Component

The consumers of digital service providers may be companies, organizations, or individuals. Examples of companies acting as consumers are electric power providers receiving automatic consumption measurements form censor platforms and newspapers buying pictures, news, and other topics from content providers.

The consumers in digital markets play an essential role in the digital economy not only as consumers of digital goods but also as a source of feedback to designers and providers of the goods that may be used to improve the product. The importance of market feedback is emphasized in ▶ Chap. 9. Closely related to market adoption is the effort by the authorities to regulate both the digital product and the marketing of it.

Consumer adoption (or user adoption) of information and communication technologies and digital services is a key element to apprehend the creation of dependencies in the digital economy ecosystem. Consumer adoption is a measure of how and at what rate consumers are adopting a specific digital service. Some aspects concerning consumer adoption rate can be summarized as follows:

- Obviously, the technology or digital service must be adopted by some initial consumers to have any impact on the market evolution. If there are too few initial consumers, then evolution may stagnate, and the technology or service may disappear from the market. Examples of this are videophones only enhancing ordinary telephony by showing videos of the speakers while talking and the

Teletex service for transmitting documents over telephone networks. The videophone service required expensive user terminals and offered the users only small advantages compared to the simple and cheap telephone service. Moreover, the videophone service was subject to strong network effects: the first videophone has zero value since there are no other communication partners. The timing of the introduction of Teletex was bad, and the service was almost immediately substituted by the free-of-charge e-mail service over Internet.
- Early market adoption is particularly important if the market growth depends on network effects (see ▶ Chap. 18). Social services, such as Facebook, are examples of services that are subject to strong network effects having difficulty attracting early users.
- The adoption of a technology or digital service may depend on other technologies or digital services to be widespread and fully adopted by consumers. For instance, Uber would have never become a success without the high adoption rate of smartphones and wireless Internet access. The video-on-demand service requires broadband access by users and depends on optical network technologies for sufficient traffic capacity in the network and for access to the database.
- When a technology or digital service starts to attract consumers and the use of it increases, it may trigger the evolution of new technologies or services. The two most obvious examples are Internet and mobile networks prompting the entire evolution of digital services. A less obvious example is touchscreens for mobile terminals stimulating the development of apps.
- New dependencies and entirely new stakeholders may appear as the digital service evolves and gets adopted by even more users. Offline use of credit cards prompted new operators to offer automatic card reader facilities for direct payment in shops and hotels. This has further stimulated the evolution of card readers in petrol pumps, parking meters, public toilet locks, and payment automata in public transport. Apps on mobile phones are now taking over several of the applications previously supported by credit cards.

Hence, analyzing the targeted technology or digital service in isolation will not predict how attractive it will be—several other services and functionalities needed for the adoption of a technology or a digital service must also be considered. All these interdependencies make up the ecosystem of the digital service. A quantitative consumer adoption model based on the Bass equation is presented in ▶ Sect. 18.2.

4.7 Authorities as Ecosystem Components

The digital economy ecosystem also consists of social and legal aspects concerning conditions for marketing and use of digital services, including how technologies and digital services are regulated by the government. Legal regulations of digital services may not only influence the content of these services but also how they are adopted by the consumers. Such legal regulations may also have an impact on the visibility, development, and use of related digital services. Examples of the impact of legal aspects on the digital economy are the regulations of cryptocurrencies and sharing services such as Uber (Court of Justice of the European Union, 2017) and Airbnb (Tuohey, 2018). The decision by the European Court of Justice (ECJ) to classify Uber as a transport company has significant bearing on the business operations of Uber.

The authorities also follow the businesses conducts of the large corporations in the digital economy closely to uncover, for example, tax evasion, unethical or illegal exploitation of personal information gathered about consumers and users, infringements or circumventions of competition laws and regulations, building of lock-in barriers to create monopoly advantages, unsustainable environmental footprint and use of energy, exploitation of workforce, and negligence regarding child work. Most of the large corporations in the digital economy have been accused of misconduct in one or several of these areas. However, it has been difficult to alter the behavior of these corporations, though criticisms from authorities and the public, and sometimes legal proceedings, have forced the corporations to alter their business conduct in some cases.

The role of the authorities as watchdogs in the digital business sector is, therefore, important to avoid concentration of too much power on just a few stakeholders in the digital economy.

4.8 Conclusions

The ecosystem metaphor is an important tool for strategic planning in the digital economy. The ecosystem analysis reveals, among others, stakeholders that may influence the business performance directly or indirectly, the type and strength of the interactions with these stakeholders, and possible vulnerabilities and weaknesses with the chosen business model.

The ecosystem does not only consist of cooperating and competing companies but also less obvious stakeholders such as consumers and authorities. To estimate the performance of the company or the mere survivability of it in the marketplace, public opinion and government regulations must also be considered.

Some ecosystem aspects are related to the technology such as the underlying Internet and access technology, own computer infrastructure and computer infrastructure owned by other parties (e.g., cloud services), and the development environment for apps and other software and hardware components.

The aspects outlined in this chapter are applied in ▶ Chap. 19 where several case studies are presented.

❓ Questions
1. Which information and communication technologies (ICTs) does Dropbox depend on?
2. What digital services depend on Dropbox?
3. What impact has the authorities on the business operations of Google?

✅ Answers

1. Internet, smartphones, personal computers, cheap mass storage of data, cryptography, digital payment solutions, and mobile apps.
2. Cloud storage, file sharing, file synchronization, and project collaboration.
3. Google's business operations have been under investigation by both the US authorities and the EU. Authorities in the USA have filed a lawsuit against Google in 2020. The EU has fined Google several times in the past decade for a total of €8 billion.

▶ Exercises

1. Describe the ecosystem for Apples App store.
2. Describe the ecosystem of Uber.

✅ Answers

1. Apple, app developers using the app development platform of Apple, third parties required for management of the particular app (e.g., providers of supplementary content, payment systems, cloud computing), mobile network operators and the technological platform they offer, other network providers, smartphone manufacturers (e.g., operating system), standards organizations (e.g., 3GPP) specifying the basic technology supporting apps and other content, regulatory authorities (e.g., violations of law and license conditions), and app users (e.g., usefulness of app, cost of usage).
2. Uber depends on technologies such as the smartphone, mobile broadband networks (e.g., 4G and 5G), GPS, and digital payment system, among others. In addition, Uber depends on local authorities and the legislations in the areas they operate. Since Uber hires drivers as a part of their business model, they will have formal contracts with these drivers and may also be dependent on labor unions and other local rules.

References

Audestad, J. A. (2007). Internet as a multiple graph structure: The role of the transport layer. *Information Security Technical Report, 12*(1).
Court of Justice of the European Union. (2017, December 20). *The service provided by Uber connecting with non-professional drivers is covered by services in the field of transport*.
Durlauf, S. N. (1998). What should policymakers know about economic complexity? *The Washington Quarterly, 21*(1).
Gara, T. (2014). Skype's incredible rise, in one image. *The Wall Street Journal*.
Lafferty, K. D., & Morris, A. K. (1996). Altered behavior of parasitized killifish increases susceptibility to predation by bird final hosts. *Ecology, 77*(5).
Moore, J. F.. (1993, May–June). *Predators and prey: A new ecology of competition*. Harvard Business Review.
Muegge, S. (2013, February). *Platforms, communities, and business ecosystems: Lessons learned about technology entrepreneurship in an interconnected world*. Technology Innovation Management Review.
Tuohey, P. (2018, January 10). Cities and state are struggling to regulate Airbnb. *The Hill*.

Digital Market Evolution

Contents

5.1 Telecommunications as Natural Monopoly – 62

5.2 De-monopolization of User Equipment – 63

5.3 De-monopolization of Mobile Network Operations – 64

5.4 De-monopolization of All Telecommunications Operations – 66

5.5 Resellers and Virtual Network Operators – 68

5.6 Conclusions – 71

References – 72

© The Author(s), under exclusive license to Springer Nature Switzerland AG 2021
H. Øverby, J. A. Audestad, *Introduction to Digital Economics*, Classroom Companion: Business,
https://doi.org/10.1007/978-3-030-78237-5_5

> **Learning Objectives**
>
> After completing this chapter, you should be able to:
> - Explain the process leading to de-monopolization of telecommunications in Europe.
> - Understand the consequences de-monopolization has on the market structure in telecommunications.
> - Explain the difference between the three concepts: reseller, virtual network operator, and mobile virtual network operator.

5.1 Telecommunications as Natural Monopoly

The telecommunications industry has undergone an evolution in market structure from monopoly to competition market as illustrated in ◘ Fig. 5.1. This process is referred to as the *de-monopolization* of the telecommunications market. Other often used terms are *market deregulation* and *market liberalization*. This chapter describes how this evolution took place in the European Economic Area (EEA).

The evolution in EEA took place in three steps:
1. The market for retail sales of user equipment was opened for competition during the period 1985–1987.
2. Competition was introduced for mobile network operation, first in the UK (1982) and about 10 years later in other EEA countries (1991).
3. Full competition on all aspects of telephone network operation in Europe was introduced in 1998 (in 1996 in the USA).

Traditionally, most telecommunications operators in Europe were state-owned monopolies. There were also privately owned telephone and telegraph companies, but these companies had monopolistic rights to offer telecommunications services in particular regions of the country. The argument in favor of monopolies was that it would be more expensive for the users if there were more than one telephone operator in the region because of the large investments in telecommunication

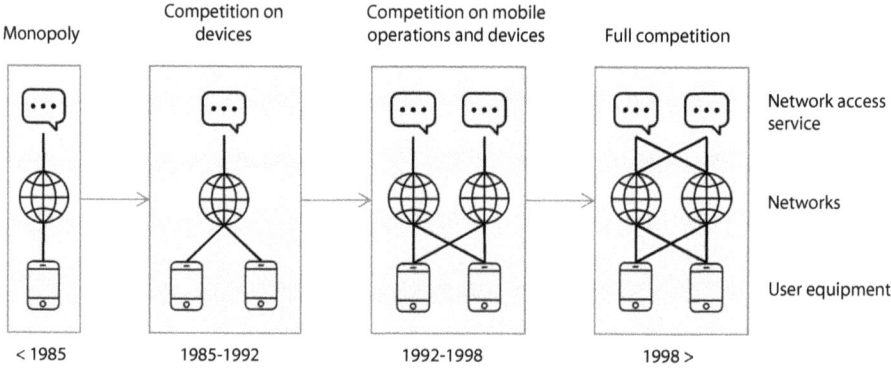

◘ **Fig. 5.1** Evolution of the telecommunications business. (Authors' own figure)

infrastructures required. Moreover, the technology used prior to the 1980s (electromechanical telephone exchanges interconnected by coaxial cables and radio relays) had an economic lifetime of several decades, often as much as 50 years. Therefore, it was deemed inefficient to allow several telecommunications carriers to build their own communication networks delivering the same set of services. Telecommunications was then regarded as a natural monopoly.

The state monopoly owned the network, offered the few services supported by the network, and sold or rented out telephones, local switchboards, data modems, and other terminal equipment. These telecommunications carriers were called *vertically integrated monopolies*. Consumers usually had one choice concerning network provider, telecommunications service, and type of user equipment. The governments also decided the charges the subscribers had to pay for subscriptions and use of the services.

The situation was more complex for long-distance communication systems such as intercontinental submarine cables and satellite systems. Several consortia owned competing intercontinental cable systems, and the international organization Intelsat was a competitor to these systems offering an alternative for long-distance interconnections over geostationary satellites. These systems were not subject for debate in the de-monopolization discussion that followed.

During the late 1980s, it was questioned whether it would be better to open up for full competition in telecommunications considering the rapid evolution of digital networks and digital switching, the growing need for computer communications, and advances in mobile network technologies. This came at the same time as the internationalization of the industry started in general. Many companies expanded to become international corporations with factories in several countries. This evolution also triggered the governments to consider opening up national monopolies for full competition to enhance innovation and making services and industrial products cheaper for the consumers. De-monopolization and the belief in free markets became the *zeitgeist* of the late 1980s. However, the process to transform the monopolistic telephone operators into competitive businesses in a competitive market took a long time because new competition laws and market legislation had first to be put in place and enough time had to be allowed for the monopolies to reconfigure their business models to face a situation where they had to fight for market size and revenues.

5.2 De-monopolization of User Equipment

In the early 1980s, the first public data networks were put into operation, and the first automatic mobile networks were up and running. The number of different types of user equipment had exploded, and the monopolies were too bureaucratic and too inexpert to handle this profusion of new equipment. Responding to this, starting from about 1985, the authorities opened the sale of user equipment for free competition; however, the equipment had to be approved by the telecom operator or a separate regulatory authority before the new device could be connected to the network to ensure that the equipment met international and national performance standards.

The number of independent retailers of various types of user equipment grew rapidly; in particular, for sales of ordinary telephones and mobile phones. An important offspring of the deregulation was that the telecommunications operators no longer owned the telephone apparatus, the data modem, or the local switchboard at the user premises as they did before sale of user equipment was opened up for competition. This equipment was regarded as a technical extension of the network and, as such, an integral part of the network. After the deregulation, the operator's responsibility and ownership of equipment ended at the network interface device (NID) on the wall of the house; this technology is often referred to as "wire-to-the-wall" and, in the optical age, "fiber-to-the-premises." The manufacturers could now build the data modem into, for example, computers, fax machines, and copying machines. This simplified the use of data communications but had little impact on the number of users of data communications until the Internet was incorporated in the portfolio of the telecommunications operators in the mid-1990s.

> **Definitions 5.1**
> Terms often used in the literature related to the local wire, cable, or fiber interconnecting the subscriber and the telecommunications network are the following:
> - *The local loop* is the connection from the local telephone exchange (or Internet router) to the premises of the subscriber.
> - *The last mile* refers to the same part of the connection.
> - *Network interface device (NID)* is the demarcation point between the local loop and the internal wiring at the user's premises. The responsibilities of the operator end at the NID.

The first regulatory authorities were established during this period to ensure fair competition and to avoid that the telecommunications monopolies misused their market power to hinder other retailers to establish their independent businesses. The regulatory authorities also issued licenses for sale of equipment and followed up that the retailers had access to enough technical expertise for installation and maintenance of equipment.

5.3 De-monopolization of Mobile Network Operations

In 1981, the Nordic Mobile Telephone (NMT) had just been put into operation in the Nordic countries. NMT was the first cellular system offering automatic roaming and undisruptive handover of calls when the mobile terminal moved into a new cell. Already in 1982, NMT was about to become the preferred common European land mobile system. British Telecom participated in this project. In 1982, Prime Minister Margaret Thatcher and her government decided there should be full competition on mobile communications in the UK with two independent operators.

5.3 · De-monopolization of Mobile Network Operations

This implied that the UK had to choose a system other than NMT; otherwise, one of the competitors would have too big advantage. Europe was then left with four incompatible automatic land mobile systems: NMT in Norway, Finland, Sweden, Denmark, Iceland, Spain, the Netherlands, and Switzerland; TACS in the UK and Ireland; C Netz in Germany; and Radiocom 2000 in France.

This was, in fact, the major incentive for the Netherlands to suggest in 1982 that Europe should develop a new pan-European digital mobile system—the Global System for Mobile Communications (GSM). GSM was originally an abbreviation for the name of the group developing the technology—Groupe Spécial Mobile. In 1992, the GSM system was put into operation, and EU and EFTA decided that each country should have at least two competing land mobile networks. GSM was an ideal place where the de-monopolization of telecommunications could start. The countries developing the GSM standard had already agreed that the whole telecommunications business should be de-monopolized soon. GSM was a completely new network where all operators had to build the network infrastructure from scratch. The new infrastructure consists of base stations, telephone exchanges supporting entirely new functions, and entirely new databases for subscription handling and location management. The only advantage the telephone monopolies had was transmission lines that could be used to interconnect the new devices, thereby reducing the need for investments in basic infrastructure; however, by simple regulatory requirements, all mobile operators in the region had equal opportunities to lease such lines from the monopoly operator for the same price as a subsidiary of the monopoly operator.

The fixed network operators would remain monopolies offering fixed telephone services. Hence, from 1992 onward, consumers could choose between at least two providers of mobile telecommunications services in Europe.

A mobile operator established in one country could now also establish subsidiaries in other countries, thereby increasing the market of potential subscribers and, as a result, enhancing its business prospects and boosting its financial value. Several mobile telecommunications companies then rapidly developed into large international conglomerates.

One particularly amusing strategic dilemma that this situation led to is illustrated in ▶ Box 5.1.

Box 5.1 Competitive Dilemma

◘ Figure 5.2 illustrates the competitive dilemma many mobile services operators are facing, using the mobile telephony market in Norway and Sweden as an example.

Telia and Telenor are dominating mobile operators Sweden and Norway, with market shares (in terms of subscribers) of about 35% and 60%, respectively (per 2019). Telenor is a minority operator in Sweden, and Telia is a minority operator in Norway with market share of 19% and 33%, respectively. This leads to a situation where the operators have to instigate different strategies in the two countries. In Sweden, the strategy of Telia is to hinder Telenor to capture market shares, while the strategy of Telia in Norway is to capture as much of the market from Telenor

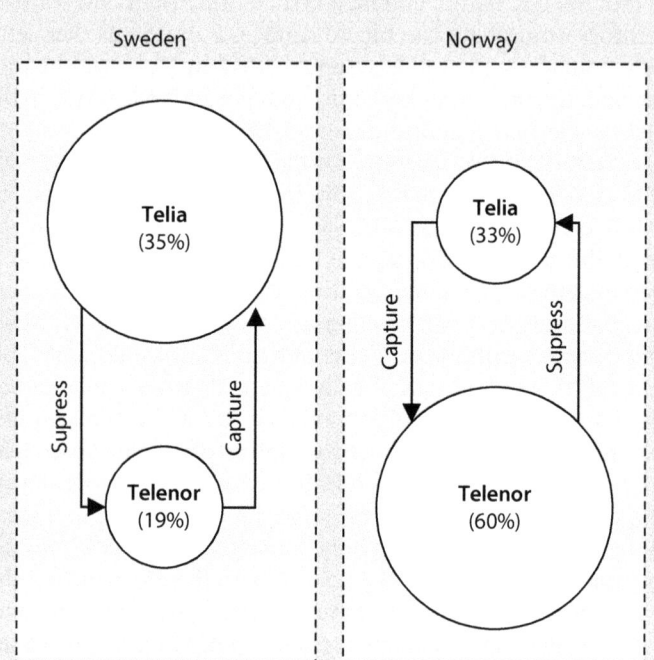

● **Fig. 5.2** A strategic dilemma between Telia and Telenor. The markets shares are based on 2019 figures published by NKOM (Norwegian market) and PTS (Swedish market). (Authors' own figure)

as possible. The strategy is, of course, the same for Telenor: gain market shares in Sweden and protect its market shares in Norway. The two strategies are incompatible, and the mobile services operator must master each of them.

5.4 De-monopolization of All Telecommunications Operations

In 1998, the EU opened all aspects of telecommunications for full competition. The process toward full deregulation had started already in 1987 by the Green Paper on the Development of the Common Market for Telecommunications Equipment and Services (Lando & The European community's telecommunications deregulation, 1994). One important requirement and a first step toward full deregulation was that the countries separated the telecommunications operator from the telecommunications policy maker. Previously, the telecommunications operator (or PTT as it was called in many European countries[1]) had both roles. The earlier monopole operator was referred to as the *incumbent operator*.

---

1 PTT = Post, Telephone, and Telegraph

5.4 · De-monopolization of All Telecommunications Operations

Definition 5.2
The telephone operator (or carrier) that existed before de-monopolization is usually referred to as the *incumbent operator* (or just the *incumbent*) to distinguish it from new operators. The incumbent had the advantage of having built the network infrastructure from "monopoly money" or by government subsidies. This advantage had to be eliminated by govern regulations before real competition could take place.

Note that in 1998, fixed-telephone services were still regarded as the most important business in the telecommunications industry despite that mobile phone and data services were growing rapidly. Mobile communications had already been de-monopolized. The Internet had existed for several years as an independent network not owned by anyone. In 1998, Internet had just started to be included in the business portfolio of the telecommunications operators in Europe but was still regarded as a rather minor addition to their portfolio. Almost unrecognizably, the Internet had started to replace the X.25 data network as carrier for data communication services. While the network operators could levy differentiated charges on the services offered by the telephone network (local calls, long-distance calls, international calls, calls to value-added services, and so on), it turned out that this was not possible for Internet services. The revenue basis of the telecommunications industry was about to change.

Both the Internet and the mobile phone have altered the business landscape of telecommunications entirely. Now, about 20 years after de-monopolization, the fixed telephone service is about to be replaced by cellular mobile networks, and the telephone service, fixed or mobile, is itself soon incorporated as one out of numerous data services on the Internet using voice over IP technology. This is the convergence of technologies and services described in ▶ Chap. 3.

The deregulation process took several years because the telecommunications network was regarded as a public utility that was best served by the old state monopolies (the incumbents). Moreover, it was a long and difficult process to establish the rules and procedures for regulating the market so that new entrants had a fair chance to compete with the incumbents. As already mentioned, the GSM network was an exception because this was a new network and the cost of building the network was regarded to be the same for all competitors. If the incumbent also owned a mobile network, this network had to be commercially separated from the telephone network, and no cross subsidizing and other value exchange was allowed between them. Moreover, if required by the competitor, the incumbent had to provide leased lines, at a competitive price, as feeder lines to base stations and other equipment.

In the USA, the telecommunication market was opened for free competition in 1996. The rules governing the competition were stated in the Telecommunications Act of 1996. Note that the divestiture of AT&T in 1984 was not de-monopolization of telecommunications in the USA. AT&T was broken up into seven regional monopolies offering telecommunications services in non-overlapping regions. The purpose was to reduce the market power AT&T had built up over several years. Telecommunications still existed as a monopoly business until 1996.

After 1998, anyone in the EEA could become a network operator, service provider, or retailer of user equipment. However, the stakeholders in this market were subject to some regulatory restrictions related to the competition between network operators—including virtual network operators—on price, performance, customer care, and quality of service. These regulations included mandatory cooperation between network operators to ensure full connectivity between users of competing networks at reasonable prices and quality of service and non-discrimination of application service providers accessing the network, in particular, preventing network operators from giving advantages to application service providers owned by themselves.

To understand the present situation, it is important to note that the deregulation of 1998 had to do with the telephone network only. The driving force for the de-monopolization was the political idea that a competitive market would be more efficient and offer lower prices than the monopoly. This conclusion may be true for fixed and mobile telephone operation, but the development of Internet services has shown that this is not always true. A concern for policy makers now is that free competition has led to the undesirable situation that several companies in the data or Internet business have had a tremendous increase in market value and revenues during the last few years. Some of these companies have also become ad hoc monopolies in their market segments (e.g., Google, Facebook, and Netflix) by acquisitions of competitors. These companies also benefit from strong network effects, thereby resulting in robust lock-in barriers for users (see ▶ Chap. 12).

The deregulation of telecommunications has also generated a new form of competition in the global telecommunications industry. Until 1998, the old monopolies existed within a single country, but after 1998, these companies could also start operations in other countries. Making the situation even more complex, two new types of operators have arrived: resellers and virtual network operators.

5.5 Resellers and Virtual Network Operators

Resellers and virtual network operators are two stakeholders in the telecommunications market that are direct results of the de-monopolization of this business area. These concepts are defined as follows.

Definition 5.3
The *reseller* buys bulk traffic from other network operators and resells it to its own customers.

Definition 5.4
A *virtual network operator* (VNO) does not own its own access and network infrastructure but uses the infrastructure owned by other network operators.

5.5 · Resellers and Virtual Network Operators

Definition 5.5
The *mobile virtual network operator* (MVNO) is a VNO offering mobile services.

The resellers buy bulk traffic capacity and call time from telecommunications carriers and resell it to their customers with profit. Reselling is particularly popular in the mobile market. The reseller does not own any network infrastructure. In the mobile market, they may issue their own SIM. The profit is generated from discounts they obtain by buying large quantities of traffic capacity and by combining telecommunications services with other services or goods, e.g., service packaging, price profiles, and value-added services. The reseller is the single point of contact for their customers independently of the operators from which the reseller buys traffic capacity. The resellers are in control of their own systems for customer care, billing, marketing, and sales, either owning these facilities themselves or outsourcing them to specialized providers of such services.

The mobile market was opened for resellers in Europe in 1992, just after the first GSM network was put into operation.

The virtual network operator (VNO) buy access to the network infrastructure of network operators (NOs) owning their own network. The most common VNOs are the mobile virtual network operator (MVNO). They deliver their services to their customers using the radio network infrastructure of mobile network operators (MNOs) owning base stations and other mobile network infrastructure. The MVNO issues its own SIMs, operates its own Home Subscription Server (HSS) for subscription and location management, and has at least one Internet gateway router and/or telephone gateway exchange for access to the network of the MNO. The configuration is shown in ◘ Fig. 5.3 for an MVNO offering 4G services. Data packets from the mobile terminal are then routed from the base station via the gateway router (GW) into the Internet, and data packets coming from the

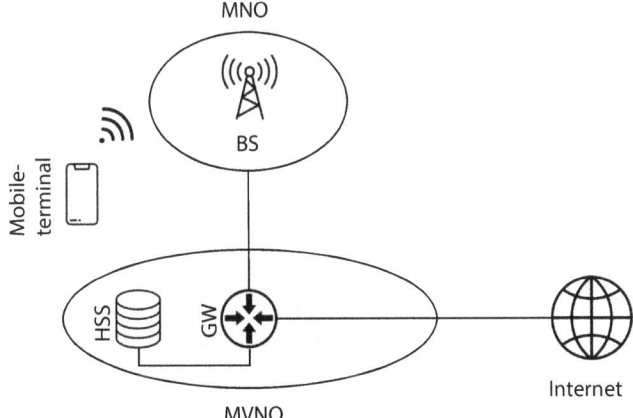

◘ **Fig. 5.3** Network with MVNO. (Authors' own figure)

internet are routed to the gateway router before they are routed into the network of the MNO and delivered to the mobile terminal over the base station.

What makes the MVNO different from a reseller is that the MVNO owns some network infrastructure, while the reseller does not. The actual MNO serving the MVNO is not visible for the customers, and the MVNO has roaming agreements with other MNOs independently of the MNO serving the MVNO.

MVNOs are particularly interesting because there are so many of them. The first MVNO (Sense Communications) was established in Denmark in 1997 and in Norway and Sweden in 1999. In 2014, there were 943 MVNOs worldwide (The global MVNO landscape, 2012–2014, 2014).

The number of MNOs in a region is limited by the amount of radio spectrum available, and the dominating mobile operators in EEA are obliged by EU directives to offer services to both resellers and MVNOs to enhance competitions in the mobile market. The effect of competition between MNOs and MVNOs may not be obvious as illustrated in the example below.

▶ **Example. Competition and Mobile Virtual Network Operators**

Initially, there was strong resistance from mobile network operators (MNOs) to allow virtual mobile network operators (MVNOs) into their networks. They were afraid of increased competition without really appreciating the difference between market share and revenue share. The size and value of mobile operators are measured in terms of market shares and not in terms of revenue shares.

◘ Figure 5.4 shows the case of two competing network operators (MNO1 and MNO2) and an MVNO leasing infrastructure from MNO1. The MVNO pays a leasing fee to MNO1 for using its infrastructure.

The effect of the MVNO is illustrated by the following simple numerical example, illustrated in ◘ Fig. 5.5: Suppose that the market consists of three million subscribers and is equally shared between the two MNOs before the MVNO enters the market. The revenue per user is 1000 money units. Then the revenue for each of the two MNOs will be 1.5 billion money units initially.

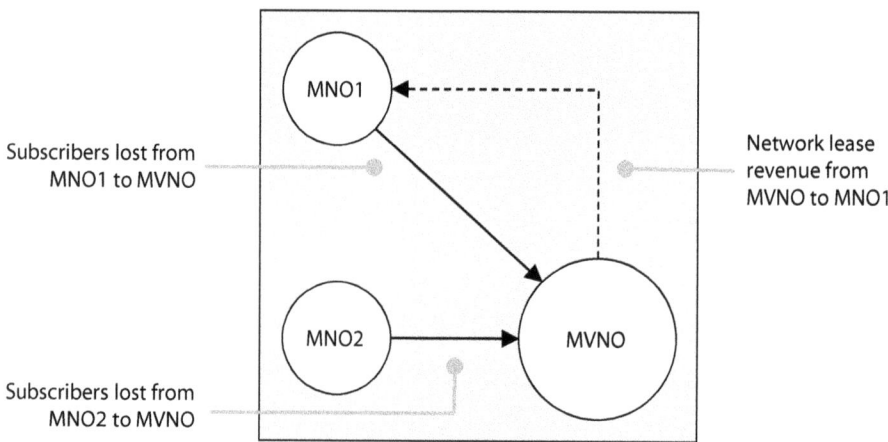

◘ Fig. 5.4 Competing network operators. (Authors' own figure)

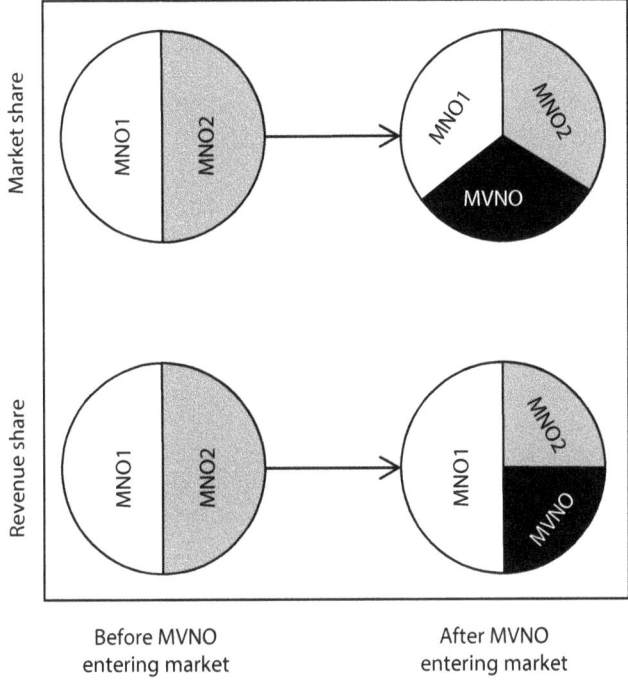

Fig. 5.5 Market shares and revenues for mobile network operator (MNO) 1 and 2 and mobile virtual network operator (MVNO). (Authors' own figure)

At some time after the MVNO entered the market, the two MNOs and the MVNO have one million subscribers each generating 1000 money units each; that is, MNO1 and MNO2 have both lost 0.5 million subscribers to the MVNO. Suppose next that the rent the MVNO has to pay for using the network of MNO1 is 500 money units per subscriber, then the revenues of MNO1 will be 1 billon from own subscribers plus 0.50 billion from the MVNO; that is, the revenues of MNO1 is 1.5 billion money units. The revenues of MNO2 are 1 billion money units.

Compared to the situation that existed before the MVNO entered the market, the revenues of MNO1 have stayed the same, while the revenues of MNO2 have become 0.5 billion money unit smaller. This simple example shows that even if the MVNO is winning many customers from MNO1, housing the MVNO may still be a good business for MNO1 since a large proportion of the revenues of the MVNO is fed back to MNO1 in the form of network leases. Some of these revenues are revenues lost by MNO2 to the MVNO. The result is that MNO2 always loses both market share and revenues. ◄

5.6 Conclusions

Telecommunications was a monopoly business up to about 1985: the operator owned and sold or rented out the user equipment, owned the network, and offered all services available on the network. Thereafter, it took about 10 years until the

telecommunications market was completely liberalized. After 1998, the telecommunications market has been broken up into three major sectors:
- Development and retail of user equipment.
- Network operation.
- Service, applications, and content provision.

There is full competition within each of these sectors. However, network operations are subject to certain regulation to ensure interoperability between customers subscribing to different networks.

It is expensive to build and operate telecommunications networks. Therefore, two types of operators not owning network infrastructure have been allowed into the market (in particular, the mobile market): resellers of traffic and virtual network operators. These operators increase competition and make the market richer for the users.

Questions
1. What is the key source of revenues for resellers?
2. What are the sources of revenues for mobile network operators?
3. Why may renting out a communication network be a good business?

Answers
1. Discounts for buying large amounts of traffic time from ordinary operators.
2. Subscription fees, traffic fees, sales of bulk traffic to resellers, rents from virtual network operators.
3. Increased revenues due to rental fees, and that competitor users churn to the MVNO renting the network.

References

Lando, S. D., et al. (1994). *Fordham Law Review, 62*.
The global MVNO landscape, 2012–2014. (2014, 12 June) *GSMA intelligence*.

Digital Goods and Services

Contents

6.1 Definitions – 74

6.2 Zero Marginal Cost – 78

6.3 Classification of Digital Goods – 80

6.4 Zero Average Revenue per User – 83

6.5 Digital Commodities – 84

6.6 Transaction Costs – 85

6.7 Bundling – 85

6.8 Conclusions – 86

References – 89

© The Author(s), under exclusive license to Springer Nature Switzerland AG 2021
H. Øverby, J. A. Audestad, *Introduction to Digital Economics*, Classroom Companion: Business,
https://doi.org/10.1007/978-3-030-78237-5_6

Learning Objectives

After completing this chapter, you should be able to:
- Explain the concepts of marginal cost, exclusivity, commodities, and transaction costs for digital services.
- Explain why some digital goods and services can be offered free of charge.
- Understand why service bundling is particularly simple for digital goods and services.

6.1 Definitions

Everything in the digital economy can be mapped down to the production, circulation, trade, and use of digital goods and services. The definitions of digital good and digital service are related and sometimes overlapping concepts but are also different in several aspects.

> **Definition 6.1**
> A *digital good* is a networked zero marginal cost virtual object having value for some individuals or organizations.

A digital good has, in addition, the following properties (Fournier, 2014):
- The virtual object is intangible but can be stored as data on a digital medium, e.g., the consumer's hard disk or smartphone or in the cloud.
- The virtual object can be replicated without any incurred cost; that is, the marginal production cost of the object is zero as explained in ▶ Sect. 6.2.
- The format of the virtual object must be such that it can be delivered to consumers over the Internet, or in other words, the virtual object is networked.
- The virtual object must have financial, psychological, or other value for the consumer (individuals or organizations). Virtual objects without value for anyone are not included in our definition.

Examples of digital goods that satisfy this definition include Microsoft Word documents, music tracks on Spotify, webpages on the Internet, apps on iPhone, Wikipedia articles, e-mails, data stored on electronic bank accounts, private data stored on Dropbox accounts, and the list of apartments on an Airbnb web page. These goods are all virtual objects; they have value for someone; they can be replicated without any cost; and they can be delivered to consumers over the Internet. Examples of non-digital goods are computers, mobile phones, and mobile base stations. These goods have value for someone, but none of them are virtual objects; they have non-zero marginal cost and cannot be sent over the Internet.

> **Definition 6.2**
> A *digital service* is a networked zero marginal cost service that has value for individuals or organizations.

6.1 · Definitions

Services are intangible by nature. Digital services include posting news on social media, electronic banking, Internet access, multiplayer online gaming, web browsing, and composing and sending e-mails. The difference between a digital good and a digital service is somewhat blurry. This is illustrated by two examples. The data on a Facebook account is a digital good, while the use of Facebook for any purpose is a digital service. Music tracks stored on Spotify's servers are digital goods, while the use of Spotify to listen to music is a digital service.

Network access and transmission of data over fixed and mobile networks, as well as data storage and data processing, are also digital services. These services are not only digital services in their own right but are also enablers for other digital goods and services. As such, they are also called *enabling* or *fundamental technologies*. This means that the value proposition of all other digital goods and services depend critically on these technologies. Moreover, the providers of digital goods and services usually benefit from the enabling technologies without investing directly in them. For example, Facebook uses the worldwide Internet to support its value proposition but has not contributed to the development and management of the Internet as such. Offering enabling services as a commercial product has become a new business arena referred to as Anything as a Service (XaaS), also known as cloud computing. Cloud computing and XaaS were described in ▶ Sect. 4.4 in the context of business ecosystems. ▶ Box 6.1 lists some examples of XaaS.

Box 6.1 Anything as a Service

The XaaS concept is a generic name for several commercially available types of enabling services. The most common are Software as a Service (SaaS), Platform as a Service (PaaS), and Infrastructure as a Service (IaaS). Different combinations of enabling services are illustrated in ◘ Fig. 6.1.

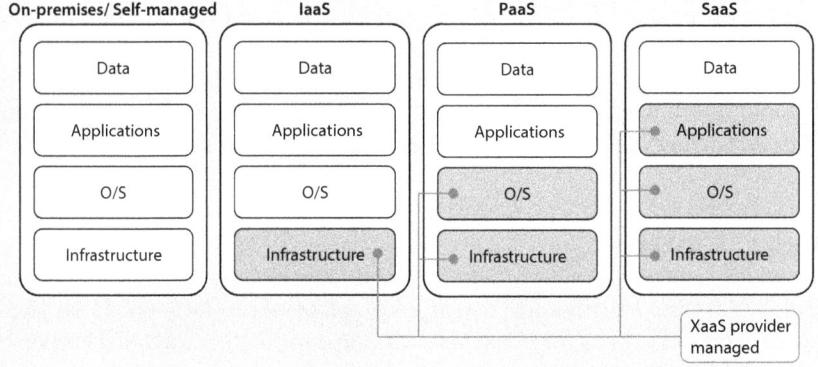

◘ **Fig. 6.1** Examples of XaaS. From on-premises systems where everything is self-managed (left) to SaaS where only data is self-managed. (Authors' own figure)

Dropbox is an example of an IaaS offering storage of data for anyone in one of their data centers. The user can access the data via the Internet from anywhere and at any time. App Engine of Google is a PaaS platform where app developers can develop software for the web applications. Vortex is an SaaS offering gaming services. Using Vortex, the player need not install, store, or process the game in the player's own computer since all processing is done in Vortex servers.

Blockchain technology is also offered as a service called Blockchain as a Service (BaaS). Consumers buy access to BaaS without installing the complex processing software needed to support the service. Amazon, Oracle, and IBM are examples of companies offering BaaS.

XaaS has changed the way in which companies invest in ICT. Companies buying services from an XaaS provider need no longer bind capital on long-term investments since the use of XaaS converts these investments into short-term running costs. The capital costs of offering XaaS may be huge since XaaS usually requires large investments in computing infrastructure and support of fast and reliable communication networks to handle many simultaneous customers and process huge amounts of data.

Digital goods and services are different from physical products (or tangible goods). Physical products have presence in the physical domain, while digital goods are built up by sequences of bits and exist only as pieces of software or data stored on computers or other storage devices. Digital goods and services may be combined to form larger and more complex digital goods and services before being offered to consumers. One simple example is the use of the secure digital payment solution offered by Google Play where the same platform is used to support the app software, to pay the developer for use of the app, and to collect payments from the user. A similar but more complex example is to use smartphones as authentication tokens for secure access to bank accounts (see ▶ Box 6.2). This case involves the primary service provider (the bank), the authentication provider (the mobile operator), and one or more clearinghouses which supervise and guarantee the validity of the authentication process. This example illustrates that a new digital good or service may be constructed by linking digital goods and services delivered by several independent stakeholders, in this case, banking, mobile operation, clearinghouse technology, and Internet operation. The ecosystem of the new product may then become complex consisting of elements from the ecosystem of each stakeholder.

Box 6.2 E-Banking
E-banking (online banking or Internet banking) is the provision of digital banking services using the Internet and mobile devices. The consumer can access their bank data and perform bank operations at any time and from any geographical location. E-banking has disrupted the traditional banking services by providing permanent access to the bank from anywhere and at

reduced transaction costs. Some banks are "virtual banks," meaning that they only offer online e-bank services and are only present on the Internet.

For an e-bank, it is essential to provide strong security measures including the use of strong cryptographic protocols for both message transfer and user authentication. To provide a complete e-banking service, cooperation between stakeholders at different business levels is necessary. This is illustrated in ◘ Fig. 6.2. The user is accessing their e-bank application through their laptop over the Internet and is authenticated via their smartphone. In Norway, this authentication service is called *Mobile Bank ID*.

The authentication of the user takes place over the GSM/3G/4G/5G network by first authenticating the smartphone of the user and, thereafter, sending a onetime password via SMS. The onetime password is then returned to the bank from the laptop to complete the authentication process. The independent stakeholders are the bank, the authentication provider, the mobile network operator, and the Internet provider. Note that cooperation between different business layers and within the same business layer is needed to provide a complete e-banking service. For example, mobile authentication may take place over two mobile networks: the home network of the user and a visited network if the user accesses the bank from another country.

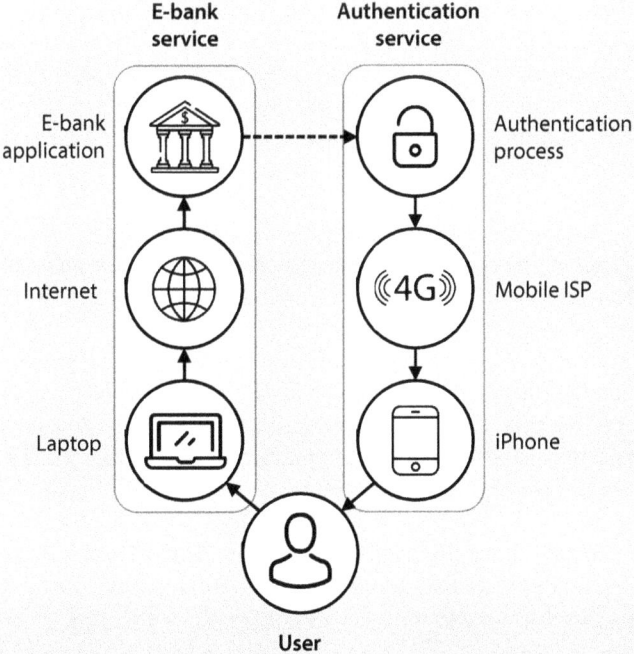

◘ Fig. 6.2 E-banking. (Authors' own figure)

Digital goods and services do not degrade as a function of time—they will continue to exist far into the future with the same quality as when they were created because of their digital nature. This is different from physical goods which normally degrade over time.

For simplicity, we will hereafter use the term "digital goods" instead of "digital goods and services" if the meaning is clear from the context.

6.2 Zero Marginal Cost

A key characteristic of digital goods is that they have zero marginal cost. Digital goods can be reproduced with no additional cost.

> **Definition 6.3**
> Marginal cost is the cost of producing one additional unit of a good or service. Digital goods and services have zero marginal cost.

Let us estimate the cost of producing one additional copy of an app. If the app has been downloaded and installed, say, 10,000 times on different smartphones, what is the cost of the next download? In a networked system, the app software is downloaded from the app server and transmitted over the Internet to the smartphone where it is installed. There are certain costs associated with these operations, for example, a small amount of electric energy is required for processing the app in the server and installing it in the smartphone. Similarly, there are some small costs associated with sending the app software over the Internet (amount of electric energy consumption per message and the share of fixed costs associated with sending a single message over the network). These costs are tiny so that, for all practical purposes, the cost of installing one additional copy of the app is zero.

Repeating the same arguments, we again conclude that the costs of processing an extra trade transaction on Amazon, posting a new message on Facebook, or downloading a video on YouTube are zero.

On the other hand, the marginal cost is not zero for physical goods. The cost of production then includes the cost of raw materials (e.g., steel or plastic), workforce, and logistics. Note that some e-commerce businesses selling physical products online, such as Amazon, do not have zero marginal cost because of the shipping of the physical goods. However, the marginal cost of the digital trade transaction is zero.

Digital goods may have high fixed costs since some of them are expensive to develop, build, and operate. The development of software may cost millions of US dollars, require development teams with hundreds of people, and take several years from idea to finished product. The development of the computer game *Grand Theft Auto V* (released in 2013) cost $265 million, while *Star Wars: The Old Republic* (released in 2011) cost more than $200 million (List of most expensive video games to develop, 2020). On the other hand, there are examples of digital goods with low fixed costs, for example, the computer game *Minecraft* and many apps for iPhone

6.2 · Zero Marginal Cost

or Android. Some of them are very simple digital services that have been developed by a single person over a relatively brief timeframe.

An interesting example is telecommunications networks. It costs billions of US dollars to build and run these networks. On the other hand, the networks transport several exabytes (10^{18} bytes) of information each second so that the cost per byte is negligible, several magnitudes smaller than a cent. Hence, the marginal cost for sending an additional message over the expensive telecommunications infrastructure is, for all practical purposes, zero. The marginal cost of telecommunications services is thus zero, and the pricing of telecommunications services cannot be based on usage.

High fixed costs do not always mean that the consumer must pay for the good. This depends on the business model of the company. The running costs of Facebook and Google are very high. These costs are not covered by direct payments from the consumers but, indirectly, by selling advertisement space. This is made possible by collecting huge amounts of personal data from the users and selling these data to marketers for targeting the advertisements or to other data processing corporations using them for other purposes. Such business practices are subject to obvious privacy concerns.

The relative gap between fixed and marginal costs is descriptive for digital goods. For example, the major cost of an app is the development of the app. The time taken to develop an app can be anything from a few days to several years. As we have seen, the marginal cost of a digital good (e.g., the app) is zero so that the cost of installing the app is also zero, and every new sale of the app contributes directly to revenues. Copies of the app can even be distributed for free without any financial loss for the developer. When total sales have matched the costs of developing the app, the remaining sales are pure profit.

Under these conditions, the average cost of a copy of the digital good equals:

$$AC = \frac{F}{n} + MC = \frac{F}{n},$$

where AC is the average cost, F is the fixed costs, n is the number of copies of the good produced during its lifetime, and MC is the marginal cost. ◘ Figure 6.3 shows the average cost as a function of n. Observe that the average cost approaches zero as n gets large.

Economies of scale are the cost advantages that companies obtain as the number of units produced increases. This is so because the fixed cost per unit decreases as the production volume increases as shown in ◘ Fig. 6.3 and may tend to zero if the number of units produced is large. Companies producing physical goods benefit from cost advantages as the number of units produced increases only up to a certain point. The marginal cost per unit produced is independent of production volume and sets a lower limit for the cost of the product. Moreover, expanding the production beyond a certain threshold may also necessitate that more production infrastructure must be built, thereby increasing the cost of administration and support-functions so that the benefits from economies of scale are marginalized. This is different in the digital economy. This is so because the marginal cost is zero and that there is no limit to the number of units that can be produced without

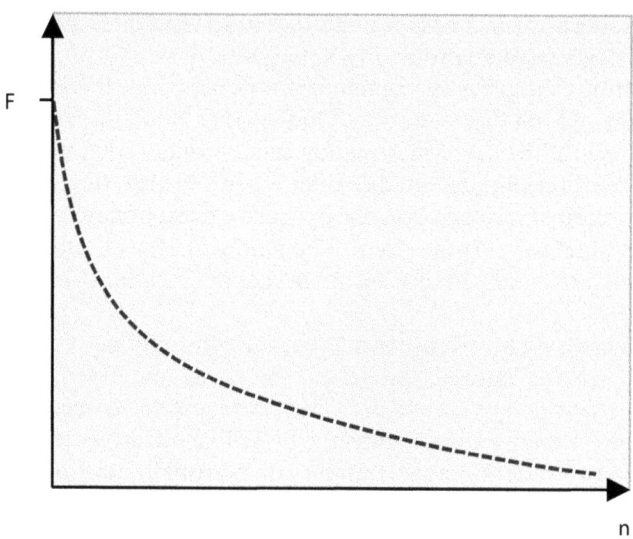

Fig. 6.3 The average cost as a function of the number of units produced. (Authors' own figure)

increasing the fixed costs. Hence, the cost per unit produced will be zero independently of the production volume. This is one of the reasons why companies producing digital goods and service get so big.

6.3 Classification of Digital Goods

Goods can, in general, be classified either as private goods, public goods, club goods, or common-pool resources (Stiglitz, 2015). This classification depends on whether a certain good is rival/non-rival or excludable/non-excludable.

> **Definition 6.3**
> A good is classified as *rival* if it is reduced in quantity after consumption or if the usage of the good prevents others from using it. A *non-rival* good is the opposite of a rival good; it is neither reduced by consumption nor does the usage of the good prevent others from using it. An *excludable* good is such that it is possible to prevent consumers from accessing or using the good. A *non-excludable* good is such that consumers cannot be prevented from accessing or using the good.

From these characteristics, four different types of goods can be defined as shown in ▪ Table 6.1.

Digital goods are non-rival by nature—the consumption of a digital good by a user does not reduce the quantity available to other users of the same digital good.

6.3 · Classification of Digital Goods

Table 6.1 Different types of goods. (Authors' own compilation)

	Rival	Excludable	Examples
Private goods	Yes	Yes	Cars, food, mobile phones
Common-pool resources	Yes	No	Fish, forests, wild berries
Club goods	No	Yes	Cinemas, cable TV, private parks
Public goods	No	No	Air, national defense, knowledge

For example, a user reading a webpage does not reduce the availability of that webpage for other users. A Spotify subscription gives a user access to Spotify, but this does not prevent other users from accessing Spotify. A user accessing the Internet does not reduce the availability of the Internet for other users. The latter is true with some limitations since webservers and the Internet have a maximum capacity. However, most computer and communication systems today are provisioned to handle high demands. In this book, digital goods and services are assumed to be non-rival in most practical cases.

Digital goods can either be excludable or non-excludable. Excludability means that access to the good can be regulated. On the other hand, if a good is non-excludable, a user cannot be denied access to the good. Digital goods that are widespread on the Internet are non-excludable. Examples are free music, news, and content on free web pages. Digital goods that have restricted access are excludable. Examples include access to specific magazines and journals, copyrighted music and movies, and licensed software. Excludable goods can be accessed by, for example, accepting a paid subscription plan or enjoying a club membership. The illegal copying of copyrighted material might result in excludable content becoming non-excludable—copies become abundant and available for everyone.

> Digital goods and services are non-rival by nature. Digital goods and services can be either excludable or non-excludable.

Figure 6.4 shows examples of digital goods classified according to the type of good defined in Table 6.1. Note that all the digital goods in the example are non-rival. Access to Wikipedia articles is non-excludable since the website is open and available for anyone. Gmail is an open and free service available for anyone who registers for an account. Spotify is both excludable and non-excludable at the same time. Its basic service is free for anyone registering for Spotify; however, Spotify's premium service is accessible only by paid subscription. Internet access is excludable since the users must pay for Internet access. However, Internet access may also be non-excludable; access to the Internet may be free and open to anyone in airports and shopping malls and on trains and other public transport. Access to Net-

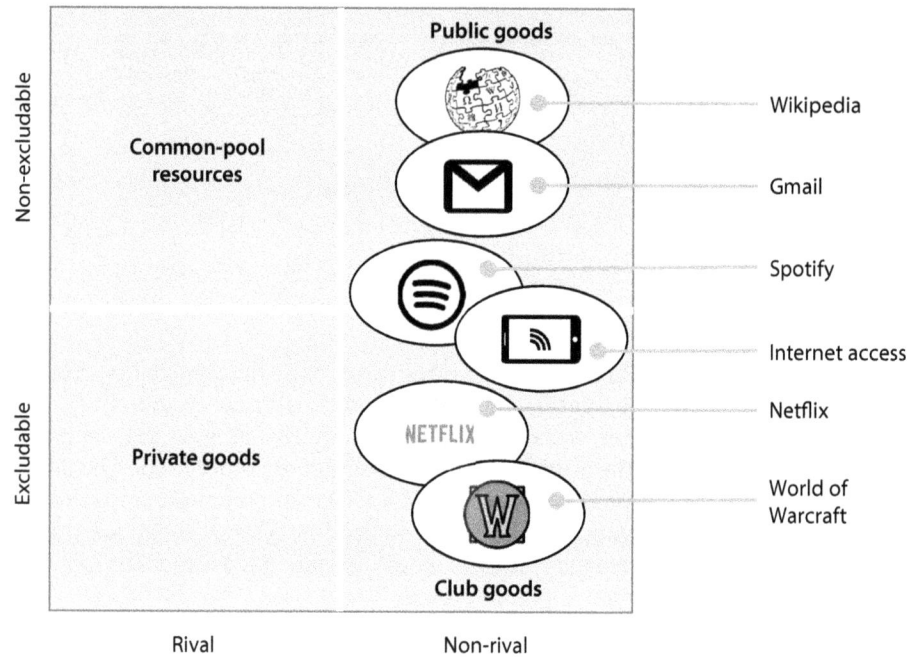

☐ **Fig. 6.4** Classification of digital goods. (Authors' own figure)

flix and *World of Warcraft* is excludable—a paid subscription plan is required for using both these services.

If a digital good is both non-rival and non-excludable, it is classified as a public good. Public goods occupy a special place in economic theory. They are often prone to market failure resulting in governmental regulation or other market interactions to make the market function properly. One of the reasons for market failure is the *free rider problem*. Public goods can be accessed by anyone without paying for it. There are, therefore, no incentives for private actors to provide these goods; likewise, there are no incentives for users to pay for access or usage to maintain and uphold the good. One example is Wikipedia offering a free encyclopedia on the Internet. There are few or no incentives for private actors to financially support or invest in Wikipedia. Wikipedia relies primarily on two sources of income for sustaining its operations: financial donations from benefactors and voluntary work by authors who write and update articles.

A common-pool resource is prone to *the tragedy of the commons*, in which common resources get overused and depleted. Even though individuals act in their own self-interest, it is the collective behavior of all individuals that may lead to overuse or depletion. Examples of the tragedy of the commons are overfishing in the seas and air pollution. The tragedy of the commons also has impacts on the digital economy even though digital goods and services are non-rival by nature. Since digital goods and services have zero marginal cost and, therefore, close to unlimited supply, the tragedy of the commons takes different appearances in the digital economy, resulting in publishing of unwanted and illegal information and content, spam, denial of service attacks, and service abuse (Gapper, 2017).

6.4 Zero Average Revenue per User

Average revenue per user (ARPU) is an important financial indicator in economics. The ARPU states how much revenue an average user is generating over a specific period of time. For instance, the monthly ARPU for mobile subscribers in the USA is about $40. Total revenue for a mobile service provider is the ARPU multiplied by the number of subscribers. The mobile service provider will focus on increasing its total revenue by increasing both the ARPU and the number of subscribers.

In the digital economy, several companies operate with zero average return per user (ARPU = 0), in which case the company does not receive any revenue from the consumers at all. Since the marginal cost is zero, the cost to attach users is also zero. This applies to all competitors offering the same service so that, to compete, goods are offered for free to the consumer by all of them. The suppliers do not compete on price but on user experience. In this economy, supply-demand curves are meaningless.

The main challenge for many companies in the digital economy is, therefore, to get revenue for its operations from sources other than consumers. A few companies have succeeded in this effort, for example, Facebook, Google, and Twitter. Their main source of revenue is advertisements: the more they know about their consumers, the more attractive they are as marketing channels.

Note that ARPU = 0 is not a universal rule applicable to all digital services. Netflix, for example, has an ARPU >0 because consumers pay to access the service.

> **Box 6.3 Facebook and ARPU = 0**
> Facebook is the world-leading social networking service with currently more than two billion users. None of the users pay anything for using their services so that ARPU = 0. Yet, Facebook's revenue is over $40 billion for 2017, increased from $27 billion in 2016 and $18 billion in 2015. In 2018, Facebook is among the six most valued companies in the world, according to market capitalization (◘ Fig. 6.5).

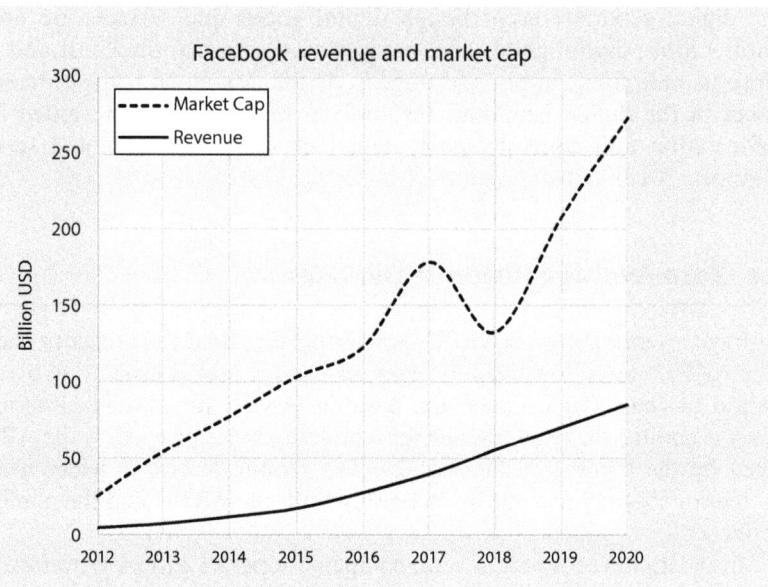

• **Fig. 6.5** Facebook revenue and market cap 2012–2020. (Authors' own figure)

How is it possible for Facebook to reach such a financial position when it does not earn anything from its users? The answers to this question are related to network effects and multi-sided platforms (see ▶ Chaps. 9 and 10).

6.5 Digital Commodities

Commoditization is the process by which digital goods (or any good or service in general) end up being indistinguishable from a consumer's point of view. Competing goods will look the same to the user—it is impossible to differentiate between the goods even though they are produced by different manufacturers. The only distinguishing factor for a commoditized good is the price. It is, for example, impossible for consumers to distinguish between lubrication oils from different refineries or electricity produced by different power plants—only the price can be used as a distinguishing factor.

Several, but not all, digital goods have been commoditized. Examples of digital commodities are Internet access and transport of bits, storage of data, processing of data, international news bulletins, and, to some extent, certain types of software products (e.g., word editing and spreadsheet software).

Digital goods that have been commoditized compete only on price. A fierce competition among companies providing digital commodities tends to push the price to zero because of the zero-marginal cost property of digital goods. Standard microeconomic theory on perfect markets also predicts this outcome. However, at price equal to zero, it is a challenge for companies to be profitable. Most of them will run out of business as revenues decrease and profits turn negative. This is a strategic dilemma for several companies in the digital economy. To avoid a price war resulting in zero revenue, companies may differentiate their goods from the competitors by making them unique for customers, for example, newspapers offering customized news alerts. The newspaper may then generate revenue from these customers. Another option is to apply creative business models that operate under condition that the service is provided for free while the revenues are obtained from other sources—Google and Facebook employ such business models.

Some digital goods become commodities because of standards. Standards force providers to deliver indistinguishable digital goods, for example, compatible Bluetooth access to mobile phones, hearing aids, and household gadgets. Digital goods also tend to become commodities over time. This may be the result of the harmonization of competing goods. An example is word editing software. In the 1990s, editing products from different suppliers supported different functions. Today, word editing software packages are so similar that they have become digital commodities.

6.6 Transaction Costs

The transaction cost is the cost associated with the process of selling and buying. Transaction costs can be divided into three categories:

- *Search and information costs* are the costs of searching for a particular good and determining its price and properties.
- *Bargaining costs* are the collective costs for the consumer and the provider to agree on the terms of the contract. This includes the price and delivery conditions of the good.
- *Policing and enforcement costs* are the costs of sticking to the agreement and taking appropriate action if the agreement is not upheld by either party.

An example is trading of physical goods on eBay. The buyer first searches for products they want to buy among offers made by various sellers (search and information costs). This is done on eBay's website. When the buyer has decided which item to buy, buyer and seller will negotiate price and delivery conditions (bargaining costs). If something is wrong with the received product, the buyer will enforce contractual rights by taking direct contact with the seller (policing and enforcement costs). eBay may also be involved in the dispute if the buyer and seller do not agree.

Amazon, eBay, and Alibaba lower the transaction costs by offering efficient search processes using web or mobile apps.

6.7 Bundling

Product or service bundling means that several products or services are combined and offered for sale as a single package. One example is the Microsoft Office 365 package. This package contains the digital services Word, Excel, PowerPoint, OneNote, Outlook, Publisher, and Access. Another example is cable television subscriptions where the user may subscribe to various bundles of television channels. The cable television provider may also extend the package to include audio broad-

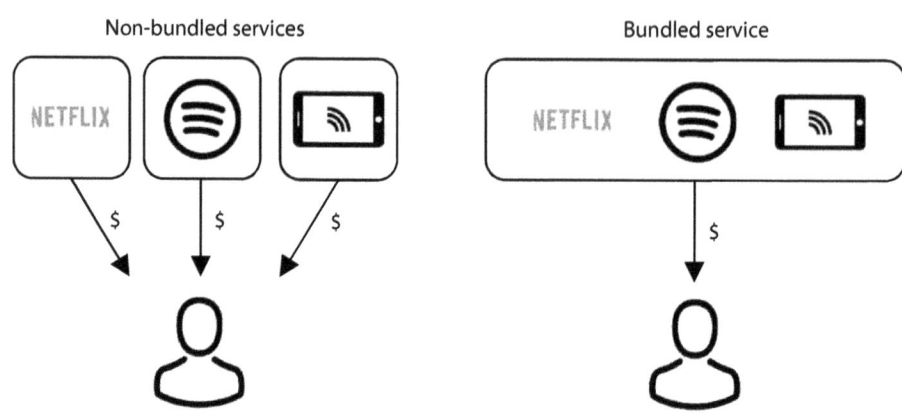

Fig. 6.6 Example of a bundle of the services Netflix, Spotify, and network access. (Authors' own figure)

casting, streaming of movies and music, broadband Internet access over Wi-Fi, and VoIP. This is exemplified in Fig. 6.6.

Pure bundling means that consumers can only buy the bundled package without the opportunity to buy the single products or services in the package. Mixed bundling means that a consumer has the option to buy the package as well as the single products or services constituting the package. In general, the price of the bundle is lower than the sum of the price of the individual services constituting the package.

Bundling is a strategy for providers to increase sales. In the digital economy, bundling is common and particularly efficient because of the zero marginal cost property—it does not cost the provider anything adding another service it already owns to the package. The consumer may find this business model attractive since an additional service in the bundle contributes to increased value for the consumer and, hence, an increased willingness to pay for the bundle.

The digital economy has also enabled the unbundling of previously bundled goods and services. Unbundling has become common in the music industry. Apple iTunes, for example, unbundles CD albums offering each music track as an independent product. The customer may then buy a single track rather than buying a complete album. It also allows the consumer to build their own personal playing lists containing songs from several albums. The benefit for the music industry is that this increases sales without generating additional costs since the marginal cost of providing a complete album or just a single track is zero in both cases.

6.8 Conclusions

The most important characteristics of digital goods and services are summarized as follows:
- The marginal cost of production and distribution of digital goods and services is zero.

6.8 · Conclusions

- Digital goods and services are non-rival; that is, the availability is not reduced by consumption and usage.
- Digital goods and services may be excludable or non-excludable depending on commercial conditions of usage.
- Several, but not all, digital goods and services are commodities; that is, they can only be distinguished by price. In some market segments, the price for the product is zero, and price cannot be used as differentiating factor.
- It is easy to bundle digital goods and services in flexible packets. If the provider owns all components of the bundle and all components are digital goods, then the cost of bundling is zero. In this case, the customers may create their own bundles, for example, playing lists for music and collection of television channels.

▶ Exercises

1. Digital Services
   Which of the following are digital goods or services?
   1. The *New York Times* web page
   2. Internet access over a 4G mobile network
   3. A compact disc (CD)
   4. HBO subscription
   5. An Apple iPhone

2. Computer Game Development
   A computer game costs $100 million to develop (fixed costs). The game is sold to consumers of $50 per copy. Assume that the marginal cost is zero. How many copies must be sold to cover the fixed costs? How many copies must be sold to cover the fixed costs if the marginal cost of each copy is $10? Under what condition is the marginal cost zero? Under what condition is $MC > 0$?

3. Digital Commodities
   Determine if any of the following digital goods have been commoditized:
   1. Social media services
   2. E-mail clients
   3. Web browsers
   4. Cloud storage
   5. Wi-Fi Internet access

   Why have these digital goods been commoditized? If they have not been commoditized, why not?

4. Bitcoin Transaction Costs
   How does Bitcoin influence transaction costs in the digital economy? Which stakeholders are affected by Bitcoin's potential impact on transaction costs?

5. Internet Explorer
   In 2002, Internet Explorer had over 90% of the web browser market. Who were Internet Explorer's main competitors at that time? Explain how Internet Explorer got so large.

Answers

1. The following are digital services: The *NY Times* web page, Internet access, and an HBO subscription. The following are *not* digital services: a CD and an iPhone. The *NY Times* web page is considered a digital good. The content available on HBO is a digital good.

2. The number of copies sold must cover the fixed costs. If $MC = 0$, the number of copies sold to cover the fixed costs is 100,000,000 / 50 = 2,000,000 copies. If $MC = 10$, the number of copies sold to cover the fixed costs is 100,000,000 / (50 - 10) = 2,500,000 copies. The $MC = 0$ if the trade is completely digital. That is, ordering, payment, and delivery are all digital. On the other hand, the $MC > 0$ if the trade includes a physical product (e.g., DVD containing the game, a box, or a user manual).

3. Of these services, only cloud storage is fully commoditized. Social media is not commoditized. This is because the social media networks available (e.g., Twitter, Facebook, and Google+) have very different functionalities, and they do not communicate with one another. This is because of missing standards in the social media industry. E-mail clients are close to being commoditized. This is because e-mail as a service is standardized (SMTP). Hence, the functionalities of different e-mail clients are the same. The major difference between various e-mail clients is the design and interoperability with other applications (such as a calendar). Web browsers are close to being fully commoditized. This is because the web service is standardized (through the protocols HTML, HTTP, and URL). The major differences between web browsers are the design and, to some degree, the interoperability with other digital services (such as Flash and JavaScript). Cloud storage is fully commoditized. The only difference between various cloud storage services is their price. Wi-Fi Internet access is close to being fully commoditized. However, there are quality differences in Wi-Fi access (e.g., different bandwidths).

4. Bitcoin has the potential to significantly reduce transaction costs in the digital economy. Current third-party payment services—such as VISA, MasterCard, and American Express—charge transaction fees of 1.4–3.5%. Bitcoin, on the other hand, can charge as little as 0%. It is no wonder why the established financial industry views Bitcoin and other cryptocurrencies as a threat to their operations. It is VISA, MasterCard, American Express, and, to a certain degree, the banking industry, which are the competitors of Bitcoin.

5. The main competitor of Internet Explorer was Netscape. Netscape was the largest web browser in the mid-1990s. However, when Internet Explorer was launched in 1995, it started to increase its market share until it had almost a monopoly in 2002. The main reason for Internet Explorer's success was because it was free and bundled with Microsoft Windows. Few consumers took the extra trouble of installing another web browser on their PC when Internet Explorer was already installed and ready for use. This, combined with the large market share of PCs using Microsoft Windows, fueled Internet Explorer's growth. In addition, Microsoft—which provided Internet Explorer—was a much larger company than Netscape, with significantly more financial resources.

References

Fournier, L. (2014). *Merchant sharing: Towards a zero marginal cost economy*. ArXiv, 1405.2051.
Gapper, J. (2017, November 29). Facebook faces the tragedy of the commons. *Financial Times*.
List of most expensive video games to develop. (2020, December 16). *Wikipedia*.
Stiglitz, J. E. (2015). *Economics of the public sector*. W. W. Norton & Company.

Further Reading

Christensen, C. (1997). *The innovators dilemma: When new technologies cause great firms to fail*. Harvard Business School Press.

Production Models

Contents

7.1 Physical and Digital Products – 92

7.2 Basic Production Methods – 93
7.2.1 In-House Production – 93
7.2.2 Commons-Based Peer Production – 93
7.2.3 Crowdsourcing – 97

7.3 Production Tools – 98
7.3.1 Crowdfunding – 98
7.3.2 Peer-to-Peer Lending – 100
7.3.3 Free and Open-Source Software and Cloud Computing – 100

7.4 Conclusions – 101

References – 102

© The Author(s), under exclusive license to Springer Nature Switzerland AG 2021
H. Øverby, J. A. Audestad, *Introduction to Digital Economics*, Classroom Companion: Business,
https://doi.org/10.1007/978-3-030-78237-5_7

Learning Objectives

After completing this chapter, you should be able to:
- Comprehend the difference between production of physical and digital goods.
- Explain the basic production models described in this chapter and apply them in the analysis of business models.
- Understand the importance of online financing methods and open-source software for the development of digital goods.

7.1 Physical and Digital Products

Production of digital goods and services is different from standard industrial production. Standard theory of production is based on manufacturing of physical goods requiring, in addition to the actual manufacturing process, retrieval of raw material, storage facilities for products before they are delivered to the market, and logistics for transporting the products to the market. All the elements of the production process contribute to the total cost of the product as explained in ▶ Sect. 8.2. The costs associated with development and later improvements of the product are usually not included as a contribution to the direct costs of production. These costs, together with administrative and capital costs, are usually included among the common costs of running the company. The total direct cost of production is then equal to the marginal cost of producing one item of the product multiplied by the number of items produced.

Production of digital goods is different, though all the production stages mentioned above may be present. The most important characteristics of the production of digital goods include:

- The major cost contribution to a digital product is associated with developing the product itself (e.g., app, webpage, book, or program update) and investments and running costs associated with the production platform, for example, fees to cloud providers. Note that the running cost for producing some digital goods may be huge. Production of Bitcoin requires huge computer facilities consuming large amounts of energy. The same may apply to search engines and providers of massively multiplayer online games running large server platforms capable to accommodate millions of simultaneous players.
- After the product and the production platform have been developed, the cost of producing an item of the product is almost zero (zero marginal cost).
- Only one copy of the product needs to be stored. Copies of the product are produced instantly on demand.
- Distributing a single copy of the product over the Internet costs almost nothing.
- Some digital products may require "raw materials" in the form of licenses or other expenditures associated with each item, for example, copyrighted material such as music, books, and films. For these products, the marginal cost is no longer zero.

The difference between properties of digital and physical products is explained in ▶ Chap. 6.

The general characteristics of digital goods generate new ways of production. The most important difference compared to physical products is that digital products can be produced by collaboration over the Internet giving rise to entirely new production methods. In the following, production is understood to include both the development of the product and the subsequent production and delivery of the product to the customers.

> There are several ways in which digital goods can be developed and produced. Three basic production methods of digital goods are *in-house production*, *commons-based peer production* (CBPP), and *crowdsourcing*. Production based on CBPP and crowdsourcing takes place over the Internet.

The three basic production models are not independent—a company may apply a mix of them when developing and producing a digital service. Within this context, note that some digital services may be rather simple to develop requiring only few resources. This includes even big services like the World Wide Web, Facebook, Airbnb, and TCP/IP. However, other digital services require the collaboration of hundreds of people over long periods of time. Examples include the development of operating systems (e.g., UNIX and Linux), public mobile networks (GSM, 3G, 4G, and 5G), and local access networks (e.g., Wi-Fi, WiMAX, Ethernet, and Bluetooth).

7.2 Basic Production Methods

7.2.1 In-House Production

In-house production (also termed "firm-production") means that the company develops the good or service using internal resources, possibly combined with manpower contracted from other enterprises (outsourcing). In this case, the company is in control of the whole development process and owns the final digital product and intellectual property rights associated with it. This also includes the part outsourced to independent companies. In-house production is illustrated in ◘ Fig. 7.1.

In-house production is the most common approach taken by both large companies (e.g., Google, Microsoft, and Facebook) and small startups. The company organizes the work and sets up tasks in such a way that the final service or good is produced within deadline and according to accepted industry standards. In-house production may include the use of open-source software and crowdsourcing for part of the production.

7.2.2 Commons-Based Peer Production

Commons-based peer production (CBPP)—also called social production—is a way of producing goods and services in which a large number of people (collaborators) take part in the development of the product. The term was coined by Yochai

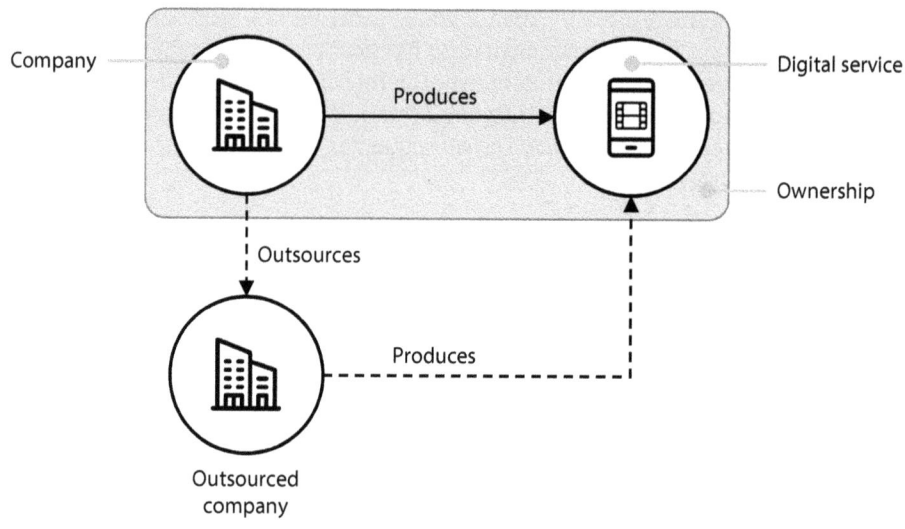

☐ **Fig. 7.1** The in-house production model. (Authors' own figure)

Benkler (Benkler, 2002). The production process takes place by use of the Internet—the commons in the context of digital products. The group of collaborators is usually self-organized (if organized at all) and without central leadership or coordination. A platform for gathering the contributions from each collaborator into a final digital service must be established before the collaboration starts. The platform is used throughout the production of the digital service to organize and divide work between the collaborators. The contributing collaborators are not organized by a firm as in the in-house production model. Often, the collaborators do not receive any financial rewards for their contribution. ☐ Figure 7.2 illustrates the CBPP model.

The most famous example of the CBPP model is the operating system Linux in which hundreds of computer scientists contributed to the evolution of the Linux software over many years. Wikipedia is also the result of the CBPP model—no one is coordinating the content or the evolution of the encyclopedia. Arbitrary readers are checking the validity of the articles, correcting errors, adding novel material, and writing new articles.

The Internet itself is also a result of the CBPP model. Anyone can submit proposals for new protocols, procedures, and functionalities of the Internet in memoranda called Requests for Comments (RFCs). The work is loosely organized by the Internet Society (ISOC) and the Internet Engineering Task Force (IETF), which are both non-profit organizations in which anyone—individuals as well as industries and organizations—can be members. The acceptance and implementation of new proposals depend entirely upon how the business opportunities and other prospects of the new proposal are assessed by users and providers of Internet hardware, software, and services. Some of the new products may be short-lived (e.g., the real-time transport protocol XTP developed to speed up data exchange in distributed processing systems), while others may exist for generations (e.g., HTTP and TCP).

7.2 · Basic Production Methods

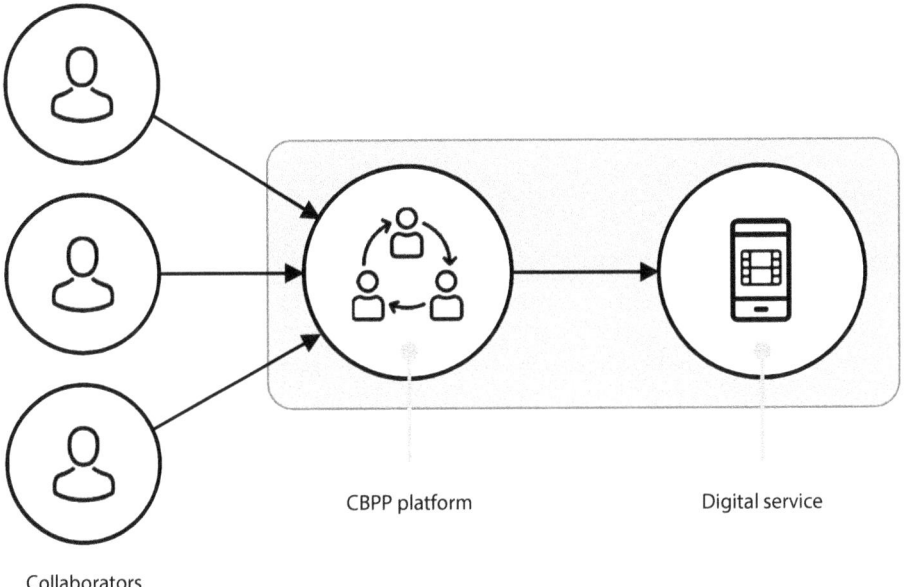

Fig. 7.2 The commons-based peer production model. (Authors' own figure)

Below follow examples of peer production initiatives in four different fields: software development, production of encyclopedia, proofreading of scanned books, and open hardware design.

> **▶ Example 7.1 Linux and GNU**
>
> Linux is a Unix-like operating system suitable for a wide range of computing devices: mainframe computers, smartphones, servers, personal computers, and several other types of electronic devices. It is built on free and open-source software. Linus Torvalds started the development of the platform in 1991. The idea was to develop an operating system like Unix consisting entirely of free software that could be loaded down by anyone free of charge. Since then, several hundred computer scientists have contributed to the development of the software, and in several countries and regions, there exist loosely knit Linux User Groups promoting the software, assisting new users installing the software, and providing technical assistance and training. Anyone may contribute to the evolution of the software but without levying any wages for the work.
>
> The goal of the GNU project is to provide an environment for collaborative software development and distribution of free software. The distribution of the software is subject to GNU General Public License (GGPL), allowing users to run, share, and modify the software (also called copyleft conditions, (see ▶ https://www.gnu.org/copyleft/). The license guarantees that there are no hidden intellectual property rights or other restrictions of usage associated with the software or other products licensed by GNU such as specifications, design descriptions, and hardware. The Linux kernel and several other free software packages not developed in the GNU project itself are

distributed with the GNU General Public License. GNU Free Documentation License (GFDL) is a similar license for free documentation (e.g., textbooks and manuals) allowing users the right to copy, modify, and distribute the text. New software or texts produced and submitted under GGPL or GFDL should also be freely available subject to copyleft conditions.

The production of the content of Wikipedia is a result of peer production over the Internet. ◄

► Example 7.2 Wikipedia

Anyone may contribute to the content of the encyclopedia by producing new articles, adding new material to existing articles, and deleting, modifying, or correcting existing articles. The Wikipedia Foundation is not a licensing organization itself but a platform on which contributors can publish their work. The content of Wikipedia is licensed using the Creative Commons (CC) license. This license is similar to GFDL but contains rules by which otherwise copyrighted material (e.g., pictures) can be used in other contexts. The rules may be different in the various language editions.

By the end of 2020, the English Wikipedia contained about 6.2 million articles and is among the 15 most visited website on the Internet (See ► https://stats.wikimedia.org/EN/TablesWikipediaEN.htm). ◄

► Example 7.3 Project Gutenberg and Distributed Proofreaders

Project Gutenberg is digitizing public domain books and other texts for free public access as e-books. Public domain books are books where the intellectual property rights have expired or otherwise not applicable.

As of 2019, the project has digitized about 60,000 books. The scanning and preparation of the books were first done by the founder of the project, Michal Hart, alone, but the project attracted soon several volunteers scanning and preparing books and other texts for the project. Since Hart died in 2011, the project is run entirely by volunteers.

When scanning the books, it is likely that errors occur because the scanner may misinterpret a letter or a group of letters. Proofreading is required to correct these errors. In 2000, Charles Franks opened the website Distributed Proofreaders where volunteers could proofread the texts produced by the Gutenberg Project. Several thousand volunteers have since joined the project. Distributed Proofreaders have prepared about 40,000 texts for Project Gutenberg. ◄

► Example 7.4 RepRap Project

The RepRap project was initiated by the University of Bath, England, for developing low-cost 3D printers using various thermoplastic materials. The project now includes several hundred participants all over the world developing free 3D printing software and hardware design and experimenting with new materials suitable for printing. RepRap is an open design project releasing design details via the GNU General Public License. This includes free open-source software, design details, and hardware. The goal is to develop desktop manufacturing systems affordable and useful for everyone for, among others, producing household artifacts. ◄

7.2 · Basic Production Methods

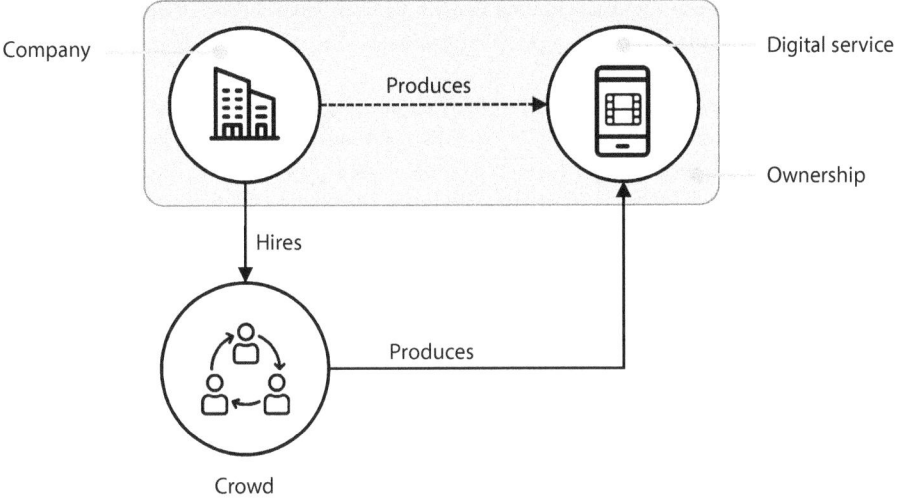

Fig. 7.3 The crowdsourcing production model. (Authors' own figure)

7.2.3 Crowdsourcing

In the crowdsourcing production model, organizations and individuals produce digital services by inspiring the public to contribute to the project. This seems somewhat similar to outsourcing; however, the difference between outsourcing and crowdsourcing is that outsourcing implies that the work is contracted out to another company on strict commercial and juridical conditions, whereas crowdsourcing implies that the work is done by arbitrary groups of individuals without formalized participation. The result of the work may then be more arbitrary but may also lead to better, cheaper, and more versatile solutions. Since there may be many participants in the project, it is likely that design flaws are discovered at an early stage and that better and cheaper designs are found. The crowdsourcing production model is illustrated in ◘ Fig. 7.3.

Crowdsourcing is a form of peer production. The difference is that CBPP may follow arbitrary development paths sometimes resulting in a viable product, whereas a crowdsourcing project aims at developing a predefined product. Crowdsourcing may be used in any stage of product development from the initial idea to development, production, testing, and marketing. The prerequisite is that the collaboration can take place over the Internet. A company may use crowdsourcing at all stages of production or only parts of production, leading to a final digital service.

Next follows some examples of crowdsourcing initiatives.

> ▶ **Example 7.5 Crowdsourcing Using Contests**
> Contests are important methods to trigger crowdsourcing events. One example is the CAESAR competition in which the goal was to develop new encryption methods. The contest started in 2012, and individual researchers or groups of researchers proposed new algorithms which were tested against cyberattack and other weaknesses by the par-

ticipants in the contest. Six winning algorithms were announced in March 2019 after several rounds of eliminating proposed candidates. The winning algorithms are candidates for new cryptographic standards.

In 2009, Netflix used a similar contest to improve its recommendation algorithm. The winner received one million US dollars (Jackson, 2017). The large premium was then the obvious motive to participate. Microsoft used crowdsourcing to test the security of the Windows 8 software. This included both detecting security bugs ($100,000) and methods to correct them ($50,000) (Bell, 2013). ◄

▶ **Example 7.6 Crowdsourcing Using Collaboration Platforms**

The business models of Topcoder and Clickworkers are based entirely on crowdsourcing.

The core business of Topcoder is to run a collaborative computer platform and to organize communities of individual coworkers. Computer scientists, system designers, and software engineers may join these communities and participate in various projects the company is developing for their clients. The company also uses online annual tournaments called Topcoder Open where members of the community compete in solving particular problems in various fields of computer science.

Clickworker offers "micro-jobs" to volunteers. Potential collaborators register in the community run by the company and are allocated jobs in accordance with their reported skills and earlier accomplishments. The company pays for the jobs each individual does for them. These jobs range over a large field of problem areas, for example, software development, proofreading of books and manuals, information gathering, and processing of unstructured data. The participants are connected to the company on a freelance basis, and they decide themselves when and how much they want to work. ◄

7.3 Production Tools

The most important challenges related to design and production of digital goods are financing the development and reducing the running production costs. For new startups, it may be difficult to persuade banks, venture capitalists, and other investors to put money into the project. Financing the project may then be achieved by crowdfunding or peer-to-peer lending. The development costs may be reduced by using free and open-source software, and investment and running cost may be reduced by renting processing and storage capacity from cloud providers.

7.3.1 Crowdfunding

Crowdfunding is a way to raise funds for projects or startups by inviting people to invest in the venture. The interactions take place over the Internet. The investors usually receive shares in the startup or company owning the project equal to the amount of money they have invested. Most fund-raising events are small but some of them are huge. In 2018, a Cayman Island startup raised more than 4 billion US dollars for developing a blockchain platform (Rooney, 2018).

Crowdfunding may refer to several types of funding mechanisms (Hellmann et al., 2019).
- The most widely used method is *peer-to-peer lending* (see next).
- *Equity-based crowdfunding* implies ownership of securities in the company or project. These are then usually high-risk investments.
- In *reward-based crowdfunding*, the investors receive services or other benefits as reward for their investments. In this case, there is no guarantee that the compensation will match the size of the investment.
- *Donation crowdfunding* is mainly used for supporting charitable causes, and the donor does usually not receive any compensation for the investment.

There were more than 2000 crowdfunding platforms in 2016 (Drake, 2017). Kickstarter is one of the most successful of these platforms.

▶ **Example 7.7 Kickstarter**

Kickstarter is an example of a crowdfunding organization. Project owners publish and describe their project on the Kickstarter website. People from all over the world may choose to fund the projects they like, often with as little as $1. There may be thousands of different investors on a single project. The project will start if the project achieves its funding goals. Kickstarter projects can be anything from game developments and app design to the creation of books, music, art, and films. All projects awaiting funding are listed on their homepage. On Friday, January 10, 2020, there were 467,867 projects asking for funding on the Kickstarter website, 3630 of them were software projects. When a project is funded and the project owner has completed the project, the funders will receive a reward based on the allocated funding, e.g., a copy of the creative work.
◘ Figure 7.4 illustrates the creative and funding process of Kickstarter.

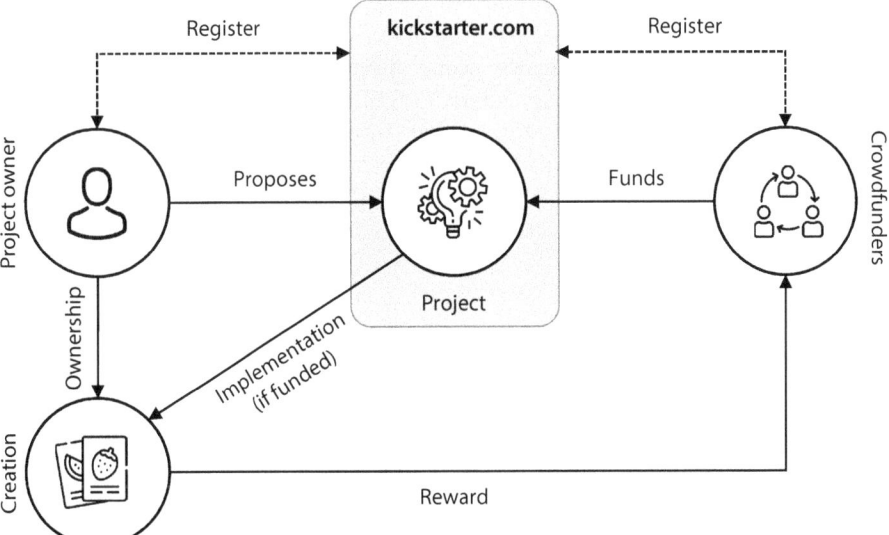

◘ **Fig. 7.4** The creative and funding process of Kickstarter. (Authors' own figure)

Kickstarter apply a 5% fee on the collected funding as a source of revenue. Crowdfunding has been particularly popular in the video game and traditional table-top game industry, and several games have been funded using the Kickstarter website. ◄

7.3.2 Peer-to-Peer Lending

Peer-to-peer lending (P2P lending or crowdlending) means that individuals lend money directly to other individuals or businesses. Startups may have problems financing the project by traditional bank loans because of the high risk associated with the project. In such cases, peer-to-peer lending is an alternative way of financing the project.

Companies mediating in peer-to-peer lending transactions run match-making platforms where borrowers and lenders may register for a certain fee. The intermediating company does not offer loans using its own money and is thus not a regular financial institution.[1] The company may, however, offer services such as credit checking, registering the transaction details, and assisting in resolving disputes. The intermediators are value networks as defined in ► Sect. 8.3, matching people or firms lacking capital to initiate a project and potential lenders.

The interest rates on peer-to-peer loans are generally lower than for bank loans but higher than the interest rates on bank deposits. Moreover, it has been reported that this market is less volatile than the stock market, and an investor targeting peer-to-peer lending will typically diversify the funds over many borrowers to reduce risks and increase the return on investments (Roth, 2012). People are then encouraged to invest money in peer-to-peer lending rather than in stock market securities. The Australian peer-to-peer lending company SocietyOne reports that they passed $800 million in lending by the end of 2019.

In some cases, the interest rates are very low and sometimes even zero, in particular, if the cause is charity or investments in projects in developing countries (Brook, 2007), for example, using the peer-to-peer platform of Kiva.

Peer-to-peer lending stands for about 73% of all crowdfunding for small- and medium-size businesses according to a report from the Emerge Partnership (ITU) (A review of Micro, Small and Medium Enterprises in the ICT Sector. Emerge Partnership (ITU). 2016).

Unlike bank loans, peer-to-peer lending is usually not protected by government guarantees.

7.3.3 Free and Open-Source Software and Cloud Computing

Free and open-source software (FOSS) is an initiative for the collaborative development of software. Free and open-source software is an important ingredient in commons-based peer production. The source code of the free and open-source

---

[1] Some of these companies may also have banking licenses, for example, the UK company Zopa.

software is made available to other developers along with a license allowing them to use, modify, and redistribute the software. The license is issued by the copyright holder of the software and approved by, for example, the nonprofit organization Free Software Foundation. The GNU General Public License mentioned in ▶ Example 7.1 is one such license.

The use of the software may be free or subject to a small fee. There are thousands of licensed open-source software packages covering fields such as grid computing, web browsing, file systems, 3D animation, and firewalls. Linux and Android are among the most successful open-source projects. In fact, most of the Internet runs on open-source software.

Cloud computing is also a major component in the production model of several small- and medium-size enterprises and startups. The main advantage for a provider of digital services to use cloud computing is that both investments in computer infrastructure and running costs associated with operation and maintenance are reduced. There is also no need for the service provider to have deep insight in computer science in order to design, promote, and deliver the service.

Other advantages of cloud computing are that it is easier for the user to adjust resources to fluctuating needs, and the technology offers increased reliability because data may be mirrored on several redundant sites, more and better cybersecurity protection, access to high-speed computing resources with low latency, and state-of-the-art data speed, streaming capabilities, and protocols (What is cloud computing? A beginner's guide. Microsoft Azure).

7.4 Conclusions

The traditional production method is in-house production in which the entire production of the good takes place within the company. This method is used for almost all physical products. This is also the dominating production method in the digital economy. Microsoft, Facebook, Google, Netflix, and all the other big companies in the digital economy base their production method on in-house production.

The Internet has created more flexible production methods based on collaboration over the network. Commons-based peer production (CBPP) is founded on voluntary participation and takes place without (or with only little) central coordination. This has led to large projects such as Linux, digitization of books and documents, development of free and open-source software (FOSS), and production of technical standards end recipes. CBPP has created vast amounts of freely available resources such as statistics, encyclopedia, software, and digital books and documents.

Crowdsourcing implies that a firm invites individuals to participate in the development or production of a good. The project is managed by the firm, but the work is done by a group of arbitrary individuals. Crowdsourcing does not depend on the Internet but is facilitated by it.

Investments in and financing of new products also take place over the Internet in terms of crowdfunding and peer-to-peer lending by bypassing traditional banking and investment procedures.

? Questions
1. Who owns a service produced using the CBPP model?
2. How can services produced using the CBBP model generate revenues?
3. What are the main challenges of the crowdsourcing production model?
4. Discuss whether the crowdsourcing production model can produce digital services of the same quality as the in-house production model.

✓ Answers
1. Anyone who participates in the development of the product may be an owner of it. In some cases, the product is marketed and maintained by a group of volunteers (e.g., Linux, Gutenberg Project). In many cases, no one owns the product.
2. In most cases, CBPP does not generate revenues since the product is offered for free. In some cases, the project may receive donations (e.g., Wikipedia) or generate revenues from ads, complementary services (e.g., consultancy services or seminars), or services built on the CBPP service.
3. Challenges are:
    - Coordinating the work
    - Scheduling and planning tasks
    - Attracting the right workforce and expertise
    - Quality management

4. Crowdsourcing may produce better results, more innovative solutions, and better quality.

References

Bell, L. (2013, June 20). Microsoft offers a $100,000 bug bounty for cracking Windows 8.1. *The Enquirer*.

Benkler, Y. (2002). Coase's Penguin or Linux and the Nature of the Firm. *The Yale Law Journal, 112*(3).

Brook, Y.. (2007, August 20). The morality of moneylending: A short history. *The Objective Standard*.

Drake, D. (2017, December 6). 2000 Global Crowdfunding Sites to Choose from by 2016. *The Huffington Post*.

Hellmann, T., Mospitan, I., & Vulkan, N. (2019, September). *Be careful what you ask for: Fundraising srategies inequity crowdfunding*. NBER Working Paper No. w26275

Jackson, D. (2017, July 7). The Netflix prize: How a $1 million contest changed binge-watching forever. *Thrillist*.

Rooney, K. (2018, May 31). A blockchain start-up just raised $4 billion without a live product. *CNBC*.

Roth, J.D. (2012, November 16). Taking a peek at peer-to-peer lending. *Time*.

Further Reading

Benkler, Y. (2006). *The wealth of networks: How social production transforms markets and freedom*. Yale University Press.

Jemielniak, D., & Przegaliska, A. (2020). *Collaborative society*. MIT Press.

Value Creation Models and Competitive Strategy

Contents

8.1 Introduction – 104

8.2 Value Chain – 105

8.3 Value Shop – 106

8.4 Value Network – 108

8.5 Competitive Forces – 111
8.5.1 Porter's Five Forces – 111
8.5.2 Porter's Five Forces Applied to the Digital Economy – 112

8.6 Competition, Cooperation, and Coopetition – 116

8.7 Conclusions – 119

References – 121

© The Author(s), under exclusive license to Springer Nature Switzerland AG 2021
H. Øverby, J. A. Audestad, *Introduction to Digital Economics*, Classroom Companion: Business,
https://doi.org/10.1007/978-3-030-78237-5_8

Learning Objectives

After completing this chapter, you should be able to:
- Identify whether an enterprise or business sector is a value chain, shop, or network, or a combination of these.
- Understand the concepts competition, cooperation, and coopetition in the digital economy.
- Use Porter's five forces model in strategic analysis and planning.

8.1 Introduction

There are several models explaining how value is created within a company. The classical and perhaps most influential paper concerning the strategy of industrial companies was written by Michal Porter in 1979 (Porter, 1985). Porter's model was developed for analyzing the industrial company's conversion of raw material into final tangible products sold to consumers. These companies are categorized as value chains (▶ Sect. 8.2) because the production follows a linear chain of transformations. In 1998, Stabell and Fjeldstad published a paper proposing two additional types of companies using completely different ways to produce their product: value shops (▶ Sect. 8.3) and value networks (▶ Sect. 8.4) (Stabell & Fjeldstad, 1998). This chapter discusses and compares all three value creation models and provides a broad overview of how the business strategies are different in the three value creation models.

Most companies in the digital economy are value networks. The value network is closely related to multisided platforms (MSPs) as discussed in ▶ Chap. 10. The following sections briefly review all three value models to show the differences between them, however, with emphasis on the value network. The value models presented in this chapter are supplemental to the production models presented in ▶ Chap. 7—production models and value models describe different aspects of the business operations of a company.

Competition is closely related to value creation. Competitive forces acting upon a company producing digital goods are considered in ▶ Sect. 8.5, while ▶ Sect. 8.6 discusses different aspects of competition and cooperation in the digital economy.

As most economic models, these models are only crude but useful approximations of reality. They are useful in the sense that they identify some issues that matters to fully understand the roots of value creation and competition. Or as the British statistician George Box reminds us in an aphorism attributed to him: "…all models are approximations. Essentially, all models are wrong, but some are useful. However, the approximate nature of the model must always be borne in mind" (Box & Draper, 1987).

8.2 Value Chain

Definition 8.1
The *value chain* can, in its simplest form, be represented as a linear chain consisting of three elements: logistics in (retrieval of raw material, components, or services), the production of goods, and logistics out (delivering goods to the market). In addition, there is a need for common activities such as management, buildings, inventory, storage facilities, and research.

The value chain is illustrated in ◘ Fig. 8.1. The factory producing physical goods is a value chain. The actual chain modeling a factory may contain more elements in a series than the three basic elements in the definition (Porter included also marketing and promotion and services in the chain).

The value chain is just a model by which it is easier to understand the economy and strategy of the classical industrial organization producing tangible goods. The value chain has been analyzed in depth by Michael Porter and other economists.

The logic behind the value chain is that the cost of a single item of a good can be computed as the sum of the cost of raw materials needed for each item (m), the cost of producing a single item (p), and the cost of shipping the item to the market (s). This sum is the direct cost (marginal cost) of the good. The total cost per item is then the sum of the direct costs and the cost of the common activities (A) per item. If the total production is n items, the common activities represent a cost of A/n per item. The total cost per item is then:

$$c = m + p + s + A/n.$$

The major strategy of the chain is to reduce the cost per item. From the equation, it is obvious that this entails reducing the cost of raw materials, production, marketing and sales, and the common cost. The marginal cost (or incremental cost) as $n \to \infty$ is then:

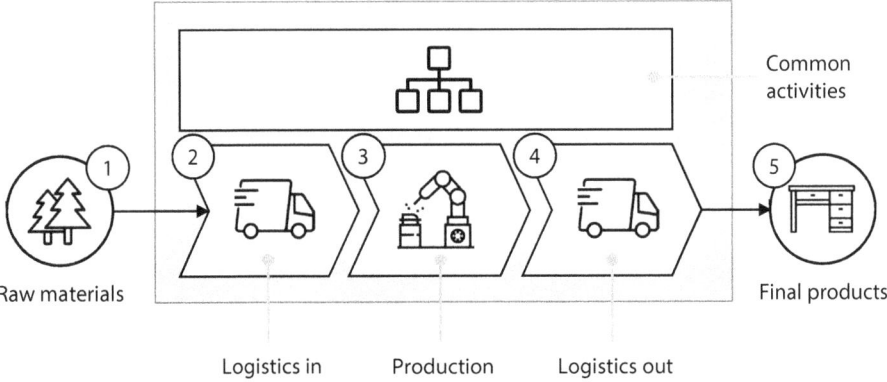

◘ **Fig. 8.1** The value chain. (Authors' own figure)

$$\text{MC} = m + p + s > 0.$$

This is the lowest achievable cost per item. Note that this is different from digital services in which the marginal cost can be zero (MC = 0) as explained in ▶ Chap. 6. This emphasizes the difference between the industrial economy (non-zero marginal cost) and the digital economy (zero marginal cost).

Reducing the cost of raw materials can be done by bargaining for lower prices and utilizing the raw materials better. One example is to increase the yield when producing large semiconductor wafers, thus making each wafer cheaper. However, the cost of producing large silicon crystals with few defects is expensive so that there is a balance between the optimum purity of the crystals and yield. A second example is to develop mechanical structures requiring less material for the same structural strength. The cooling towers of nuclear plants are shaped such that they require less concrete than a cylinder with the same cooling capacity—their shape just makes the towers cheaper and has nothing to do with the physical or chemical processes of the reactor. A third example is to replace existing raw material with new material that is more easily available. This requires research into new materials, for example, to produce semiconductors that are more heat-resistant or to find materials that can replace indium in touchscreens.

The cost of production is reduced by, for example, inventing new production methods that are faster and more power effective, require less manpower (e.g., using robots instead of people), or reduce waste. Maintenance and renewal of machines are also important factors. Sometimes, better algorithms will do the trick. A German company producing printed cards for the electronics industry developed an algorithm for finding the shortest path (also called the "travelling salesman problem") for the movements of the robot drilling the holes into the card, thereby reducing the time it took to produce a single card (and hence, reducing the price per card).

Out-logistics costs may be reduced, for example, by just-in-time production, whereby storage requirements and the need for binding capital over a long period are reduced.

8.3 Value Shop

Definition 8.2
The *value shop* is a problem-solving organization such as consultants, health services, engineering companies, and architects.

Value shops earn more money the better and faster they can solve a problem. Their most important competitive market force is their reputation. Shops may exist within networks or chains. Some examples are the advertisement department of newspapers, the consultative sales department of telecommunications operators, the R&D departments of the pharmaceutical industry, the design departments of

8.3 · Value Shop

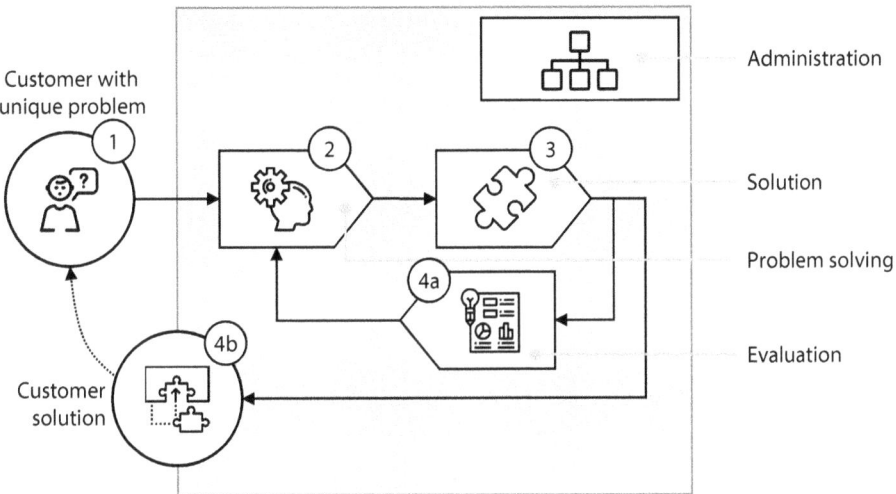

Fig. 8.2 The value shop. (Authors' own figure)

automobile manufacturers, and the pilot-training centers of airlines. The shop may, of course, be outsourced to independent companies. For instance, the newspaper may outsource all its advertisement activities, including small ads.

Universities and schools are also value shops, as they perform research, teaching, and innovation. All these activities are problem-solving tasks; the researcher must find solutions to new challenges, and the educator must adapt and develop their teaching to target a specific group of students. Reputation is the most important market force for both activities.

The value shop is illustrated in Fig. 8.2. The value shop receives problems from its customers and solves them using its internal competence and experience from previous projects. The value shop may also draw upon external resources to solve complex problems requiring specific expertise that the value shop does not have. After solving the problem, a solution is presented to the customer. The value shop will then evaluate its performance and solution and build experience. Clever solutions will also contribute to the reputation of the value shop.

Value shops depend on customers or clients who have problems they cannot solve themselves. There are several mechanisms allowing a value shop to solve problems better or faster than the client himself, including:
- The shop knows more about the problem than the client.
- The shop possesses specialized methods to deal with the problem.
- The employees are expert professionals in the relevant field.
- The shop can form flexible project teams and is able to reorganize quickly to solve new problems.

Value shops compete to attract clients with problems to solve. Competition among value shops depends not only on price but also on reputation. A lawyer with a good reputation can take higher fees for consultations and still get more clients than lesser-known or cheaper lawyers. If the shop's reputation is destroyed, the company may be out of business quickly. This happened to Arthur Andersen after the Enron scandal (Fox, 2002). The company was then accused of accountant fraud and complicity in hiding large deficits from public view. Though the Supreme Court acquitted Arthur Andersen for any misconduct, the company was not able to enter the consultancy market afterward.

8.4 Value Network

Definition 8.3
A *value network* is a business mediating between members of a market.

The mediation relationships in the value network can be represented as links between interacting stakeholders. These links form a network called a *value network* since the network itself creates value for the business controlling or operating the network. ◘ Figure 8.3 shows a general model of a value network. Value networks consist of four components:
- An organization that provides the services
- Customers or users in the network
- Services enabling interaction between the customers or users
- Contracts that permit customers or users access to the services

Note that the value network is not necessarily a physical network or a business that owns a physical network. The value network is an entirely abstract concept. The concept implies that the value network establishes, for example, an abstract network of selling and buying relationships between its customers or users. However, there are cases where the value network also owns a physical network, e.g., a telecommunications network, but such ownership is not a requirement for being a

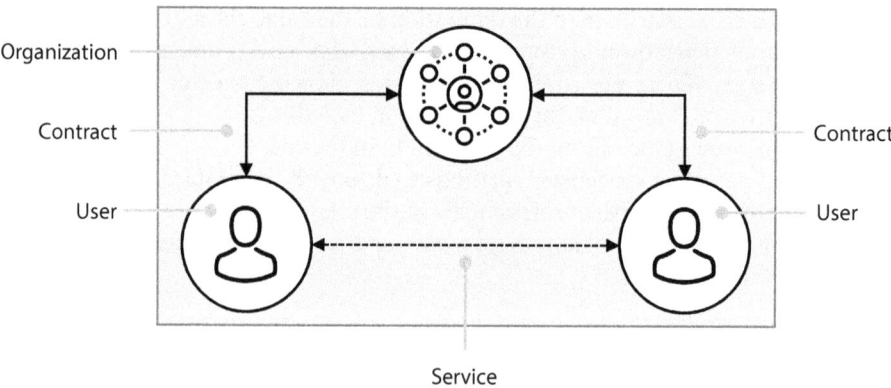

◘ **Fig. 8.3** The value network. (Authors' own figure)

8.4 · Value Network

value network. Note that in such cases, the mediation network and the physical network may be two different things. In the telephone network, the mediating network consists of people calling one another and not the telecommunications network itself. The physical telephone network just enables or supports the network of relationships between the users of the network. The same applies to e-mail and social media—the telecommunications network is an enabler for the value network associated with these services. Example of value network not operating a physical network is the newspaper mediating between readers and advertisers.

> The value network is not a physical network but an abstract network of relationships between stakeholders.

Figure 8.4 shows four examples of value networks: (1) *NY Times*, which mediates between the readers of the newspaper and the merchants advertising merchandise and services; (2) eBay, which mediates between the sellers and buyers of goods; (3) Facebook, which mediates between the users of the social media and the advertisers; and (4) Kickstarter, which mediates between the project owners and the funders. Note that these examples are simplified pictures of the actual business only emphasizing the mediation principles by suppressing all other business activities taking place in the company.

Next, let us discuss some particular characteristics of value networks. The market behavior of some mediation services is different from most other services. A simple bank facility has two types of customers: those depositing funds are paid by the bank for being a customer, while those loaning funds must pay the bank for being a customer. The price of advertisements depends on the number of readers of the newspaper—the more readers, the more the newspaper can charge for each advertisement.

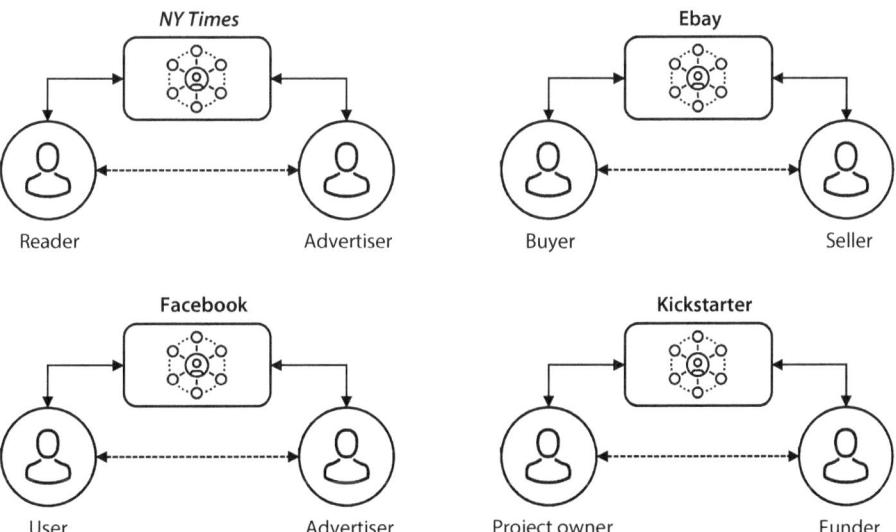

Fig. 8.4 Examples of value networks. (Authors' own figure)

Customers or users may be people or organizations. The users may be of the same category; for example, friends on Facebook. The users may also be of different categories; for example, a newspaper is mediating between readers and advertisers. The latter is an example of a multisided platform with strong cross-side network effects (see ▶ Chap. 10). The same applies to commercial television and social network services such as Facebook and Twitter. Their revenue from advertisements is directly related to the number of people using their services.

As just explained, the competitive strength of several value networks depends not only on the quality of the product they deliver but also on the number of users they have been able to capture and, in particular, how these users stimulate other people to become members of the network. These are the network effects discussed in ▶ Chap. 9. The awareness and popularity of a product is sometimes related to the diffusion of information of the product via channels other than advertisement such as word-of-mouth. The "like" button on Facebook and other social media is another mechanism for increasing the recognition of a product.

Many of the largest companies in the digital economy base their businesses on the value network. Examples of value network companies among the top five companies in the world according to market cap include Facebook, Amazon, and Google. One of the most important reasons why these value networks tend to get so big is just the network effects.

Networks often produce goods that are not stored but consumed immediately. For instance, it is not possible to store the following for later use: empty seats in aircraft or trains, surplus energy, unused bits on the Internet, or empty space in the cargo hold of a truck.

Value networks may offer mutual benefits to its members. This is the idea behind clubs of different kinds (e.g., literary, musical, bonus programs, sports)—the more members, the bigger the benefit. The insurance company can offer better security at a lower price if many people are using the same insurance company. One reason why they may lower the price is that the more customers of the same type they have, the smaller the uncertainty (or variance) of the stochastic product they are selling (this is called the law of large numbers in statistics).

The cost of one item of a service in a value network can be expressed as follows:

$$c = m + \frac{A}{n}$$

Here, m is the *direct cost* (marginal cost) per item, A are the *common costs* associated with a product, and n is the *number of items* produced. How to measure or compute these three variables is discussed next.

Direct cost (m) In many cases, the direct cost per item is zero (also referred to as the zero marginal cost property) as discussed in ▶ Chap. 6. The cost of producing and sending one more bit in the telecommunications network is negligible. The cost of one additional passenger on an airplane is almost negligible. The cost of producing and delivering one copy of an electronic book is negligible. The cost of adding a new user to social media, such as Twitter or Facebook, is also negligible. On the other hand, the marginal cost of a physical book is considerable and includes paper cost, printing cost, storage cost, and shipment cost. In this case, the printing of the book is done in a value chain, and the cost is as described in ▶ Sect. 8.2.

Common costs (*A*) Since the direct costs are often negligible, the dominant costs of the value network are the common (or fixed) costs. These costs are the total cost of running the company and producing and marketing the services. This is contrary to value chains, in which the direct cost often is the dominant cost. This also indicates that the strategy of value networks and value chains are different.

Number of items (*n*) What is the volume of production? For a producer of digital books, this is obviously the number of digital books sold. For an airliner, this may be the average number of passengers per flight. In a communication network, it may be the number of subscriptions. It may also be the average traffic carried by the network (e.g., in terms of the average number of bits sent per unit of time or the average relative traffic load). Therefore, the number of items may not be a unique concept in network businesses. To make it even more complicated, the business may serve a multisided market in which it is difficult to define what a produced item is, for example, what is the product produced by Facebook—the number of users; the amount of information stored about the users; the number of advertisers; and the number of advertisements? Nevertheless, the formula shows that if the direct costs are very small, such as for many digital goods and services, and the fixed costs can be divided on many items, then the marginal cost is also negligible. This shows that the zero marginal cost property is common in value networks.

❯ In several value networks, the cost of producing one item of a good or service is zero.

8.5 Competitive Forces

8.5.1 Porter's Five Forces

One important strategic evaluation of both tangible and digital markets is the five forces model proposed by Porter, illustrated in ◘ Fig. 8.5 (Porter, 1979). The purpose of the model is to identify which external forces that may act on a company and how these forces may influence the market performance of that company. Based on this knowledge, the company may develop strategies that counteract the competitive challenges inflicted by external influence. The model was developed for strategic analysis of industrial companies that are designed as value chains. However, the theory can be easily adapted to analyze competition in the digital economy as shown in the next section. The five forces are:

- Competitive rivalry is the same as standard competition between providers of identical goods.
- Threat that new entrants may enter the market making it less profitable for existing providers of the good.

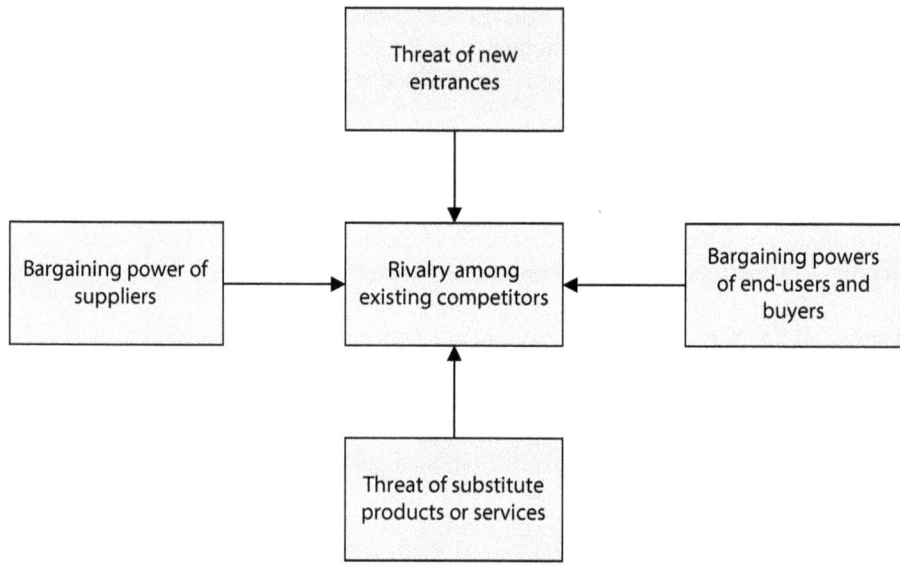

● **Fig. 8.5** Porter's five forces. (Authors' own figure)

— Bargaining power of end users and buyers is related to network externalities such as user feedback and the influence users may have on the price of goods and the consumption of freemium or free goods.
— Bargaining power of suppliers has to do with the price they may charge for raw materials, semi-products, contents, and services needed in the production of the good. It also includes the availability of raw materials and other inputs the company needs.
— Threat from substitutes is that the good may be replaced by an entirely different product offering the same or better user satisfaction.

▶ Section 8.5.2 is an adaption of Porter's theory to digital markets. The model also includes a sixth force (or rather three such forces) that also may have strong impact on the market performance of a company.

8.5.2 Porter's Five Forces Applied to the Digital Economy

Competitive rivalry takes place between companies sharing the same market. Competition in the digital economy may be on price as in non-digital markets, but not always, for example, when the price is zero as it is for several digital goods and services. Competitive rivalry in the digital economy is complex. In some segments, competition takes place between companies offering digital services and companies offering traditional services. This includes e-commerce markets for physical goods, in which the online shop (e.g., Amazon) may have advantages since it is accessible anytime from anywhere and offers products that are not found in the shelves of traditional shops. The advantage of traditional shops is that the customer can see, touch, taste, and smell the product.

Competition may take place between companies offering similar digital services, for example, Facebook and Myspace. In some of these markets, strong network effects may result in de facto monopolies where one of the competitors captures the whole or most of the market (as in the case of Facebook versus Myspace). In other cases, several competitors may share the market, each having market shares that are stable over long periods of time, for example, mobile network operators.

Competition may also take place between companies offering entirely different services to their users. One example is Facebook offering social networking and Google offering email and web browsing. They do not compete for users but for money from the advertising business. This situation may arise in multisided markets (see ▶ Chap. 10). Another example is MasterCard serving two markets: cardholders and merchants. Since the card is accepted almost everywhere, there is no competition with other credit card companies for attracting new merchants. The competition is for attracting new cardholders. Airbnb offer services in two market segments: hosts and guests. Airbnb is subject to competition in both segments, for example, from hotels and travel agencies.

New entrants may establish themselves in existing markets. In this context, the concern is about companies producing the same or equivalent goods and services. New entrants producing substitutions are considered below. The general effect of new entrants is that the profitability of the market for each manufacturer or service provider is reduced. In cases where investments are high, competition may lead to the formation of oligopolies, resulting in complex and unstable forms of competition. The mobile communications markets are oligopolies with few competitors. In other cases, it may be virtually impossible for new competitors to enter the market because strong network effects may have created high lock-in barriers. This is the case for many social media.

End users and buyers may put additional pressure on the companies, for example, by creating special interest groups which press for lower prices or better and more reliable products or for abandoning certain products altogether (examples from non-digital markets are whale meat and furs). The buyers may also use new distribution channels. One example is that more and more people are making purchases over the Internet, thereby reducing the market for physical shops. Loyalty programs are sometimes instigated to reduce the bargaining power of the customers (e.g., bonus programs of airlines).

Since the use of social media and web browsing creates enormous amounts of data about the users of the service, the service provider may be able to extract information about the user that may violate personal integrity protection laws or are regarded as ethically unacceptable. This may then cause users to switch to alternative suppliers or use the service in a way that is less profitable for the supplier. There have been reactions against Facebook for having misused customer trust (Confessore, 2018).

Suppliers in value chains deliver raw materials, components, or semi-finished products. Suppliers in the digital economy may provide technical support or services, for example, processing and mass storage, access to the Internet, software, content, or service supplements. The suppliers are in the position to bargain for prices, offering different qualities of service to different companies, control access to facilities and content, and so on. Net neutrality (see ▶ Chap. 21) delimits the capabilities that the Internet service providers have to discriminate against different users of the network.

Substitutes are products that may replace other products which offer the same or an equivalent experience. For example, seafood may replace meat as nourishment. In the digital economy, substitutes have become a strong market force. Examples of substitutes include mobile phones substituting fixed telephone services, and video streaming replacing broadcast services. The most competitive advantage of mobile phone manufacturers was originally the design of the radio modules of the phone, and competition took place between traditional radio manufacturers. However, as the mobile phones developed into smartphones (or handheld computers), the competitive advantage changed to the ability to design complex software that supports the new functionality, thereby inspiring computer manufacturers to enter the market. The smartphone then became a substitute for simple mobile phones produced by a new type of manufacturer. Other examples of substitutes in the digital economy are e-books substituting paper books, MP3 players substituting CDs as a medium for the dissemination of music, and streaming services on smartphone replacing the MP3 players.

Later, a sixth force was added to Porter's model. Different authors attributed different interpretations of what this force is (Brandenburger & Nalebuff, 1995):
– Complementors
– Government
– The public

In a strategic analysis of the company, it is recommended to consider all three alternatives because they will all have an impact on the company's strategy.

Complementors are companies that produce or sell products for which the demand is positively correlated to the demand of a given product. These products are called *complementary products*. Complementarity may be either unilateral or bilateral. Unilateral complementarity occurs when the product of one company depends on the product from the other company but not vice versa. Bilateral complementarity means that each product cannot exist without the other product. Examples of complementors and complementary products are shown in ◘ Table 8.1.

Governments decide rules for competition and oversee that the rules are followed. In the telecommunications market, regulations may include license of operation, maximum and minimum price of services and subscriptions, conditions for lease of network resources, use of the frequency spectrum, conditions for interconnectivity of customers in different networks, and number portability. Governments may also regulate the business of application service providers, for example, via licensing, taxation, law regulations, and censorship.

8.5 · Competitive Forces

Table 8.1 Complementors. (Authors' compilation)

Complementors and complementary products	Type (unilateral or bilateral)
Intel (hardware) and Microsoft (software)	Bilateral: both companies depend on each other to provide a complete service
DVD players and DVDs	Bilateral
Printers and ink cartridges	Bilateral
Apps and smartphones	Unilateral: smartphones offer services that do not involve the use of apps
Skype and ISPs	Unilateral: Skype depends on ISPs for Internet access, while ISPs do not depend on Skype to offer Internet access

The public is made up of more than just users and buyers. Society has numerous written and unwritten rules that may influence the market of a company. Some of these rules are ethical; for example, a company may sell products which are made by suppliers who employ child workers, cause pollution, or prohibit workers to form labor organizations. This company may meet strong hostility in the market. Recently, strong public opposition forced shops to stop selling clothes with certain types of fur.

Case Study 8.1 Netflix

Table 8.2 shows a simple analysis of the film and video streaming services of Netflix using Porter's five forces model plus the three versions of the sixth force.

Table 8.2 Competitive forces and threats. (Authors' compilation)

Type	Threat
Competition	Cinemas, broadcast corporations, Disney +, Amazon Prime, Redbox, Hulu Plus, and several other providers of equivalent services
New entrants	Any new provider of streaming services may capture market shares from Netflix
Bargaining power of users	Because of competition, the bargaining power of uses is mainly on price
Bargaining power of suppliers	Distributors of films may withdraw their contract with Netflix as The Walt Disney Company is doing in favor of its own streaming service Disney +. Film studios may also negotiate higher prices and special conditions for delivery of content. They can also ban Netflix from buying their content

(continued)

Table 8.2 (continued)	
Type	Threat
Substitutes	BitTorrent technology (See for example BitTorrent on Wikipedia) based on P2P distributed file sharing (Popcorn Time was a serious threat to Netflix before it was discontinued for legal reasons in 2014 (Idland et al., 2015)). The technology is still a threat to Netflix if intellectual property rights can be solved in a satisfactory way
Complementors	Film studios and video producers for delivery of content and ISPs for distribution of the streaming service
Government	Accusation of tax evasion, high energy usage, and traffic stress on the broadband networks. Some countries (e.g., Iran and China) block access to Netflix. Censorship of content
The public	The public may react to the content of films and shows. One problem for Netflix is that it provides global services and is subject to reactions from different cultures restricting what is regarded as universally acceptable content

8.6 Competition, Cooperation, and Coopetition

▶ Section 4.3 contains a layered business model for the Internet consisting of a network layer accommodating the infrastructure providers and the network service providers (ISPs); a transport layer (or equipment layer) which is the business arena of the manufacturers of user equipment and providers of cloud services; and an application layer containing applications, services, and content. In the layered Internet model, there is *competition* between companies within all three business layers. Companies usually compete within the same business layer and not between different business layers. At the same time, companies operating in digital markets *cooperate*. Companies at different layers must obviously cooperate to provide digital services to consumers. For example, an electronic newspaper needs the support of ISPs to deliver the newspaper to its readers. This is called *vertical cooperation*. Companies in the digital economy may also cooperate at the same business layer (*horizontal cooperation*). Since companies compete within the same business layer, such companies may both compete and cooperate at the same time. This is called *coopetition* (Shapiro & Varian, 1999).

Definition 8.4
Companies *compete* within the same business layer. The companies may *cooperate* both within the same business layer (*horizontal cooperation*) and across business layers (*vertical cooperation*). *Coopetition* implies that a company simultaneously competes and cooperates with other companies within the same business layer.

8.6 · Competition, Cooperation, and Coopetition

The concepts are exemplified in ▶ Case Study 8.2.

Coopetition is particularly important in developing new systems and services as explained in ▶ Example 8.1.

> ▶ **Example 8.1 Coopetition and Crowdsourcing: Developing New Systems or Services**
>
> Some of the largest systems or most complex services of the information and communication technology have been developed jointly by operators and industries that later have become competitors offering services to customers, building infrastructures, or producing user equipment and infrastructure components. This is an example of coopetition in the digital economy.
>
> The largest effort of this kind is the development of standards for mobile communications (the 3GPP project). The 3GPP project is manpowered by participants from more than 700 member organizations, comprising equipment manufacturers, authorities, research organizations, and network and service providers. Other examples are distributed processing (e.g., the CORBA project), specification of local area networks (e.g., the IEEE Standardization Association), and cloud computing (e.g., the RECAP project of the EU). Research groups that are open for participation by anyone are also established to improve and upgrade existing technologies such as the Internet, the World Wide Web, and local area network standards.
>
> There are several motives for this type of cooperation:
>
> The science community prefers that standards should be public and open for anyone to exploit. In several cases, this is also supported by governments because open standards enhance competition and avoid formation of monopolies. For equipment manufacturers, the potential market for internationally accepted standards is large, offering good profit margins. For network operators and other infrastructure providers, the standard opens new opportunities to expand their businesses to new markets.
>
> The aim of these projects is usually to define systems and technologies that can be implemented in a global market. This implies that industries and researchers from all over the world are invited to cooperate developing the standard. Experience has also shown that if the prospects of the project are promising, it is not difficult to voluntarily man such projects. Moreover, it is simpler to attract highly specialized expertise to solve specific problems if the development process is open for anyone.
>
> The cost to develop these standards is huge and requires large resources, in particular, manpower. The estimated cost of developing a mobile network standard (e.g., 5G) is more than $1 billion and may require several thousand man-years of professional work. Cooperation reduces the development costs for both individual manufacturers and operators.
>
> The solutions these projects end up with usually meet high performance and technology standards and are better than solutions developed by a single stakeholder.
>
> This type of cooperative development of standards is an example of crowdsourcing (see ▶ Sect. 7.2.3). The projects are managed by an organization (e.g., 3GPP, ETSI, or the World Wide Web Forum), and the goal is usually defined in vague terms and within an unclear timeframe, for example, developing the next-generation mobile system or developing new security algorithms for protecting web services. The final shape and the details of the end product are defined as the project progresses, and the end product may be very different from the product that was initially anticipated. This type of crowd-

sourcing takes full advantage of the technological evolution since the work can change direction as new technological advances emerge. The best example is the mobile standards which have been enhanced with new features (e.g., GPRS in GSM and HSPA in 3G) or become an entirely new standard (e.g., 4G) as soon as the mobile phone had achieved enough computational power to support these features.

The participation in these projects is entirely voluntarily, and the amount of work each participant contributes to the project varies among the different participants. There are also free-riders who do not contribute to the development of the project but implement and make business on the results of the project.

As the complexity of ICT projects have increased, more and more of the evolution of the technology has been achieved through this type of cooperative endeavor. ◄

Case Study 8.2 Chat Services and Competition, Cooperation, and Coopetition

◘ Figure 8.6 illustrates the concepts of competition, cooperation, and coopetition. The figure shows how a user of a chat service can choose between various providers at all three business levels independently. The user may choose among different equipment supporting chat services (Apple iPhone, Samsung Galaxy, or Google Pixel), select one of several ISPs (Telenor, Telia, or TDC), and select one out of four chat applications (Skype, WeChat, WhatsApp, and Messenger). Each chat application can be used with any combination of user equipment and ISP. However, chat applications are not necessarily compatible—if a user selects Skype, they cannot chat directly with another user using WeChat. This is because there is no standard among chat applications; therefore, they cannot interoperate.

On each business level (ASP, user equipment, and ISP), companies compete to attract users. Skype competes with WeChat, WhatsApp, and Messenger; Telenor competes with Telia and TDC; Apple competes with Samsung and Google. On the other hand, Skype does not compete with Telenor, Telia, or TDC since they are at different business layers. This is a truth with modifications since

Telenor is also an ASP offering a chat application through its SMS service. However, in its role as an ISP, Telenor does not compete with Skype.

To provide a complete digital good or service, it is necessary for companies at different business layers to cooperate. For instance, cooperation between Skype, Telenor, and Apple iPhone is required to provide the chat service to some users, while Telia, Samsung, and WeChat must cooperate to provide chat services to other users. This is *vertical cooperation*. These companies may have or not have formalized cooperation agreements between them. In any case, through standards, contracts, and agreements, they each provide elements of the complete digital service.

A Telenor subscriber can communicate with a Telia subscriber, a TDC subscriber, or a subscriber of any other ISP. International agreements enforce cooperation between ISPs to ensure interoperability between operators located in different countries and within the same country. For the chat service, this implies that a customer using an iPhone may be a subscriber of Telenor, while the server providing the chat service is attached to the network of Telia. It is for the benefit of the market and the users that companies in the same business layer cooperate. This is called *horizontal cooperation*.

These companies also compete for the same customers. As explained above, this market behavior is called *coopetition*.

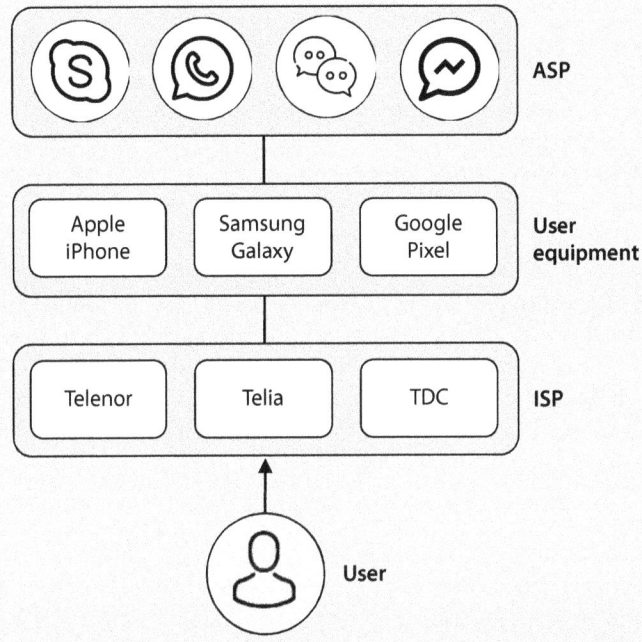

Fig. 8.6 Competition, cooperation, and coopetition in digital markets. (Authors' own figure)

8.7 Conclusions

Based on the way in which value is created, three types of enterprises have been defined:
- Value chains transforming raw material into physical products
- Value shops solving problems for their clients
- Value networks mediating between the stakeholders in the market

Many businesses in the digital economy are value networks. One characteristic of value networks in the digital economy, making them different from other value creation models, is that the cost of producing an additional item is zero—or that the marginal cost is zero. This property allows them to exploit new business models such as freemium where some basic products are offered for free, while money is charged for additional features, and multisided markets where some user groups are not charged for the service they receive, while other user groups must pay for the services.

▶ The marginal cost of products produced in a value chain is always larger than zero. The marginal cost of products produced in several value networks, particularly in the digital economy, is zero.

It has also been shown how the five forces model of Porter—originally developed for value chains—can be modified to also apply to value networks. The model can then be used as a valuable tool in analyzing business strategies for value networks.

The Internet is a layered network consisting of a transport network transferring information in form of bits, processing equipment connected to the network, and applications running on the processors. This structure gives rise to three independent types of stakeholders: Internet service providers, equipment manufacturers, and application service providers. There is cooperation between stakeholders at each of these layers to provide services to the users, and no competition between stakeholders on different layers. Competition takes place between stakeholders on the same layer. However, stakeholders at the same layer may also cooperate, for example, to interconnect users over multiple networks, to offer complex services consisting of several components, and to develop and standardize new technologies.

❓ Questions

1. Are the following businesses primarily a value chain, value shop, or a value network?
   (a) Johns Hopkins Hospital
   (b) AXA
   (c) Harvard University
   (d) BMW
   (e) Apple iPhone
   (f) Apple App Store
   (g) Twitter

2. Which of the user groups, if any, contribute to the revenues of:
   (a) The newspaper?
   (b) The social network service?
   (c) The stockbroker?
   (d) Wikipedia?

3. How does vertical cooperation between online video and music streaming providers and Internet service providers take place?

✅ Answers

1. Value generation model
   (a) Value shop
   (b) Value network (insurance company)
   (c) Value shop

(d) Value chain
   (e) Value chain (producing iPhones)
   (f) Value network (mediating between app designers and app users)
   (g) Value network

2. Revenues
   (a) Usually both the readers and the advertisers. In many cases, the major (and sometimes all) revenue comes from advertisers.
   (b) Users of the social service do not pay for the usage of the service. The revenue comes from other sources, mainly advertisers.
   (c) Both buyers and sellers of stocks pay a fee to the stockbroker.
   (d) Neither readers nor authors contribute with revenues.

3. The music streaming provider (e.g., Spotify) may have subscription for broadband access with several network providers in different parts of the world to offer streaming services to millions of simultaneous users. The streaming service provider may also rent storage facilities in the network to provide low latency services and reduce the traffic load on the network. This may become one of the applications of edge computing in mobile 5G network (for more information, see Wikipedia article on edge computing).

References

Box, G., & Draper, N. (1987). *Empirical model-building and response surfaces*. Wiley. The quotation is found on page 424.
Brandenburger, M., & Nalebuff, B. J. (1995). The right game: Use game theory to shape strategy. *Harvard Business Review, 73*(4).
Confessore N. Cambridge Analytica and Facebook. The scandal and the fallout so far. *The New York Times*. April 4, 2018.
Fox, L. (2002). *Enron: The rise and fall*. Wiley.
Idland, E., Øverby, H., & Audestad, J. (2015). Economic markets for video streaming services: A case study of NetFlix and Popcorn Time. NIKT.
Porter, M. E. How competitive forces shape strategy. Harvard Business Review. March/April 1979.
Porter, M. E. (1985). *Competitive advantage: Creating and sustaining superior performance*. Simon and Schuster.
Shapiro, C., & Varian, H. R. (1999). *Information rules: A strategy guide to the network economy*. Harvard Business School Press.
Stabell, C. B., & Fjeldstad, Ø. D. (1998). Configuring value for competitive advantage: On chains, shops, and networks. *Strategic Management Journal, 19*, 413–437.

Further Reading
Porter, M. E. (1985). *Competitive advantage: Creating and sustaining superior performance*. Simon and Schuster.
Stabell, C. B., & Fjeldstad, Ø. D. (1998). Configuring value for competitive advantage: On chains, shops, and networks. *Strategic Management Journal, 19*, 413–437.

Network Effects

Contents

9.1 Introduction – 124

9.2 Positive and Negative Network Effects – 124

9.3 Characteristics of Network Effects – 131

9.4 Direct and Indirect Network Effects – 135

9.5 Same-Side and Cross-Side Network Effects – 135

9.6 Estimating the Value of Networks – 136
9.6.1 Size of Networks – 136
9.6.2 Sarnoff's Law – 137
9.6.3 Metcalfe's Law and Odlyzko-Tilly's Law – 139
9.6.4 Reed's Law – 141
9.6.5 Summary and Comparison of Network Laws – 142

9.7 Conclusions – 144

References – 147

© The Author(s), under exclusive license to Springer Nature Switzerland AG 2021
H. Øverby, J. A. Audestad, *Introduction to Digital Economics*, Classroom Companion: Business,
https://doi.org/10.1007/978-3-030-78237-5_9

Learning Objectives

After completing this chapter, you should be able to:
- Identify network effects associated with a particular digital service and the impact the network effects may have on the temporal evolution of the market.
- Explain how positive network effects may cause slow initial adaptation of new services and that this may be mitigated by stimulating early market growth by offering the service for free initially.
- Demonstrate how the value of networks of different types can be estimated and use this knowledge in strategic planning.

9.1 Introduction

Definition 9.1 Network Effect
The *network effect* (also called network *externality* or *demand-side economies of scale*) is the effect that the number of users or amount of usage of a service has on the value of that service as perceived individually by each user (Arthur, 1990).

The network effect is the value a new user adds to existing users in a network (Shapiro & Varian, 1999). A related term is *supply-side economies of scale*, which is the effect the number of users or units produced has on the costs of production. Supply-side economies of scale are different from network effects—the former describes the cost advantages of being large, while the latter describes the value of having many users. This section considers the demand-side economies of scale—the network effect.

Sometimes a distinction is made between network effect and network externality. Network externality is then used as the general term referring to all types of feedback from the market (i.e., negative or positive), while network effect is only used in the case where this feedback causes an increase in value of the network (i.e., positive). Since the nature of positive and negative network effects are essentially the same, we will use the term network effect referring to both positive and negative changes in value and, if a distinction is necessary, refer to them as positive or negative network effects.

9.2 Positive and Negative Network Effects

Network effects may be visualized using undirected networks illustrated in ◘ Fig. 9.1. Network A has 3 nodes and 3 links, network B has 7 nodes and 11 links, and network C has 11 nodes and 21 links. The nodes may be individual consumers or users of a specific digital service, and the links may represent the interaction between the users, e.g., trading, communication, or any other common interest. Not every pair of node needs to be connected in these networks. Networks may be

9.2 · Positive and Negative Network Effects

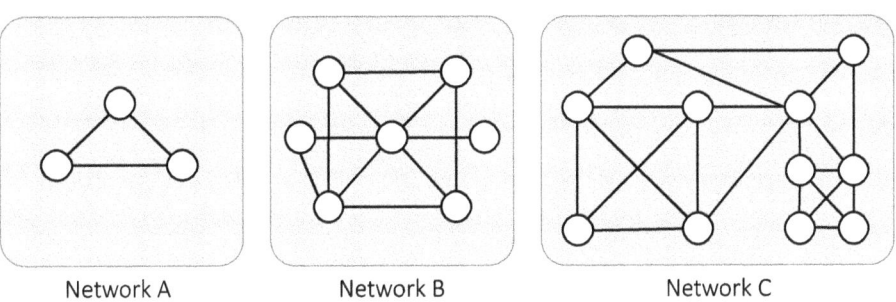

Network A   Network B   Network C

◘ **Fig. 9.1** Undirected networks. (Authors' own figure)

small—as those depicted in ◘ Fig. 9.1—or large such as Facebook, with more than two billion nodes (users). The number of links is a measure of the value of a network and is the essential mechanism creating network effects. Another important concept of networks is the distance between two arbitrary nodes; that is, the smallest number of links that must be traversed when travelling from one node to the other. This distance is important when evaluating how fast innovations diffuse in networks. The concept is discussed in ▶ Box 9.1.

Box 9.1   Six Degrees of Separation

Six degrees of separation is the concept that any human being is (at the most) six intermediaries away from any other human on Earth. That is, anyone can connect to any other person through a chain of friends with a maximum of six hops. This is illustrated in ◘ Fig. 9.2. While by some considered to be an urban myth, research has shown that the six degrees of separation concept is valid in many social networks.

The theories of a "shrinking world" were first popularized by the Hungarian author Frigyes Karinthy in 1929. Karinthy argued that the modern world at that time was shrinking, primarily because of recent innovations in communications such as the telegraph, radio, and telephone. In his paper "The Small World Problem" published in the journal *Psychology Today* in 1967, Stanley Milgram showed experimentally that this was indeed true. He found that the average social distance between two randomly chosen individuals in the USA was 5.2 (Milgram, 1967). His observations later became known as the "six degrees of separation" concept. Stanley Milgram did not use this term himself; the popularization of the term is attributed to John Guare and his play "Six Degrees of Separation" from 1990.

Other concepts related to the "six degrees of separation" are the Erdös number describing the collaboration distance to the mathematician Paul Erdös based on shared publications (The Erdös Number Project. Oakland University., n.d.) and the Bacon number describing the distance to the American actor Kevin Bacon based on shared movie appearances. The collaboration distances are amazingly small even between people having published in completely different fields of mathematics. One of the authors (Audestad) has a collaboration distance 4 to Erdös and 5 to Einstein!

Facebook has analyzed the average degree of separation between any two users of the network and found that this distance has decreased from 5.28 in 2008 to 4.74 in 2011 and 4.57 in February 2016. In the Watts-Strogatz model, which produces random graphs with small-world properties, the average path length between two nodes is calculated using the formula $\ln N / \ln K$, in which N is total number of nodes and K is the average number of links per node. For Facebook, with 2.2 billion users (nodes) in 2018 and 150 number of friends (links) per user as suggested by Dunbar's number (see ▶ Box 9.2), the average path length is calculated as:

$\ln N / \ln K = \ln 2.2 \times 10^9 / \ln 150 \approx 4.29$

in good agreement with the observed numbers presented above.

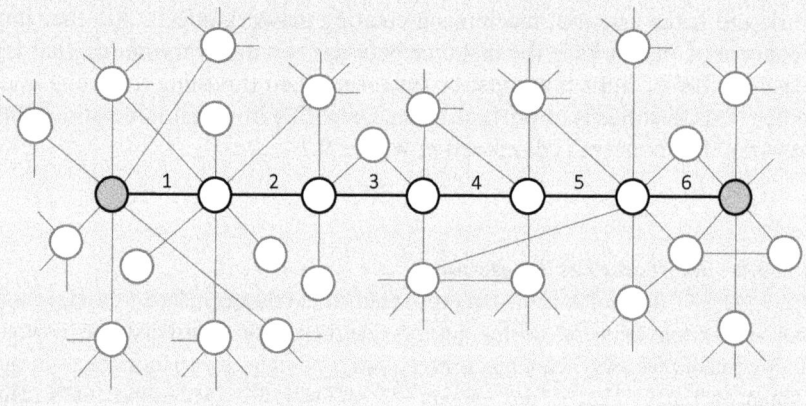

Fig. 9.2 Social network. (Authors' own figure)

Another concept that has to do with the size of human groups is the Dunbar number; see ▶ Box 9.2. The concept is used later in this chapter to evaluate the strength of certain networks.

Box 9.2 Dunbar's Number
Robin Dunbar is a British anthropologist that studied the volume of the neocortex of various animals and their corresponding social group sizes. Based on his findings, he predicted the number of people with whom a human can maintain a stable relationship. His initial studies suggested a number between 100 and 250, but he later argued for 150 as a mean group size for communities with high incentives to stay together. The latter was based on studies on human societies, both existing and historical. Dunbar's number is, then, 150. It is argued that this is the number of people an individual can call a "friend,"

9.2 · Positive and Negative Network Effects

which translates informally to "people you would not feel embarrassed about joining uninvited for a drink if you happened to bump into them in a bar" (Dunbar, 1998).

Dunbar's number has been applied to social media, business management, military studies, and workplace organization. The number has been used to study social networks such as Facebook and Myspace. The average user on Facebook has 155 friends, which is close to Dunbar's number (Knapton, 2016). As quoted by Dunbar:

"The interesting thing is that you can have 1,500 friends, but when you actually look at traffic on sites, you see people maintain the same inner circle of around 150 people that we observe in the real world." (Knapton, 2016)

Dunbar's number and his studies of the size of social groups give empirical input to analytical network models such as Metcalfe's law. The communication and formation of social circles might not be that different in social media as it is in the real world. One way of dividing people's social circle is shown in ◘ Fig. 9.3, in which five social groups are outlined: family and very close friends, close friends, friends, acquaintances, and strangers.

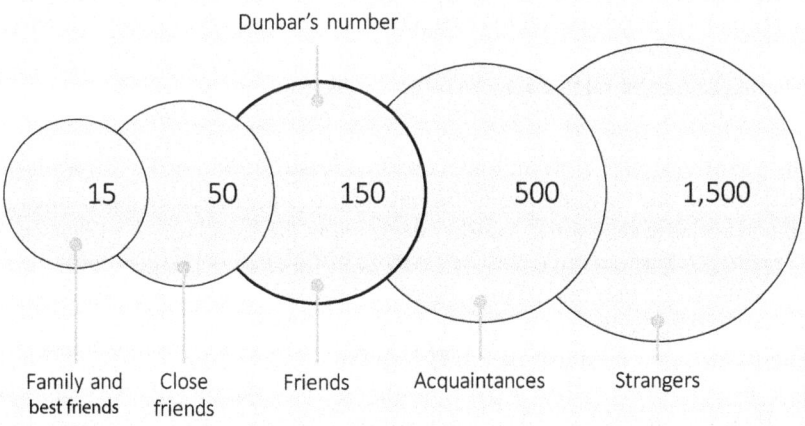

◘ **Fig. 9.3** Size of human groups. (Authors' own figure)

We may define two types of network effects: positive network effects and negative network effects.

Definition 9.2 Positive Network Effect
The network effect is *positive* if the market feedback causes a perceived increase in value (e.g., more users) that stimulates further increase in value (users).

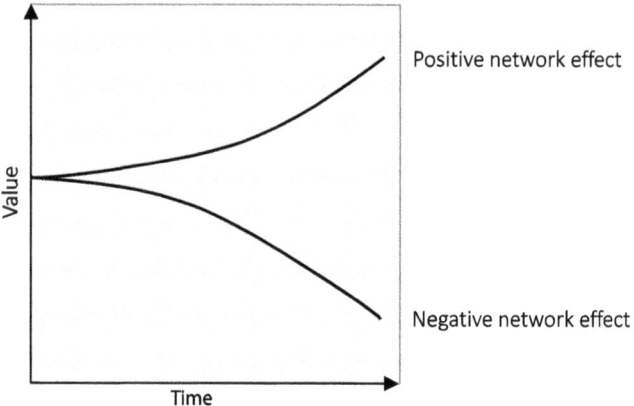

Fig. 9.4 Result of positive and negative network effects. (Authors' own figure)

Facebook is an example where the value of the network increases as the number of users increases. The positive network effect is caused by positive feedback from the market.

> **Definition 9.3 Negative Network Effect**
> The network effect is *negative* if the market feedback causes a perceived decrease in value (e.g., fewer users) that stimulates further decrease in value (users).

Negative network effects occur, for example, toward the end of life for multiplayer online games: if the number of players leaving the game increases, more players are stimulated to leave the game. Another example is the standard war between VHS and Betamax where positive network effects in favor of VHS generated negative network effects for Betamax. This type of negative network effect is also driven by a positive market feedback (Øverby & Audestad, 2019).

These two cases are illustrated in Fig. 9.4.

The network effect is also negative if an increased number of users cause more dissatisfaction with the service, for example, because of traffic congestion in Internet routers or servers of social media. This case is a little more complicated than the previous one. If there are alternative providers offering the same or replaceable services, this may stimulate the users to switch to another provider. Take the competition between Netflix and Popcorn Time as example. Because of congestions in the servers of Netflix in 2014 and first half of 2015, several users switched to Popcorn Time even though Popcorn Time was illegal in most countries. This reduced the congestion on the Netflix servers so that the traffic toward Netflix again increased causing new congestion. This caused the traffic toward Netflix and Popcorn Time to oscillate (Idland et al., 2016). This situation ended in mid-2015 when the Popcorn Time service was taken down in most countries for legal reasons, and the capacity of the Netflix servers had been improved.

The outcome of this type of negative network effect can be that the market enters a chaotic or oscillating state where the market dominance is oscillating between two or more providers. The outcome may also be that the market reaches a tripping point where it collapses and is thereafter rebuilt (e.g., the housing bubble in 2008). Note that oscillating or quasi-stable markets are also subject to positive feedback from the market.

Negative network effects may be generated by negative reviews and low ratings of the product, inferior experience expressed by friends, few active users, or users leaving the product stimulating others to do the same. Things that may amplify negative networks effects are insufficient advertisements (invisibility), poor user experience, technical issues (such as complex login), freeze-out, congestion, long response times, disturbing differential delays, interruptions, and frequent downtimes.

Positive network effects may include high ratings, high product visibility (bandwagon effect), and excellent user satisfaction as expressed by friends (word of mouth).

Observe again that network effects, whether positive or negative, are caused by *positive feedback* from the market.

Feedback implies that some part of the output from a system is routed back to the input of the same system and thus causes an effect on the output. Feedback theory is important in almost all fields of science: physics, chemistry, technology, social sciences, medicine, economics, and so on. The first deep analysis of feedback phenomena in natural systems was done by the American mathematician and physicist Norbert Wiener (Wiener, 1948). There are two types of feedback: positive feedback and negative feedback. These are well-defined technical terms.

Definition 9.4 Positive Feedback
Positive feedback is such that if there is a deviation in the output in one or the other direction, the feedback will make this deviation larger. In other words:
- The feedback is positive if more of A (input) produces more of B (output) and more of B produces more of A and so on until all of A has been consumed.
- The feedback is also positive if less of A causes less of B and less of B causes less of A until there is no more A left.

The most important observation is that positive feedback is the cause of both negative and positive network effects.

Positive feedback may also result in periodic or irregular oscillations. This is utilized in, for example, high frequency oscillators producing radio carrier waves for television broadcasting. Applied to economics, this may be the cause of certain types of business phenomena such as repeated economic crashes because of unsustainable growth. One common reason for oscillations in the market (and in several other cases such as hunter/prey ecosystems) is long delay in the feedback loop. One example is the "pork cycle" in the early twentieth century where the demand and supply of pork meat were out of phase by one year because deficiency (and high price) of pork meat in one year caused overproduction (and low price) the next year. Another example is higher education where the delay is several years causing the labor market to fluctuate between surplus and shortage of expertise in certain areas: the students choose a particular education based on the observed prospect of getting a job in that field at the start of the study. When they finish the education several years later, the labor market may have changed considerably.

> **Definition 9.5 Negative Feedback**
> Negative feedback, on the other hand, reduces the deviations and tends to bring the output toward a stable equilibrium and keep it there. If there is an increase in the input A causing an increase in the output B, then this increase in B will cause a reduction in A bringing B back close to equilibrium. Similarly, a decrease in A causing a decrease in B will cause an increase in A again bringing B back close to equilibrium. The feedback will then counteract any deviation of the output B away from its equilibrium state. Market stability is one of the basic assumptions in traditional microeconomic theory where competition leads to perfect market equilibrium. In this theory, the market is stabilized by negative feedback loops counteracting any deviation from equilibrium.

Most markets for digital goods and services are subject to positive or negative network effects and, hence, subject to positive feedback. This implies that mainstream economic equilibrium theory does not apply to such markets.

> The points made above are so important (and sometimes misinterpreted) that it is worthwhile to summarize them. Do not confuse the terms "positive (negative) network effect" and "positive (negative) feedback." Positive and negative network effects are both driven by *positive feedback* from the market. *Negative feedback* from the market results in equilibrium markets, while *positive feedback* results in non-equilibrium markets. Positive network effects will drive the market into saturation such as the mobile market. In this market, everyone sooner or later owns a mobile phone. Negative network effect will initiate a vicious spiral, in which customers are leaving the market and the company serving it may face bankruptcy.

Figure 9.5 illustrates how positive feedback stimulates positive network effects: new users adopting the digital service stimulate other users to do the same, resulting in a positive network effect that further stimulates the growth of the service. The final state of most of these markets is that every user has adopted the service or bought the good—the market ends up being saturated and cannot increase anymore.

In some markets where competition exists between two or more supplementary goods (e.g., VHS and Betamax; see ▶ Chap. 11), one of the goods may become the good that most customers prefer, generating a negative network effect on the other product that finally squeezes it out of the market. Another way of expressing this is that positive feedback in a competitive market may imply that the strong gets stronger and the weak gets weaker, also called the Matthew effect, a term coined by the sociologist Robert K. Merton (Merton, 1968). In this way, the network effects in competitive markets often produce winner-take-all markets, where one of the

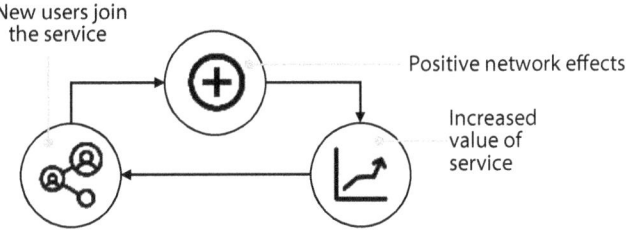

Fig. 9.5 Positive feedback. (Authors' own figure)

suppliers becomes a de facto monopoly after all competitors have been squeezed out of the market. Positive feedback may govern the evolution of a single technology (search engines), the evolution of a digital service (the World Wide Web), and the competition between technologies or companies providing digital services (Facebook vs Myspace).

9.3 Characteristics of Network Effects

The network effect may be *time-dependent* and may even change from positive to negative as the number of users of the game or service increases. One example is an interactive video game in which the gaming experience of the early game attracts more players. When the number of players increases, the game may become overcrowded, causing players to leave the game, thereby shifting the network effect from positive to negative.

The network effect is measured by the amount of interactions or number of links in the network. This is proportional to the amount of use of the network resources which in turn is proportional to the time or amount of attention invested in the network by the users. Remember that attention is a scarce resource in much demand by the providers since user attention means opportunities for the providers to sell goods and services and thereby generate revenues.

The *strength of the network effect* is thus a direct measure of the number of links that each new user adds to the network. This is shown in ◘ Fig. 9.6, in which a new user (node) joining the network connects to three existing users, thereby adding three new links to the network. It is not uncommon that a new user connects to all other users in the network. If a new user connects to exactly one other user in the network, there are no network effects. This is equal to the Sarnoff type of network in ▶ Sect. 9.6.2.

Value networks in general and many digital services have strong network effects. Examples include Facebook, Twitter, YouTube, Uber, Airbnb, Skype, MMOGs (e.g., *World of Warcraft*), and smartphone app ecosystems.

Links between users may have *different strengths* depending on the importance of the relationship and volume of interaction between the users. Users may also have different importance in the network depending on how connected they are. *Central users* are users with a high number of links, while *marginal users* are users with a low number of links.

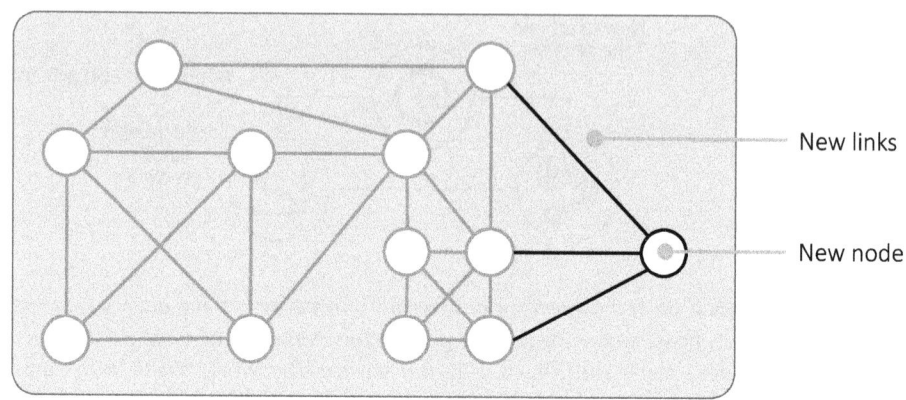

Fig. 9.6 Adding a new node and links to a network. (Authors' own figure)

A network may also be *clustered*, meaning that there exist clusters of networks within the network. One example of this is social media, where individuals residing within a country are more connected with each other than with individuals outside their country. Furthermore, within the same country, people are more connected with each other within the same town or city. Clusters may also appear among families, friends, and other socioeconomic groups, for example, workplaces and people that have similar interest. This leads to networks of networks with potentially many layers of clusters.

Networks are often modeled as undirected (or symmetrical) networks. However, the interaction between two users may be *asymmetric*—a user sends more information to another user than he receives in return. Asymmetric users are widespread in digital services like YouTube and Twitter, where relatively few users are generating content that is spread to the rest of the network.

▪ Figure 9.7 shows two competing social networking services (A and B). The figure introduces the terminology of Frank Bass—imitators and innovators (see ▶ Chap. 18). The buying habit of *imitators* is that they listen to advice from others (i.e., word-of-mouth) and are therefore likely to buy the version of the product owned by most other people. The imitator in the figure therefore chooses social network service A. The *innovators* do not listen to advice and buy the product of their liking. The imitators then represent a network effect, in which the value of the product as perceived by the imitators increases as more people use the service. The buying habits of innovators are not ruled by network effects.

Note that the "network" in this context does not refer to physical networks but to relational networks between users; for example, between players of the same online game, people and organizations exchanging emails, family groups, or friends on Facebook. For digital services, the underlying physical network is, however, a prerequisite for the existence of the social network. However, sometimes, network effect may refer to the popularity or ill repute of the physical network.

▪ Figure 9.8 illustrates one of the strategic dilemmas associated with strong network effects. The figure shows two curves. The S-shaped curve is the evolution of a market with only imitators, and the second curve shows the evolution if there

9.3 · Characteristics of Network Effects

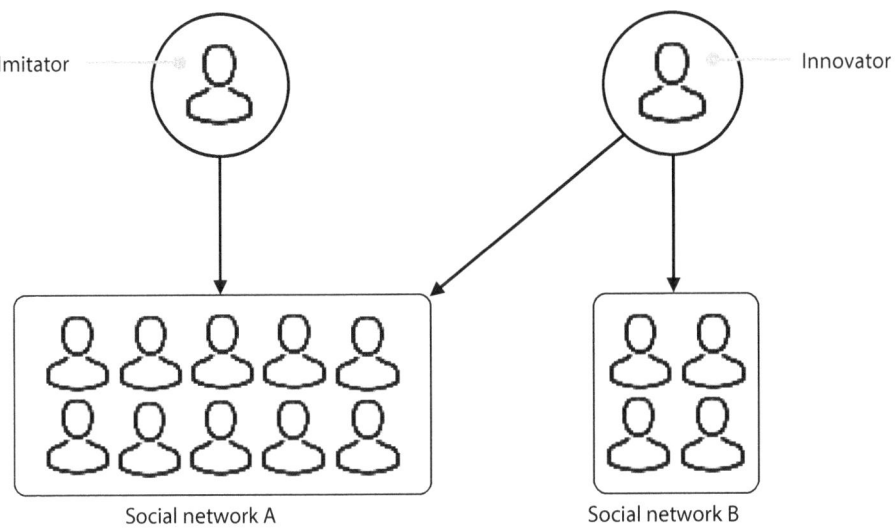

Fig. 9.7 Network effects in social network services. (Authors' own figure)

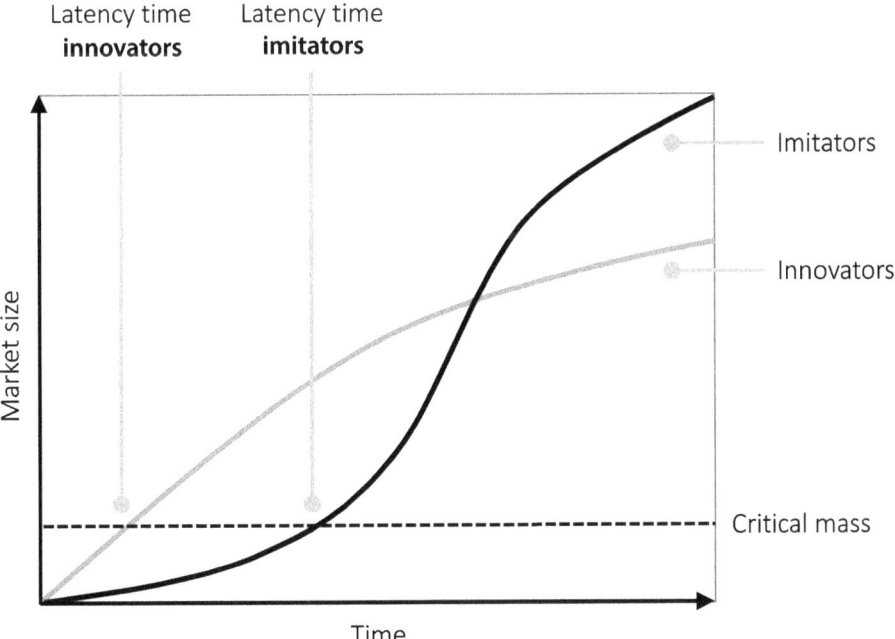

Fig. 9.8 Market evolution if all customers are imitators or innovators. (Authors' own figure)

are only innovators. As indicated above, the imitators inflict strong network effects on the market evolution, while no such effects are present in the case of only innovators.

Observe that the initial market growth is extremely slow if all customers are imitators. It may take several years before the market has reached a *critical mass* for which the market penetration is commercially sustainable (represented by the dotted line). This is the *latency* associated with the market. Moreover, if there are no initial customers at all, the market never starts to increase—there is no one there to inspire other customers to buy or use the service. The long latency is the most difficult strategic dilemma in markets with strong network effects—the supplier may abandon the product because of the slow initial growth. On the other hand, the market with only innovators grows rapidly initially and has low latency. This point is considered in more detail in ▶ Chap. 18 where the solution of the Bass equation is presented.

After a digital service or good with strong network effects reaches its critical mass, it usually undergoes a period of rapid growth until the market approaches saturation. The strategic dilemma is how to reach critical mass in a brief period. If this period is too long, there is a certain possibility that the service will be prematurely terminated. ◘ Figure 9.9 shows the number of active monthly users on Facebook for the period from 2004 to 2015 (Roberts, n.d.). Observe that critical mass was reached in 2008, after 4 years of slow growth. Thereafter, Facebook grew rapidly. Other social network services, such as Twitter, have undergone a similar evolution.

Network effects range from concrete and easily identifiable ones to vague and less obvious occurrences. Easily identifiable network effects are those where physical objects or users interact directly with each other. Examples include telephone networks, computer networks, social media, and multiplayer online gaming. These networks usually exhibit strong direct network effects, meaning that the network of users is highly connected.

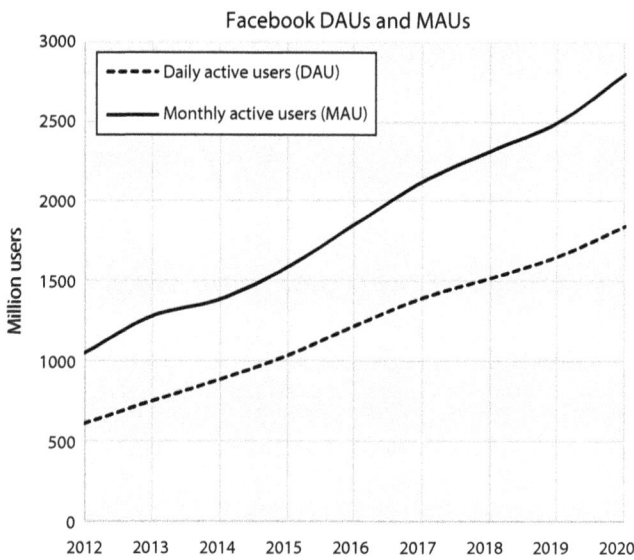

◘ **Fig. 9.9** Facebook users in the period from 2004 to 2015. (Authors' own figure)

On the other end of the scale are vague and less obvious network effects. These include bandwagon effects and tech-performance network effects. *Bandwagon effects* include the social pressure to join a service or buy a good because everyone else is using it. *Tech-performance network effects* include the effect that an increased number of users have on the performance of a technology or service. Tech-performance network effects are in general easier to identify and measure compared to bandwagon effects. An example of tech-performance network effects is peer-to-peer file sharing services such as BitTorrent. New users joining the BitTorrent network result in, on average, reduced download times and potentially an increased amount of available content for other users of the service. Bandwagon and tech-performance network effects are usually indirect.

Another type of network effects is *data network effects*, in which data collected about users or user behavior is used to improve digital services. Google Search is an example of data network effects since each search query contributes to refining the Google Search algorithm. Another example is recommendation systems based on input or feedback from users.

9.4 Direct and Indirect Network Effects

Network effects may be direct or indirect: *direct network effects* take place when users induce value on other users by the means of direct interaction between the users; *indirect network effects* take place when the aggregated behavior of the users induces value on other users. For example, in the case of positive direct network effects, users benefit from other users in the network because they have more options for direct interaction. In the case of positive indirect network effects, users benefit from other users because they, collectively, provide value that is somehow appreciated by all users in the network without any direct interaction between the users taking place. Examples of direct network effects are interactions among members of social media, between smartphone users, and between buyers and sellers in multisided markets. Examples of indirect network effects are improvements of service quality due to user feedback, product reviews, and bandwagon effects.

9.5 Same-Side and Cross-Side Network Effects

In a network, there may be same-side or cross-side network effects. *Same-side network effects* imply that an increased number of users lead to an increase in value for other users in the same user group. Examples are telephones, social networks, and multiplayer online games. These networks are made up from direct or indirect contact among the users of the service.

Cross-side network effects imply that an increase in the number of users in one user group enhances value in other user groups. These network effects arise only in multisided markets (see ▶ Chap. 10). One example is computers and software—without software, there is no value in the computer, and without computers, there is nowhere to run the software. A little less obvious example is smartphones and apps: the availability of apps increases the value of the smartphone beyond that of voice and message communications. A final example is third-party content or service providers in social media. The availability of, for instance, games on Facebook increases the value for Facebook users as well as the value for the providers of these games. In this case, there are positive cross-side network effects.

Note that both same-side and cross-side network effects may be direct or indirect and positive or negative. Hence, theoretically, there exist eight different types of network effects—any combination of positive/negative, direct/indirect, and same-side/cross-side network effects.

Analysis of network effects associated with digital services includes identification of all positive, negative, direct, indirect, same-side, and cross-side network effects and the estimation of the strength of these effects. A suitable tool for performing such analysis is the stakeholder relationship model (SRM) presented in ▶ Chap. 19. The strength of network effects may be quantified using, for example, Metcalfe's law.

9.6 Estimating the Value of Networks

9.6.1 Size of Networks

This section provides simple mathematical arguments concerning the impact that network effects may have on the value of various types of digital goods or services depending on the way in which users interact. First, observe that in a population or network of n individuals, there are:
- n singletons.
- n^2 pairs (assuming $n \gg 1$ and counting all one-way interactions between individuals)
- 2^n groups (also assuming $n \gg 1$)

Based on this observation, different laws estimating the value of digital services are presented next. In the following text, $V(n)$ is a measure for the total value of a digital service or network, and n is the total number of users. Value in this context is an abstract concept that can be a measure of, for example, revenues, market capitalization, volume of transactions between users, or time spent using a service.

Common representations of value are the number of links between users in the network and the number of groups a user can be member of. These are the basis for the calculation of the various network laws. Note that, in the presented models, $V(n)$ depends only on the number of users, n. As a general note, the value of a company or a service depends also on other tangible and intangible assets such as cash, securities, property, equipment, design value, brand recognition, and organizational value. However, these variables are not considered in the following calculations; the focus here is solely on the value that arises because of the number of users.

9.6 · Estimating the Value of Networks

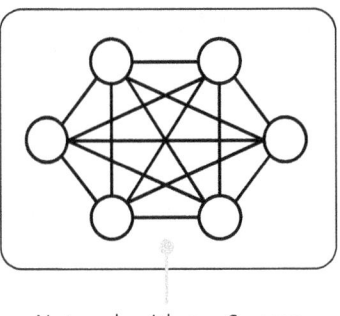
Network with n = 6 users

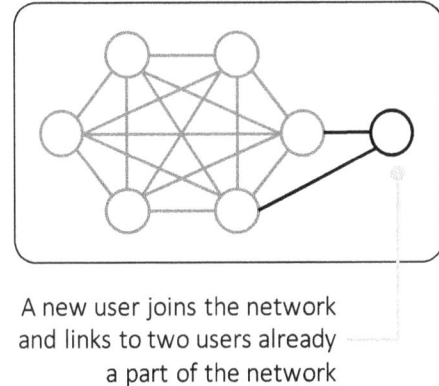
A new user joins the network and links to two users already a part of the network

Fig. 9.10 A new user joins the network. (Authors' own figure)

The value each new user adds to the network, or the network effect generated by a single user, is given as:

$$F(n) = V'(n) = \frac{dV(n)}{dn}.$$

When a new user joins a network, they link to other users that are already a part of the network. This is illustrated in **Fig. 9.10**.

The tilde notation "~" is used to indicate the growth rate of the value of a network. For example, $V(n) \sim n$ indicates that the value of the network grows (at most) as fast as cn, where c is a constant. This is equivalent of the "big O notation," $O(n) = cn$, commonly used to assess the growth rate of algorithms in mathematics and computer science.

9.6.2 Sarnoff's Law

Sarnoff's law is about the value of broadcast networks such as radio and television broadcast networks. In such networks, one sender transmits information to a group of n receivers. Sarnoff claimed that there is no additional value for new customers to join the network because others have done so in the past. For the supplier, the value of the network is the number of customers connected to it, that is:

$$V_{Sarnoff}(n) \sim n,$$

in which $V(n)$ is the value of the network and n is the number of devices connected to the network. The value added by a new user to the network (network effect or feedback term) is $F_{Sarnoff}(n) = V'_{Sarnoff}(n) \sim 1$. Hence, there is no network effect in this case. Every new user adds only a single link to the network. This is shown in **Fig. 9.11**, in which the number of customers equals the number of links in the network which, in turn, equals the total value of the network. The value of a company providing a broadcast service depends on the number of customers only since

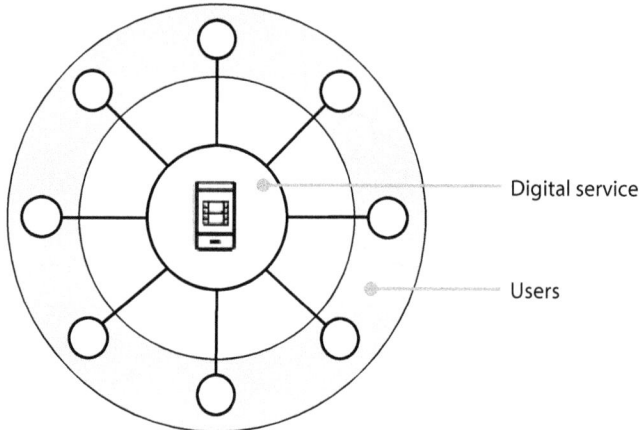

Fig. 9.11 A broadcast network. (Authors' own figure)

each customer provides a fixed income to the company. There is no other value created in these networks.

The law is named after David Sarnoff (1891–1971), an American pioneer of radio and television manufacturing and broadcast. Sarnoff spent most of his career in the Radio Corporation of America (RCA) and the National Broadcasting Company (NBC) and was one of the most influential businessmen in the early days of radio and television.

Sarnoff's law applies to all kinds of broadcast networks in which there is no interaction or exchange of value between users or customers. The only interaction in a broadcast network takes place between the provider of the service and the users. In addition to radio and television broadcast networks, there are several examples of other digital services in which there is no network effect, for example:

— In **Google Search,** a user does not benefit from using the search engine because other people are using it. Therefore, there are no direct network effects stimulating people to use the search engine so that, in this respect, Google Search is a Sarnoff network. However, there may be a weak indirect network effect, hardly recognized by the users, since search habits of the users contribute to refinement of the engine's search algorithm which, in turn, results in more accurate search results for other users. On the other hand, Google is a multisided platform, where the users of Google Search generate a strong cross-side network effect for the advertisement business of Google since the number of people using the search engine determines the fees that Google can charge advertisers.
— **Netflix** uses a subscription-based business model. Each subscriber contributes to the value of Netflix by paying regular subscription fees. There is no interaction or exchange of value between Netflix subscribers. On the other hand, Netflix was initially subject to negative network effects (word-of-mouth) and loss of users to the illegal Popcorn Time because of overloaded databases (Idland et al., 2016).
— The value of **Wikipedia** depends entirely on the volume and quality of the articles in the encyclopedia. There is no interaction between readers, writers, and benefactors and thus no feedback effects prompting new readers of Wikipedia.

The value of Wikipedia for the reader is the volume and correctness of the content. The value is independent of who else is reading this content and the number of writers and benefactors. Wikipedia is a special case where the network laws do not apply—even Sarnoff's law—since the value is independent of the number of users.

9.6.3 Metcalfe's Law and Odlyzko-Tilly's Law

Fax machines, telephones, and email accounts are more valuable when more equipment of the same type is connected to the network. Robert Metcalfe, one of the inventors of Ethernet, suggested in 1980 that the value of an Ethernet network would be proportional to the number of possible transactions between compatible devices connected to the network, that is:

$$V_{Metcalfe}(n) \sim n^2,$$

in which n is the number of devices. The law assumes that all possible interactions are equally valuable and probable. For small networks, such as Ethernet, this is a reasonable assumption. This is illustrated in ◘ Fig. 9.12, in which all nodes are connected to each other in a network consisting of six nodes. The number of links in the network in ◘ Fig. 9.12 is 15 which, according to Metcalf's law, is a measure for the value of the network. Note that the number of links in a network with n nodes, where all nodes are connected to each other, is $n(n-1)/2 \sim n^2$, from which Metcalf's law follows directly.

Later, it was argued that Metcalfe's law is also valid for social media network, such as Facebook, Twitter, and other digital services in which the most important feature is interactions between individuals. A recent paper (Zhang et al., 2015) indicates that Facebook follows Metcalfe's law quite accurately and that the value can

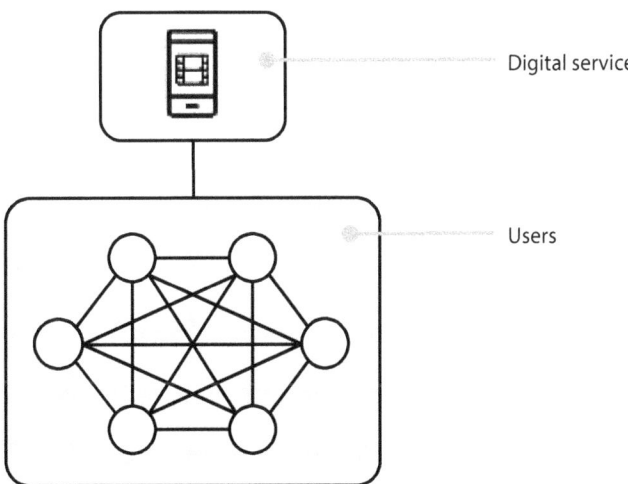

◘ **Fig. 9.12** A network where all nodes connect to each other. (Authors' own figure)

be calculated as $V(n) = 5.7 \times 10^{-9} \times n^2 \sim n^2$. However, this conclusion depends on how value is defined and how the number of users is counted.

The network effect (or feedback term) of Metcalfe's law is $F_{Metcalfe}(n) \sim n$. This is the most commonly used value for network effects in economic research. The value was, in fact, used long before Metcalfe suggested it in 1980. This feedback value is the basis for the diffusion model of Frank Bass from 1969 (see ▶ Chap. 18).

Andrew Odlyzko and his coworkers have argued that Metcalfe's law is incorrect—in particular, concerning social media networks—since Metcalfe's law assumes that all possible transactions have equal value. In a large population, Metcalfe's law gives an overestimation of the value of the network since each individual will only interact with a small number of other individuals, and not all interactions between them will be equally strong. Based on this argument, Odlyzko and Tilly proposed the alternative law:

$$V_{O-T}(n) \sim n \ln n.$$

This law is called Odlyzko-Tilly's law. The network effect is now reduced to $F_{O-T}(n) \sim \ln n$.

Box 9.4 Derivation of Odlyzko-Tilly's Law

Odlyzko-Tilly's law is derived applying Zipf's principle to the frequency of interactions an individual has with other individuals. Zipf's principle is an empirical law based on the observation that several sequences in nature and society (e.g., frequency of words, size of cities, and length of rivers) follow a rank distribution (called a "Pareto distribution" in statistics) in which the most frequent or largest item is twice as frequent or large as the second item in the sequence, three times as frequent or large as the third item, and so on.

By applying this ranking principle on interactions between people, the total number of transactions T between one individual and all other individuals is:

$$T = c + \frac{c}{2} + \frac{c}{3} + \cdots + \frac{c}{n} \sim c \ln n \sim \ln n.$$

Applying Zipf's ranking principle, the assumption is that an individual has c transactions with the person who is closest to him, only half as many with the next closest person, one-third as many with the third closest, and so on. The value of the network is then $V_{O-T}(n) = nT \sim n \ln n$.

Another way to derive Odlyzko-Tilly's law is based on the connectivity of random graphs. First, assume that individuals are nodes in a random graph and that the interactions between the individuals are the links in the graph; that is, two individuals interacting with each other are connected by a link, while there is no link between two individuals who are *not* interacting with each other. The simplest random graph is the Erdős-Rényi (ER) graph. In ER graphs, the probability, p, that a link exists between any two nodes is the same for all pairs of nodes in the network.

9.6 · Estimating the Value of Networks

It can be shown that the ER graph becomes connected if $p = c \ln n/n$ for some constant c. This threshold is sharp. If the link probability is increasing slightly slower with increasing n, for example, $p = c \ln n/n^a$, $a > 1 + \varepsilon$ and ε is an arbitrarily small number, large parts of the graph will be unconnected. If the probability is increasing slightly faster with increasing n, for example, $p = c \ln n/n^a$, $a < 1 - \varepsilon$ and ε is an arbitrarily small number, the graph will be tightly connected. It is reasonable to assume that the graph representing relationships between people is connected—there exists a path from one person to another either directly or via other people. This path is rather short, as revealed by observations made by Milgram, leading to his law of six degrees of separation; that is, the distance between people is seldom more than six links, in which a link is from one person to another person personally know. Since each of us has few direct links to other people, it is reasonable to assume that the graph is lightly connected so that $p \sim \ln n/n$ is a good approximation of the link probability of the relationship graph between people. Since there are n^2 possible links, the total number of links N and the value of the network $V(n) \sim N$ is $V_{O-T}(n) \sim N \sim n^2 \ln n/n = n \ln n$, and, again, Odlyzko-Tilly's law has been derived.

9.6.4 Reed's Law

In massive multiplayer online games (MMOGs), the players form groups. The number of possible groups among n players is $N \sim 2^n$ (assuming that n is large). Therefore, it is reasonable to assume that the value of a digital service in which groups are formed is:

$$V_{Reed}(n) \sim 2^n.$$

This is Reed's law (Reed, 2001). Reed is an American computer scientist and one of the developers of the TCP and UDP protocols.

Reed's law determines, in general, the value of a network in which interactions take place in groups. Again, we may use Odlyzko's argument that the contribution from large groups is too big and the actual network effect of group formation is smaller than what is predicted by Reed's law. One way to modify Reed's law is to use Dunbar's number, which is the average number of people an individual knows (see ▶ Box 9.2). A commonly used value of Dunbar's number D is 150.

Let us set the maximum size of a group that can be formed by people—for example, in an online game—as equal to D (=150). The number of groups smaller than D that can be formed by n people is:

$$N \sim \sum_{k=1}^{D} \binom{n}{k} \sim n^D,$$

in which the binominal coefficient is the number of groups of k people that can be formed by n people. For large n, $n^2 \ll n^D \ll 2^n$. The value of the network is then:

$$V_{Reed-mod}(n) \sim N \sim n^D.$$

To see that this is a reasonable assumption, note that by Reed's law, the value of the network doubles when a new customer is connected to the network because $V_{Reed}(n+1) \sim 2^{n+1} = 2 \times 2^n = 2 \times V_{Reed}(n)$. This vastly overestimates the value that a single person may have on the network. In the modified case, the value increases more modestly:

$$V_{Reed-mod}(n+1) \sim (1+D/n)V_{Reed-mod}(n).$$

> **Box 9.5 Derivation of the Modified Law**
> The formula follows from the observation that:
>
> $$N = \sum_{k=1}^{D}\binom{n}{k} = \sum_{k=1}^{D}\frac{n!}{k!(n-k)!} = \sum_{k=1}^{D}\frac{n(n-1)\cdots(n-k+1)}{k!}$$
>
> and that $\binom{n}{k} < \binom{n}{D}$ for $k < D$ and $D < n/2$ (Pascal's triangle). Hence,
>
> $$N = \sum_{k=1}^{D}\binom{n}{k} < D\binom{n}{D} = D\frac{n(n-1)\cdots(n-D+1)}{D!} < D\frac{n^D}{D!} \sim n^D$$
>
> using the "big O notation" and the fact that $D \ll n$.

9.6.5 Summary and Comparison of Network Laws

■ Table 9.1 summarizes the network laws presented above. These laws cover a broad array of different networks with very different underlying value production mechanisms.

Reed suggests that Sarnoff's law, Metcalfe's law, and Reed's law may be used to analyze the effect of merging two network companies. The value of the merged company may then either be proportional to:
- The sum of users of the two companies (Sarnoff), leading to a linear increase in value
- The increased number of possible interactions between users enabled by the merger (Metcalfe), leading to a quadratic increase in value
- The number of groups that can be formed among users in the new company (Reed), leading to an exponential increase in value

9.6 · Estimating the Value of Networks

Table 9.1 Network laws. (Authors' compilation)

Law	Value of network (V)	Network effect (F)
Sarnoff's law	n	1
Odlyzko-Tilly's law	$n \ln n$	$\ln n$
Metcalfe's law	n^2	n
Reed's law	2^n	2^n
Modified Reed's law	n^D	n^{D-1}

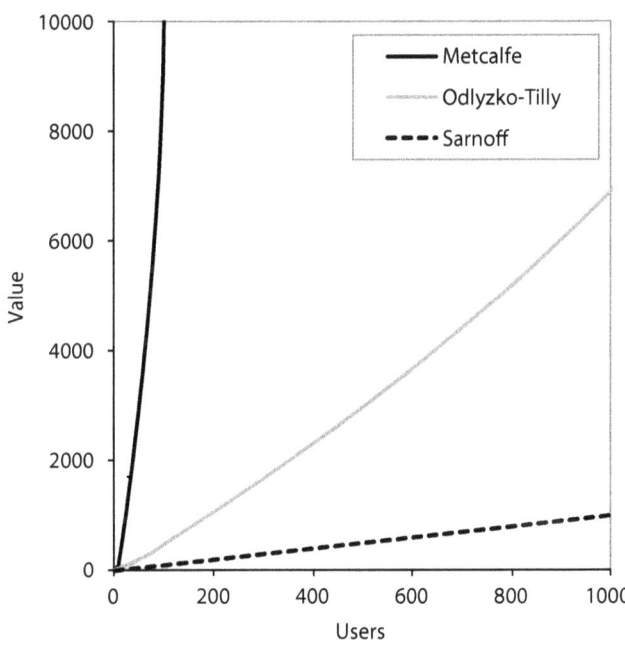

Fig. 9.13 Numerical examples of Metcalfe's, Odlyzko-Tilly's, and Sarnoff's law. (Authors' own figure)

This simple analysis may then, in some cases, uncover otherwise hidden values and, in other cases, avoid overoptimistic valuations of the new company.

■ Figure 9.13 shows numerical examples of Metcalfe's, Odlyzko-Tilly's, and Sarnoff's law using a linear scale. Observe the significant differences in value as a function of the number of users for the three laws. Reed's law and the modified Reed's law have not been plotted since they both increase so fast that they are significantly steeper than Metcalfe's law and would, therefore, almost overlap with the vertical axis.

9.7 Conclusions

The key messages in this chapter can be summarized as follows.
- In some markets, the temporal evolution of the market is stimulated by positive feedback from the market. This is what is called network effects. The most important source causing feedback is the number of customers joining or leaving the market.
- The network effect is positive if an increase in the number of customers causes further increase in the number of customers.
- The network effect is negative if customers leaving the market stimulate other users to do the same. The network effect is also negative if an increase in the number of customers reduces the quality of the service, stimulating users to leave the market.
- The market may oscillate or become chaotic if there is significant delay from cause to action.
- Both negative and positive network effects are caused by positive feedback from the network. Negative feedback stabilizes the market at a nominal level; that is, counteracting any fluctuations away from stability.

Network effects are common in the digital economy and are, as such, important for strategic business analysis in several digital markets. An important observation is that markets with strong positive network effects grow very slowly initially and may be abandoned prematurely.

The network effects depend on the interactions between the customers. There are three basic types of markets:
- There is no interaction between customers—leading to Sarnoff's law.
- The customers interact in pairs—leading to Metcalf's and Odlyzko-Tilly's laws.
- The customers interact in groups—leading to Reed's law.

? Questions

1. Assume that Network A in ◘ Fig. 9.1 grows to Network B and finally to Network C. Assume that each link has a value equal to 1. Applying the definition of network effects, how does the value per user increase as this network evolves?
2. Snapchat is a social media service available for smartphones.
   (a) Identify network effects in Snapchat (positive, negative, direct, indirect, cross-side, and same-side network effects).
   (b) How are network effects in Snapchat different from network effects in Facebook?
3. Does Sarnoff's law give an accurate valuation of Instagram?
4. Draw two graphs—one linear and one logarithmic—that show the network effect as a function of the number of users using (1) Sarnoff's law, (2) Metcalfe's law, and (3) Odlyzko-Tilly's law. How would you interpret the graphs? (The network effect is defined in ▶ Sect. 9.6.1.)

9.7 · Conclusions

5. Assume two competing social media companies, A and B, with $N_A = 10$ million users and $N_B = 20$ million users. Assume that these two companies plan to merge, making a new company, C, with $N_C = N_A + N_B = 30$ million users. Assume further that the valuation of the companies depends on the number of users only. What is the total gain (in percentage) from such a merger when estimating the company's value using:
   (a) Sarnoff's law?
   (b) Metcalfe's law?
   (c) Odlyzko-Tilly's law?

6. Consider a social media network that you are a part of (e.g., Facebook, Twitter, or Snapchat).
   (a) How many users are there in total in the chosen social media network?
   (b) How many users do you link to in the chosen social media network?
   (c) How will you rank and quantify the importance of your links?
   (d) Does Metcalfe's law or Odlyzko-Tilly's law best describe the value that the social media network offers to you?

7. Facebook has, by 2018, approximately 2.2 billion monthly active users.
   (a) Based on this number, calculate the total value of Facebook. You can use the formula $V(n) = 5.7 \times 10^{-9} \times n^2$.
   (b) What does this value represent?
   (c) How many users does Facebook need to have for a total value of 1?

8. Which of the three laws (Sarnoff, Metcalfe, and Reed) are valid for the valuation of the following digital services: Google Search, Gmail, *World of Warcraft*, Wikipedia, Netflix, Twitter, YouTube, eBay, and Facebook?

✅ Answers

1. Assuming that the value of the network is the number of links per user, we find:
   1. Network A: $3/3 = 1$.
   2. Network B: $11/7 = 1.57$.
   3. Network C: $21/11 = 1.9$.
   The network effect is positive since the value increases as the number of users increases.

2. Snapchat is used for photo sharing, videos chat, and instant messaging.
   1. Snapchat is subject to positive network effect (the number of users). This is a direct same-side network effect. Snapchat also offers advertisements. There is then a direct cross-side network effect from the number of users to the advertisers.
   2. Facebook (more than 2.2 billion users) is much larger than Snapchat (about 230 million users). In accordance with Metcalf's and Odlyzko-Tilly's laws, the network effects of Snapchat are much weaker than for Facebook.

3. Instagram is a value network mediating between users sharing photos and videos and is not a broadcast network. Therefore, Sarnoff's law does not apply to Instagram.

4. The strength of the feedback is defined as the value each user adds to the network. The feedback function is shown in ◘ Fig. 9.13 for the linear case.

- In Sarnoff's law, the value that each user adds to the network is 1; that is, there is no feedback in this case.
- In Odlyzko-Tilly's law, the additional value each new user adds to the network increases as $\ln n$ as the number of users increases. For a large network such as Facebook, the user adds approximately 20 units of value to the network.
- In Metcalf's law, the additional value that each user adds to the network is n. For Facebook, this is approximately 2 billion, that is, 100 million times more than Odlyzko-Tilly's law.

5. The gain is defined as:

$$\text{Gain} = \frac{\text{Value C}}{\text{Value A} + \text{Value B}} - 1$$

The result is shown in the table.

Value model	Company A 10,000 users	Company B 20,000 users	Company C 30,000 users	Gain in percent
Sarnoff	10,000	20,000	30,000	0
Metcalf	1×10^{14}	4×10^{14}	9×10^{14}	80
Odlyzko-tilly	1.6×10^{8}	3.4×10^{8}	5.2×10^{8}	4

6. Look for information on Wikipedia or the web for your choice of social media network.
7. Value of Facebook.

$$V(\text{Facebook}) = 5.6 \times 10^{-9} \times (2.2 \times 10^{9})^2 = 27.6 \times 10^{9}$$

   (a) This value can be a measure for (i.e., proportional to) the number of user interactions, revenues, or stock market value.
   (b) To have value 1, the number of users must be:

$$n = \sqrt{\frac{1}{5.7 \times 10^{-9}}} = 13.245.$$

8. Value model:
   1. Google Search: Sarnoff (no interaction between users).
   2. Gmail: Sarnoff (there are other email services).
   3. *World of Warcraft*: Reed (formation of groups of players).
   4. Wikipedia: none of them—the value of Wikipedia is independent of the number of users.
   5. Netflix: Sarnoff (no interaction between users).
   6. Twitter: Metcalf (depends on the number of followers).
   7. YouTube: Metcalf (number of viewers depends on the number of videos producers).
   8. eBay: Metcalf (depends on the size of the marketplace).
   9. Facebook: Metcalf (depends on the number of friends).

References

Arthur, W.B. (1990). *Positive feedbacks in the economy*. Scientific American, No. 262.

Dunbar, R. (1998). *Grooming, gossip, and the evolution of language*. Harvard University Press.

Idland, E., Øverby, H., & Audestad, J. (2016, November 23–25). *Economic Markets for Video Streaming Services: A Case Study of Netflix and Popcorn Time*. NIK 2016, Ålesund, Norway.

Knapton, S. (2016, January 20). Facebook users have 155 friends – But would trust just four in a crisis. *The Telegraph*.

Merton, R. K. (1968, January 5). The Matthew Effect in Science. *Science, 159*.

Milgram, S. (1967). *The small world problem*. Psychology Today, No. 2.

Odlyzko, A., & Briscoe, B. (2006, July 1). *Metcalfe's law is wrong*. IEEE Spectrum: Technology, Engineering, and Science News.

Øverby, H., & Audestad, J. A. (2019) *Temporal market evolution of interactive games*. SSRN. Available at https://ssrn.com/abstract=3412902

Reed, D. P. (2001, February). *The law of the pack*. Harvard Business Review.

Roberts, P. (n.d.). *The most important Facebook statistics for 2017*. Our Social Times, Cambridge.

Shapiro, C., & Varian, H. R. (1999). *Information rules: A strategic guide to the network economy*. Harvard Business School Press.

The Erdös Number Project. Oakland University.

Wiener, N. (1948). *Cybernetics: Or control and communication in the animal and the machine*. MIT Press.

Zhang, X.-Z., Liu, J.-J., & Xu, Z.-W. (2015). Tencent Facebook Data Validate Metcalfe's Law. *Journal of Computer Science and Technology, 30*(2).

Further Reading

Dorogovtsev, S. N., & Mendes, J. F. F. (2003). *Evolution of networks: From biological nets to the internet and WWW*. Oxford University Press.

Multisided Platforms

Contents

10.1 Introduction – 150

10.2 Characteristics of Multisided Platforms – 151
10.2.1 Network Effects – 152
10.2.2 Pricing – 152
10.2.3 Competition – 152
10.2.4 Business Ecosystem – 153
10.2.5 Market Regulations – 153

10.3 Network Effects and MSPs – 153

10.4 Business Ecosystem and MSPs – 158

10.5 Trade Process of MSPs and Resellers – 159

10.6 Conclusions – 161

References – 163

© The Author(s), under exclusive license to Springer Nature Switzerland AG 2021
H. Øverby, J. A. Audestad, *Introduction to Digital Economics*, Classroom Companion: Business,
https://doi.org/10.1007/978-3-030-78237-5_10

Learning Objectives

After completing this chapter, you should be able to:
- Identify the different user groups of a multisided platform.
- Identify the value proposition for each user group and the combined effect on the aggregate business offered by the platform.
- Analyze same-side and cross-side network effects governing the evolution of the different services offered by the platform.

10.1 Introduction

In a multisided platform (MSP), two or more distinct user groups interact to produce mutual benefits for each other. In many practical cases, there are just two groups, in which case, the multisided platform becomes a two-sided platform. There is no essential difference between two-sided and multisided platforms. The most important difference is that the multisided platform consists of many more business roles and interactions between these roles. This chapter will therefore mainly discuss two-sided platforms, keeping in mind that the theory is valid also for multisided platforms. For simplicity, we will also refer to two-sided platform as MSP.

> **Definition 10.1 Multisided Platform**
> A multisided platform (MSP) enables direct interactions between two or more distinct user groups in which all user groups are affiliated with the MSP (Hagiu & Wright, 2015).

The MSP is one of the most profitable innovations of the digital economy. Some of the largest companies in the digital economy base their business models on an MSP, including Google, Facebook, and eBay. Some MSPs have even become market leaders in their industry since there is tremendous value in connecting different user groups. Still, there seems to be a considerable potential for new MSPs in several business and industry sectors, as well as in the public domain.

A comprehensive overview of the literature on the economics of multisided platforms is presented by Sanchez-Carlas and Leon (Sanchez-Cartas & Leon, 2018). The overview shows that the general approach to dynamic behavior of platforms is based on standard supply and demand theory and agent-based behavior theory. These methods provide insight into important areas such as pricing and price dependence between the different markets supported by the platform, the origin of network effects, coupling between platform services, behavior of users, competition between platforms offering equivalent services, problems associated with regulations, and formation of de facto monopolies.

In this chapter, the focus is on the temporal evolution of multisided platforms triggered by strong network effects and not on pricing and competition in equilibrium markets. Several of these markets are usually not in equilibrium because they have not reached saturation where growth has stagnated (e.g., most social media platforms). Moreover, some of the platforms (e.g., Facebook) have become de facto monopolies. In these cases, standard supply/demand theories do not apply.

10.2 Characteristics of Multisided Platforms

MSPs offer several benefits to the users, including:

- They offer uniform, simple, and secure login procedures and ease of use.
- They offer simple and transparent ways of connecting customers with matching interests through built-in matchmaking mechanisms, for example, matching suppliers and consumers in a trade process or providing information to marketers to support targeted and precise advertisement campaigns.
- They offer efficient transaction management, thereby simplifying search, reducing management costs, and streamlining administrative and payment processes.
- They may also assist in trust-building between users within the same group or between users in different groups.

The MSP is related to the concept of value networks described in ▶ Chap. 8 since the value network is an organization or company offering mediation services either within a single group or between different groups, in which case, the value network is equivalent to an MSP. ▶ Chapter 8 explains the strategy of value networks in general. In this chapter, the attention is on the mediation activity itself and the techno-economic platform supporting it.

It is assumed that the mediation between the user groups is *asymmetric*. Asymmetry means that the platform is serving two or more user groups with different motives for using the platform services. ◘ Table 10.1 shows examples of MSPs.

There are two main types of MSPs: *digital MSPs* and *tangible MSPs*. Digital MSPs mediate the exchange of digital goods and services, while tangible MSPs mediate the exchange of physical goods and non-digital services. Facebook and

◘ Table 10.1 Examples of MSPs. (Authors' compilation)

MSP	Type of business	User groups	Platform type
New York Times	Newspaper	Readers and advertisers	Digital
eBay	Electronic marketplace	Sellers and buyers	Tangible
Facebook	Social networking service	Users and advertisers	Digital
Uber	Sharing service	Drivers and passengers	Tangible
Airbnb	Sharing service	Hosts and guests	Tangible
MasterCard	Point-of-sale transactions	Merchants and cardholders	Digital
Kickstarter	Crowdfunding	Borrowers and investors	Digital

MasterCard are examples of digital MSPs, whereas Uber and Airbnb are examples of tangible MSPs. Tangible MSPs have also been termed online-to-offline (O2O) MSPs (McAfee & Brynjolfsson, 2017). ◘ Table 10.1 lists some two-sided platform businesses.

Some of the major characteristics of MSPs are associated with network effects, pricing, competition, business ecosystem, and market regulation (Ardolino et al., 2020).

10.2.1 Network Effects

The MSP may be subject to complex network effects not only involving each user group but also between user groups. Network effects are so important for MSPs that they are discussed in more detail in ▶ Sect. 10.3. The network effects may sometimes lead to winner-take-all markets where one platform supplier after some time becomes a de facto monopoly.

10.2.2 Pricing

The pricing model and, hence, the way revenues are generated may be complex. For example, one user group are offered platform services for free, while other customer groups must pay for the services they receive (e.g., Facebook and Google Search); customers may pay per interaction or amount of service they receive, or they may pay a fixed monthly subscription fee (e.g., eBay and Airbnb); customers may pay for some types of services and receive other services free of charge (electronic newspaper); or any combination thereof.

It is a common feature of MSPs that some user groups subsidize the other user groups by levying differentiated charges among the user groups. Sometimes, the MSP gets all its revenues from only one user group while providing services for free to other user groups.

An MSP often benefits from a reduced price of the goods or services mediated between the sellers and the buyers. This is because low prices mean more sales and, potentially, more buyers of the goods, increasing the usage of the platform and, in turn, add value to the platform in terms of increased cross-side network effects. In this respect, MSPs have incentives to reduce prices in the business areas in which they operate.

In several of these pricing regimes, supply/demand theories are meaningless since the two variables are decoupled in market segments where the good is traded for free.

10.2.3 Competition

Three basic types of competition are identified for MSPs. The platform may compete directly with other platforms offering the same services (e.g., between Facebook and Myspace and between electronic newspapers) or compete with entirely different platforms for certain types of customers. Facebook and Google compete for attracting advertisers to their platform even though the two platforms belong to completely different business segments. This type of competition may seem counterintuitive but is the most important competitive challenge for several platform operators. Finally, there may also be competition between the customers of the same type (e.g., between drivers offering services over the Uber platform). This makes competition in the MSP business more complex than in most other businesses.

One particularly interesting group competing in the advertisement business is the influencers promoting various products on their blogs over social media platforms (e.g., Facebook, Instagram, and YouTube). The influencers run two-sided platforms (readers and advertiser) on the Internet without owning any kind of infrastructure except their own smartphones, tablets, cameras, or personal computers.

10.2.4 Business Ecosystem

Because of competition as just explained, the ecosystem for MSPs is more complex than other businesses. For this reason, the MSP must sometimes include other businesses in their ecosystem analysis that are seemingly unrelated to the primary business areas of the platform making the overall business model more complex and unpredictable. Because of the complex interactions among the various types of customers, the use of standard business modeling tools may not capture all strategic issues related to MSPs. Business models often fail to take the effects of interactions between user groups (e.g., cross-side network effects) into account but rather treat them as independent business segments. One way of characterizing the MSP in terms of its ecosystem is considered in ▶ Sect. 10.4.

10.2.5 Market Regulations

The mere existence of two or more user groups and sometimes also strong network effects both within the same user group and between the various groups make it difficult to find one regulatory regime that supports fair competition and avoids formation of monopolies. Facebook is a de facto monopoly in the segment of social media services but not in the advertisement segment. Moreover, intricate competition and complex ecosystem make it even harder to regulate MSP businesses. The complexity itself may make it difficult to identify what needs to be regulated, what can in fact be regulated, what are the actual effects of regulation, and how can lock-in be avoided.

10.3 Network Effects and MSPs

Network effects (see ▶ Chap. 9 for a general discussion of network effects) play an essential role in MSPs as illustrated in ◘ Fig. 10.1 for a two-sided platform. Here, there are two distinct user groups. The platform mediates between these two user

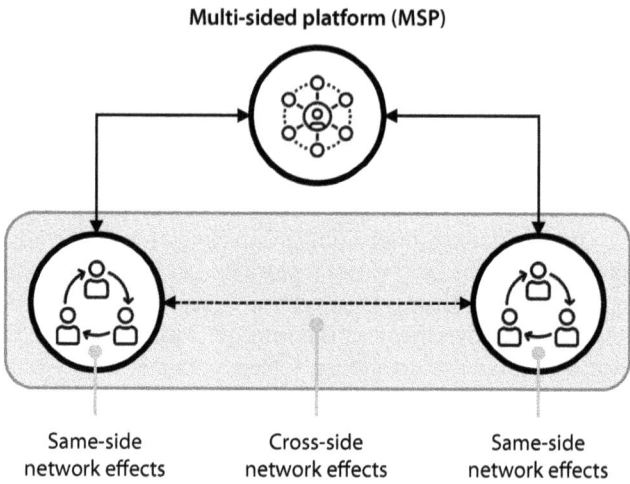

Fig. 10.1 Network effects in a two-sided platform. (Authors' own figure)

groups as well as between users within each user group. If the network effect involves only one side, it is called a *same-side network effect*. If it has an impact on the other side, it is called a *cross-side network effect*. Positive, negative, direct, and indirect network effects may be present within user groups and between user groups. The dynamics of an MSP may be complex since there are dependencies and network effects within user groups and between user groups.

It is worthwhile to repeat that network effects are positive feedbacks from the market and that the mere nature of positive feedback is such that the market cannot be in equilibrium unless the market is saturated (there are no more potential customers). Therefore, equilibrium theory is not applicable to markets where network effects are present.

The Bass equation (see ▶ Chap. 18) is an example of how the market evolves if there are same-side network effects present. The outcome a simple cross-side network effect has on the temporal market evolution is analyzed in ▶ Box 10.1 using a simple mathematical model.

Box 10.1 Dynamics of Markets with Cross-Side Network Effects

A simple mathematical model for the temporal evolution of a two-sided platform with a single cross-side network effect is shown in ◘ Fig. 10.2. This simple model can easily be extended to models with multiple same-side and cross-side network effects and more than two types of customers.

There are two types of customers, A and B. Initially there are N potential customers of type A and M potential customers of type B. Customers of type A adopts the platform service offered to them at a fixed rate p, symbolized by a valve controlled by the parameter p. The adoption rate of customers of type B is proportional to the number of customers of type A, i.e., the adoption rate of type-B customers is qA. This is a cross-side network effect from customer-side A to customer-side B. The flow parameters p and q are assumed to

10.3 · Network Effects and MSPs

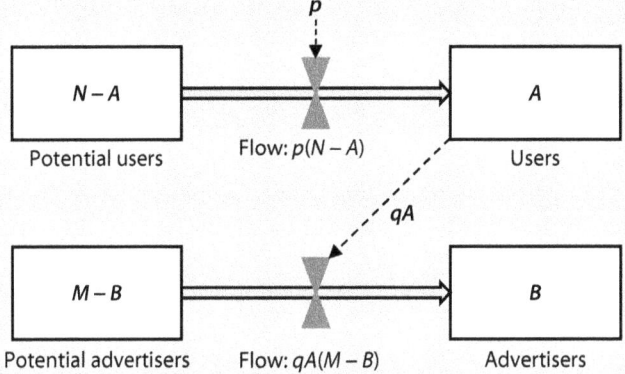

Fig. 10.2 Two-sided platform with cross-side network effects. (Authors' own figure)

be constants; otherwise, the equations cannot be solved analytically. The flow parameters may depend on other factors such as price, service promotion, and visibility. This is not included in this simple model where the aim is to show how the growth in one customer segment may influence the growth in the other customer segment.

The flow rate of customers is equal to the number of users adopting the service per unit time. This is, by definition, equal to the time derivative of the number of customers having adopted the service at given time. Hence, the flow of customers of type $A = dA/dt = p(N - A)$ and the flow of customers of type $B = dB/dt = qA(M - B)$, where $N - A$ and $M - B$ are potential customers who have not adopted the services yet. This gives the following set of coupled first-order differential equations for the evolution of the two markets:

$$\frac{dA}{dt} = p(N - A),$$

$$\frac{dB}{dt} = qA(M - B).$$

The first equation is solved immediately giving:

$$A = N\left(1 - e^{-pt}\right).$$

Inserting this in the second equation gives:

$$\frac{dB}{dt} = qN\left(1 - e^{-pt}\right)(M - B)$$

with solution:

$$B = M - Me^{-q(Nt + A/p)}.$$

For small t, B increases as:

$$B = \frac{MNpqt^2}{2},$$

which is much slower than linear increase for small values of t.

The evolution of the relative market size (A/N and B/M) is shown in ◘ Fig. 10.3. The abscissa is the time in years, the ordinate is the relative number of customers, and the flow parameters in the example are $p = 0.17$ and $qN = 0.21$.

Because of the feedback from customer-side A to customer-side B, the growth of type-B customers will follow an S-curve and lagging the growth curve for type-A customers. In the example, it takes about 6 months until 10% of the market of type-A customers has been captured. At that time, only about 0.5% of the potential market of type-B customers has been captured. It takes 2 years to capture 10% of the market of type-B customers. If the revenues depend only on the number of type-B customers, the cross-side network effect may result in too small revenues to sustain the service initially. The service may then be prematurely terminated.

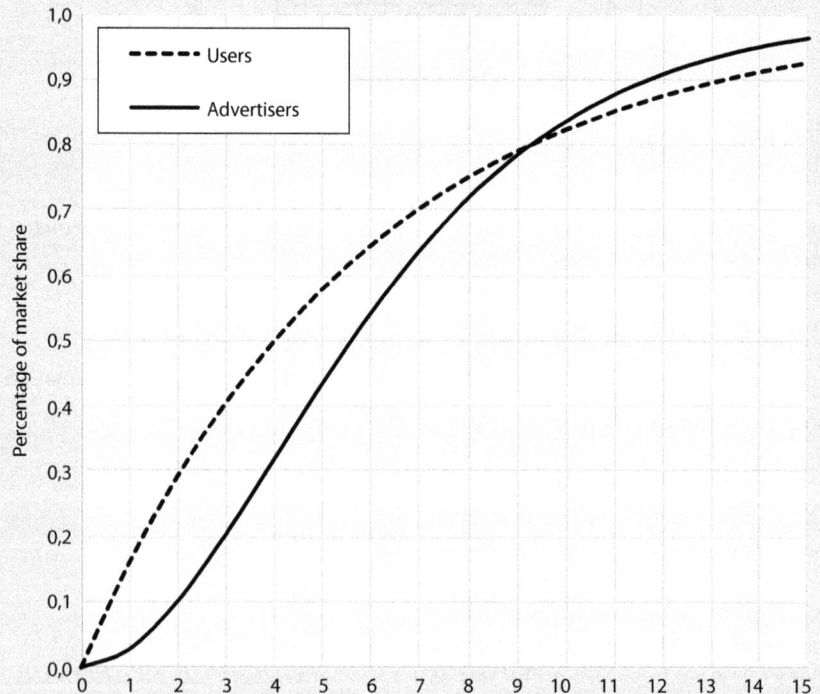

Fig. 10.3 Temporal market evolution for a two-sided platform. The parameters used are $p = 0.17$ and $qN = 0.21$. (Authors' own figure). The abscissa is the time in years

10.3 · Network Effects and MSPs

Case Study 10.1 Growth of Facebook

The theory in ▶ Box 10.1 can be used to study the temporal evolution of Facebook. ◘ Figure 10.4 shows the evolution of users and revenue of Facebook from 2008 to 2019 (Facebook's annual revenue from 2009 to 2019, 2019; Number of monthly active Facebook users worldwide as of 4th quarter 2019, 2020). The revenues are assumed to be proportional to the potential number of advertisers. The theoretical curves are calculated using the formulas of ▶ Box 10.1 with parameters $N = 7.8 \times 10^9$ (the current world population), $M = 1.9 \times 10^8$ (the current worldwide number of companies—as estimated by ▶ datapo.com), $p = 3.7 \times 10^{-2}$, $qN = 1.9 \times 10^{-2}$, and the average revenue generated per advertiser is 10 USD. The similarity between theoretical and observed curves is striking.

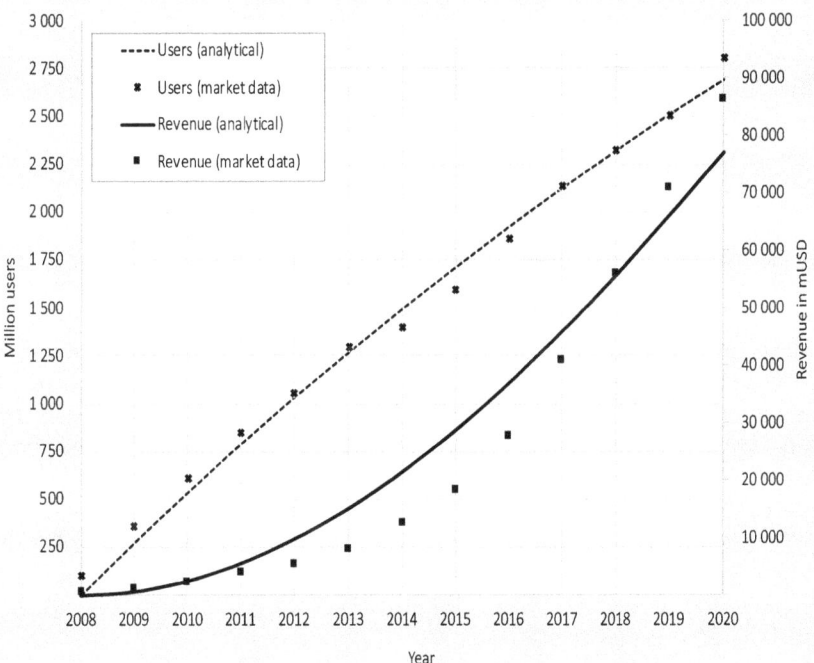

◘ **Fig. 10.4** Market and revenue evolution of Facebook. (Authors' own figure)

The simple model in ▶ Box 10.1 shows that the network effects may lead to slow service adoption by one (or even both) user groups in two-sided markets. Strategically, this may deceive the platform provider to believe that this user group will not adopt the service and, therefore, prematurely abandon it. This is a general problem associated with positive network effects as explained in ▶ Chap. 8 and shown mathematically in ▶ Chap. 18. This problem is particularly vital if the revenues of the platform provider depend mainly on the service of the customer group subject to the positive network effects. The revenues of Facebook depend almost entirely on the number of advertisers they can capture, which, in turn, depends strongly on the number or users of the social platform. For this reason, the revenues of Facebook increased slowly initially as shown in ► Case Study 10.1.

The networks effects of MSPs consisting of ordinary users and advertisers (e.g., Facebook) can then be summarized as follows. The number of ordinary users enforces a strong positive network effect on the number of advertisers. The number of advertises, on the other hand, will have little or no effect on the number of ordinary users so that the there is only cross-side network effects in the direction from users to advertisers. There are no network effects among advertisers though some of them may be competitors. Among the ordinary users, there are strong positive network effects; this is a major cause of growth of this type of MSPs.

In the electronic marketplace consisting of sellers and buyers (e.g., eBay), the sellers prefer many buyers, and the buyers prefer many sellers. Therefore, this platform has positive cross-side network effects. On the other hand, the existence of many sellers means increased competition among seller, possibly generating a weak negative same-side network effect. There is generally no same-side positive network effect concerning buyers; however, weak network effects may be present generated by user reviews and word of mouth.

10.4 Business Ecosystem and MSPs

One generic model for MSPs consists of six types of stakeholders in addition to the platform itself: content providers, advertisers, developers, professionals, merchants, and consumers (Gautier & Lemesch, 2020). A platform may offer services to all six categories or to only some of them. Similarly, several stakeholders belonging to the same category receiving similar or different services from the platform may be connected to the platform so that the overall ecosystem of the MSP may be overly complex. The configuration is shown in ◘ Fig. 10.5.

Content providers may use the platform for streaming of media (Spotify), offering specialized content to certain user groups (e.g., via Facebook), production and publishing of digital content (e.g., Google's YouTube and Amazon's Kindle), and support of video games (Facebook).

Advertisers use the platform for marketing, promotion, campaigns, publicity, and targeted and personalized advertisements, usually based on information the platform has gathered about each individual customer. This is a primary business of, for example, Facebook and Google.

Developers use the platform to develop new services or goods, most notably, apps for Apple's App Store and Google's Play Store.

Professionals are companies or organization receiving services that are used in their own production of digital or physical goods, for example, cloud computing, production of statistics (e.g., based on user data from Facebook, Google, or Amazon), online accounting support, collaboration services (e.g., iWork from Apple), document sharing, backup and security services (e.g., WorkDocs from Amazon), and physical or digital delivery services.

10.5 · Trade Process of MSPs and Resellers

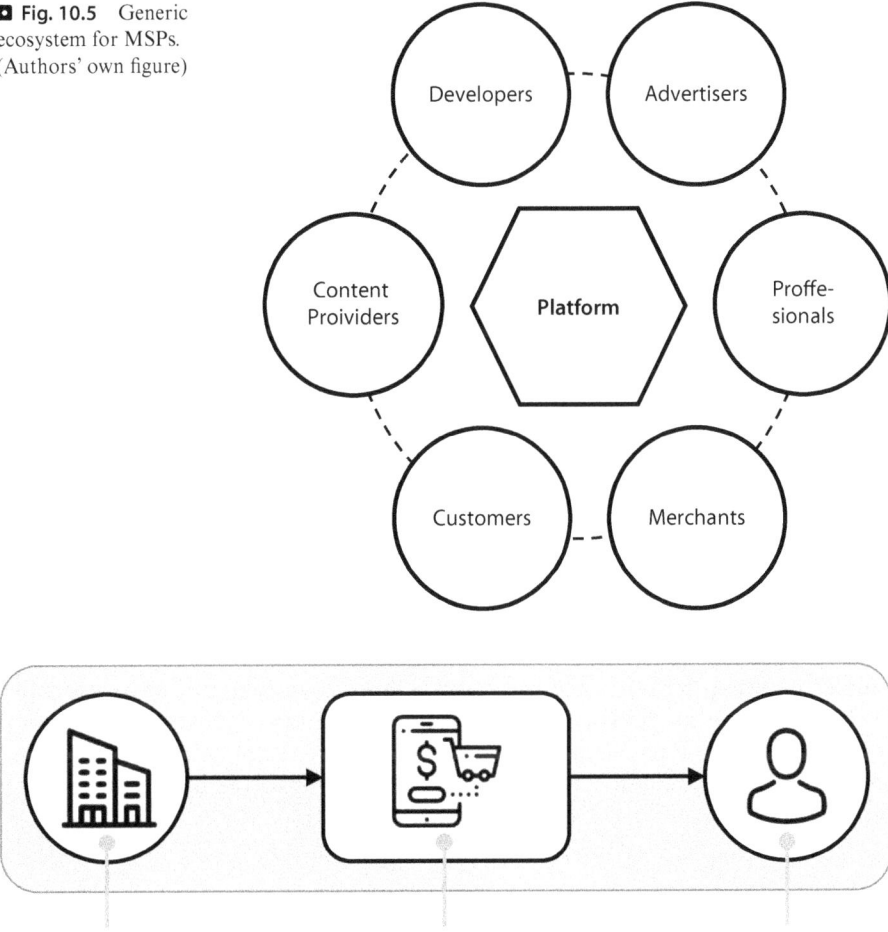

Fig. 10.5 Generic ecosystem for MSPs. (Authors' own figure)

Fig. 10.6 The reseller. (Authors' own figure)

Merchants use the platform for online shopping and payment of both physical and digital goods.

Consumers are the end users of digital services using smartphones, tablets, and other computers to access and process the information, or they are the receivers of physical goods ordered over a digital platform.

10.5 Trade Process of MSPs and Resellers

The MSP is one of several ways to organize a company. Another common type of organization is the *reseller* illustrated in ◘ Fig. 10.6. The reseller purchases goods and services from a producer and resells these goods and services to the buyer. The buyer receives the goods and services from the reseller, who, in turn, receives payment from the buyer.

One important requirement for being an MSP is that the platform enables a direct contact between the user groups attached to it. An electronic marketplace, such as eBay, is different from a supermarket in this respect. The supermarket is not an MSP since there is no direct contact between the shopper and the supplier. The supermarket is a reseller. On the other hand, eBay may sell the same goods as the supermarket, but eBay is an MSP since there is direct contact between supplier and buyer. For similar reasons, a taxi company is not an MSP, while Uber is.

An example of a reseller is Amazon: Amazon buys books from publishers and resells them to readers in the same way as any other bookstore. Resellers of telecommunications services are another example of resellers—they purchase bulk traffic capacity from a network operator and resell it in subscription packages to the customers.

The MSP platform may be quite simple. It may consist of a single app loaded down from the Internet and processed on the smartphones of the supplier and the customer. In other cases, the platform may be complex such as the platforms of Google and Facebook. The MSPs may then be companies ranging in size from one-person enterprises to large corporations. Most sharing economies are two-sided or multisided platforms.

◻ Figure 10.7 illustrates a trade process for an MSP. The MSP mediates contact between the seller and the buyer. Observe the similarities between the MSP and the value network in ▶ Chap. 8. The trade—including the flow of goods, services, and payment—is done directly between the seller and the buyer and facilitated by the MSP. The MSP is not directly involved in the exchange of goods.

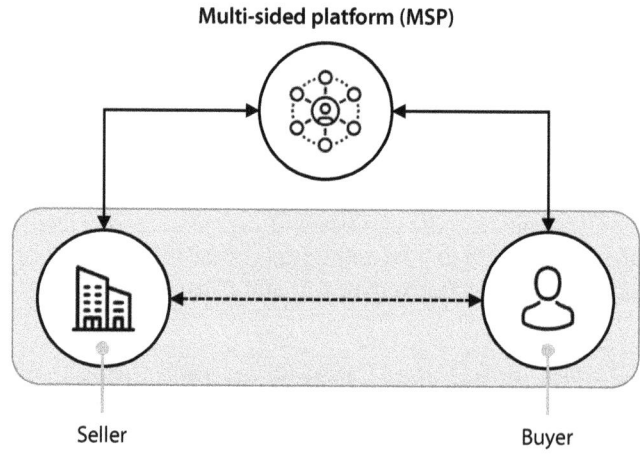

◻ **Fig. 10.7** The trade process of multisided platforms. (Authors' own figure)

10.6 Conclusions

The multisided platform (MSP) provides services to two or more user or customer groups at the same time. To be an MSP, there must be interactions between the groups providing benefits for each user group. The interactions between the groups are the cross-side network effects. This gives rise to complex business ecosystems consisting of several types of stakeholders and the numerous interactions between them. This makes the analysis of MSPs considerably more complex than businesses offering services to a homogenous group of customers.

Most businesses in the digital economy are multisided platforms. Therefore, the understanding of how interactions take place in these platforms is essential in the analysis of price formation within each individual user group, how the platform configuration generates revenues, and how competition takes place in the MSP market. Competition is particularly challenging since competition may take place not only between similar platforms but also with platforms in different business segments, for example, Facebook and Google compete for attracting advertisers.

Several MSPs offer services for free to some user groups, while other user groups pay for the services. This flexibility is one reason for being an MSP. The revenues of the MSP are then determined by the strength of the cross-side network effect these users impose on the customers paying for the services. In such cases, standard economic demand/supply analysis may be meaningless.

Finally, several MSPs are de facto monopolies in one of their business segments (e.g., as social medium) while competing in other segments.

❓ Question 10.1 Three-Sided Markets

Postmates is a logistics company mediating between companies having goods to deliver, engaging couriers for delivering the goods, and customers. Illustrate Postmates as an MSP and its associated user groups. Identify same-side and cross-side network effects within and between user groups. Which of the user groups contribute to Postmates' revenues?

❓ Question 10.2 Multisided Platform Laws

Discuss whether Metcalfe's law and Odlyzko-Tilly's law can be applied to multisided platforms.

❓ Question 10.3 YouTube

What is the ecosystem of YouTube? Who generates the revenues? Identify cross-side and same-side network effects.

✅ Answer 10.1

The configuration of Postmates is shown in the figure. The platform serves three user groups: companies (restaurants and merchants) selling the goods, the couriers transporting the good to the customers, and the customers ordering the good. Referring to ◘ Fig. 10.5, these correspond to merchants, professionals, and customers. The companies selling the goods contribute with revenue to Postmates. Postmates pays

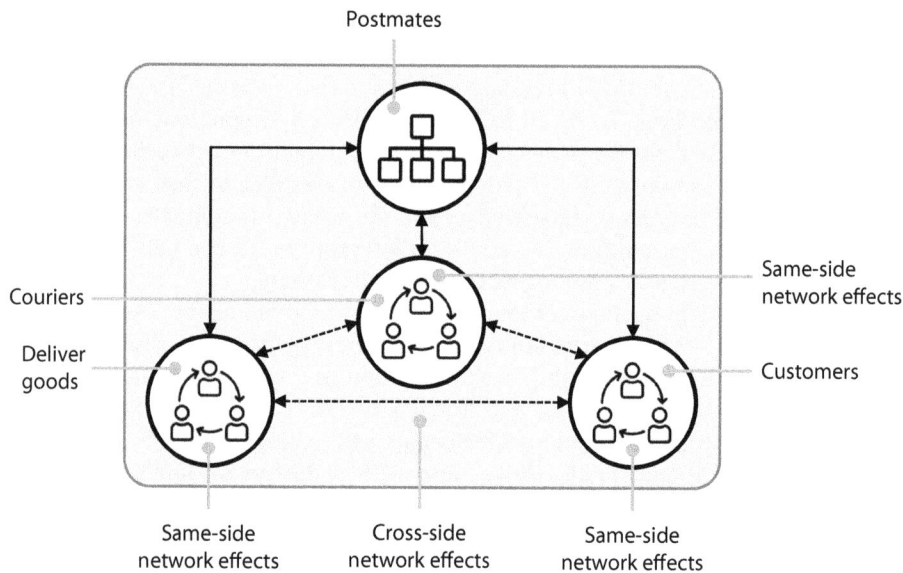

Fig. 10.8 Network effects in Postmates

the couriers for transporting the goods. The customers pay the company delivering the good, where the price also covers the cost of engaging couriers.

There are cross-side network effects between all three groups. The more sellers, the more customers, and the more couriers. The more customers, the more seller, and the more couriers. There are no significant same-side network effects (● Fig. 10.8).

✓ Answer 10.2
Yes. In an MSP, there are cross-side network effects. Metcalfe's law or Odlyzko-Tilly's can be applied to calculate the strength of the network effects or the value that each user group represents. In ► Box 10.1 and ► Case Study 10.1, Metcalf's law was used to do this.

✓ Answer 10.3
The stakeholders are uploaders, users receiving free services, viewers paying for premium services, content providers channeling information through YouTube, and advertisers. The revenues are coming from advertisers and viewers paying for premium services.

Cross-side network effects:
- The more uploaders, the more viewers.
- The more viewers, the more uploaders.
- The more viewers, the more advertisers.

Same-side network effect: uploaders stimulate other uploaders.

References

Ardolino, M., Saccani, N., Adrodegari, F., & Perona, M. (2020). A business model framework to characterize digital multisided markets. *Journal of Open Business: Technology, Markets, and Complexity, 6*, 1–23.

Facebook's annual revenue from 2009 to 2019. Statista, 2019.

Gautier, A., & Lemesch, J. (2020, January). Mergers in the digital economy. CESifo working paper No. 8056.

Hagiu, A., & Wright, J. (2015). Multi-sided platforms. *International Journal of Industrial Organization, 43*, 162–174.

McAfee, & Brynjolfsson, E. (2017). *Machine, platform, crowd: Harnessing our digital future*. W. W. Norton & Company.

Number of monthly active Facebook users worldwide as of 4th quarter 2019. Statista, 2020.

Sanchez-Cartas, J. M., & Leon, G. (2018). *Multi-sided platforms and markets: A literature review*. Universidad Politecnica.

Path Dependence

Contents

11.1 Definitions – 166

11.2 Competition and Path Dependence – 168

11.3 Impact of Churning – 169

11.4 Path Dependence and Lock-In – 172

11.5 Conclusions – 174

References – 176

© The Author(s), under exclusive license to Springer Nature Switzerland AG 2021
H. Øverby, J. A. Audestad, *Introduction to Digital Economics*, Classroom Companion: Business,
https://doi.org/10.1007/978-3-030-78237-5_11

Learning Objectives
After completing this chapter, you should be able to:
- Understand the concepts of diminishing returns, increasing returns, and path dependence in the context of the digital economy.
- Explain why some economic systems—contrary to standard microeconomic theory—may end up in one out of several equilibrium states depending on internal and external forces acting on the market.
- Analyze how path dependence is generated by positive feedback from the market or by external forces.

11.1 Definitions

The general assumption in conventional economic theory is that the markets are controlled by negative feedback that reduces any deviation away from market equilibrium. This is referred to as markets with *diminishing returns* in standard economic theory. These markets are in fine-tuned dynamic equilibrium, in which no change takes place in the composition of the market. The law of diminishing returns ensures that this equilibrium state always will be reached and that this state always is the best choice.

> **Definition 11.1 Law of Diminishing Returns**
> If additional units of one production factor are employed, with all other held constant, the output generated by each additional unit will eventually decrease (Bannock et al., 1998).

The traditional view in microeconomics is that the market is governed by the balance between supply and demand and that all competitors have perfect knowledge about the market. In this simple market theory, an evolving market (e.g., the mobile phone market) will end up in a single predetermined equilibrium state, regardless of initial conditions and events taking place as the market evolves. In accordance with the law of diminishing return, any deviation away from this equilibrium will quickly be counteracted by negative feedback such that the market returns to the equilibrium state. If a new competitor is added to the market, the market will initially be out of balance but will soon reach a new equilibrium state uniquely determined by the new number of competitors.

In 1990, Brian Arthur wrote an article in *Scientific American* in which he claimed that many dynamic markets will not settle in an equilibrium state predicted by conventional economic theory (Arthur, 1990). This is the case for products where there is positive feedback from the market (or network effects; see ▶ Chap. 8) resulting in increasing returns (sales stimulate more sales). As explained above, diminishing returns imply that the market contains a single stable equilibrium state. The evolution of markets with increasing returns due to market feedback is different. Already in 1986, Arthur and coworkers had shown mathematically—using a method called

11.1 · Definitions

Polya urns—that, in general, several equilibrium states may exist in systems with positive feedback (Brian et al., 1986). This implies that these systems may settle in an arbitrary equilibrium state depending on initial conditions or internal and external forces acting on the system. This is called *path dependence* or "history matters" (Liebowitz & Margolis, 1995). The chosen equilibrium is quite arbitrary and may not be the best choice. This is contrary to standard economic theory postulating that the market's choice is always best.

> **Definition 11.2 Path Dependence**
> *Path dependence* means that the path of evolution of the market of a good depends on the initial state of the market (e.g., number of early adopters), network effects (e.g., bandwagon effects), and external events taking place during the evolution of the market (e.g., product visibility and searching costs). The different paths may end up in different equilibrium states.

Network effects are common in the digital economy. Therefore, it is reasonable to assume that path dependence will be common in digital markets and that these markets may end up in one out of several equilibrium states. There is no universal rule by which the market picks any such state as in standard economic theory: the choice is quite arbitrary. The path the evolution will follow depends on customer preferences, random external events, actions taken by stakeholders, and the timing of these random events.

> **Definition 11.3 Law of Increasing Returns in Classical Economic Theory**
> The *law of increasing returns* in classical economy states that the returns from one period to the next are more than proportionate. This is also referred to as *economies of scale* (Bannock et al., 1998).

The law of increasing returns implies that if the returns during a period T are R, then the returns during the next period T are larger than R. One common cause of increasing returns in the production industry is that the revenues per unit produced increase because the production cost per unit is reduced as the production volume increases (at least up to a certain point). Sometimes this law is referred to as *the law of diminishing cost*.

The law of increasing returns must be treated differently in the digital economy since the cost of production is of no relevance for most digital goods. As explained in ▶ Chap. 6, the marginal cost of digital goods is zero so that the cost of producing one unit of a digital good is also zero. In the digital economy, increasing returns, therefore, usually mean that the number of users adopting a digital good during a period T is larger than the number of users who adopted the good during the previous period of length T. Returns do not refer to revenues in terms of money or valuables since, because the marginal cost is zero, the revenue per user may also be zero (ARPU = 0; see ▶ Chap. 6). As explained in ▶ Chap. 9, increasing returns are driven by positive feedback from the market, or in other words, increased market advantages generate further advantages.

A different definition of increasing returns is then appropriate for the digital economy.

> **Definition 11.4 Law of Increasing Returns in the Digital Economy**
> *Increasing returns* in the digital economy is generated by positive feedback; that is, if a company or product gains some advantage (e.g., increasing number of customers or more sales), it gains further advantages. These advantages may not generate direct revenues for the company, though they may generate indirect revenues (Arthur, 1990).

Different forces may drive competition in different directions. Such forces may be:
- External forces, for example, where one of the candidates is more visible and easier to find than the competitors (e.g., VHS vs Betamax, where more VHS than Betamax recorders were displayed in the shops)
- Internal forces, for example, network effects (bandwagon effects, word of mouth, "likes" buttons) in which people's preference for a product increases as other people buy it (e.g., Facebook vs Myspace)

The outcome is that new customers are more likely to choose one of the suppliers in favor of the competitors and that there eventually is a net churn of users from the competitors to this supplier. In some cases, this leads to the situation where one of the competitors captures the whole market. This is called a *winner-takes-all market*.

11.2 Competition and Path Dependence

Competition in digital markets with zero marginal costs (e.g., Facebook vs Myspace) or between technologies designed to different standards (e.g., VHS vs Betamax) may be subject to path dependence. Usually, only one of the competitors will survive so that the number of possible equilibrium states is equal to the number of competitors, for example, two for the VHS vs Betamax. It is not possible to predict beforehand which of the competitors will be the winner.

The evolution of multisided platforms is a little more complex. Facebook is a multisided platform where one of the business sectors is social networking services. In the competition with Myspace, arbitrary events generated a path in which Facebook ended up as a de facto monopoly for social networking services (see ▶ Case Study 11.2). Facebook is not a de facto monopoly in the other market segments of the platform. In the advertising market, it competes with several other companies, most notably, Google. These market segments will end up in a state which, for Facebook, depends on the number of users of the social networking services and, for Google, the number of people using the search engine. Neither of them will become a monopoly in the advertisement sector since both are important advertisement channels targeting different user groups.

One of the most analyzed examples of the competitive war between technological standards is the competition between VHS and Betamax. The case is also used as pedagogic example of path dependence because it illustrates in a simple way how path dependence may arise and lead to a winner-takes-all situation (see the Wikipedia article for more details (Wikipedia, n.d.)).

> **Case Study 11.1 Videotape Format War**
>
> VHS and Betamax were two competing standards for video cassette recorders (VCR) in the late 1970s and the early 1980s. They were incompatible standards since cassettes designed to the VHS standard did not work with Betamax and vice versa. After intense competition, it became clear in the early 1980s that VHS won the videotape format war and eventually captured 100% of the market.
>
> Betamax was developed by SONY and released on the consumer market in May 1975 in Japan and on the US market the following November. VHS was developed by Matsushita (now Panasonic) and released in 1976 in Japan and 1977 in the USA. The market for VCRs, offering a new form of home entertainment, grew quickly.
>
> Betamax had the first mover advantage since it was the only VCR available in the USA during the first year. Introduction of VHS in the USA in 1977 triggered full competition between Betamax and VHS. Standard microeconomic theory predicts that both standards would prevail and share the market. However, it turned out that VHS and Betamax were operating in a market with strong network effects which, eventually, became a winner-takes-all market.
>
> The VHS cassette could record longer TV shows than the Betamax cassette due to its larger size. Of particular importance was the fact that VHS could record a complete football match (up to 3 hours) on a single cassette. This, combined with lower prices, shifted the market share leadership from Betamax to VHS in the late 1970s. As a secondary effect, the number of VHS recorders on display in retailer shops gradually increased, resulting in a bandwagon effect in favor of VHS.
>
> This led producers of movies and other content to favor VHS. In the beginning, content producers made their titles available on both Betamax and VHS; however, when VHS took the market lead, they gradually stopped producing content for Betamax, strengthening the position of VHS. Finally, VHS was locked into the path of dominating the VCR market entirely.

11.3 Impact of Churning

In markets with several competitors offering similar services, users may, from time to time, change their affiliation with one supplier for another. This is called *churning*. Churning is common in the mobile phone market. Churning causes fluctuations in the market shares of each mobile network operator but has kept the distribution of average market shares rather stable over long periods of time. This is so because the churn from one operator to another has on average been equal to the churn in the opposite direction.

In other markets—for example, VHS vs Betamax and Facebook vs Myspace—this is not the case, and a net churn in favor of one supplier takes place.

▶ Box 11.1 contains a simple mathematical model for competition between two technologies (e.g., VHS vs Betamax) showing the impact churning has on the growth and decline of the two technologies.

Box 11.1 Mathematical Model for the Temporal Evolution of Markets with Churning

This is a simple mathematical model for the temporal evolution of a winner-takes-all market (e.g., VHS vs Betamax). For simplicity, assume that the adoption rate (p) for new customers is the same for both technologies. This does not change the validity of the arguments: it just makes the computation simpler.

There is a bandwagon effect causing a net churning flow from technology 2 (e.g., Betamax) to technology 1 (e.g., VHS). The model is shown in ◘ Fig. 11.1.

The differential equations for the dynamics of this system are:

$$\frac{dA}{dt} = p(N - A - B) + rB,$$

$$\frac{dB}{dt} = p(N - A - B) - rB,$$

in which dA/dt and dB/dt are the change in the number of users of technology 1 and technology 2, respectively, $N - A - B$ is the number of users that have not adopted any of the technologies at time t,

and rB is the flow of churners technology 1 receive from technology 2. Since p is the adoption rate, $p(N - A - B)$ is the total number of new adopters per unit time adopting either technology 1 or technology 2.

Adding the two differential equations gives:

$$\frac{dA}{dt} + \frac{dB}{dt} = \frac{d(A+B)}{dt} = 2p(N - A - B).$$

This is a separable differential equation in $A + B$ with solution:

$$A + B = N\left(1 - e^{-2pt}\right).$$

Inserting this in the second equation yields a linear differential equation for B:

$$\frac{dB}{dt} + rB = pNe^{-2pt}$$

with solution:

$$B = \frac{pN}{2p - r}\left(e^{-rt} - e^{-2pt}\right).$$

This gives for A:

11.3 · Impact of Churning

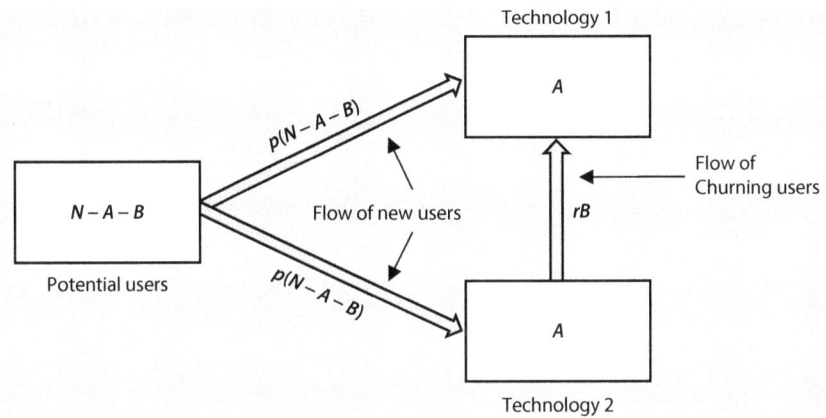

Fig. 11.1 Mathematical model with churning from technology 2 to technology 1. (Authors' own figure)

$$A = N\left(1 - e^{-2pt}\right) - B = N - \frac{N}{2p - r}\left[pe^{-rt} + (p - r)e^{-2pt}\right].$$

Figure 11.2 shows the evolution of the market for $p = 0.5$ and $r = 0.1$. The ordinate is the market share ($A/N, B/N$), and the abscissa is the number of years after the technology was introduced.

In this model, there is a net churning from technology 2 to technology 1, and technology 1 captures the whole market in the end. If the net churning had been from technology 1 to technology 2, then technology 2 would have captured the whole market. The alternative the market chooses cannot be predicted by standard economic theory. Both alternatives are stable equilibria, and which of them is finally chosen is path dependent.

The theoretical market evolution shown in Fig. 11.2 is not too different from the actual evolution of the VHS and Betamax markets as described in ▶ Case Study 11.1. After about 4 years VHS had captured almost 60% of the US market, and after 13 years VHS controlled more than 90% of that market.

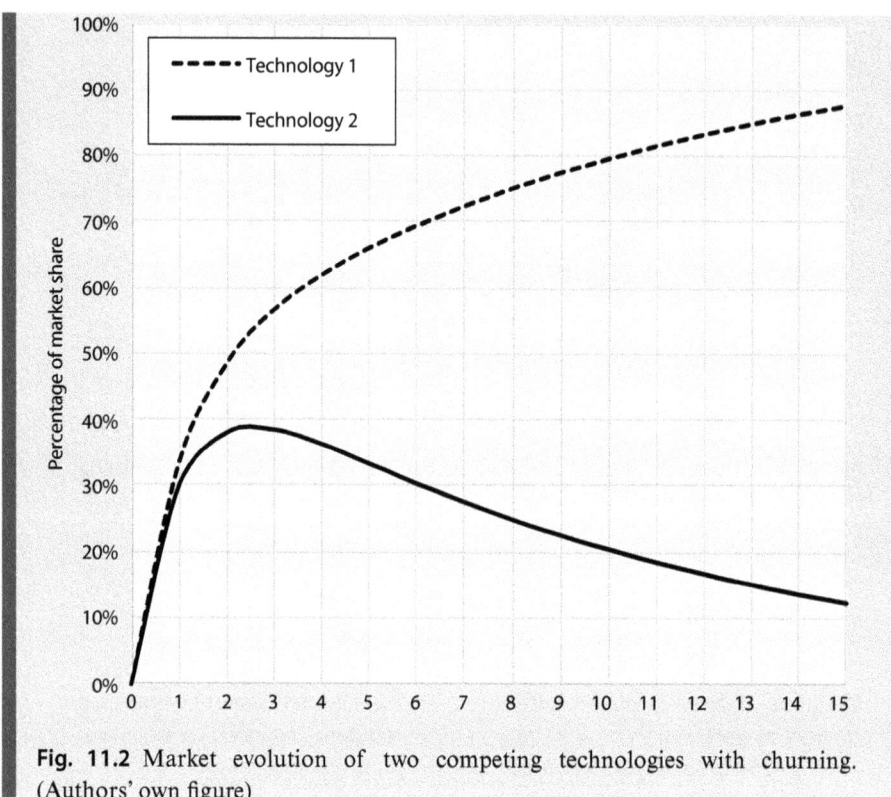

Fig. 11.2 Market evolution of two competing technologies with churning. (Authors' own figure)

11.4 Path Dependence and Lock-In

Path dependence may cause strong vendor lock-in in which one supplier dominates the market entirely. In such markets, it is almost impossible for new vendors to enter the market to offer a competing product. VHS vs Betamax is such a case. Another case is Facebook vs Myspace.

The process of lock-in in a market shared by two services is illustrated in ◘ Fig. 11.3. Initially, Service A has a small lead in market size compared to Service B. At some point in time, an external event boosts the popularity of Service B. This event may be caused by a successful advertisement campaign for Service B, word of mouth in which people start sharing positive experiences on Service B, or new features added to Service B making it more attractive. It is hard to predict what triggers a positive feedback event. However, the event gives Service B a boost in market size, and as network effects trigger the users of Service A to churn to service B, the market size of service B increases further, while that of service A

11.4 · Path Dependence and Lock-In

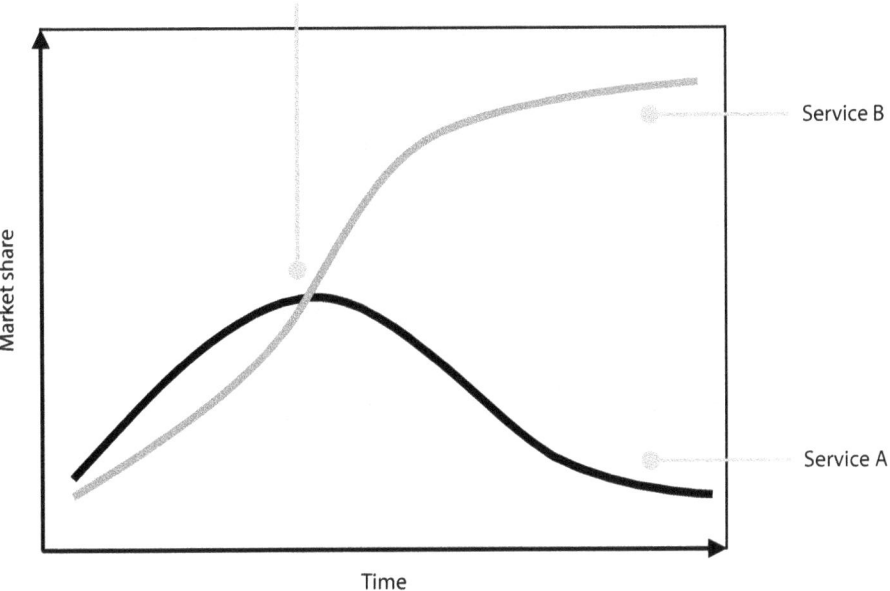

☐ **Fig. 11.3** Path-dependent evolution with one positive feedback event. (Authors' own figure)

becomes smaller. Eventually, Service B will capture the whole market. This is called *lock-in* if it, afterward, is almost impossible for anyone to compete with service B (see ► Chap. 12).

As an illustration of this concept, the competition between Facebook and Myspace is described in ► Case Study 11.2.

Case Study 11.2 Facebook vs Myspace

Facebook vs Myspace is a recent example of path dependence. Either of the two companies could have ended up as the market leader. However, early events triggered Facebook to take the lead and suppress the future growth of Myspace. Myspace was inaugurated on August 1, 2003, while Facebook was used for the first time on February 4, 2004. The early versions of Myspace and Facebook were rather similar from a user's point of view. Myspace had a market lead on Facebook until 2008, most likely caused by being first to the market. There is no evident reason why Facebook should have taken the lead in 2008. One possible explanation is that Myspace was a less-flexible service, building most of the Myspace content in-house, and focusing on music and entertainment. On the other hand, Facebook had a more open and flexible platform that allowed third-party providers to create content. They also focused on a social networking experience in which the users themselves created content for one another.

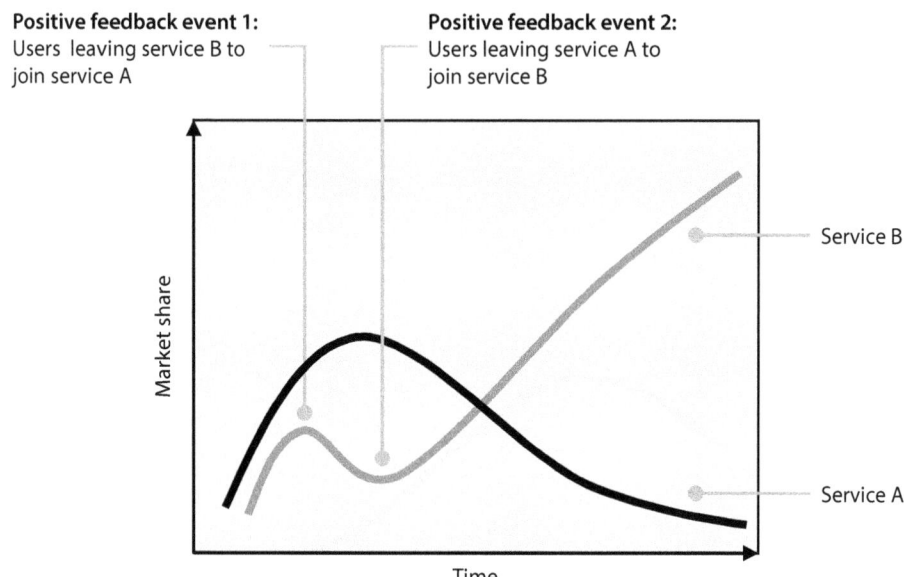

Fig. 11.4 Path dependent evolution with two positive feedback events. (Authors' own figure)

A succession of several events may alter the market, as shown in Fig. 11.4. In this example, a positive feedback event boosts the popularity of Service A (positive feedback event 1). The increased number of customers overloads the capacity of Service A, resulting in a negative network effect eventually reducing the number of users of Service A (positive feedback event 2). Service B may first lose users to service A, but later receive users from Service A when the popularity of Service A declines. The popularity of Service B is also boosted by positive feedback events, for example, after having introduced new features.

11.5 Conclusions

We have seen that several business cases in the digital economy cannot be explained by standard microeconomic theory. Microeconomic theory postulates that the market always ends up in a single predetermined equilibrium. Two cases analyzed in this chapter, VHS vs Betamax and Facebook vs Myspace, both end up being a winner-takes-all market. Either of the competitors could have won the market war so that there are two stable market equilibria in this case. That Facebook and VHS won the competition is just luck and help from external events working in their favor. The evolution of these markets is said to be path dependent.

Path dependence is caused by positive feedback from the market stimulating growth of some competitors resulting in loss of market shares for other competitors. Sometimes, one of the competitors will capture he whole market. As we have

11.5 · Conclusions

seen in this and previous chapters, positive feedback is common in the digital economy. Therefore, it is particularly important to be aware of path dependence and the influence it may have on both establishment of new businesses and competing with other businesses in the digital economy.

❓ Questions
1. AltaVista was launched in 1996 and Google was introduced on the international market in 1999. What happened to the two search engines? (See, e.g., Wikipedia articles on search engines).
2. Can the "likes" button trigger path dependency? Explain.
3. May path dependence explain why similar businesses, e.g., car dealers, tend to agglomerate geographically?

✅ Answers
1. AltaVista was inaugurated in December 1995, while Google appeared on the international market in 1999. AltaVista had an obvious first mover advantage over Google. Already in early 1996, 45% of the users preferred AltaVista for web search. In 2000, about 1 year after Google started operation, AltaVista had still 17% of the market, while Google had only 7%. Since then, the usage of AltaVista declined rapidly and soon more or less disappeared from the market, while Google increased their grip on the market and soon became the leading search engine, currently, with a market share of more than 60%. The reasons were that Google offered a more efficient search algorithm (causing positive network effects changing the path of evolution in favor of Google) and that AltaVista was taken over by Yahoo! (external path-changing event where the brand name disappeared from the market).
2. Yes. The "likes" button is a positive feedback mechanism from the market where a positive response may increase the popularity of a Facebook page (positive network effect), while a negative response may reduce the popularity of the page (negative network effect). See ▶ Chap. 9 for definitions of positive and negative network effects and positive and negative feedback.
3. Several factors causing agglomeration have been suggested:
   - If there are several similar vendors selling similar products (e.g., cars, shoes), more customers are attracted to the area and hence increasing the sales for each vendor.
   - It may be easier to attract workers with specialized skills to the region.
   - It may stimulate cooperation reducing development costs and enhancing research.
   - It is more likely that easily available support facilities will be established in the same area.

   These factors may then generate positive network effects attracting new businesses to the same area. It has been claimed that Silicon Valley grew up in this way.

References

Arthur, W. B. (1990). Positive feedbacks in the economy. *Scientific American, 262*, 92–99.
Bannock, G., Baxter, R. E., & Davis, E. (1998). *The penguin dictionary of economics* (6th ed.). Penguin Books.
Brian, A. W., Ermoliev, Y. M., & Kaniovski, Y. M. (1986). Strong laws for a class of path-dependent stochastic processes with applications. In V. I. Arkin, A. Shiraev, & R. Wets (Eds.), *Stochastic optimization* (Lecture notes in control and information sciences) (Vol. 81). Springer.
Liebowitz, S. J., & Margolis, S. E. (1995). Path dependence, lock-in, and history. *Journal of Law, Economics and Organization, 11*(1), 205–226.
Wikipedia. (n.d.). Videotape format war.

Further Reading

Arthur, W. B. (1994). *Increasing returns and path dependence in the economy*. University of Michigan Press.

Lock-In and Switching Costs

Contents

12.1	Introduction – 179	
12.2	Switching Costs – 180	
12.3	**Lock-In Mechanisms – 181**	
12.3.1	Spare Parts, System Updates, and Maintenance – 181	
12.3.2	Training – 181	
12.3.3	Incompatibility and Compatibility – 181	
12.3.4	Potential Loss of Information – 183	
12.3.5	Investments and Economic Lifetime – 183	
12.3.6	Difficult-to-Terminate Contracts – 183	
12.3.7	Loyalty Programs – 184	
12.3.8	Bundling – 184	
12.3.9	Search Algorithms – 184	
12.3.10	Product Tying – 185	

© The Author(s), under exclusive license to Springer Nature Switzerland AG 2021
H. Øverby, J. A. Audestad, *Introduction to Digital Economics*, Classroom Companion: Business,
https://doi.org/10.1007/978-3-030-78237-5_12

12.4	Lock-In Cycle – 185
12.5	Network Effects and Lock-In Cycle – 186
12.6	Lock-In and Market Regulations – 188
12.7	Conclusions – 191
	References – 192

Learning Objectives

After completing this chapter, you should be able to:
- Identify and classify lock-in mechanisms associated with a digital technology or service.
- Explain how network effects may cause lock-in and sometimes also winner-takes-all situations.
- Identify whether or not lock-in effects can be eliminated by market regulations.

12.1 Introduction

▶ Chapter 9 explains why network effects may cause lock-in in certain markets, and ▶ Chap. 11 illustrates how path dependence generated by network effects may drive the market into such states. This chapter considers more closely mechanism that can be deployed to acquire and maintain lock-in.

> **Definition 12.1 Lock-In**
> *Lock-in* incorporates all mechanisms that a company may use to keep its customers by establishing barriers to prevent customers to switch to another supplier. This is referred to as *vendor lock-in* (focusing on the vendor instigating lock-in), *customer lock-in* (focusing on the customer being locked in), or *proprietary lock-in* (focusing on the product or service into which lock-in takes place).

We will use the term lock-in for all three terms since they only display different perspectives of the same phenomenon.

Acquiring new customers is expensive since it often involves intensive marketing and expensive price campaigns. Therefore, the vendor must do whatever is possible to keep the customers. Churning is defined to be the act that a customer abandons the service offered by one provider for a competing service offered by another provider. Vendors want to reduce churning as much as possible by exploiting various lock-in mechanisms, for example, by making it expensive or inconvenient for users to switch to other suppliers.

Note that lock-in may lead to de facto monopolies such as in the standards war between Betamax and VHS (see ▶ Chap. 11). Lock-in combined with path dependence is also the reason why Facebook, and not Myspace, became the leading social networking medium on Internet. The wisdom is that the level of lock-in for a digital service significantly influences the evolution of market shares, competition, and formation of monopolies.

12.2 Switching Costs

> **Definition 12.2 Switching Costs**
> *Switching costs* are the direct and indirect costs for suppliers to capture customers from a competitor (*vendor switching costs*) and for a customer to switch to a new supplier of a good or service (*consumer switching costs*). The *total switching cost* is the sum of the cost for the supplier and the cost for the customer.

If the vendor's switching cost is V and the customer's switching cost is C, then the total switching cost is $S = V + C$.

For the vendor, there are two strategies (Amarsy, 2015):
1. To capture new customers, the vendor must make the switching cost for potentially new consumers as small as possible. In practice, this means that the vendor must compensate for expenses or inconveniences the customer may have for swapping supplier. This makes the switching costs for the vendor high.
2. On the other hand, the vendor must make the switching cost as high as possible for its own customer to discourage them from switching to a competitor. The switching costs should be so high that competitors are discouraged from trying to capture the customer.

In oligopolies, this may sometimes cause conflicting strategies, particularly, if the switching costs are purely monetary as illustrated in ▶ Example 12.1.

> **▶ Example 12.1 Competition in the Mobile Phone Market**
> Until about 2010, it was common for mobile operators to sell mobile phones to new customers for a much lower price than the actual market price for mobile phones to capture new customers. This reduced the switching costs for the consumer but increased them for the supplier. The total switching cost was unchanged. Since the mobile market is an oligopoly, the mobile operators were forced to play a prisoner's dilemma game, in which all suppliers were compelled to use the same pricing strategy (see ▶ Chap. 13 where prisoner's dilemma is explained). If not, they would capture fewer new customers, and the cost for own customers to switch to a competitor would be small. When the market for smartphones approached saturation, this practice was terminated, and the consumers had to pay the market price for smartphones. One reason for the new strategy was, of cause, that the operators had realized that subsidizing the phones was a bad strategy in markets that were saturated, as the mobile market in Europe had become at that time. In an oligopoly market where there are few new customers to capture, this strategy will not stimulate growth. The strategy will reduce the expenses of the customers but increase the costs and reduce the revenues of the mobile operators. ◄

The switching cost for the consumer is composed of several elements such as fees for terminating a subscription (now mostly nonexistent because of market regulation), lost advantages (conditional savings and discounts), additional work (installation and training of staff), possible loss of information (incompatible formats), hidden costs (additional equipment or functionality not included in the offer), inconvenience (updating cooperating systems, customers, or address lists), and surprises (the offer is not as good as promised). Some of the switching costs are direct costs (e.g., exit fees, training, or additional equipment), and some are psychological, emotional, or social ("the pain of losing an advantage is stronger than the pleasure of gaining the same advantage" (Kahneman & Tversky, 1992)).

The switching costs for the vendor may be introductory price offers (first month free of charge), discounts on equipment (mobile phone for a low price), training assistance (free training course for key employees), or free additional features (antivirus protection or backup storage).

12.3 Lock-In Mechanisms

A company may employ different strategies to lock in its users. Here are some of the main strategies (Shapiro & Varian, 1999).

12.3.1 Spare Parts, System Updates, and Maintenance

Systems where availability and dependability are critically important (e.g., power distribution, telecommunications, airlines, and large computer systems), it must be easy to obtain spare parts to keep the system up and running. The company may have a separate store of spare parts and skilled maintenance personnel, or they may have a contract with the equipment manufacturer to supply spare parts and repair at short notice. All this costs money. This leads to lock-in for the system owner because switching to a new supplier while the existing system is still in operation means a double set of spare parts (and related maintenance contracts).

12.3.2 Training

The situation is much the same as for spare parts. A new system—for example, a new type of aircraft—may require extensive training of staff for operations and maintenance. The same applies for a change of computer platforms from, for example, Microsoft to Mac, in which lock-in mechanisms usually favor Microsoft since they have the biggest market share.

12.3.3 Incompatibility and Compatibility

There are several examples where incompatible formats, procedures, or technologies may lead to lock-in. Some examples of lock-in caused by incompatibility are in
▶ Example 12.2. A more complex case is backward compatibility since it sometimes is used to avoid lock-in, while in other cases, backward compatibility creates lock-in.
▶ Example 12.3 discusses the effect backward compatibility may have on lock-in.

▶ Example 12.2 Lock-In by Incompatibility

Lock-in by incompatibility is best exemplified by the lock-in strategy of Microsoft known as *embrace*, *extend*, and *extinguish* (EEE) (See Wikipedia article: Embrace, extend, and extinguish):

- Embrace: base the product on a public standard also used by competitors.
- Extend: add features not in the standard that cause interoperability problems with other products based on the same standard.
- Extinguish: because of dominant market shares, the new product may become a de facto standard squeezing out competitors not having access to the extensions. The users are then locked into a Microsoft product.

App Store and Google Play Store are incompatible marketplaces for software applications for smartphones, and since the platforms are incompatible, the user cannot switch from an Android telephone to an Apple platform (or vice versa) without losing downloaded apps—the two marketplaces require incompatible types of smartphones.

Skype is an over-the-top technology incompatible with voice-over-IP (VoIP) technologies such as the technology used in 4G and 5G mobile systems. Both parties in a conversation need Skype software to encode and decode the speech samples. Skype is indistinguishable from other web services and is therefore not subject to specific user charges. This cause lock-in to Skype services, particularly, for long-distance telephone calls. Skype is just one example of incompatible file formats causing lock-in to a particular technology. ◀

▶ Example 12.3 Avoiding and Creating Lock-In by Backward Compatibility

One important aspect of standardization is built-in backward compatibility. This means that a new version of equipment or software can operate smoothly together with earlier versions. In many protocols (e.g., IP), the first information element in the format is the version number, allowing the computer to switch to the appropriate software for reading remaining parameters (e.g., IPv4 or IPv6). Equipping computers with software for both IPv4 and IPv6, lock-in to a particular network technology is avoided.

Backward compatibility of mobile phones is beneficial both for network operators and users—network operators may smoothly build out the network with new technology, and the users need not buy new phones to continue using the network. Some backward compatibility in mobile systems is built into the specifications (e.g., offering GSM, 3G, 4G, and 5G in the same network). Some backward compatibility is implemented by the manufacturers so that the same phone can be used in networks using different network technologies (e.g., 3G and the American CDMA standard and 2G, 3G, 4G, and 5G networks where the smartphone can attach to either of these technologies), hence making roaming independent of network technology. Other examples of backward compatibility are game consoles, reuse of fixed network technologies in mobile networks, and radios (DAB radios can receive both digital signals and analog FM signals). In these examples, backward compatibility does not cause lock-in; on the contrary, backward compatibility reduces or even eliminates switching costs.

Backward compatibility is also related to the "grandfather clause" where an existing standard (or system) continues to be in force after a new standard (or system) replacing

12.3 · Lock-In Mechanisms

it has been put into operation. The "grandfather" of mobile communications, GSM, is still used together with 3G, 4G, and 5G mobile systems. The MARISAT system, owned by COMSAT General, for satellite communications to ships was adopted by the intergovernmental organization INMARSAT as its first satellite system in parallel with systems developed by the organization itself to allow smooth transition from one technology to another and to avoid unnecessary lock-in to the old technology.

Microsoft products (e.g., Windows, Word, PowerPoint, and Excel) support backward compatibility. The backward compatibility of Microsoft products is beneficial for users of computer systems because it guarantees that documents written several years ago can still be read and modified using the current standard. The motive is obviously to make the Microsoft products more attractive and to increase the lock-in of Microsoft users.

Backward compatibility may then in some cases cause lock-in (e.g., to Microsoft products), while in other cases, backward compatibility reduces the switching costs of the users and does not lead to lock-in (e.g., mobile communications networks). ◄

12.3.4 Potential Loss of Information

If a company changes its computer platform, the new system may not support the old software. This may result in loss of information or instigate major work to be done to convert the software. Even if this is not the case, the belief that information may be lost for some unspecified reason may be enough to cause lock-in. Database systems tend to grow because of the fear that the removal of an old database may cause loss of information or that deleted information may turn out to be useful after it has been removed.

12.3.5 Investments and Economic Lifetime

Most expensive equipment and systems usually have long technical and economic lifetimes and cannot be replaced without substantial cost. The manufacturer of the system may then earn money on maintenance, by upgrading the system with new functionality and by expanding the system. This is the case, for example, for telecommunications equipment—long equipment lifetime (GSM is, for example, almost 30 years old and still in operation), together with expensive training and maintenance, may be an efficient lock-in of network operators over long periods of time.

12.3.6 Difficult-to-Terminate Contracts

Suppliers of services may impose real or perceived penalties upon customers trying to terminate the contract. Examples are:
- Loss of interests on savings.
- Paying back expenses for expensive training if the employer decides to quit the company before the end of a contractual period.
- Binding time for mobile subscriptions; see ► Example 12.4.

> ▶ **Example 12.4 SIM-Lock**
>
> SIM-lock implies that the smartphone will not accept a SIM from a different mobile operator either permanently or for a limited period. This is referred to as SIM-lock. Switching to another operator then implies that the customer must buy a new phone or pay a fee to the original operator to unlock the SIM. In the early years of mobile communications, such subscription contracts were common. This was one reason why operators heavily subsidize mobile phones, thereby reducing the direct switching costs for subscribers churning from a competing operator. This practice is now usually regulated by the authorities stimulating competition and reducing the power of dominating operators. In some countries, binding is not allowed at all, while in other countries, binding is allowed for a limited time (e.g., 1 year). A supplement to SIM-lock is to offer, as part of the subscription contract, non-transferrable insurance of the phone in case of damage. ◀

12.3.7 Loyalty Programs

Loyalty programs are used by, for example, airlines, hotels, and retailers to stimulate customers to purchase their services rather than those of competitors. Club membership is similar. Club members may get access to goods and services not available for non-members, or they may gain other advantages (e.g., lower price, priority, or gift certificates).

12.3.8 Bundling

Several suppliers bundle different products to make their offer more attractive, for example, offering television, on-demand streaming services, Internet access, telephony, and proprietary content (e.g., free music lists and movies) as one subscription. The interface equipment may also be owned by the provider or designed to proprietary standards so that switching also compels the customer to buy new hardware. The customer may also lose access to content.

12.3.9 Search Algorithms

This has to do with the inconvenience (cost and time) it takes a customer to find a particular product among millions of other products. By implementing efficient search algorithms, a company may ease the search for products causing lock-in of the customers. Amazon and eBay are businesses in the digital economy benefiting from efficient search algorithms. The same applies to Airbnb, Uber, booking services, and streaming of music, films, and video. The search algorithm is particularly useful to identify rare products in the long tail and stimulate sales of these products (e.g., Amazon).

Retailers may also benefit from efficient search algorithms picking out potential customers of a product. The retailer may then target advertisements and sales promotions directly at the customer. Facebook, Google, and influencers lock in advertisers and marketers by offering such algorithms. This is the reason why Facebook is so big in the advertisement business.

12.3.10 Product Tying

Product tying implies that the customer must purchase another product (called the tied product) in addition to the product the customer wants to buy. In some cases, this may lead to lock-in. For example, Apple initially sold iPhones in the USA together with a 2-year contract with the carrier Cingular (now AT&T) locking the customers involuntarily to this carrier (Honan, 2007). Microsoft Windows and Internet Explorer are also tied, making the market for independent browsers difficult because the strong lock-in of Microsoft Windows induces strong lock-in also of Internet Explorer. Product tying is generally forbidden in the USA, Europe, and elsewhere but is sometimes difficult to stop (Microsoft).

Google's suite of apps is also a tied good but, since it is free for manufacturers of mobile phones to install the apps and for users to download them, is not regarded by the US Supreme Court to be illegal. On the contrary, the Court found that the practice of Google was beneficial for innovation and sales of mobile devices in general (Sidak, 2015).

12.4 Lock-In Cycle

Shapiro and Varian illustrate the dynamics of lock-in using the simple diagram shown in ◘ Fig. 12.1 (Shapiro & Varian, 1999). The *lock-in cycle* is as follows:

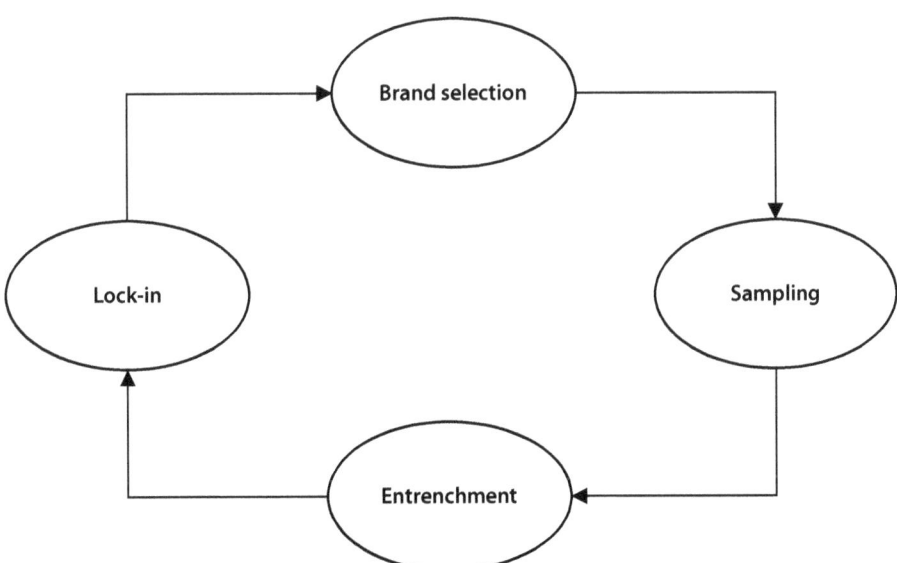

◘ **Fig. 12.1** The lock-in cycle. (Authors' own figure)

- The cycle starts when the user chooses a new product (*brand selection phase*). This can be anything from becoming a user of a social networking service, subscribing to music streaming services, building a new 5G mobile network, or purchasing a new smartphone. For the supplier, it is important to be more visible in the market and have a better reputation than the competitors. This then increases the likelihood that this supplier is among the brands the customer may investigate further.
- In the *sampling phase*, the customer may start using the new brand if it is available without binding conditions or, in case of large purchases, start negotiating price, amount, delivery conditions, and other contractual conditions with one or more suppliers. The supplier may offer inducements that stimulate the user to try the product, for example, offer the service for free for some time or offer free samples of the product. This may also include compensating costs associated with switching from another supplier. On the other hand, the customer should consider both the likelihood and consequence of being locked into a particular product and estimate the costs of later switching to another supplier.
- The *entrenchment phase* is entered when the customer chooses a particular brand. The strategy for the supplier is to build in mechanisms or incentives that gradually increase the switching cost of the customer. Note that a competitor can always compensate for pecuniary switching costs as explained above. Therefore, the most efficient lock-in mechanisms are those associated with irrecoverable loss (real or imagined) of assets such as information.
- In the *lock-in phase*, the customer switching cost has become substantial, discouraging the customer to switch to another supplier.

The suppliers may use the lock-in cycle as a tool in strategic analysis and planning. Decisions taken at each stage of the cycle may influence the growth of the future customer base and revenues. In the brand selection and sampling stages, it is important to attract lucrative customers and avoid customers that generate insignificant revenues. In the entrenchment phase, the supplier must build in mechanisms that discourage the customer to switch to another supplier, for example, making the customer dependent of information and procedures that cannot be provided by the competitors.

The diagram may then be used to visualize how path dependence occurs and traps the customer in different lock-in states.

12.5 Network Effects and Lock-In Cycle

Network effects, as explained in ▶ Chaps. 9 and 11, are among the strongest lock-in mechanisms, often resulting in de facto monopolies. This is usually not a vendor-controlled lock-in, but one that is caused by natural, strong positive feedback from the market in favor of a particular service or technology (e.g., Facebook vs Myspace).

The most prominent example of a company benefitting from strong network effects is Facebook. Facebook has grown into a monopoly because of strong network effects associated with the proficiency of effective formation of groups of

12.5 · Network Effects and Lock-In Cycle

"friends" and rapid dissemination of information within the groups. It has become virtually impossible for other suppliers to launch a similar or better service. To do so, the supplier must offer something that gives the users better experiences and must be able to build up communities at least as professionally as Facebook. It must also be possible for the users to move at least part of their Facebook content to the new website to switch to the new service provider. Otherwise, the users may lose information they have built up over time. For the users, loss of information may be a strong reason for not switching to a similar service offered by another supplier.

YouTube attracts users—both viewers and publishers—because of the popularity of the service (bandwagon effect) and strong network effects associated with reviews, recommendations by other viewers, and ratings. This also leads to lock-in since it is both difficult and expensive for competitors to build up a competing service that will give users access to such a volume of video content and provide so much visibility to publishers of new video material.

Lock-in to a technology is also often caused by network effects. The two most quoted examples are the adoption of the QWERTY keyboard (see ▶ Box 12.1) and VHS as a video cassette standard (see ▶ Chap. 11).

Box 12.1 The QWERTY Keyboard

Most of the keyboards in use today follow the QWERTY layout. This layout was generally adopted in the late nineteenth century after the success of the Remington 2 typewriter. The specific QWERTY layout was selected to make the typewriters work as smoothly as possible and to avoid jamming of the metal bars in the machine when two letters were typed in fast succession. Enforcing a standard, such as the QWERTY layout for keyboards, is beneficial—though not necessary—for both keyboard users and keyboard manufacturers. However, since the QWERTY layout became dominant, it was hard for competing layouts to enter the market since switching costs built up as more and more users adopted and were trained for the QWERTY layout. The layout is shown in ◘ Fig. 12.2.

The competing DVORAK layout (◘ Fig. 12.3) was patented in 1936 by Dr. August Dvorak. It is, by many, believed to be superior to the QWERTY layout, in terms of typing speed. However, when it was launched, it failed to get any market foothold due to high switching costs and the lock-in of QWERTY. Since the QWERTY layout had a dominating position in the market, it was hard to convince both users to learn and manufacturers to produce keyboards with the DVORAK layout. Today, almost all PCs, laptops, and smartphones use the QWERTY layout.

The choice of the QWERTY keyboard layout as a standard is also an example of path dependence. The early decision to adopt the QWERTY layout, which was perfectly logical at that time, locked keyboard designs into a path which would be extremely hard, if not impossible, to leave. Adopting the DVORAK keyboard layout would have been better for the society at large (though this conjecture is contested by, e.g., S. J. Liebowitz and S. E. Margoliz (Liebowitz & Margoliz, 1994)); however, the switching costs are currently too big for revitalizing DVORAK.

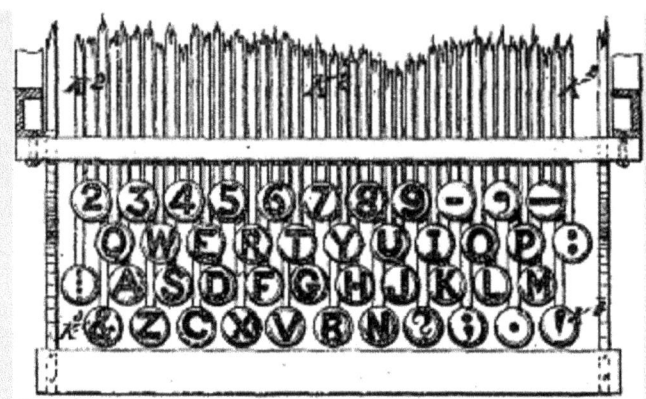

Fig. 12.2 The original QWERTY layout (By C.L. Sholes - U.S. Patent No. 207,559, Public Domain). Note that the "0" and "1" is intentionally missing to simplify design. The "0" can be reproduced as a "O," while a "1" can be reproduced as an "l" or an "I." (Source: Public Domain, ▶ https://en.wikipedia.org/wiki/QWERTY#/media/File:QWERTY_1878.png)

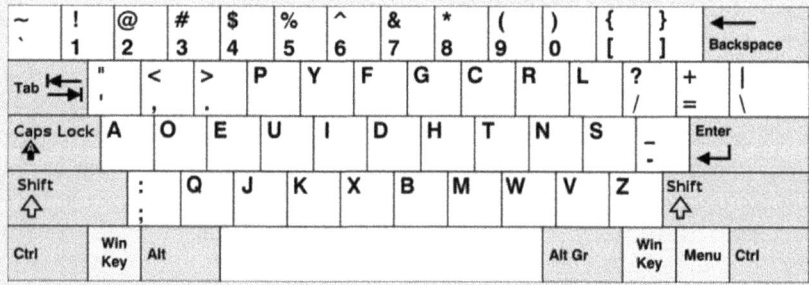

Fig. 12.3 The original DVORAK keyboard layout. (Source: Public domain, ▶ https://en.wikipedia.org/wiki/Dvorak_keyboard_layout#/media/File:KB_United_States_Dvorak.svg)

12.6 Lock-In and Market Regulations

One of the most important aspects of market regulation is to reduce the lock-in capabilities of service providers to enhance competition. Examples of such regulations include:
- Forbidding binding time for subscriptions (e.g., in telecommunications)
- Prohibiting loss of advantages (e.g., in insurance)
- Obligating number portability in telecommunications

The last item may require some explanation. Both fixed and mobile telephone numbers have historically uniquely identified both the operator and the subscriber

12.6 · Lock-In and Market Regulations

connected to the network. If there is more than one telephone operator in a country, each operator is, therefore, assigned different series of national telephone numbers. In this regime, the subscriber will get a new telephone number if he or she moves the subscription from one operator to another. This is inconvenient for the subscriber and causes lock-in since it may entail that hundreds of friends and other contacts must be updated about the new number. To avoid this type of lock-in, the regulatory authorities in several countries introduced number portability as a mandatory requirement around 2000. This implies that the subscriber keeps the same number if the subscription is moved to another operator. The networks must then be updated with facilities that route the calls to new destinations without any involvement of the users of the telephone network.

In telecommunications, some providers, particularly, incumbent or dominating operators, are facing a particular form of lock-in, namely, that they must continue to offer network services long after these services have ceased to be profitable. This is usually a public duty enforced by the authorities. Network providers must, for example, still offer fix telephone services even though more and more of the users are switching to mobile phones as their only telephone subscription, and mobile network operators must still support GSM even though they offer full national coverage with 4G technology.

◘ Table 12.1 summarizes how regulation can be applied to avoid lock-in and undesirable market behavior. The effect of the switching barriers is also indicated in terms of two broad categories:
- Economical barrier implies that there are considerable economic expenses associated with crossing the barrier.
- Psychological barrier implies that the major switching cost is associated with lack of knowledge of the outcome of the switching, for example, fear for losing information built up over time.

In some cases, it is impossible to regulate the market such that the switching barriers disappear, for example, expenses associated with spare parts, training, possible loss of information, and equipment lifetime. In other cases, switching costs may be reduced or eliminated by appropriate regulations.
- Termination of contracts without any expenses or inconveniences for the customer is in many cases made compulsory by regulations, for example, forbidding or limiting the use of SIM lock or requiring that advantages gained as customers are transferrable to new providers (e.g., in the insurance business).
- Bundling of services is also regulated in several countries. One case is associated with incumbents, that is, operators that were state monopolies before the general liberalization of telecommunications in 1998. To avoid that the incumbents misuse their market power, restrictions may be put on how these companies bundle their services in subscription packages, for example, combining telephony, Internet, mobile phone, and television in one subscription and thereby capturing all the individual markets. The physical connection, called the" local loop," from the subscriber to the local exchange is usually owned by the incumbent. To allow other operators to access the subscribers without digging new cable ducts, the market regulations require that the incumbent allowed other

Table 12.1 Lock-in and regulations in the digital economy. (Authors' compilation)

Lock-in mechanism	Regulation	Switching barriers if not regulated	Regulatory actions
Spare parts and maintenance	Impossible	Expensive for the customer	
Training	Impossible	Expensive for the customer	
Incompatibility	Some regulations but mostly unregulated	Expensive for the customer unless in regulated cases	Interoperability is required by law in certain cases (telecommunications networks) and between ASPs and ISPs
Loss of information	Impossible	May be expensive for customer; in many cases psychological barriers	
Economical lifetime	Impossible	Expensive for customer	
Contracts	Possible	May be expensive for customer	May be regulated by law (SIM-lock and number portability)
Loyalty programs	Possible	Psychological barrier	Some loyalty programs may be illegal by law
Bundling	Possible	Psychological barrier	May be illegal by law in some cases, e.g., bundling of ASP services provided by market dominating ISPs
Search algorithms	Possible	Convenient for the customer	Not regulated
Product tying	Possible	May be impossible to escape in many cases	Generally forbidden but there are exceptions

operators to use the incumbent's connection. This is called *local-loop unbundling* (LLU). LLU became mandatory in the USA in 1996 (Telecommunications Act of 1996) and the European Union in 2001.

– It is difficult to regulate markets with strong network effects. The reason is that the network effects tend to create de facto monopolies. If antitrust legislation is used to divide such monopolies into two or more independent competitors, the same network effects are again likely to turn this market into a new monopoly with only one of these companies surviving the competition. For the same reasons, it is also fruitless to economically or regulatory stimulate a new competitor to enter the market. In most cases, the market dominance of the existing monopoly is so strong that the newcomer will never grow to become a real competitor, or if it starts growing because the network effects are in favor of the newcomer, it may capture the whole market and become a new monopoly squeezing the old monopoly out of the market.

12.7 Conclusions

The key message is that lock-in is common in the digital economy. For vendors, there are two strategies:
1. To keep customers by making the switching costs for the customers (barriers to leave) as high as possible
2. To capture customers from competitors by making the switching cost for customers from competitors (barriers to enter) as small as possible

These strategies may be conflicting, particularly, in oligopoly markets. In some cases, this may lead to a prisoner's dilemma where the switching barriers for the customers are low, while the vendors carry all switching costs.

If there is a choice between two or more incompatible technological standards offering the same services to the consumers, such as VHS vs Betamax and QWERTY vs DVORAK, the market eventually chooses just one of them. This is a strong case of lock-in resulting in a winner-takes-all situation. To end up in this state depends on luck, random events, and network effects, or in other words, the selection of final state is path dependent.

Providers of social networking services may also end up as de facto monopolies (e.g., Facebook). Switching barriers in favor of the provider are built up by the users themselves by creating and joining communities of users: the more communities a user is member of, the larger is the psychological barrier to leave. Facebook is a good example of a case where there are no monetary barriers against switching but huge psychological ones.

❓ Questions
1. Which lock-in mechanisms tie a mobile network operator to the manufacturer of mobile networks?
2. Which lock-in mechanisms tie users to mobile network operators?
3. Are there any lock-in mechanisms binding users to Spotify?
4. Are there any lock-in mechanisms binding advertisers to Facebook?

✅ Answers
1. The most important mechanisms are:
   - Spare parts, maintenance, and system updates
   - Training
   - Economic lifetime

2. This depends on the country.
   - SIM-lock may be legal in some countries but illegal in others,
   - Number portability may be mandatory in some countries but not in others.
   - Service bundling may be legal or illegal.
   - The mobile operator may offer loyalty programs of some kind.
   - The operator may offer cloud services (computation or storage) that are net transferrable.

3. If the user switches to another music provider, the user loses the playing lists since they are not transferrable. The user also loses access to Spotify Codes and the opportunity to share playlists and other content.
4. The advantages of Facebook are the large number of users and the accurate knowledge about the users that the advertisers may use to target the advertisements. This is not a strong lock-in since there are no switching costs. The advertisers have several other advertisement channels. If an advertiser abandons Facebook for some reason, this may not cause significant reduction in sales because the same customers may be reached via other channels.

References

Amarsy, N. Switching costs: 6 ways to lock customers into your ecosystem. *Strategyzer*, July 27, 2015.
Honan, M. Apple unveiling iPhone. *PC World*, January 9, 2007.
Kahneman, D., & Tversky, A. (1992). Advances in prospect theory: Cumulative representation of uncertainty. *Journal of Risk and Uncertainty, 5*(4), 297–323.
Liebowitz, S. J., & Margoliz, S. E. (1994). Network externality: An unknown tragedy. *Journal of Economic Perspectives, 8*(2), 133–150.
Shapiro, C., & Varian, H. R. (1999). *Information rules: A strategic guide to the network economy*. Harvard Business School Press.
Sidak, J. G. (2015). Do free mobile apps harm consumers? *San Diego Law Review, 52*, 619–694.

Further Reading

Shapiro, C., & Varian, H. R. (1999). *Information rules: A strategic guide to network economy*. Harvard Business School Press.

Digital Monopolies and Oligopolies

Contents

13.1 Definition of Market Types – 194

13.2 Formation of Monopolies – 198

13.3 Formation of Oligopolies – 201

13.4 Conclusions – 205

References – 206

© The Author(s), under exclusive license to Springer Nature Switzerland AG 2021
H. Øverby, J. A. Audestad, *Introduction to Digital Economics*, Classroom Companion: Business,
https://doi.org/10.1007/978-3-030-78237-5_13

Learning Objectives

After completing this chapter, you should be able to:
- Identify which types of markets a digital enterprise is simultaneously serving.
- Explain how digital monopolies are formed.
- Perform strategic planning of a digital service based on market type.

13.1 Definition of Market Types

Before examining the formation of monopolies and oligopolies in the digital economy, we start with a short review of some basic market types. The market type refers to the sales of a particular good or service and not the company selling it. The company may be present in several market types offering different products in each type of market. In multisided markets (see ▶ Chap. 10), interactions exist between the different markets served by the platform, making the business model complex.

> **Definition 13.1 Monopoly**
> In the *monopoly* market, there is only one seller of the good, and there are no substitutes that the buyers may choose instead. In standard microeconomic theory, the monopoly may then alone determine prices and maximize its revenues.

What makes this definition problematic in the digital economy is that the price of several of the products offered in digital monopoly markets is zero; that is, there are no revenues generated by the customer in these markets. Some of the most lucrative companies in the digital economy are monopolies in one or more of their market segments offering services free of charge (e.g., Facebook and Google). Analyzing these markets using supply-demand curves is meaningless since the marginal cost of these goods are zero and, hence, independent of the volume of production (see ▶ Chap. 6).

We may distinguish between three types of monopolies:
- That a company is a *de jure monopoly* means that the company is protected against competition by law.
- That a company is a *natural monopoly* implies that the market is best served by a single supplier rather than being shared among several suppliers; for example, if the market is shared by several companies, the prices of the good may be higher (and production less effective) than if the market is served by only one company.
- That a company is a de facto *monopoly* means that the company has captured almost the whole market and that the barrier to entry is so high that new entrants are discouraged to try.

Natural monopolies and de facto monopolies are often considered to be the same thing. However, the two market types are different. The provider of the fixed telecommunications infrastructure may be a natural monopoly since it may be more expensive for the users if there are two or more competing providers offering identical infrastructure services. It is then the cost of infrastructure that justifies the natural monopoly in this case. Facebook is not a natural monopoly because the existence of several competing "facebooks" will neither cause additional costs for the customers nor reduce the versatility of the services offered to the users. Facebook has become a de facto monopoly; it is certainly not a natural (or necessary) monopoly.

A particular form of monopoly is the *territorial cartel*. These are businesses that operate as a monopoly within a region, for example, a country. Before the market was opened for competition, the telephone operators were regional cartels by this definition. When the AT&T (the US telephone operator owning most of the telephone infrastructure in the USA) was split into regional operating companies (the "Baby Bells") in 1982, these companies became regional cartels. Since these companies were not real competitors, they established a common research center, Bellcore, to share costs concerning telecommunications research. After liberalization of telecommunications in 1998 in Europe (1996 in the USA), regional cartels have almost disappeared from the telecommunications industry.

Definition 13.2 Oligopoly
In the *oligopoly* market, there are only a few sellers of the same product. Actions taken by a single competitor (e.g., lowering the price or offer complementary goods) may change the composition of the market; that is, redistributing market shares. If there are only two competitors, the market is called a *duopoly*.

One common strategy in oligopoly markets is that each firm must be aware of actions taken by the other firms (on, e.g., price and marketing) and respond accordingly. Actions taken by each company may then have direct impact on prices, competitive strength, and customer behavior. Examples of oligopolies in the digital economy are:
- Only a few mobile network operators offer services in each country forming local oligopolies.
- Visa and MasterCard share most of the international credit cards market.
- Microsoft and Apple are the dominating producers of operating systems for personal computers.
- Intel and Advanced Micro Devices manufacture most of the CPUs used in desktop computers.
- ARINC and SITA share the market for ground station-to-aircraft communications in Europe.

Definition 13.3 Monopolistic Competition
Monopolistic competition implies that there are many sellers in the same marketplace offering differentiated products, for example, shoes with different designs, materials, and quality. Other examples are restaurants and producers of cheese, soap, cars, and clothing.

The products in a monopolistic market may serve the same purpose, but differentiation makes the products unique so that they are not exact substitutes. The prices of products from one supplier are, in general, independent of the prices set by other suppliers.

In the digital economy, the markets for smartphones, personal computers, and television sets are monopolistic markets. The market for streaming services with a few big and many small competitors may also be regarded as a combination of monopolistic market and oligopoly.

> **Definition 13.4 Perfect Competition**
> *Perfect competition* is a theoretical model that describes markets with many sellers and buyers, where both sellers and buyers have perfect information about prices and customer preferences. Opposed to the oligopoly, the actions of a single competitor will not change the composition of the market.

In a perfect market, the products are indistinguishable, there is no transaction cost associated with the sales process, and there are no externalities that may favor some competitors or change the market rules. Real markets are only crude approximations of this model. Almost perfect competition may exist in commodity markets with many suppliers and undifferentiated goods where price is the only factor distinguishing the products from different suppliers. In the digital economy, perfect competition occurs in markets for digital freelance services—webpage design, brand design, visual design, writing, and translation services.

The above market types are related to the seller side only. There are also markets where the market behavior is determined by the number of buyers, that is, if there is only one or just a few buyers. There are several examples of such markets in the digital economy. All of them are multisided platforms (see ▶ Chap. 10).

> **Definition 13.5 Monopsony**
> A *monopsony* is a market with many sellers and only one buyer.

In the digital economy, the sellers in the monopsony are content providers, often independent artists, who see the monopsony provider as the only channel through which they can distribute their art. A monopsony with both buying and selling sides controls the whole market monopolistically, buying content cheaply and reselling it with considerable profit.

Example of a (de facto) monopsony in a multisided market is the video sharing service of YouTube. The three most important customer groups are producers of video clips, viewers, and advertisers. As monopsony, YouTube is a channel for pro-

13.1 · Definition of Market Types

ducers to distribute video clips to the viewers. Production and distribution of the video content is free of charge. As a monopoly, the video clips are provided to the viewers, also free of charge. Revenues are generated by the advertisers. The advertising market may either be regarded as an oligopoly if only the advertisement channels provided by the dominating stakeholders in the digital economy are counted or as a market with monopolistic competition if both large, small, and non-digital advertisement channels are counted.

Definition 13.6 Oligopsony
The *oligopsony* is similar to the monopsony. The only difference is that there are more than one (but just a few) buyers in the oligopsony market, while there is only one in the monopsony market.

The current music streaming market is an oligopsony with three major resellers: Spotify, Apple Music, and SoundCloud. The customers in this market are single artists and producers. Publishers of e-books are also an oligopsony with a few publishers dominating the market. The strategy of the oligopsony with both a buying and a selling side is more complicated than that of the oligopoly since it competes in two interacting markets at the same time: competing as buyer of content and competing as resellers of the same content.

◘ Table 13.1 and ◘ Fig. 13.1 summarize the various market models defined above. The table characterizes the markets in terms of the number of sellers, the number of buyers, and the barriers of entry.

◘ **Table 13.1** Market types. (Authors' compilation)

Market type	Number of sellers	Number of buyers	Barriers to entry	Examples in digital economy
Monopoly	One	Many	Impossible	Facebook
Oligopoly	Few	Many	High	Mobile network operators (MNO)
Monopolistic competition	Many	Many	Open	Smartphones manufacturers
Perfect competition	Many	Many	Open	Digital freelance services
Oligopsony	Many	Few	High	Spotify
Monopsony	Many	One	Impossible	YouTube

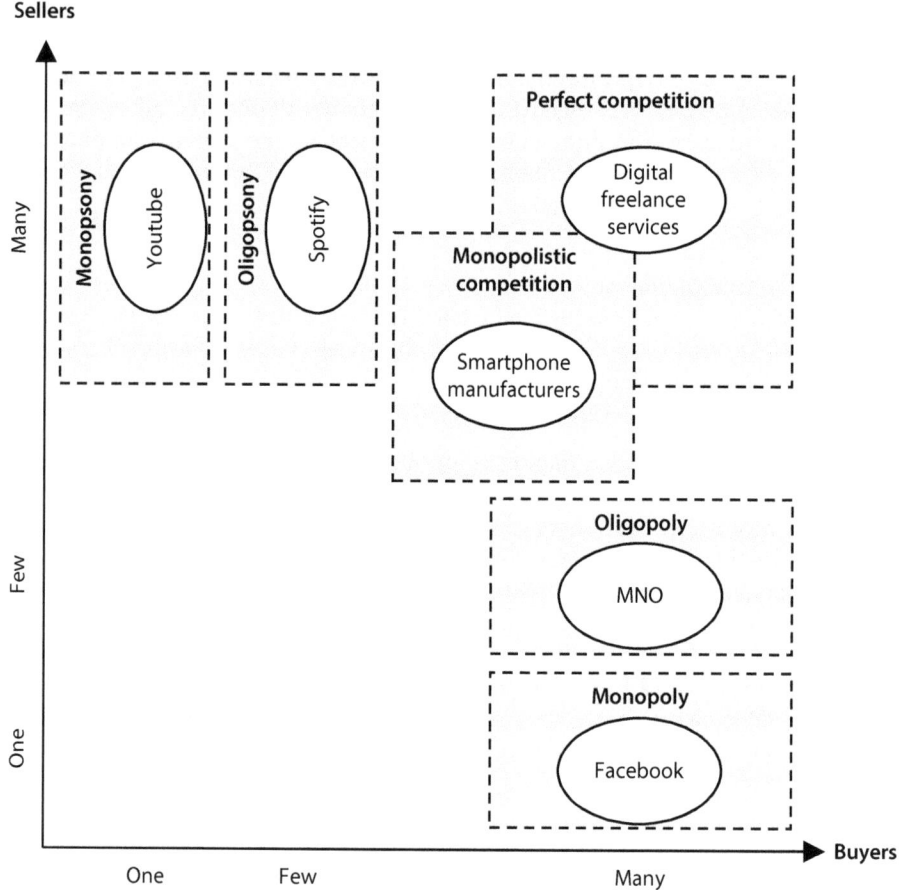

◻ Fig. 13.1 Market types. (Authors' own figure)

13.2 Formation of Monopolies

Until 1998, the telecommunications businesses in most countries were government-granted monopolies (or de jure monopolies). Full competition was introduced in Europe in 1998, allowing anyone to become a network or service provider (ISP). To prevent the incumbent (the former monopolist) from misusing its market power built up on historical government money, the fairness of competition was strictly regulated by the government. The regulations impede the incumbent from buying up competitors or forcing them out of the market with unfair pricing or other obstructions of their business. The regulations contain technical and commercial conditions for how newcomers can interconnect their networks to the network of the incumbent, also allowing the newcomers to operate as resellers or virtual network operators (VNOs). Despite the regulations, monopolies have arisen in the ICT businesses, especially in information service markets. These newcomers (e.g., Facebook, YouTube, and Twitter) are referred to as natural monopolies or de facto monopolies.

13.2 · Formation of Monopolies

The term natural monopoly was formally defined by William Baumol as "[a]n industry in which multi-firm production is more costly than production by a monopoly" (Baumol et al., 1982). The natural monopoly has 100% market share. The closely related term "de facto monopoly" implies that the company may not have 100% market share but will have nearly so over a substantial amount of time. Therefore, the de facto monopoly is not a true monopoly.

Path dependence caused by strong network effects may, at one point, work in favor of one of the competitors who eventually will capture most of the market (see ▶ Chap. 11). This happened in the competition between Facebook and Myspace, in which Facebook took the lead in 2008. Myspace is still active, having about one million registered users, while Facebook has 2.2 billion users and is a de facto monopoly, as it is more than 2000 times bigger than its competitor. Note that the same person may be a registered user of Myspace and Facebook at the same time. Membership in one social media network does not exclude simultaneous membership in a competing social media network.

As explained in ▶ Chap. 12, lock-in implies that it is difficult for a newcomer to capture market shares in a market dominated by a de facto monopoly. Though Myspace is still active and offers competitive services to Facebook, lock-in in favor of Facebook hampers Myspace to capture significant market shares from Facebook.

Cost may be a factor in some cases. In the VCR standards war, two incompatible standards are more inefficient as compared to one standard. VHS and Betamax are almost identical as seen from the user's viewpoint provided that the same films are available on both standards for approximately the same price. However, the filmmakers may view it differently; they must produce two versions of the same film for two incompatible media. This is both expensive and cumbersome for the production side and will eventually lead to higher prices; therefore, the market eventually develops into a de facto monopoly since bandwagon effects, for example, that one of the products are more visible in advertisements and, in displays in shops, may work in favor of one of the technologies (see ▶ Chap. 11 for more details).

Sometimes, companies with large market shares—for example, Google—may be mistaken to be de facto monopolies. In the search engine market, Google has 92% of the market, and the rest is divided between Bing (2.5%), Yahoo! (1.5%), Baidu (1.5%) (China), and several other search engines with less than 1% market share each (Search engine market share worldwide: Dec 2019–Dec 2020. StatCounter). The web browser market is shared between Google Chrome (64%), Safari (18%), Mozilla Firefox (4.5%), Samsung Internet (3%), and several other browsers with small market shares (Browser market share worldwide: Dec 2019–Dec 2020. StatCounter). In the search engine market, Google is strictly not a de facto monopoly since there is still considerable room for competition, and there are no strong lock-in mechanisms that bind the user to one particular search engine. The market shares in the search engine market have also been rather stable for a long period of time. The browser market is certainly not a de facto monopoly, though it is dominated by one large provider almost four times bigger than the next largest provider.

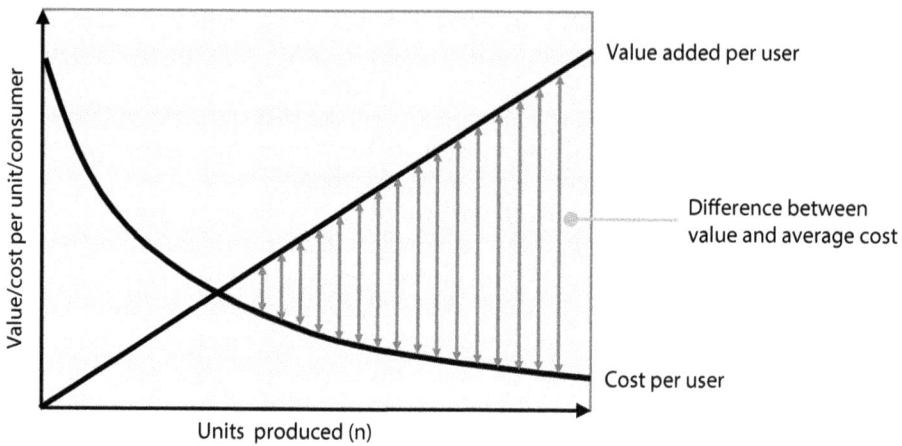

Fig. 13.2 Difference in value as a function of units produced. (Authors' own figure)

A contributing cause of formation of de facto monopolies in the digital economy is the increased gap between value and cost as more and more users adopt a digital service. This is illustrated in Fig. 13.2 for digital services with strong network effects obeying Metcalf's law (see ▶ Chap. 9). As explained earlier, many digital services and goods have zero marginal cost. This implies that the cost curve approaches zero as the production volume (n) (e.g., the number of users in social media) increases. On the other hand, the value of the digital service—and, hence, the revenues of the company offering the service—increases linearly as a function of the number of users (Metcalf's law). The result is a big gap—a value surplus—between value and cost, as depicted in Fig. 13.2. The value gap increases as the production volume increases and gives companies with large n a strong financial position. This can be seen in, for example, the profit margins of many companies producing digital services, which often range from 25% to 50%—well above the normal industry standard. Digital companies may use this profit margin for more growth; for example, developing and improving existing services, creating new services, and/or acquiring competing or supplementary businesses.

> **Case Study 13.1 Creation of a Monopoly: Facebook**
>
> The forerunner for Facebook, the website Facemash, was created in 2003 at Harvard University. The website was first only available for students at Harvard College but expanded to other universities in 2004. In 2008 after almost 5 years, it became a universally available website on the international market where users could form and participate in social groups exchanging experiences, news, comments, views, pictures, and other information. Already in 2009, it had surpassed Myspace in the number of users, exceeding 500 million users in July 2010 (Zuckerberg makes it official: Facebook hits 500 million members, 2010). The company had then become a monopoly in the social services business:

there were no real competitors that could match it in growth and market impact.

From 2008, the growth of Facebook has been governed by strong network effects creating lock-in with high barriers for competitors to enter the same market. The barriers created by Facebook were not economic but psychological. The major concern for the users is that they may lose all information they have produced and collected, as well as being chopped off from the network of interactions with friends and other user they have built up.

The primary service of Facebook is free of charge for the users. This makes the entry barriers for competitors even higher: the competitors cannot provide the same service cheaper, leaving them with the alternatives to pay users for joining their platform to differentiate them on price or offer a better customer experience with less exploitation of personal data. This will require enormous efforts and ingenuity and is extremely expensive.

The platform is designed such that Facebook can extract enormous amounts of data about the users such as personal data (gender, age, geographic location, work, etc.), political preferences, network of friends and contacts, habits, motivations, cultural preferences, and so on and so forth. Facebook sells information based on this knowledge to marketers and other organizations utilizing the information for statistics, trend analysis, sociological studies, lobbying, opinion shaping, surveillance, and other purposes. It is this sale of personal information that generates the revenues of Facebook.

Facebook does not meet competition on its social networking platform: it has long ago become a de facto monopoly. The competition Facebook encounter is on advertisements. It turns out that it is a leading stakeholder in this respect also. As of January 2019, 94% of marketers worldwide were using Facebook for advertising, and 74% were using its subsidiary Instagram. In contrast, 59% were using Twitter, 58% LinkedIn, and 54% YouTube. All other social media combined were used by less than 50% of the marketers (Leading social media platforms used by marketers worldwide as of January 2019. Statista).

Social media earns money on advertisements because of a strong cross-side network effect caused by the large number of users as explained in ▶ Chap. 10. This effect is particularly large for Facebook since it has the largest number of users and, perhaps most important, that it can discover and store more personal information about the users than other social media, facilitating marketers to target their advertisements precisely at individual users.

13.3 Formation of Oligopolies

Mobile communications and streaming services are two examples of oligopolistic markets in digital economics.

In 1992, mobile communication was deregulated in Europe, and, stimulated by the governments, two or three operators in each country acquired license to offer GSM services. Competition was later enhanced by allowing resellers to buy bulk traffic from the mobile network operators and reselling it to their own customers at a lower price than the network operator. Another category of competitors is mobile virtual network operators (MVNOs) owning some infrastructure such as subscription and location management databases and gateway exchanges but leasing radio access infrastructure from ordinary mobile network operators. The mobile market is not big enough to support many operators of different types so that mobile telecommunications within a country has become an oligopoly.

There are several reasons why mobile communications is an oligopoly market. The most important (and often overlooked) reason is that the frequency spectrum allocated to mobile communications is rather narrow and can only be sliced into a rather small number of slots broad enough to support a single operator. This then limits the number of operators that can build their own network in a region or country. Each mobile network operator must then be granted a license for using a particular slice of the available spectrum.

The second reason why there are so few mobile network operators is that it is expensive to build and manage mobile network infrastructures, in particular, since the licensing authorities may require that the network cover a certain percentage of the population (e.g., everyone) and not just the most profitable parts of the country. Resellers and MVNOs require only small capital investments and are easier to establish, and the mobile network operators are forced by government regulations to let them buy bulk traffic or lease infrastructure to affordable prices, thereby enhancing competition.

Streaming services are serving two markets: the provider of information to be streamed and the receiver of the streamed content. In music streaming, there are a few big providers, where Spotify, Apple Music, and SoundCloud are the most prominent. These providers are, on the oligopsony side, trying to capture artists and record labels on exclusive contracts and, on the oligopoly side, trying to capture listeners using different business models. This includes offering a combination of freemium and premium services (Spotify), creating communities of artists and listeners (SoundCloud), and offering access to a vast library of songs (Apple Music).

The competition between oligopolies is difficult because decisions made by one stakeholder may have direct impact on prices, competition, and market shares and, thus, changing the market composition entirely. One particular problem is that the competitors may fall into the prisoner's dilemma trap. The prisoner's dilemma is one of the most studied games in game theory (See the Wikipedia articles on "Game theory" and "Prisoner's dilemma" for more details). The payoff matrix for the prisoner's dilemma game for a duopoly is illustrated in ◘ Fig. 13.3. There are two competitors, firm A and firm B, competing for the same customers. Both firms know that the other firm is likely to lower the price to attract customers from its competitor. The decision each firm is facing is then either to keep the price unchanged or lower the price. The pros and cons for this decision are summarized in the payoff matrix as shown in figure.

- If the two firms do not change the price, the situation remains unchanged.
- If firm A decides to lower the price, then firm A may gain so many customers from firm B that its revenue becomes larger than it was before, while the reve-

13.3 · Formation of Oligopolies

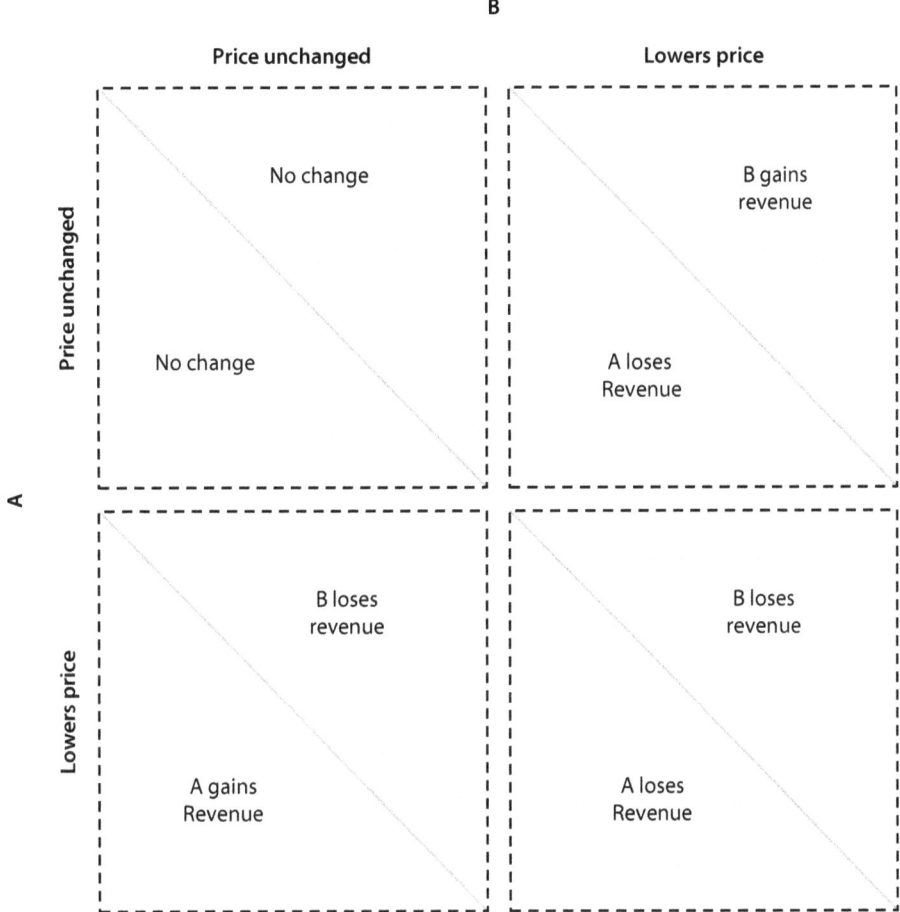

☐ **Fig. 13.3** Payoff matrix for the prisoner's dilemma game. (Authors' own figure)

nues of firm B will drop considerably; firm B may even be pushed out of the market.
- Firm A also knows that if firm B lowers the price and firm A does not, firm A will face the same destiny.
- If both firms lower the price, the market size of the two firms will be unchanged, but the revenues have become smaller for both firms because the user pay less for the service.

The worst outcome for firm A happens if it keeps the same price, while firm B lowers the price. At the same time, the best outcome for firm A happens if it lowers the price and firm B does not. So, what shall firm A do? The likely outcome (called the *Nash equilibrium*) is that firm A lowers the price and, by the same reasoning, firm B does the same. This benefits the users, but the revenues of both firms are now lower, and the business is less profitable.

The discussion above applies to two competing companies but can easily be extended to an oligopoly consisting of more than two companies.

An iterated prisoner's dilemma game is a game which is played several times in succession. Price war is one outcome of iterated prisoner's dilemma games where each competitor tries to follow the actions taken by the other competitors. One example is the continuous price war between regional gasoline stations: if one station reduces the gasoline price, then all the other stations are likely to do the same.

In the early days of mobile communications, price war forced the operators to offer heavily subsidized mobile phones to the customers. Since the mobile communication business is an oligopoly, all operators had to choose this strategy; otherwise, they would soon be out of business. The strategy had one advantage, namely, that it increased the adoption rate of mobile phones causing the market to increase rapidly. As the market matured, the practice changed because it simply meant less revenue for the operators and did not create any new market opportunities. The competition then changed, and the operators began to offer complex subscription packets consisting of various combinations of price, bandwidth, data volume, and other features to differentiate one another. The market then became more like monopolistic competition.

Case Study 13.2 The Mobile App Duopoly

Several companies offer mobile apps, but the market is dominated by only two of them: Apple's App Store and Google Play. The app market is thus a duopoly. The apps are designed for two types of smartphone technologies:

— App Store apps can only be loaded down on iPhones and some other Apple products. The apps are running on the closed-source iOS operating system of Apple. The market share of iPhone is approximately 15% of the international smartphone market.
— Google Play apps can be loaded down on smartphones with the open-source Android operating system of Google. Android phones are produced and marketed by several independent manufacturers. The market share of Android smartphones is about 85%. The market share for Google Play is then 5.7 times larger than that of App Store since the market for apps is the same as the market for operating system technologies.

Several of the apps are available for both iPhones and Android smartphones. Some apps are available only for one of the technologies. Google Play was designed as a production platform for independent app developers. Initially, App Store was proprietary but was soon opened for independent developers to produce their own apps directly on the platform.

The business models of Apple and Google are different as is evident from the statistics for mobile apps shown in ◘ Table 13.2 (Nelson, 2018). The data are for the third quarter of 2018.

Both app stores contain approximately the same number of apps. The

◻ Table 13.2 Mobile apps statistics. (Authors' compilation)

	Number of mobile apps (millions)	Mobile apps revenues (billion $)	Mobile apps downloads (billions)	Revenue per download ($)
App Store	2.2	12.0	7.6	1.6
Google Play	2.8	6.2	19.5	0.32

majority of the most popular apps (e.g., Facebook, Instagram, YouTube, Uber, and Google Maps) are available in both stores. The table shows that Apple acquires 66% of the total revenues from the app market (12 out of 18.6 billion $), while only 33% of all downloaded apps are from App Store. Other statistics show that iPhone users spend almost twice as much on paid apps than Android users (Blair, 2019). This is one reason why Apple, despite having a much smaller market share, earns more on apps than Google. Other reasons are associated with different charges for developers and share of revenues per app.

The apps duopoly is obviously much more complicated than other duopolies since there is no simple relationship between market shares and revenues.

13.4 Conclusions

The two dominating market forms in digital economy are de facto monopolies and oligopolies. De facto monopolies emerge in markets with strong positive network effects as explained in ▶ Chap. 9. The monopoly builds huge barriers so that it is almost impossible for new entrants to compete with them. Standard economic theory is obviously not applicable to these monopolies in cases where the services are offered free of charge for the customers since, in such cases, supply-demand curves are meaningless.

Oligopolies are formed in markets where there is room for only few competitors, for example, mobile network operations. In cases such as streaming services, there may be many competitors, but just a few of them are big enough to dominate the market. These markets may then also be regarded as oligopoly markets, though they may become markets with monopolistic competition if the suppliers are able to differentiate their products. In such markets, both big and small enterprises may live peacefully together.

Another feature that makes digital enterprises more complicated than standard industrial enterprises is that they often are multisided platforms serving two or more interacting markets. The digital enterprise may then be a monopoly in one market and an oligopoly in another. Services may be offered for free to one group of users, while other user groups pay for the product where the price depends on the number of users receiving free services (cross-side network effect). Therefore, decisions taken in one market segment also depend on decisions taken in the other market segment, rendering business modeling and strategic planning intricate.

Monopsony and oligopsony markets have also appeared in the digital economy, for example, enterprises offering streaming services where the enterprise buys content from artists and resells it to their own customers.

❓ Questions

1. Facebook is a multisided platform offering services in several market segments; three of them are social networking services, advertisements, and third-party services. How will you characterize each of them?
2. The credit card market is served by two-sided platforms. Who are the two customer groups served by credit card companies? What type of market do they represent?
3. Why can we model the advertisement market of enterprises in the digital economy both as an oligopoly and as a market with monopolistic competition?

✅ Answers

1. Social networking, de facto monopoly; advertisements, monopolistic competition because there are several competitors offering different advertisement services to different user segments (see also Question 3); third parties, oligopsony buying content from third parties and reselling it to social networking consumers.
2. The customer groups are card users and merchants. Both user groups are buying the service from the companies. Since there are few credit card companies, both markets are oligopoly markets.
3. The advertisement market in the digital economy is dominated by a few big companies and several small ones. The market may then be modeled as an oligopoly since it is only the companies with large market shares in the advertisement market that can manipulate the evolution of the market. On the other hand, the total advertisement market also contains a large number of non-digital companies (e.g., newspapers and journals) reaching different segments of the population. The advertisement market can then also be modeled as a market with monopolistic competition because each stakeholder may offer marketers access to different segments of the population (e.g., different age groups) and to special interest groups.

References

Baumol, W. J., Panzar, J. C., & Willig, R. D. (1982). *Contestable markets and the theory of industry structure*. Harcourt Brace Jovanovich.
Blair, I. (2019). Mobile app download and usage statistics. BuildFire.
Nelson, R. Global app revenue topped $18 billion last quarter, up 23% year-over-year. *Sensor Tower*. October 10, 2018.
Zuckerberg makes it official: Facebook hits 500 million members. *TechCrunch*. July 4, 2010.

Mergers and Acquisitions

Contents

14.1 Definitions – 208

14.2 Motivations for M&A – 210

14.3 Types of Integration – 212

14.4 Conclusions – 214

References – 215

© The Author(s), under exclusive license to Springer Nature Switzerland AG 2021
H. Øverby, J. A. Audestad, *Introduction to Digital Economics*, Classroom Companion: Business,
https://doi.org/10.1007/978-3-030-78237-5_14

Learning Objectives

After completing this chapter, you should be able to:
- Explain the difference between merger, hostile acquisition, reverse takeover, and backflip.
- Understand the concepts of horizontal integration, vertical backward integration, and vertical forward acquisition.
- Explain how mergers and acquisitions have shaped digital markets.

14.1 Definitions

▶ Chapter 13 argued that several companies in the digital economy progress towards de facto monopolies over time. The main reason for this is strong positive network effects caused by positive market feedback. Large companies have an advantage by just being large and tend to capture even more consumers—both new consumers joining the market and consumers from its competitors. The result is an increased market size for the largest company in the market and reduced market size for the rest. This phenomenon is called *organic growth (Locket et al., 2011)*.
◘ Figure 14.1 exemplifies this for Facebook, in which a growth from 360 million MAU (monthly active users) in 2009 to 608 million MAU in 2010 due to users churning from competing social media and new users that have not used a social media previously join the service. In this period (2009–2010), Facebook performed few acquisitions (only one in 2009 and ten in 2010), and most of them were of technical nature. Hence, the growth in users came only from either churning users or new users. Note that ◘ Fig. 14.1 presents the net increase in users—in the period some users may have left Facebook for competing social media and vice versa. However, the net flow of MAU from 2009 to 2010 was positive. Also note that there are no or few detailed data whether the increase in Facebook users was from churning or new users—only the net increase is reported in official statistics. Most probably, the complete picture is complex and involves churning across every social media at the time, new users joining, and existing users quitting social media altogether.

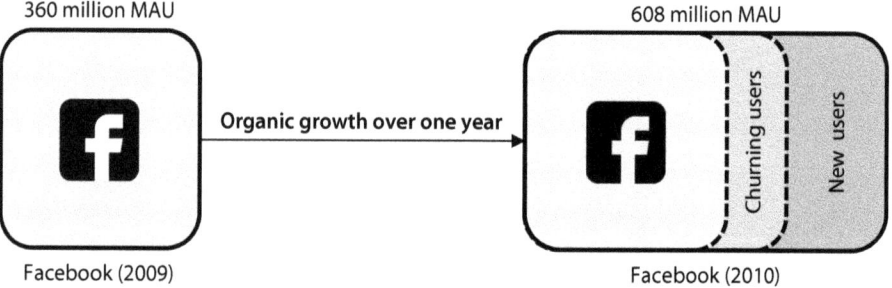

◘ **Fig. 14.1** Facebook organic growth from 2009 to 2010. (Authors' own figure)

14.1 · Definitions

> **Definition 14.1 Organic Growth**
> Organic growth is growth generated by the company's own assets and not from growth that comes from acquiring other companies. The organic growth may be positive or negative.

However, there is another way for companies to grow, namely, through *mergers and acquisitions* (M&A).

> **Definition 14.2 Mergers and Acquisitions**
> A *merger* is a legal consolidation of two enterprises into one where both enterprises cooperate equally in the merger, whereas an *acquisition* implies that one company (the acquirer) takes control of another company (the target company) by ownership of stocks, assets, or equities of that company. Acquisition is also referred to as *takeover* (Bannock et al., 1998).

In commercial terms, merger and acquisition are often treated as synonymous because both result in a consolidation of two companies. This is exemplified in ◘ Fig. 14.2 for the 2014 Facebook acquisition of WhatsApp (Deutsch, 2020). The result is a company with joint assets, employees, and customer base from the merged or acquired companies. Facebook acquired WhatsApp—a competing social media with about 500 million MAU—for $19 Billion. It is one of the largest acquisitions ever performed and has changed the business landscape in the social media market toward increased concentration (less competition).

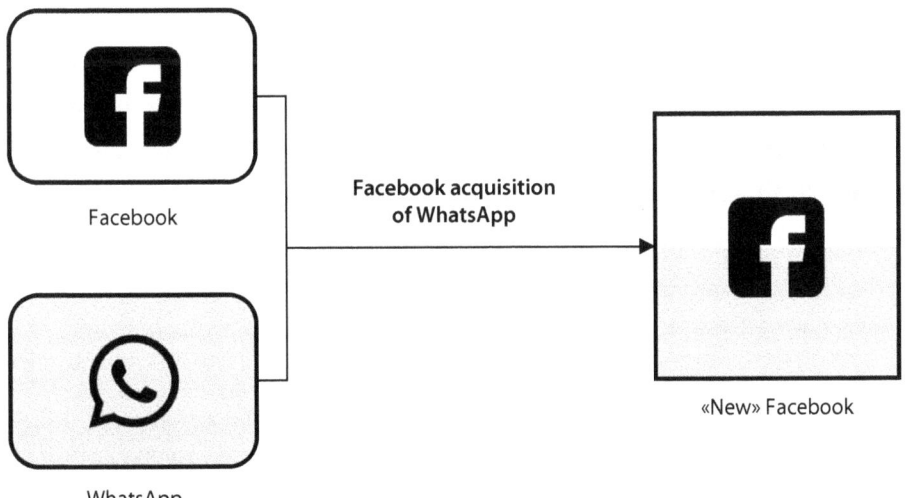

◘ **Fig. 14.2** The 2014 Facebook acquisition of WhatsApp. (Authors' own figure)

Acquisition or takeover can be divided into four categories depending upon how the acquisition takes place: friendly, hostile, reverse, or backflip.

- *Friendly takeover* means that the takeover is agreed by the management and the stockholders of both companies. However, the takeover is initiated by one of the companies making it technically different from a merger. In practice, there is no difference between mergers and friendly acquisitions. The Facebook acquisition of WhatsApp is an example of a friendly takeover (Deutsch, 2020).
- *Hostile takeover* implies that the management of the target company is unwilling to accept the takeover, but for some reason, the takeover nevertheless takes place. Methods may include offering a price well over the market value of the company, persuading enough stockholders to vote for a new and friendly management, or buying stocks directly or via intermediaries to gain control of the company. See, for example, Oracle's acquisition of PeopleSoft (Daines et al., 2006).
- *Reverse takeover* is a term used for takeover of a public company by a private company so that the private company can go public bypassing the complex process of going public itself. One example from digital economy is the reverse takeover of the public US mobile operator Metro PLC by the privately owned T-Mobile USA (Deutsche Telecom) to form the new public company T-Mobile US, the third largest mobile operator in the USA (Garza, 2013).
- *Backflip takeover* is an acquisition where the acquirer makes itself a subsidiary of the acquired company, usually because the brand name of the acquired company is better known. The Danish video game producer Interceptor Entertainment acquired the American company 3D Realms in 2014; moved its headquarters to Aalborg, Denmark; and continued its business under the name 3D Realms (Handrahan, 2014).

14.2 Motivations for M&A

Mergers and acquisitions are complex and expensive undertakings. Hence, the involved companies must have clear business motivations when initiating M&A. The overall motivation is that the outcome will benefit business operations for the involved companies compared to the situation before the M&A. This may include one or several of the following:

- Getting rid of a competitor by first acquiring and then shutting down the competitor; also referred to as *killer* or *zombie acquisition* (Argentesi et al., 2020).
- Increasing the user base by merging the markets of the two companies. The motive for a mobile network operator to acquire a mobile network operator in another geographical region is to increase the user base and, as result, increase both revenues and value on the stock exchange.
- Achieving economy of scale advantages since merging two companies often reduces common costs for administration, research, marketing, inventory, and other expenses.

14.2 · Motivations for M&A

- Getting control of larger parts of the production and delivery chain; for example, a mobile network operator acquiring retailers selling smartphones, tablets, and other terminal equipment.
- Increasing market shares, for example, by attaching a competitor as a subsidiary.
- Increasing revenues by absorbing a competitor and use the increased market power to set prices and thereby raising the revenues to more than the previous sum of revenues of the two companies.
- Improving geographical diversification by acquiring similar companies offering the same service or good in a different geographical region.
- Increasing the product portfolio, for example, offering video games as a supplement on a social media platform.
- Utilizing synergy between different product categories, for example, acquiring companies producing complementary products.
- Acquiring new skills and technologies, for example, buying promising startup companies or manufacturers of highly specialized equipment or services.
- Expanding into new profitable market segments. This is one of the reasons why Google bought YouTube.
- Marketing under a more recognized brand. This is often the motive behind backflip takeovers as explained above.
- Developing a promising concept, for example, by buying startups.
- Acquiring access to patents, protected content, shielded brand names, and other IPR.

In the digital economy, there have been particularly many M&A as shown in ◘ Table 14.1. Many of these companies have expanded into almost all areas of ICT, becoming digital conglomerates. These companies are constantly scanning the market for potential acquisitions to increase the value of their business operations.

◘ **Table 14.1** Mergers and acquisitions in the digital economy. (Authors' compilation)

Company	Number of acquisitions (by the end of 2020)	Notable acquisitions
Google	240	YouTube for $1.65 billion in 2006
Microsoft	225	LinkedIn for $26 billion in 2016
Apple	121	Beats electronics for $3 billion in 2014
Amazon	103	Whole foods market for $13.7 billion in 2017
Facebook	89	WhatsApp for $19 billion in 2014
eBay	62	Skype for $2.6 billion in 2005

An examination of the acquisitions carried out by Amazon, Facebook, Google, Microsoft, and Apple from 2015 to 2017 (a total of 175 acquisitions) indicates that the major motive has been to strengthen the core business of the company and, more rarely, to expand into new markets. Quite often the acquiring company shuts down the business of the acquired company, even if it is not a direct competitor, so that the motive apparently is to get access to core assets such as skills, technologies, processes, practices, and IPR. Sometimes, acquisition of startups seems to be substitutes for R&D. By acquiring promising startups, the project gets proper funding and can be realized in shorter time and may gain first-to-market advantages (Gautier & Lemesch, 2020).

14.3 Types of Integration

Horizontal integration and vertical integration are two types of M&A.

> **Definition 14.3 Horizontal Integration**
> *Horizontal integration* implies that a company merges with or acquires another company in the same market segment.

The motive is either to get rid of a competitor or to build a company with a larger customer base and increased economic value. Facebook's acquisition of WhatsApp in 2014 is an example of a horizontal acquisition.

> **Definition 14.4 Vertical Integration**
> The motive of *vertical integration* is to capture or secure a larger part of the company's supply chain. It is convenient to distinguish between two types of vertical integration:
> - *Backward* or *upstream vertical integration* implies that the company acquires control over suppliers producing input to the company's own product; for example, an application service provider merging with a content provider.
> - *Forward* or *downstream vertical integration* implies that the acquires control over the delivery of services to the customers; for example, a network provider (NP) offering direct access to the users—that is, integrating with an ISP.

Google's acquisition of parts of HTC in 2017 is an example of backward vertical integration since Google took control over the production of mobile phones (user equipment). Forward or downstream vertical integration implies that the company acquires control over parts of its delivery chain or enters related business domains, in which its prime services are used as an input. Examples of forward integration are big film studios (e.g., MGM) owning their own theaters and media companies merging with Internet service providers and TV satellite operators.

14.3 · Types of Integration

Case Study: Facebook Acquisitions

Facebook has acquired 89 companies since 2007. It has moved from being a social media service to a digital conglomerate with business operations in several areas of the digital economy. A few notable companies that Facebook has acquired include Instagram, WhatsApp, Oculus VR, and Parse. ◘ Figure 14.3 exemplifies these four acquisitions in the context of the types of integrations defined in ▶ Sect. 14.3:

- *Horizontal integration:* Facebook's acquisition of Instagram in 2012. Instagram is a photo-sharing app launched in 2010 and reached more than ten million users within a year. The intention was that Facebook would develop Instagram independently; however, integration with Facebook began shortly after the acquisition.
- *Horizontal integration:* Facebook's acquisition of WhatsApp in 2014. WhatsApp is offering messaging and voice-over-IP services for its users. At the time of the acquisition, WhatsApp had more than 500 million MAU. Even though Facebook and WhatsApp are not competing directly in the same market, they are both considered a part of the wider social media market. The acquisition—together with the Instagram acquisition—has increased Facebook's influence and market power in the social media market.
- *Forward vertical integration:* Facebook's acquisition of Oculus VR in 2014. Oculus VR was developing virtual reality headsets. Such devices may extend the reach of Facebook, by integrating the social media to other types of devices.
- *Backward vertical integration:* Facebook's acquisition of Parse in 2013. Parse was a mobile backend service provider. It gave Facebook new tools for developing and accessing backend systems such as data storage, login management, and push notifications.

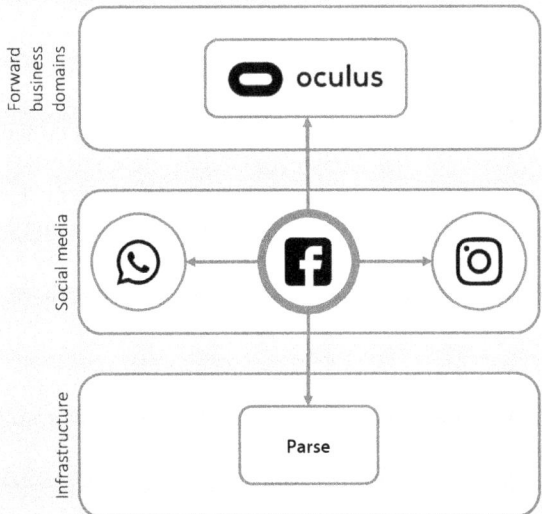

◘ **Fig. 14.3** Facebook acquisitions of Instagram, WhatsApp, Oculus VR, and Parse. (Authors' own figure)

It is easier for the authorities to check that horizontal acquisitions conform to antitrust laws and other market regulations than vertical acquisitions. However, there is one particular problem associated with regulations also in this case, namely, that many of the companies acquired by the large companies are often young and small, so that the acquisition is not regarded as a threat against healthy market evolution.

Due to the high number of M&A by companies in the digital economy, it is important to analyze market structures and, in particular, how these M&As may change competition. The role of national regulators and other governing bodies is to supervise the market evolution and to avoid the formation of de facto monopolies. The distribution of market shares and revenues is not the only factor determining whether a company will become a monopoly. The rate of growth of the number of users or market share must also be considered. If one company gets the lead in a market with strong network effects, then with time, the company may become a de facto monopoly.

14.4 Conclusions

Mergers and acquisitions are common in the digital economy in which the frequent motives have been to get rid of competitors, to get access to new technologies, to buy assets such as patents, to increase market shares, and to expand into new markets, or in short, to get bigger, more powerful, and richer. Several of the big corporations are huge conglomerates consisting of subsidiaries operating in different technological branches. One reason being that the rate of innovations after 1995, when the World Wide Web was commercialized, has been enormous. Mobile apps are examples of this innovativeness. Currently, there are almost three million apps available, and new apps are added to the app store at a rapid rate, while old once that are no longer useful disappear.

All the big corporations in the digital economy have either become de facto monopolies or are market leaders in at least one of their markets. They have become so, because there are strong network externalities in these markets that eventually work in favor of the winner and keeps the competitors small or push them out of the market. This is unavoidable organic growth. In addition, these companies grow more by buying or merging with other companies, creating commercial giants with a monopolistic core business surrounded by a large number of subsidiaries. As has been demonstrated in previous chapters, the company may not even earn money from its core business but only from its subsidiaries. Facebook is a good example.

This state of affairs is hard to regulate by the authorities to avoid market failure and concentration of power.

⊙ Exercise

Google has made more than 240 acquisitions since 2001. A selection of those include Android, YouTube, DoubleClick, GrandCentral, Motorola, and Waze. Discuss how these acquisitions have allowed for new or strengthened existing business domains of Google (you may use Wikipedia for a description of Google and the acquisitions).

⊙ Answers

The key businesses of Google are spread over several technologies: search engine, consumer services (email, software, hardware), advertisements, and enterprise services. Here follows a few of them and how they impacted Google's business operations:

1. Android Inc. was a company developing mobile phone software and operating system. It was acquired by Google to strengthen its own efforts to develop software for mobile phones, e.g., for supporting apps. Google created the Open Automotive Alliance (OAA), comprising the world's leading car manufacturers, to promote the use of Android in cars. Google improved its position as software developer by expanding the technologies of Android Inc.
2. YouTube pushed Google into the social media business. Google has, by this acquisition, become an important factor in the social media business and expanded its business area.
3. DoubleClick offered tools to advertisement agencies and media for increasing the efficiency of advertising by combining it with the search engine technology. DoubleClick was merged into the marketing platform of Google and Google Analytics to improve their own algorithms for targeting advertisements.
4. GrandCentral offered call forwarding and voicemail services. Google changed the name to Google Voice and, thereby, made its entrance into the market for voice services (e.g., VoIP and voicemail). In this case, Google bought the technology of GrandCentral.
5. Motorola Mobility produced smartphones, Bluetooth devices, cordless phones, set-top boxes, and other mobile devices. Google acquired the company to get control over its patent portfolio and, by this action, protect the Android operating system against infringements.
6. Waze is now a subsidiary of Google developing GPS navigation software. Before acquisition, Waze was a competitor to Google Maps. The acquisition therefore has strengthened the position of Google in GPS-related applications. For this reason, the acquisition is still controversial.

References

Argentesi, E., Buccirossi, P., Calvano, E., Duso, T., Marazzo, A., & Nava, S. (2020, March 4). Tech-over: Mergers and merger policy in digital markets. VoxEU & CEPR Policy Portal.

Bannock, G., Baxter, R. E., & Davis, E. (1998). *The penguin dictionary of economics*. Penguin Books.

Daines, R. M., Nair, V. B., & Drabkin, D. (2006). *Oracle's hostile takeover of PeopleSoft (A)*. Harvard Business Publishing: Education.

Deutsch, A. L. (2020). WhatsApp: The best Facebook purchase ever? *Investopedia*.
Garza, L. M. (2013, April 24). Metro PRC shareholders approve merger with T-Mobile USA. *Reuter*.
Gautier, A., & Lemesch, J. (2020, January). Mergers in the digital economy. CESifo Working Paper Series 8056, CESifo.
Handrahan, M. (2014, March 3). Interceptor Entertainment acquires 3D Realms. Gamesindustry.biz
Locket, A., Wiklund, J., Davidsson, P., & Sourafel, G. (2011). Organic and acquisitive growth: Re-examination, testing and enlarging Penrose's growth theory. *Journal of Management Studies, 48*(1), 48–74.

15

Standards

Contents

15.1 Why Standards? – 218

15.2 Standards Organizations – 220
15.2.1 ITU – 220
15.2.2 ETSI – 221
15.2.3 3GPP – 222
15.2.4 Internet Society – 223
15.2.5 World Wide Web Consortium – 224
15.2.6 Institute of Electrical and Electronics Engineers (IEEE) – 224

15.3 Market Implications of Standards – 225

15.4 Standards and Interconnectivity, Interoperability, and Backward Compatibility – 226

15.5 Standards for Trust and Security – 227

15.6 Conclusions – 229

Reference – 230

© The Author(s), under exclusive license to Springer Nature Switzerland AG 2021
H. Øverby, J. A. Audestad, *Introduction to Digital Economics*, Classroom Companion: Business,
https://doi.org/10.1007/978-3-030-78237-5_15

Learning Objectives

After completing this chapter, you should be able to:
- Explain the necessity of developing standards for systems, protocols, and other functionalities of the information and communication technology to ensure interoperability and interconnectivity between devices and systems.
- Provide examples of organizations responsible for developing different types of standards and identify the organization that is likely to have specified a standard for a particular technology.
- Analyze the impacts of standards on the market for digital services, and, in particular, why standards commoditize technologies and services.

15.1 Why Standards?

Standards are necessary to ensure interoperability between users and providers, consistency of services, protection against abuse, and maintainability of quality. In the information and communication technology (ICT), standards are critical since the ICT infrastructure consists of different types of technical equipment produced by different manufacturers from different parts of the world (e.g., network components, smartphones, and laptops). Lack of standards results in situations where international deployment of services is not possible.

The need for standards in ICT is also evident from ◘ Fig. 15.1 showing that five interfaces need to be standardized to provide interoperability:

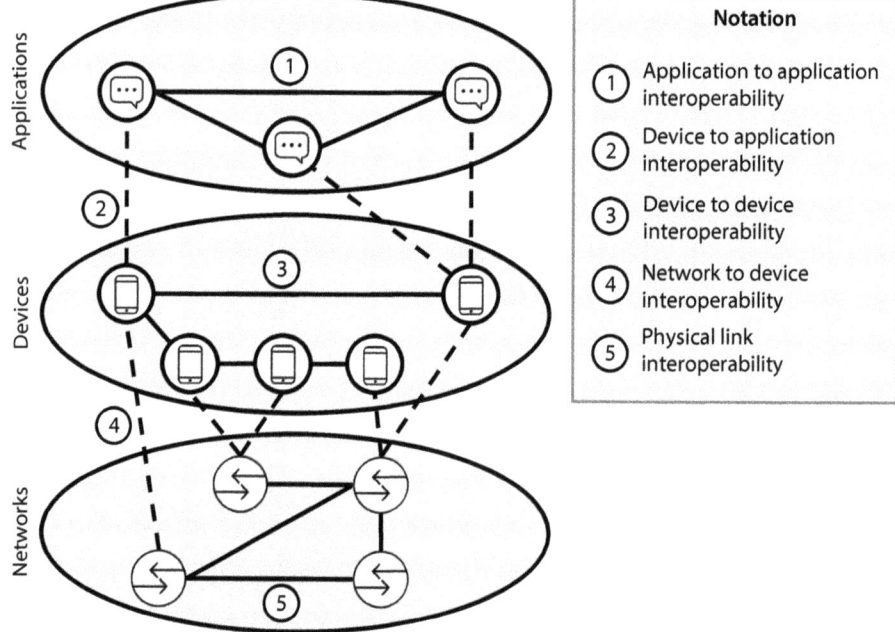

◘ Fig. 15.1 Interfaces in the digital infrastructure. (Authors' own figure)

15.1 · Why Standards?

1. Application protocols between software modules (e.g., http between browsers and webpages, streaming protocols, and e-mail protocols)
2. Application programming interfaces (APIs) for programming, downloading, and program execution and runtime management
3. Transport protocols (e.g., UDP/TCP/SCTP and the encryption protocol Transport Layer Security (TLS))
4. Access protocols (e.g., Ethernet, Wi-Fi, and 4G)
5. Internet protocols (e.g., IPv6 and the encryption protocol IPsec)

That these standards are strictly followed is particularly important for the development and sales of digital goods and services designed for the global marketplace. Standards are needed for several reasons:

- Standards are the tool by which worldwide ICT markets can be created, where the foremost prerequisite is that the devices at each end of the connection are capable of communicating irrespective of where they are located and to which ISP they are connected.
- Standards are required for creating competitive markets, for example, for end user equipment. This includes procedures for how to connect devices to the network, how different types of equipment (e.g., laptops and smartphones) can interoperate, and how to locate and identify remote equipment.
- Standards enable cooperation between stakeholders responsible for performing different tasks in the execution of certain services, for example, banking services where financial institutions may cooperate with third party service providers for trusted customer identification (e.g., ID.me), authentication (e.g., mobile operators), card verification (card issuers), and transaction managers (e.g., point of sale operators). This requires not only technical standards but also legal, economical, and managerial ones.
- Standards for distributed processing are required to allow computers to cooperate in performing a common task where the various elements of the service are executed at different computers at remote locations. This category includes concepts such as cloud computing and grid computing. Examples are the Internet itself, massively multiplayer online games, air traffic control centers, and large scientific simulation models requiring interconnection of thousands of computers in a grid to become massive supercomputers.

International ICT standards ensure interoperability between users globally. These are standards related to telecommunications networks (e.g., the Internet protocol stack and the family of mobile network standards developed by 3GPP), presentation formats (e.g., HTML), and Internet naming and addressing formats and usage (e.g., URL and URI). These standards are not subject to legal agreements between countries; that is, they are not de jure standards. On the contrary, the ICT standards are de facto standards developed by manufacturers, universities, voluntary groups, or individuals to support the international ICT infrastructure. If the proposal is valuable, it may be taken into use and thereby becoming an international standard. The World Wide Web is the most evident example, starting as a project to facilitate communications between CERN (the particle physics laboratory outside Geneva, Switzerland) and cooperating universities worldwide. Within a few years, the WWW became the de facto standard for information posting and browsing on the Internet.

The layout and content of the digital good or service itself is not usually subject to standards: there is no standard concerning the content and presentation of, for example, Facebook, Twitter, Netflix, and Apple and Android apps. To reach the market, they must only support the standards required for accessing the Internet and for interactions with the users (the World Wide Web standards).

> **Definition 15.1 Standards**
> A *de jure standard* is obligatory, for example, the use of the radio spectrum as defined in the Radio Regulations of the ITU.
>
> A de facto *standard* is a convention, procedure, or technology developed by the users of the standard (e.g., the 5G standard of 3GPP) or been selected by market forces (e.g., VHS as the standard for videocassette recorders). The de facto standard is not obligatory. A de facto standard is often referred to as *industry standard*.
>
> An *open standard* is a publicly available standard (e.g., the standards of ETSI, ITU, and 3GPP). The standard may be free of charge or be subject to a usage fee or a patent licensing fee. Most de facto standards are open standards.

15.2 Standards Organizations

There are several organizations and groups specifying and standardizing ICT infrastructures, protocols, and operations. In this section, we will just look at some of the organizations and groups having the biggest impact on the evolution of the technologies and services supported by ICT. Some of them are based on international charters (ITU, ETSI, and 3GPP), while others are nonprofit interest groups dedicated to a particular field of standardization (the Internet Society and the World Wide Web Consortium). The standards produced by these organizations and groups are open-source standards, meaning that anyone may load down and apply the standards free of charge. However, buying open-source standards from ITU and ETSI are often subject to certain fees.

15.2.1 ITU

The world's oldest standardization organization is the International Telecommunications Union (ITU). ITU was established in 1865 for the standardization of the emerging telegraph service. ITU was included as a specialized organization in the United Nations in 1947. The union is responsible for the standardization of telecommunications networks, equipment, technical interfaces, network management, services, and operations. This includes, in particular, the standards for the telephone network and mobile networks and, to a lesser degree, the standardization of the Internet and ICT. In fact, at the meeting of the

World Conference on International Telecommunications 2012 (WCIT-12), the European Parliament presented a resolution where it "Believes that the ITU, or any other single, centralized international institution (e.g., ICANN), is not the appropriate body to assert regulatory authority over the internet" (European Parliament resolution on the forthcoming World Conference on International Telecommunications (WCIT-12) of the International Telecommunication Union, and the possible expansion of the scope of international telecommunication regulations (2012/2881(RSP))). The major concern was that ITU regulations, in particular on tariffing, may undermine the principle of network neutrality. Several other countries supported this view, among others, the USA, India, Australia, and Japan. Nevertheless, a new resolution was accepted by 86 of 152 countries stating rather vaguely "to invite Member States to elaborate on their respective positions on international Internet-related technical, development and public-policy issues within the mandate of ITU at various ITU forums including, inter alia, the World Telecommunication/ICT Policy Forum, the Broadband Commission for Digital Development and ITU study groups" (International Telecommunications Union, 2012).

ITU is not the dominating organization behind the Internet today and will most probably not be so in the future because of the opposition expressed by the EU, USA, Japan, and several other technologically advanced countries. For the evolution of the Internet and digital services, the ITU may become an organization that is not generating the standards, but rather ratifying standards produced by more specialized organizations.

One of the most important tasks of ITU is to govern the use of the radio spectrum. The allocations of radio spectrum to the different services (satellites, land mobile networks, radio astronomy, radio amateurs, broadcasting, and several other uses) are revised every 3 to 4 years by the World Radiocommunications Conferences (WRC). The allocation of the frequency spectrum is an international de jure standard. Other de jure standards of ITU include allocation of country codes for telephone numbers, international mobile subscriber identities (IMSI), and international numbering and identification plans for radio communication with ships and aircraft.

15.2.2 ETSI

The European Telecommunications Standards Institute (ETSI) was established in 1988 as an offspring of the *Conférence européenne des administrations des postes et des télécommunications* (CEPT). ETSI is an independent standardization organization for the EU and associated European states (e.g., Switzerland, Norway, and Turkey). Industries and organizations of these countries are the full members of ETSI. In addition, there are several organizations and industries from other counties outside Europe that are associated members, for example, USA, Japan, People's Republic of China, India, Brazil, Australia, and Canada. Currently, ETSI has over 800 full and associated members (countries, industries, and organizations).

ETSI is now regarded as world's most influential, progressive, and successful standardization organization on all aspects of information and communications technologies, including new fields such as machine-to-machine (M2M) technologies and the Internet of Things (IoT). ETSI has taken over many of the roles ITU had previously, publishing more than 2000 standards every year.

15.2.3 3GPP

The third Generation Partnership Project (3GPP) is responsible for developing the standards for public land mobile networks 3G, 4G, 5G, and beyond. 3GPP has also taken the leadership in developing Internet standards for applications in mobile systems such as new voice-over-IP standards, the IP multimedia subsystem (IMS) for application in all-IP mobile systems, and access technologies and architectures for the Internet of Things.

3GPP is a partnership of the major standardization organizations in the USA, Europe, and Asia. The technical support team is located at the headquarters of the European Telecommunications Standards Institute (ETSI) in Sophia Antipolis, France. The standardization work is based on voluntary contributions from more than 370 member organizations.

All standards made by 3GPP can be accessed and loaded down free of charge by anyone and are, in this respect, free open-source standards (The 3GPP specifications can be loaded down free of charge from ▶ http://www.3gpp.org/specifications/releases). One of the most successful technological evolutions in ICT is the evolution of the digital mobile telephone service, starting with implementation of GSM in 1991. The events leading to the standardization of mobile communications are reviewed in ▶ Box 15.1.

Box 15.1   From GSM to 5G

Standardization of public mobile communications plays a particularly important role in the evolution of digital services. The successful standardization of GSM was also one of the major arguments for establishing ETSI. Therefore, we will describe some of the events leading to the current standards for mobile communications.

The evolution of digital mobile communications started in 1982 when 17 European countries decided to jointly specify a pan-European digital mobile network. The group set up for doing the task was named *Groupe Spécial Mobile*, GSM. Later the system the group specified was renamed the Global System for Mobile Communications, also abbreviated GSM. In 1982, several incompatible systems for land mobile systems existed or were about to be put into operation in Europe: NMT in the Nordic countries, the Netherlands, Switzerland, and Spain, TACS in the UK, C-Netz in Germany, and Radiocom 2000 in France.

To ensure that GSM was built and not put aside as an interesting future option, 13 European countries signed a memorandum of understanding (MoU) in 1987 obliging that "operational networks shall be procured in each of the countries by the network operators based on the CEPT recommendations with the objective of providing public commercial service during 1991" can be downloaded from ▶ http://www.gsmhistory.com/wp-content/uploads/2013/01/5.-GSM-MoU.pdf). Therefore, GSM operation could commence in Europe in 1991/1992. GSM was not only built out in Europe; within a few years, GSM had become the preferred mobile network standard in most of the world.

GSM is a European standard that became a worldwide de facto standard. What is more important is that the GSM standardization process became the norm by which all later mobile standards—3G, 4G, 5G, and variants thereof—are made. This includes features such as service definition, network architecture, roaming, handover, subscription module (SIM), addressing, and so on. The standardization process is also an example of an open and dedicated cooperation between companies that later would become competitors as network operators, suppliers of network equipment, and manufacturers of user terminals. This is a particular form of *coopetition*. Coopetition implies that the companies may both cooperate and compete either at the same time or at different stages of the evolution. The reasons for coopetition in developing a technological standard are several:

- Instead of one company or organization carrying the total development cost, the cost is shared between several partners; the total cost of developing the rather cheap GSM standard was more than 100 million euros and required more than 1000 man-years of expert work. The development of the 4G standard has required several times as many resources.
- A global standard makes the total market pie much bigger, and, consequently the market for each participant is also bigger.
- The economic risk of participation in projects based on standards with global market potential is much smaller than for implementing a local standard.

The work on a global mobile network standard was initiated in ITU in 1986 under the name Future Public Land Mobile Network System (FPLMNS). The work progressed very slowly, and no significant results were obtained until 1998 when the project was taken over by the newly formed organization third Generation Partnership Project, 3GPP. Since then, this cooperation has developed the 4G and 5G standards and is now expanding these standards to support new services and features.

15.2.4 Internet Society

The Internet Society is an American nonprofit organization in charge of promoting the standardization and policies of the Internet. The organization also has several offices outside the USA (e.g., in Geneva and Brussels to be close to both the UN policy group on information technology issues and the political and technological power centers of Europe). The organization has no legal influence on the ICT evolution. On the other hand, the informal influence is enormous.

The Internet Society is the home for several legally informal standardization bodies, the most important of which are:

- The Internet Engineering Task Force (IETF) is in charge of developing and promoting Internet standards. There is no formal membership of the organization, and anyone may contribute to the work by issuing Requests for Comments (RFCs) which may contain amendments or additions to existing standards or proposals for completely new standards. The proposal may be accepted by the Internet Engineering Steering Group and becoming a new Internet standard. Even so, it may be rejected or ignored by manufacturers and Internet providers and never be implemented. Being so loosely organized, the Internet may evolve in an unplanned and haphazardly way. This has so far been the major forte of the Internet.
- The Internet Architecture Board (IAB) is an informal advisory group in charge of inducing some degree of consistency on the evolution of the Internet, among others by sorting out RFCs that may become useful additions to the Internet technology. This induces some direction to the evolution of the Internet.
- The Internet Engineering Steering Group (IESG) is the forum that finally endorses new Internet standards.
- The final Internet standards are also published as RFCs. Free access for downloading of all RFCs is available via the homepage of the Internet Society.

Note that ITU plays no important role in the standardization of the Internet. On the other hand, 3GPP is playing a more and more important role, in particular, in the development of the Internet of Things.

15.2.5 World Wide Web Consortium

The World Wide Web Consortium (W3C) is an independent organization in charge of standardizing web services. The organization was established and is currently managed by the inventor of the World Wide Web, Tim Berners-Lee. The charter is to standardize and develop the WWW technology and promote WWW-derived services. This includes presentation languages (XML, HTML), formats (XForms), procedures (SOAP), and protocols (HTTP, HTTPS). The W3C standards are independent of the Internet standards. The only requirement is that the Internet exists as an underlying network for communications.

15.2.6 Institute of Electrical and Electronics Engineers (IEEE)

Institute of Electrical and Electronics Engineers Standards Association (IEEE-SA) develops standards within a broad range of technologies where telecommunication is just one of them. The most important standards are assembled in the 802-series. This series includes standards for the Ethernet, Wi-Fi, Bluetooth, Zigbee, body area networks, and other local area technologies. These technologies define how various types of equipment can be connected to the Internet or interconnected locally to form local area networks for different purposes. While all the organizations listed above are authorized standardization bodies either directly or through association with other organizations, the IEEE is not. The IEEE is rather a loosely knitted community of scientists and engineers participating in developing the standards. Despite this, IEEE-SA is one of the most influential standardization bodies in the world, having specified most of the local communications technologies surrounding us.

15.3 Market Implications of Standards

Standards have significant implications on competition and on how digital services evolve in the market. Standards are drivers of commoditization—even complex services like mobile communication and Internet access are commoditized. The user will, for example, not experience any difference using smartphones from different manufacturers or receiving the service from different mobile network operators. Commoditized services compete primarily on price and not on other features. This means that it is easy for users to switch to competing service providers since all other features except price are more or less the same. In such a market, it is difficult for the provider to lock in consumers because the switching costs both for the consumers and the supplier are small.

Other standards support diversity, for example, the standards of the World Wide Web. These standards allow application service providers to develop differentiated services satisfying various user needs. There are also commoditized services on the web, for example, e-mail and web browsing.

It is more likely that de facto monopolies develop in markets without standards or with more than one competing standard because a consumer must choose between equivalent services from different suppliers that are technically incompatible. In this case, it is expensive for the customer to switch to another supplier. Moreover, network effects may dominate in the competition so that one of the providers ends up as a monopoly. One example we have already encountered several times is the competition between the video recording standards VHS and Betamax in the 1970s and 1980s. VHS and Betamax offered similar capabilities but were not compatible since there was no common standard for video recording. VHS cassettes could not be played on a Betamax recorder and vice versa. In fact, VHS and Betamax were competing industrial standards developed by different companies. Because of network effects, both standards could not coexist in the market—over time one of the standards would outcompete the other. By the mid-1980s, it became clear that—for various reasons we will not discuss here—VHS had won this "videotape format war." All the engineering and marketing efforts put into Betamax was in vain and had no benefit for the company developing it and for society.

The narrative of VHS vs Betamax shows us that competition among standards can be expensive. The lesson from this case is that it is better for operators and manufacturers first to *cooperate* and thereafter to *compete* once the standard has been agreed upon. This has been the case for almost all ICT standards developed during the last 30 years. Suppliers of equipment or services first cooperate to develop a common standard. Once the standard is agreed upon, it is freely available for any supplier of equipment or services, also those who did not take part in the standardization process. The suppliers may then develop products and services based on this standard and compete for market shares. The benefit for the manufactures and the service suppliers is that the cost to develop the standard is small for each partner and that the total market becomes larger. This was the successful approach taken by GSM and later by 3GPP in developing the mobile standards.

There are also several examples where regional standards have been developed, forming technological cartels. Europe and the USA have often adopted different telecommunications standards, for example, the basic encoding of voice signals in the digital telephone network (PCM). These technological incompatibilities were solved by interworking units at the borders converting the formats, thereby satisfying the all-important requirement of interoperability.

Except for a few instances, GSM was not implemented in the USA, so that roaming between Europe and the USA using the same mobile phone was not possible. To respond to this inconvenience, several mobile phone retailers saw the opportunity to establish a new business, among others at airports, by leasing mobile phones to travelers to Europe.

There were also two incompatible standards for 3G systems: UMTS (specified by 3GPP) in Europe and CDMA2000 (standardized by ITU) in North America and several countries in Asia; CDMA2000 was also offered by several European mobile operators in parallel to UMTS to enhance global roaming. The first true global standard for public mobile networks was 4G specified by 3GPP and endorsed by ITU as a global standard.

15.4 Standards and Interconnectivity, Interoperability, and Backward Compatibility

Interoperability is the key feature of the Internet. Each user can communicate with any other user or webpage—on e-mail or via web browsers—independently of the technology employed by the other user. Interoperability must therefore exist between networks designed with different network technologies and between user equipment of different brands and standards. Otherwise, the Internet will split up into incompatible islands and loosing much of its value.

In the physical network, technical standards and economical and legal agreements are required to interconnect networks owned by different ISPs. Nontechnical agreements may include remuneration for transiting and terminating traffic, liabilities in case of network failure, and terms of cooperation; technical agreements may include minimum quality of service commitments such as availability, minimum guaranteed data rate, and maximum latency and data jitter.

There are two incompatible network protocols on the Internet: Internet Protocol version 4 (IPv4) and Internet Protocol version 6 (IPv6). IPv4 was specified in 1983 and is still used in several networks. IPv6 was ready for implementation in 2006, but the adoption rate has been slow until recently. IPv6 was developed to provide more addressing space than IPv4. The adoption rate of IPv6 has now increased rapidly because IPv6 is the only network protocol used in 4G and 5G mobile networks. Moreover, the addressing space of IPv4 will be too small for accommodating billions of connected IoT devices.

The Internet, therefore, consists of islands based on IPv4 and IPv6, and a technology called tunneling is used to transfer IPv6 packets across IPv4 networks and vice versa. Tunneling means that the IPv6 (IPv4) packets are imbedded in the data field of IPv4 (IPv6) packets. On the other hand, most terminal equipment contains software for both IPv4 and IPv6 so that the equipment can be connected to either type of network. This ensures interconnectivity on the Internet.

Interoperability between mobile phones (smartphones) and mobile networks is supported by backward compatibility, implying that, for example, a 4G telephone can access 2G (GSM) and 3G networks. This is achieved by implementing the radio and signaling interfaces of all three standards in the telephone. This is possible since the evolution of computers have followed Moore's law: the processing and storage capabilities of mobile phones have doubled approximately every 1.5 year. This means, for example, that the computational power of mobile phones in 2001 when 3G was introduced was approximately 60 times bigger than that of GSM phones of the same physical size. Similarly, the computational power had increased by another factor of 60 when 4G was introduced in 2010 and had increased by still another factor of 60 when 5G was introduced in 2019.

The backward compatibility of mobile phones is achieved by implementing the three standards in all phones and install algorithms by which the phone can search for and identify the type of network serving a particular area. Based on information displayed to the user, the selection of network may then be automatic or manual. To assure backward compatibility, the network operators operating a 4G network must also operate, at least, a parallel 2G network. Several operators plan to discontinue offering 3G networks since 4G offers much better and faster Internet connections and because they still offer GSM network access supporting earlier standards. However, there are operators that also have shut down their GSM networks (e.g., USA and Australia).

15.5 Standards for Trust and Security

Digital services often require cooperation between several stakeholders. One example is banking. Such configurations require that trust exists between the stakeholders and that trustworthiness can be verified to a high degree of confidence. The trust relationships may sometimes exist over several administrative domains (companies or countries) with different legislations, rules of business conduct, and regulations.

Trust may imply several things, for example (See the ISO/IEC 27000 family of standards for a detailed overview of recommendations on information security and related procedures):

- *Secure identification and authentication* of communication partners mean that the partners mutually verify the correctness of their stated identities. Methods include permanent or onetime passwords and cryptographic authentication

methods. Secure identification may include more complex procedures involving independent trusted third parties.
- *Non-repudiation* implies that the originators and receivers of information cannot deny their participation in the exchange of information. This means that the supplier of the good cannot deny having sent the electronic good, for example, deny responsibility if the good contains malware that interfere with or damages the computer of the receiver. Moreover, the supplier cannot deny having received payment for the good. On the other hand, the receiver of the goods cannot deny having received the good, possibly including encryption keys to decrypt the good. Non-repudiation may be achieved by attaching digital signatures to the messages sent; for example, attach the supplier's digital signature to the good itself and to encryption keys required for decoding encrypted goods and to attach the receiver's digital signature to messages acknowledging the receipt of the good and associated encryption key.
- *Certification* implies that a trusted third party affirms the ownership of certain cryptographic secrets such as keys used for digital signatures, authentication, and encryption.

Trust is a legally complex issue. In many contexts, trust must be based on legally binding covenants and be subject to criminal proceedings if fraud is detected. Therefore, there are few, if any, trusted third parties (TTPs) offering services outside small spheres of influence, for example, specialized enterprises protecting interactions between financial institutions and mobile network operators offering two-step authentication for clients such as banks and governments. Example of two-step authentication is cryptographic authentication of the smartphone of the client followed by onetime passwords received in SMS messages for authenticating the access attempt.

In the early years of the public Internet, it was expected that it would be a lucrative business to be a trusted third party (TTP). Several standards, for example, for public key infrastructures for secure management of RSA encryption keys, were developed for this purpose. The business potential was regarded to be huge, but all legal problems and pitfalls associated with this business turned out to be many, and the few attempts to establish such companies failed: no one would trust the trusted party! TTPs owned by governments are not trusted because the users of the TTP services may suspect that the government will use the information collected by the TTP for clandestine purposes and social control. Privately owned TTPs are not trusted because the owners of the TTP may misuse the TTP for commercial reasons, for example, interfering with the business of the user or selling information gathered by the TTP to competitors. The TTP may also represent a serious security threat because hackers may gain access to the TTP tampering with or compromising the businesses of the users of the TTP. The Dutch company DigiNotar issued certificates for public/private keys for the Dutch government's public key infrastructure program. In 2011, hackers broke into the system and issued fake certificates used for criminal purposes, for example, attacking Iranian dissidents. The company went bankrupt in 2011 as a result of the break-in (See the Wikipedia article about DigiNotar).

15.6 Conclusions

Interoperability is one of the key features of ICT. Interoperability means that all networks (mobile or fixed) are interconnected and are able to pass messages between people and machines irrespective of in which country or region of the world they are located. Interoperability also implies that equipment produced by different manufacturers can work together using standardized interfaces and protocols.

International standards for ICT are developed by several specialized standards organizations. Almost all ICT standards are de facto standards; that is, they are not mandatory but are convenient since they ensure global interconnectivity and support innovations of applications and services that otherwise would have been impossible. Just a few international ICT standards are de jure standards. Examples are the use of the frequency spectrum by different radio communication services; the formats of international identification and numbering plans for land mobile, aeronautical, and maritime services; and standards for certain services such as ground-to-air traffic control.

The standards also commoditize the technologies and services they specify, for example, wireless communication, Internet access, and World Wide Web protocols. On the other hand, these commoditized technologies support a vast number of non-standard applications opening up for a digital market consisting of a mix of millions of big and small businesses. The three basic technologies—wireless communication, Internet, and the World Wide Web—have created an enormous, innovative arena for business development.

❓ Questions

1. Which organizations are responsible for standardization and allocation of:
   (a) Telephone numbers?
   (b) E-mail addresses?
   (c) Web addresses?
   Hint: this information is found by searching the Internet.
2. How can a 4G smartphone communicate with a GSM phone for voice communication despite being designed to incompatible standards?
3. Which protocols are standardized by RFC791, RFC2616, and RFC793?

✅ Answers

1. The standardization bodies responsible for allocation of telephone numbers, e-mail addresses, and web addresses are:
   (a) ITU has standardized the general formats of international telephone numbers and is responsible for allocating unique country codes identifying the country. This code consists of the first one, two, or three digits of the international telephone number. The remaining digits (called the national telephone number) are allocated by national authorities, either a regulatory authority or the telephone network operator.
   (b) The e-mail address is written as local-name@domain-name (e.g., Joe.jones@example.edu) where domain name is accredited and registered by

the Internet Corporation for Assignment of Names and Numbers (ICANN), and the local name is allocated by the e-mail provider. The allocation principle is standardized by the Internet Engineering Task Force (IETF). The domain name identifies the host and is converted to a unique IP number for sending the e-mail over the Internet to the e-mail server.

(c) The format of the web address was proposed by Tim Berners-Lee and standardized by IETF. The format is composed of three parts as follows: ptotocol://▶ www.domain-name/index.html. The protocol is either http or https, the domain name is the same as for e-mail addresses (allocated by ICANN), and the index is the local address generated automatically by the file management system of the host computer. The index identifies the web page uniquely within the file system of the host computer.

2. The voice format is translated from the GSM format to the 4G format—and vice versa—by interworking units in the network. The same applies to conversations between 4G (or GSM) and fixed telephones, between ordinary telephones and VoIP telephones, between different standards of fixed telephones (e.g., between European and North American coding standards), and so on.

3. RFC791, IP version 4; RFC2616, http; and RFC793, TCP.

Reference

International Telecommunications Union. (2012). Final acts: world conference on international telecommunications, Dubai.

The Long Tail

Contents

16.1 Origin of the Concept: Amazon and the Long Tail – 232

16.2 Internet and the Long Tail – 233

16.3 Numerical Analysis of the Long Tail – 235

16.4 Conclusions – 239

References – 241

Learning Objectives

After completing this chapter, you should be able to:
- Understand the concept of long tail distributions.
- Identify the existence of long tails in a particular digital service.
- Evaluate the effect of the long tail on revenues.

16.1 Origin of the Concept: Amazon and the Long Tail

The long tail refers to goods and services that are in low demand individually but collectively constitute to substantial sales. The term was coined by Chris Anderson in his 2006 book, *The Long Tail: Why the Future of Business is Selling Less of More* (Anderson, 2006). Traditionally, such goods and services have been too expensive for a seller to offer to its customers. Let us take a bookstore as an example. A physical bookstore can accommodate a limited number of books, typically, between 10,000 and 100,000 books. This is because the bookstore has finite space for storing and displaying books. A bookstore offers and displays books that are believed to sell in large quantities, thereby reducing storage costs and maximizing revenues. Books believed to have few sales are not offered since the cost of holding such books does not match the forecasted revenues they may generate.

A digital bookstore does not have the same limitations as a traditional bookstore. Millions of titles can be stored in a single server and be available for anyone from anywhere. Bestsellers do not take up more space than the rarest titles. The same applies to all types of digital goods such as music, films, and video shows.

Amazon can offer millions of different books on its e-commerce channel. This is achieved as a combination of large and well-organized warehouses containing printed books, digitally stored books, on-demand printing, third-party mediation, and personalized advertising based on search and purchase history of the customers. The most popular books sold by Amazon are printed in advance and stored physically in large, efficient, and automated warehouses. These warehouses may hold what is termed "the head" of Amazon's products; that is, the books that sell the most. Other books—both bestsellers and books which are low in demand—are supplied by Amazon as e-books or are printed on demand. E-books are stored digitally, and there is almost no cost for Amazon to add an e-book to its inventory (again an example of zero marginal cost). On-demand printing means that Amazon offers physical books to customers by printing them when they are ordered by the consumer. Amazon is also a multisided platform (MSP) and mediates between third-party sellers (bookstores or authors) and customers; that is, other bookstores and authors use Amazon's digital marketplace to offer their books for sale (Hanks, 2017). These bookstores may be niche stores offering books that are low in demand. This arrangement expands Amazon's supply of books. Finally, Amazon may use the search and buying history of the customers to suggest other books, including rare books, which may interest the buyer.

The sum of these supply mechanisms results in Amazon being able to offer millions of books to the customers. The bestsellers are sold by Amazon directly by

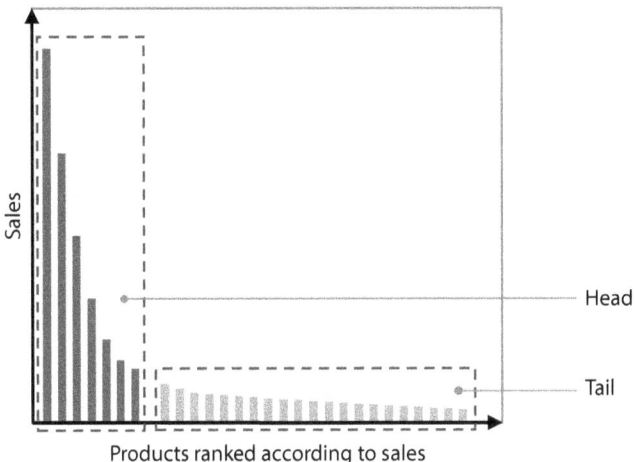

Fig. 16.1 The long tail. (Authors' own figure)

printing in advance or as e-books. Books that are low in demand are offered through a combination of third-party booksellers, e-books, and on-demand printing of digitally stored books. Hence, Amazon can accommodate the 10,000–100,000 books offered by a physical bookstore (*the head*) and, in addition, millions of other books not offered by the physical bookstore. These millions of other books that are not offered by physical bookstores constitute *the tail*—books that are low in demand individually, but collectively constitute substantial sales. This is called *the long tail of supply*.

An illustration of the long tail concept is shown in Fig. 16.1. Here, products are ranked (abscissa) according to sales (ordinate), where the top-selling products are those in the head and the books that sell the least are in the tail. Chris Anderson observed that companies like Amazon earned about half its revenue from products in the tail. Anderson based his conclusions on observations made by Brynjolfsson et al. (2003). Brynjolfsson and coworkers found, for example, that on Amazon, 2.3 million book titles were available, while the shelves of an ordinary large bookstore contained between 40,000 and 100,000 titles. They estimated that the sales of books not found in ordinary stores amounted to between 20% and 40% of the total sales of Amazon. In a new survey published in 2010, they found that 36.7% of Amazon's sales came from the long tail (Brynjolfsson et al., 2010). This is illustrated in Fig. 16.2.

16.2 Internet and the Long Tail

In a paper from 2011, Brynjolfsson et al. also argued that the long tail phenomenon is a common aspect of many Internet businesses (Brynjolfsson et al., 2011). Low production costs, cheap storage, small shipping costs, and efficient information searches are the key ingredients for long tail businesses. They emphasized the

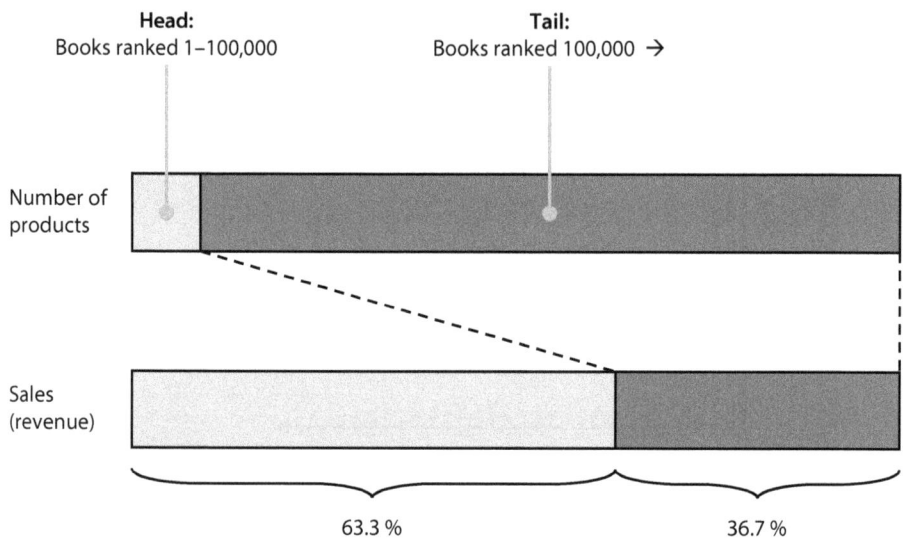

Fig. 16.2 Amazon sales. (Authors' own figure)

importance of efficient information search both on the web and on homepages of vendors such as Amazon, allowing customers to skim through millions of products using search queries based on product names, key words, product description, product category, or other information.

Offering products in the long tail is a competitive advantage for providers. This is because customers prefer variety and options when selecting products to buy. The long tail also gives the provider more relevant options for advertising and recommending similar products for the customers. Hence, companies that offer products in the long tail are rewarded by both increased sales and improved customer satisfaction by displaying a long list of products to choose from (Brynjolfsson & Saunders, 2013).

The long tail has been exploited in many digital businesses. In the music industry, the digitalization and streaming of music means that more titles can be offered to customers compared to a traditional music store. Spotify, for instance, offers access to more than 30 million songs, while the biggest record stores accommodate around 100,000 albums (equivalent to about one million songs). For Spotify, there is no cost associated with storing one extra song and making it available to users (zero marginal cost). Moreover, Spotify and other digital music provides may also de-bundle albums and sell individual songs.

> **Definition 16.1 The Long Tail**
> The long tail refers to goods and services that are in low demand individually but collectively contribute to substantial sales.

In the banking industry, the long tail has been exploited to provide microcredit to lower-class and poor people. For instance, Grameen Bank in Bangladesh offers small loans to people and private enterprises that would normally not be qualified for a loan in a regular bank.

Crowdsourcing is an example of long tail production. The long tail here is made up of all the skilled people that may contribute to a software product but are, a priori, unknown to the developer. Wikipedia encourages the regular Internet user to become an author of the encyclopedia, hence creating a long tail of contributors. Wikipedia's workforce is supplied by many contributors in a long tail of supply.

Big companies, such as Amazon, can profit from all products—both products that sell in huge numbers (head) and products that sell in small numbers (tail). However, the long tail has also made it possible for individuals to start a type of business that was not possible before. For example, individuals may now sell merchandise on eBay, offer their services on Airbnb and Uber, and sell their own books on Amazon. These individuals supply the long tail with products and services that were not previously available to consumers. Selling merchandise without a physical store was expensive before the advent of e-commerce. However, today, anyone can become an e-commerce retailer (or reseller) by setting up a web page to offer manufactured products. Such a business will find its place on the long tail among thousands of other suppliers in the same business area.

16.3 Numerical Analysis of the Long Tail

The term "long tail" alludes to statistical distributions where a large portion of occurrences are far away from the main part of the distribution. In statistics, the long tail distribution is a special case of *heavy tail distributions* defined as follows.

> **Definition 16.2 Heavy Tail Distribution and Power-Law Distribution**
> The *discrete heavy tail distribution* is a statistical distribution in which the tail of the distribution falls off more slowly than exponential decay. Any distribution of the form $f(X = k) \sim k^{-\gamma}$, where $\gamma > 1$ is a constant and the positive integer k is the running variable, is a discrete heavy tail distribution. This particular distribution is also called a *discrete power-law distribution* (Schroeder, 2009). The symbol $f(X = k)$ stands for "the frequency of occurrences that X is equal to k," and the tilde ($\sim$) means "is proportional to." If γ is small (between 1 and 2), then it is also called a *long tail distribution*.

Anderson, based on the works by Brynjolfsson et al., found that the popularity of books sold by Amazon seemed to follow a rank distribution in accordance with Zipf's law; that is, a long tail distribution with $\gamma = 1$ and where the probability drops to zero for all k larger than a certain upper threshold (the cutoff). In 2000, the number of titles available on Amazon was 2.3 million, while ordinary bookstores held, on average, about 40,000 titles. The "long tail" of Amazon then consisted of more than 2.2 million books, that is, books available on Amazon, but not in an ordinary bookstore.

> **Box 16.1 Zipf's Law**
>
> Zipf's law is based on the observation that the most frequent word in English ("the") is twice as frequent as the second-most frequent word ("of"), three times as frequent as the third-most frequent word ("and"), and so on. Zipf's law holds quite well for, at least, the first 1000 words in the English language (Schroeder, 2009). The frequency of words is then derived from the harmonic series:
>
> $$1, \frac{1}{2}, \frac{1}{3}, \frac{1}{4}, \ldots, \frac{1}{N},$$
>
> or more precisely, the frequency $f(k; N)$ of the k-th-most frequent word is:
>
> $$f(k;N) = \frac{1/k}{\sum_{j=1}^{N}(1/j)} \approx \frac{1/k}{\ln N + \gamma},$$
>
> in which N is the number of words in the English language and $\gamma \approx 0.57722\ldots$ is the Euler-Mascheroni constant. We have used the fact that:
>
> $$\sum_{k=1}^{N} \frac{1}{k} = \ln N + \gamma + O\left(\frac{1}{N}\right).$$
>
> The notation $O(1/N)$ (the "big O" notation) indicates that this term decreases at least as fast as $1/N$ as N increases. For large N, the last term can, therefore, be ignored. The statistical distribution with frequency $f(k; N)$ is also called the *Zipfian distribution*. Note that the distribution depends on the cutoff N.
>
> Zipf's law describes, in addition to word usage, the rank distribution of amazingly many natural and sociological phenomena: size of cities, size of countries (except China and India), length of rivers, size of sand grains, wealth among people, and, as we have just seen, popularity of books.

Let us then apply Zipf's law to the sale of books. The number of titles held by Amazon is 2.3 million books, while an ordinary bookstore holds about 40,000 titles. The titles held by an ordinary bookstore are, according to Zipf's law, the most popular titles, ranging from 1 to 40,000 in popularity. The titles with popularity ranging from 40,001 to 2,300,000 in popularity are the long tail. The relative number of sales of books from the long tail is then:

$$\frac{\sum_{k=1}^{2,300,000} \frac{1}{k} - \sum_{k=1}^{40,000} \frac{1}{k}}{\sum_{k=1}^{2,300,000} \frac{1}{k}} = 1 - \frac{\sum_{k=1}^{40,000} \frac{1}{k}}{\sum_{k=1}^{2,300,000} \frac{1}{k}} \approx 1 - \frac{\ln 40,000 + \gamma}{\ln 2,300,000 + \gamma} \approx 26.6\%.$$

16.3 · Numerical Analysis of the Long Tail

Hence, the long tail makes up 26.6% of all sales of books by Amazon, provided that the demand for books follows Zipf's law. Note that empirical results based on Amazon sales yielded a long tail of 36.7%. This means that Zipf's law gives a reasonable estimate of Amazon's long tail sales under the rather arbitrary assumption that 40,000 titles are in the head of the distribution.

If the tail is twice as long (4.6 million books), then the sales from the tail increase to 29.8%; that is, the sales from the first 2.3 million books in the tail amounts to 26.6% of the total sale, while the next 2.3 million books in the tail amounts to only 3.2% of the total sales. If the tail is only half as long (1.1 million books), the sales from the tail are 22.9% of the total sales.

▶ Box 16.2 contains a generalization of Ziff's law applied to infinitely long tails.

Box 16.2   Generalization of Zipf's Law

The size of the tail can be adjusted by applying a general discrete dissemination instead of Zipf's law. In a general discrete power-law distribution, the frequency of exactly k events is:

$$f(k) = \frac{k^{-\alpha}}{\zeta(\alpha)}, \alpha > 1,$$

in which $\zeta(\alpha) = \sum_{k=1}^{\infty} k^{-\alpha}$ is the Riemann zeta function of argument a. This distribution is called the *zeta distribution*.

The parameter a alludes to the size of the tail of the distribution. If the tail starts at $k = K = 40{,}001$ (as in the example with Amazon above), then the relative number of books, R, sold in the tail will be:

$$R = 1 - \frac{\sum_{k=1}^{40{,}000} k^{-\alpha}}{\zeta(\alpha)}.$$

The Zipfian distribution is the special case in which $\alpha = 1$. In this case, there must be an upper cutoff N for which $f(X > N) = 0$, and the zeta function is replaced by $\sum_{k=1}^{N} k^{-1}$. The same applies if $\alpha < 1$ since the zeta function diverges for $\alpha \leq 1$.

◘ Figure 16.3 shows the relative number of books sold in the tail (R) as a function of α. Here, the cutoff value is $N = 2{,}300{,}000$, corresponding to the number of books available on Amazon. There are 40,000 books in the head of the distribution. Observe that the relative number of books sold in the tail (R) decreases from 98.3% when $\alpha = 0$ to about 0% when $\alpha > 1.6$. For $\alpha = 0$, all book titles (both in head and tail) sell in the same numbers. In this case, sales are uniformly distributed. Furthermore, for $\alpha > 1.6$, the tail is too small to have any economic value since books in the tail collectively contribute to virtually no sales. Note that in the Zipfian distribution $\alpha = 1$, resulting in $R = 26.6\%$ as calculated above. Note that $\alpha \approx 0.94$ will match the empirical data of Amazon's sales $R = 36.7\%$ for the parameters $N = 2{,}300{,}000$ and $k = K = 40{,}001$. In other words, Amazon book sales as presented here can be modeled accurately using general discrete power-law distribution with $\alpha = 0.94$.

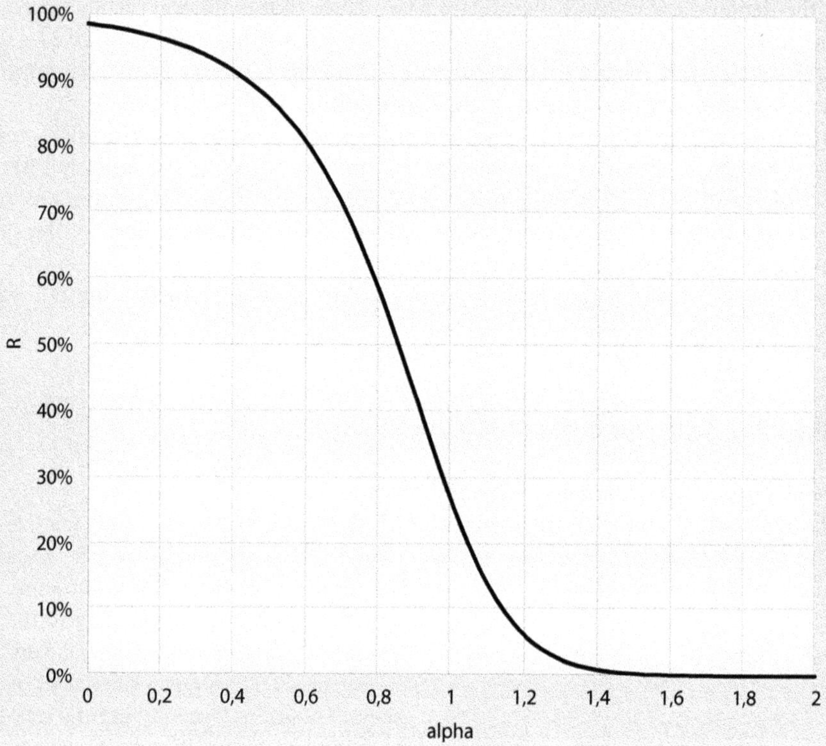

Fig. 16.3 Relative number of books in the tail as a function of alpha. (Authors' own figure)

▶ Box 16.3 is an example of the application of Zipf's law to a completely different area, namely, the vulnerability of the Internet and the World Wide Web to targeted attacks on the infrastructure. Both the Internet and the Web may be regarded as a long tail network. On the Internet, most of the routers are small and connected by communications links to few other routers, while the "tail" of the Internet consists of rather few big routers connected to thousands of other routers. In the Web, most websites are connected to few other websites. These websites make up the "head" of the Web. The "tail" of the Web consists of websites connected to very many other websites, where search engines are example of websites connected to an enormous number of websites.

> **Box 16.3 The Long Tail and the Vulnerability of Internet**
>
> Power-law distributions are not only important to determine the economic value of the long tail. These distributions are also used to evaluate the robustness and vulnerability of the Internet and digital services. In 1999, the two physicists, Albert-László Barabási and Réka Albert, discovered that the number of hyperlinks pointing into or out of webpages followed a general power-law distribution with an exponent approximately equal to 2 (Albert & Barabási, 2001). The same researchers also developed a general theory in which they demonstrated that the number of links connected to the nodes of a graph follows a power-law distribution if the graph is grown with preference. For the Web, "growth with preference" means that a new webpage is connected to another webpage with a probability proportional to the number of existing connections to that webpage. This phenomenon is called the "Barabási-Albert (BA) random graph model." Later, it was found that the size of Internet routers measured in terms of the number of connections they have with other routers also follows the same power law (Dorogovtsev & Mendes, 2001).
>
> Hence, the Internet and the Web have long tails. In these cases, the tail consists of the largest and the head consists of the smallest routers and webpages. This insight directs us toward another observation, namely, that structures like the Internet and the Web are very vulnerable to attacks against routers and webpages in the long tail. Remove several of the biggest Internet routers—there are not very many of them—and the Internet runs into severe connectivity and capacity problems; remove the search engines from the Web, and the Web falls apart. The Internet and the Web are vulnerable to targeted attacks. On the other hand, most of the routers and webpages have small connectivity, and a random attack on routers and webpages may have little overall effect on the Internet or the Web. Hence, the Internet and the Web are, at the same time, both vulnerable and robust against failures and cyberattacks (Audestad, 2007).

16.4 Conclusions

One of the most important characteristics of digital businesses is that the marginal costs of the products are zero; that is, there is no cost associated with production, storing, and distributing the good. For companies selling digital goods, it is, therefore, no practical limits to how many products they have in store. This has created a new type of business that is not practical for products requiring physical space for manufacturing, storing, and delivery. This is the long tail of products that are low in demand but collectively create considerable revenues. Amazon has successfully applied this strategy, and it is claimed that about one-third of their revenues stems from the long tail consisting of books not available in ordinary bookstores. There are several examples of businesses in the digital economy exploiting the same strategy.

Statistically the long tail distribution is related to other statistical distributions such as discrete power-law distributions, the discrete zeta distribution, the Zipfian distribution, and general discrete heavy tail distributions. For example, the long tail distribution of Amazon can be modeled using the Zipfian distribution. Using the distribution fitting the empirical data best, the expected sales from the long tail can be estimated for a variety of digital businesses so that the concept can also be used in strategic business planning.

The distribution of the size of routers on the Internet and connectivity of webpages of the World Wide Web have also long tails. This has important consequences both for the robustness and the vulnerabilities of these structures.

❓ Questions

1. How is Airbnb exploiting the long tail of demand and the long tail of supply in its business operations?
2. What are the characteristics of the long tail generated by Uber in the personal transport industry?
3. What is the probability that that the Internet contains a router with 1000 connections if the size distribution of Internet routers follows a general power law with $\alpha = 2$? To simplify calculations, you can use the fact that Riemann's zeta function with argument 2 is $\zeta(2) = \dfrac{\pi^2}{6}$. If there are ten million routers on the Internet, how many are expected to have 1000 connections? How many routers have exactly one connection?

✅ Answers

1. Airbnb allows people to rent out their homes. This is how Airbnb thereby creates a "long tail" to the supply of available vacation resorts for tourists. Airbnb contributes to the supply side of the tourist industry. Airbnb are different from hotels. They have few rooms available (typically accommodating 2–5 guests) and may be situated outside the city center, where most hotels are located. They may also be cheaper or offer facilities not available at hotels. The demand aspect of this is that people often prefer to rent unique homes, vacation homes, or rooms with bread and breakfast rather than hotels.
2. On the supply side, Uber creates a long tail in the taxi market by enabling private drivers to offer transport using their private cars. This includes that the driver may offer special service such as a ride in a sport car, limousine, van, motorcycle, and so on. On the demand side, the market for personal transport has been increased both in size and diversity.
3. Apply the general power-law distribution and observe that:

$$f(1000) = \frac{k^{-\alpha}}{\zeta(\alpha)} = \frac{1000^{-2}}{\zeta(2)} = \frac{6 \times 1000^{-2}}{\pi^2} = 6 \times 10^{-6} \pi^{-2} \approx 6.08 \times 10^{-7}$$

If there are ten million routers on the Internet, it is expected that $10^7 \times 6.08 \times 10^{-7} \approx 6$ routers have 1000 connections. The expected number of routers with one connection is:

$$10^7 \times f(1) = 10^7 \times \frac{1^{-2}}{\zeta(2)} = 6 \times 10^7 \times \pi^{-2} \approx 6{,}000{,}000$$

References

Albert, R., & Barabási, A.-L.. (2001). Statistical mechanics of complex networks. *ArXiv*.
Anderson, C. (2006). *The long tail: Why the future of business is selling less of more*. Hyperion.
Audestad, J. A. (2007). Internet as a multiple graph structure: The role of the transport layer. *Information Security Technical Report, 12*(1), 16–23.
Brynjolfsson, E., & Saunders, A. (2013). *Wired for innovation*. The MIT Press.
Brynjolfsson, E., Hu, Y., & Simester, D. (2003). Consumer surplus in the digital economy: Estimating the value of increased product variety at online booksellers. *Management Science, 49*, 1580–1596.
Brynjolfsson, E., Hu, Y., & Smith, M. D. (2010). The long tail, the changing shape of Amazon's sales distribution curve. *SSRN*.
Brynjolfsson, E., Hu, Y., & Simester, D. (2011). Hello long tail: The effect of search cost on the concentration of product sales. *SSRN*.
Dorogovtsev, S. N., & Mendes, J. F. F. (2001). *Evolution of networks: From biological nets to the internet and WWW*. Oxford University Press.
Hanks, J. (2017, April 4). Amazon doesn't do long tail. Why should you? *Practical Ecommerce*.
Schroeder, M. (2009). *Fractals, chaos, power laws: Minutes from an infinite paradise*. Dover.

Further Reading

Anderson, C. (2006). *The long tail: Why the future of business is selling less of more*. Hyperion.

Digital Markets

Contents

17.1 Market Types – 244

17.2 Stakeholders and Relationships in Digital Markets – 245

17.3 E-Commerce Markets – 247

17.4 Network Access Markets – 251

17.5 Information Service Markets – 254

17.6 Conclusions – 256

References – 258

© The Author(s), under exclusive license to Springer Nature Switzerland AG 2021
H. Øverby, J. A. Audestad, *Introduction to Digital Economics*, Classroom Companion: Business,
https://doi.org/10.1007/978-3-030-78237-5_17

Learning Objectives

After completing this chapter, you should be able to:
- Understand digital and e-commerce markets.
- Identify the different types of stakeholders in digital markets.
- Analyze network access markets and information service markets.

17.1 Market Types

A market is a mechanism for trading both tangible and intangible goods and services. Figure 17.1 classifies markets according to the type of good or service (horizontal axis) and type of channel used for trading the good or service (vertical axis). Examples of tangible goods include computers and cars. Examples of non-digital services are hairdressing and taxi rides. Online trading implies that an ICT infrastructure (the Internet) is used to carry out some or all activities associated with the trade: viewing products, bargaining prices and delivery terms, ordering, product delivery, and transfer of payment. Tangible goods and non-digital services can be traded online; however, these products cannot be delivered over the ICT infrastructure. Shipment and delivery of digital services is done online. We may then define a digital market as follows.

> **Definition 17.1 Digital Market**
> A digital market is a mechanism for *online* trading of both digital goods and digital services and tangible goods and non-digital services.

Fig. 17.1 Classification of markets. (Authors' own figure)

E-commerce is online trading of all kinds of goods and services. This includes online shopping, online payment, transfer of funds, management of supply chains, and business-to-business exchange of data. E-commerce also includes the trading of network access and information services. To classify an activity as e-commerce, it must support some sort of digital payment system.

E-commerce markets have grown to constitute an important part of the global economy following the commercial success of the World Wide Web (WWW) in the early 1990s. Two important and distinct parts of e-commerce are the online markets for network access and the online markets for information services:

- *E-commerce markets* are the business of selling goods and services over the Internet (see ▶ Sect. 17.3).
- *Network access markets* are the business of providing access to the Internet and other communication networks (see ▶ Sect. 17.4).
- *Information service markets* are the trade of content, applications, and information on the Internet (see ▶ Sect. 17.5).

Note that not all activity performed online in digital markets is e-commerce. For instance, information services may be exchanged between provider and consumer free of charge. Such an exchange of digital goods is not e-commerce since there is no payment involved.

17.2 Stakeholders and Relationships in Digital Markets

◘ Figure 17.2 shows the most important stakeholders involved in digital markets and the relationships between them. The *network provider* (NP) is the owner of the ICT infrastructure needed for online trading, encompassing fixed networks, mobile networks, Internet infrastructure, and storing and computing facilities. An infrastructure provider owning a mobile network is sometimes referred to as a "coverage" operator. The *Internet service provider* (ISP) buys access to this infrastructure from the NP and resells it to the *consumer* (C) and the *application service provider* (ASP). The consumer may use these services directly to access the Internet, make phone calls, and send SMS. The ASP uses the infrastructure access purchased from the ISP to support the distribution of content, applications, and services that the ASP produces. The ASP may also buy copyrighted content from a *content provider* (CP) such as movies, music, and news articles. The ASP uses the input from the ISP and the content provider to offer digital services and applications to the consumer.

Examples of types of services offered by ASPs are online music streaming (e.g., Spotify and Tidal), online video streaming (e.g., Netflix and HBO), digital newspapers (e.g., *The New York Times* and *Financial Times*), online banking (e.g., HSBC and Nordea), cloud storage (e.g., Dropbox and Google Drive), and social media services (e.g., Twitter and Facebook). Many of the applications and services offered by the ASP are free of charge for the consumer, for example, Google's search engine, Wikipedia, and Facebook. The ASP providing these applications must acquire revenues from other sources than the consumers. Normally, the consumer

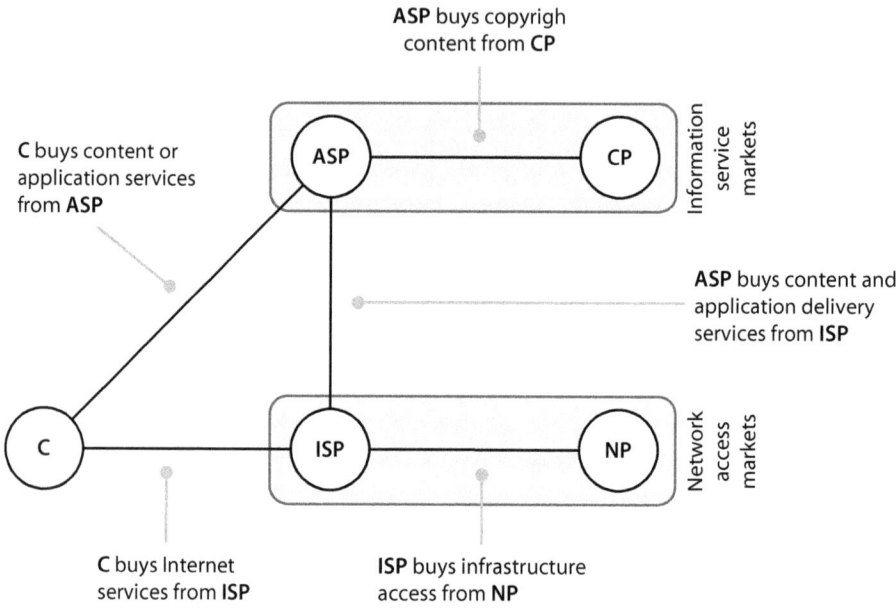

Fig. 17.2 Stakeholders and relationships in digital markets. (Authors' own figure)

pays for Internet access to the ISP. Network access markets are the business domain of the ISP and the NP, while markets for information services are the business domain of the ASP and the CP.

The model in Fig. 17.2 is a simplification of the business domain for digital services. The most important observation from this simple model is that there is a sharp separation of business domains in the provision of digital services. Not only are there many stakeholders involved in the provision of digital services, but there are also big differences in how each of them conducts their business. For instance, the NP builds and operates a physical ICT infrastructure consisting of optical fibers, mobile base stations, communication satellites, undersea cables, Internet routers, and switching centers. This infrastructure may cover a large geographical area and consist of expensive equipment. Moreover, the NP needs a staff of technicians and engineers to build and manage the ICT infrastructure. There are also huge undertakings in upgrading the ICT infrastructure since ICT tends to get outdated quickly.

The content provider produces content such as music, movies, and news articles. The business operation of the content producer is vastly different from that of the NP. The products of the content provider are usually digital and reside only on a digital storage device. These products do not need upgrades or extensive management after being produced.

Formal relationships or contracts, in terms of service-level agreements (SLAs), may exist between the stakeholders in digital markets.

17.3 · E-Commerce Markets

Definition 17.2 Service-Level Agreement
A service-level agreement (SLA) is a contract that exists between a consumer and a provider of a digital service; see ◘ Fig. 17.3. The SLA describes certain contractual terms related to the delivered service, e.g., price, delivery precision, and responsibility.

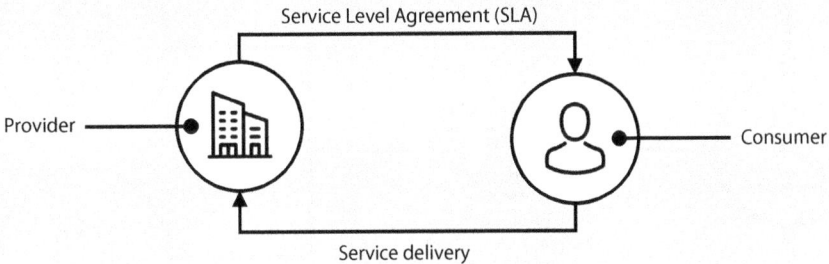

◘ **Fig. 17.3** Service-level agreement configuration. (Authors' own figure)

Most SLAs between consumers and providers are standardized. If the terms defined in the SLA are not satisfied by either party, some form of compensation might be requested.

Examples of the terms that may be covered in an SLA include specifications of maximum service delays, mean time between failures, service availability, security, and privacy. All these specifications describe the quality of the service (QoS) as perceived by the consumer. Examples of SLAs are the contract between consumers and Internet service providers for the delivery of network access, the contract between consumers and Spotify for the delivery of online music, and the contract between a provider of security alarm services and a mobile network operator.

17.3 E-Commerce Markets

E-commerce is the online trading of tangible goods, digital goods, and services. This is illustrated in ◘ Fig. 17.4. For all types of e-commerce trade, the consumer conducts and manages the trade using an online channel such as the Internet. The supplier handles the trade and ships the products or services to the consumer. Digital goods and services are delivered to the consumer over the Internet, while tangible goods are delivered to the consumer using traditional transportation.

Examples of e-commerce trading include buying books from Amazon, buying music from iTunes, purchasing electronics on eBay, and subscribing to services delivered by Spotify, Netflix, mobile network operators, and Internet access providers. In fact, all trading activities conducted online can be categorized as e-commerce. However, to categorize an exchange of goods and services between a

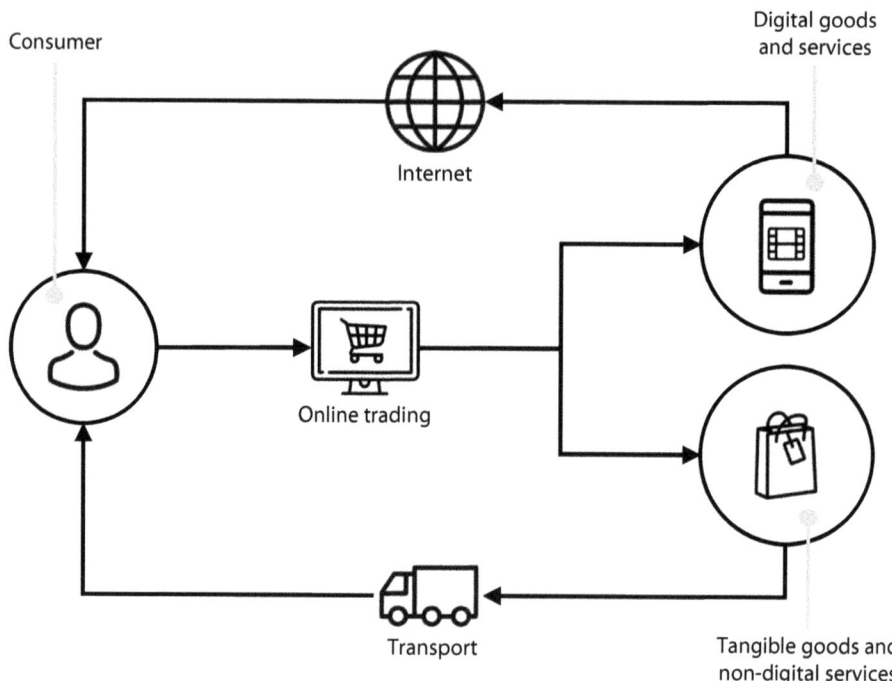

☐ **Fig. 17.4** E-commerce trading. (Authors' own figure)

supplier and a consumer as e-commerce, there must be some sort of financial activity between them. The exchange of goods and services without any financial activity is not regarded as e-commerce even though the trade is done in a digital market. One example is the use of Facebook. The use of Facebook is free of charge for the user, and, therefore, there is no financial activity between the user and Facebook. The access to and use of Facebook is not e-commerce. On the other hand, Facebook sells advertisement space to retailers and other companies as a part of their business model. This is, indeed, e-commerce in which Facebook is the supplier.

> **Definition 17.3 E-Commerce**
> E-commerce is the online trading of tangible goods and digital goods and services with some sort of financial activity.

One particular form of e-commerce is mobile commerce, or m-commerce, where all interactions between retailer and customer (viewing, ordering, shopping, and payment) take place via smartphone applications. The term was coined by Kevin Duffey in 1997. He defined m-commerce as "the delivery of electronic commerce capabilities directly into the consumer's hand, *anywhere*, via wireless technology" (Global Mobile Commerce Forum, 1997). The use of smartphones for shopping and payment services is now taking over most of the e-commerce market because

17.3 · E-Commerce Markets

of the convenience of using a smartphone for this purpose rather than personal computers (Popovic, 2019).

In the USA, about 10% of all retail is performed using e-commerce (E-commerce in the United States, Statistics and Facts, 2020). In China, which is the largest e-commerce market in the world, about 20% of all retail sales are e-commerce (Long, 2017). These numbers are from 2017, and they are expected to escalate in the near future. Similar trends are seen in most parts of the world—the share of e-commerce is increasing and is replacing traditional retail. Ecommerce News Europe reports that e-commerce increased dramatically during the COVID-19 lockdown (The impact of Covid-19 on ecommerce, 2021). According to the survey, 90% of the major companies involved in e-commerce increased their sales during this period. For 50% of them, the sales more than doubled.

Important milestones in the evolution of e-commerce were the launch of eBay and Amazon in 1995, PayPal in 1998, and Alibaba in 1999. Amazon is now among the five largest companies worldwide according to market cap. PayPal was one of the pioneers of online payment systems. Other important services and companies in the e-commerce market include Groupon (launched in 2010), Apple Pay (launched in 2014), and Google Pay (launched in 2015 as Android Pay).

There are two important requirements for successful e-commerce markets.
− To become an efficient marketplace, e-commerce requires *websites or apps* where vendors can present their items for sale and buyers can choose among products and fill their shopping trolleys. The search algorithms must be simple and based not only on product names but also keywords and product categories.
− Simple and effective *online payment systems* are crucial to the success of e-commerce. There are several different types of online payment systems; for example, credit cards (e.g., VISA and MasterCard), e-wallet (e.g., PayPal), invoice installments (e.g., Klarna), and cryptocurrencies (e.g., Bitcoin, Ethereum, and Ripple).

E-commerce market can be divided into four categories depending on whether the buyer or the seller is a professional business (denoted as "B") or a private consumer (denoted as "C"). These four types of e-commerce markets are as follows (see ◘ Fig. 17.5):
− *Business-to-Consumer* (B2C) e-commerce is the traditional market in which goods or services are sold online by professional companies to private consumers. Examples are buying books from Amazon, films from Netflix, flight tickets from Expedia, computers from Dell, and broadband subscriptions from a network operator.
− *Business-to-Business* (B2B) e-commerce is the online trading between two professional companies. B2C e-commerce and B2B e-commerce have experienced huge growth during the last decades. The main difference between B2B and B2C e-commerce is that, in B2C, small quantities of goods and services are sold to many private consumers, while in B2B, large quantities of goods and services are sold to a small number of professional businesses.
− *Consumer-to-Consumer* (C2C) e-commerce is the online trading between two private consumers. Examples of C2C e-commerce companies include eBay,

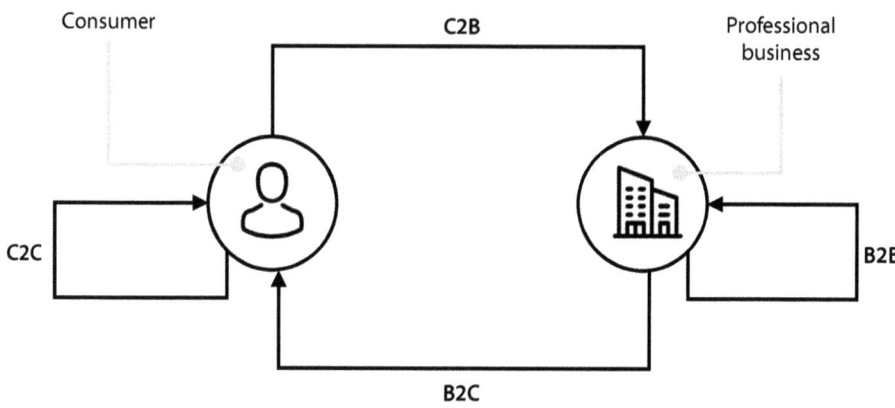

Fig. 17.5 Classification of e-commerce markets. (Authors' own figure)

Uber, and Airbnb. In fact, most of the sharing economies are C2C e-commerce. Advantages of C2C e-commerce are better utilization of resources and simpler trade opportunities for second-hand goods.
- *Consumer-to-Business* (C2B) e-commerce enables private consumers to sell digital services online to professional companies. This is the most recent supplement to e-commerce. One example of C2B e-commerce is a private consumer's web page on which manufacturers and retailers advertise their products. A blogger may have many viewers on their blog, and manufacturers or providers may find the blog to be a simple and cheap way to reach a particular audience.

Box 17.1 The Sharing Economy

The sharing economy enables consumers to sell access to property, goods, money, or services to other consumers for a certain fee. Airbnb and Uber are two of the most well-known companies in the sharing economy. The sharing economy is an example of C2C e-commerce since the trade takes place between two consumers.

A more precise term of the sharing economy is *access economy*. This is because, strictly speaking, consumers do not share goods or services but pay for access to other consumers' goods and services. The sharing economy may lead to better utilization of resources since homes, tools, or cars can be rented out when they are not used by the owner. An important requirement of sharing economy services is fast and reliable feedback from the consumers. This is required to build trust and reputation for those offering access to their assets and services.

The major difference between the sharing economy and traditional trade is that the providers are often individuals and not companies. In many countries, this means that a different set of laws and regulations govern the trade. The sharing economy is enabled by multisided platforms (see ▶ Chap. 10) and crowdsourcing (see ▶ Chap. 7). Sharing economy services use crowdsourcing as a production model and create value as a value network (see ▶ Chap. 8) or, more specifically, as a multisided platform. One example is Uber, in which people (the crowd) offer transportation services to consumers. Uber does not own taxis or cars but instead mediates between drivers and passengers. Uber is totally dependent on the crowd to provide their assets (cars) in its business model.

The sharing economy challenges legal frameworks, especially labor laws and commercial laws. Uber is, for example, forbidden in several countries, including Norway, Denmark, and Italy, due to violation of the laws concerning licensing of professional taxi drivers (Rhodes, 2017). Another example is Airbnb having met restrictions in, for example, New York City where private consumers are not allowed to rent out property on a short-term contract (less than 1 month) when the host is not present. The sharing economy enables consumers to make profits off assets they own. Sharing services have been criticized as competing under different terms than established businesses by circumventing labor protection laws and thereby providing services with lower costs compared to services produced by companies using the in-house production model.

17.4 Network Access Markets

Network access is offered jointly by the ISP (commercial) and NP (technical). This includes access to broadband Internet connections, Wi-Fi, public mobile networks, telephone services, and messaging services (e.g., email and SMS/MMS). These services are integral parts of the network and do not depend on additional services delivered by other stakeholders (e.g., ASPs or content providers).

Network access is a fundamental service—also called a foundational technology—in the digital economy. This is because the access to and delivery of digital services depends on reliable access to the Internet. Reliable access to the Internet is supported by a worldwide ICT infrastructure consisting of optical fibers, wireless base stations, Internet routers, satellite networks, and other network resources. Users access the Internet using personal computers, tablets, set-top boxes, or smartphones. The NP owns and operates the physical ICT infrastructure supporting the Internet. This includes all kinds of communication networks and associated management systems and computing and storage facilities. The ISP buys access to the infrastructure from the NP and resells this access to consumers and ASPs.

There are several examples of NPs that are also ISPs. The traditional incumbent network operator both owns the communication network and sells telephone services to consumers. To ensure fair competition among ISPs, national regulation in most countries compels the incumbent network operator to split the business operations into two independent parts: one for NP operations and one for ISP operations. Several national regulators have also forced the incumbent NP to open the ICT infrastructure for ISPs other than the ISP owned by the incumbent. These ISPs can lease the ICT infrastructure from the NP on the same terms as the ISP owned by the incumbent NP.

ISPs that do not own their own network infrastructure are called *virtual network operators* (VNOs)—or mobile virtual network operators (MVNOs) if they offer mobile services. Figure 17.6 shows an example of how a VNO (ISPB of Company B) is commercially related to the network provider (NP) owned by Company A. Both companies A and B offer services to the consumer (C) through the Internet service providers ISPA and ISPB, respectively. The major difference between them is that ISPA is owned by the company that owns the ICT infrastructure (IP), while ISPB leases access to the same infrastructure from Company A. See ▶ Chap. 5 for other aspects concerning VNOs.

Over-the-top services (OTT) are media services offered by the ASP or content provider directly over the network of the NP. OTT services require access to the Internet delivered by the ISP. However, OTT services compete with the media and communication services offered by the ISP itself. This is illustrated in Fig. 17.7,

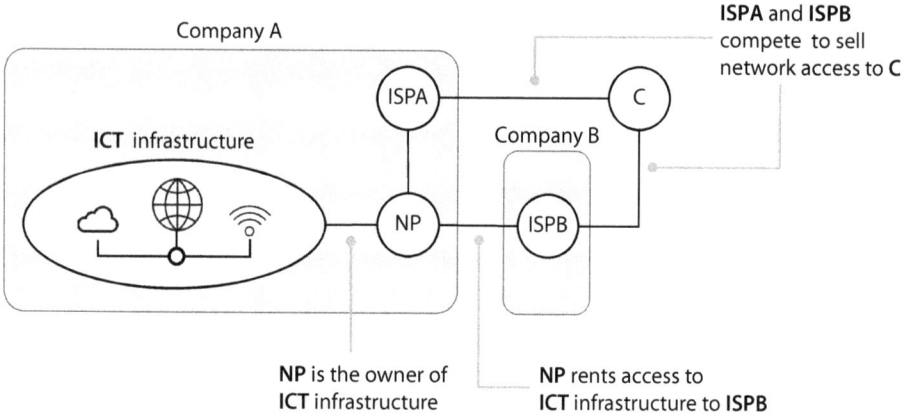

Fig. 17.6 Virtual network operator. (Authors' own figure)

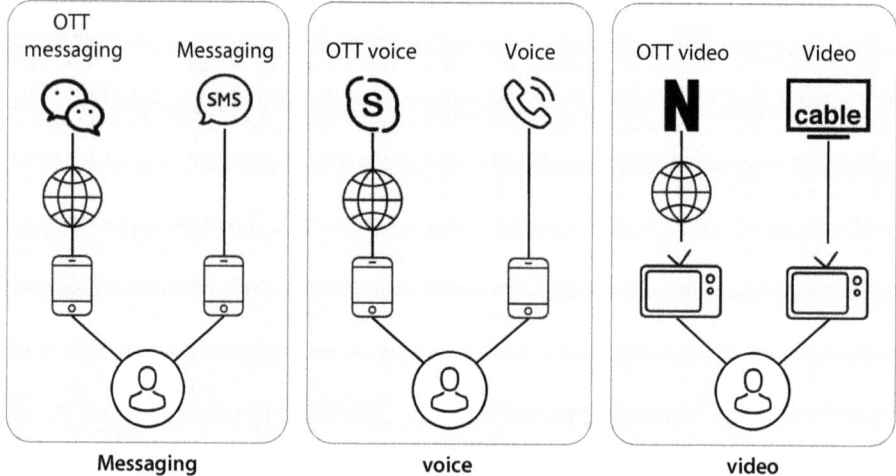

Fig. 17.7 Over-the-top services. (Authors' own figure)

in which the architecture of OTT messaging, OTT voice, and OTT film distribution is presented together with the equivalent services offered by the ISP.

A consumer may use a smartphone in combination with Internet access offered by the ISP and WeChat (an OTT messaging service) as an alternative to SMS messaging provided by the ISP. A consumer may also use Internet access combined with voice-over-IP telephone service offered by an ASP—for example, Skype—as an alternative to the telephone service offered by a mobile service provider. Similarly, Netflix may provide the same services directly over the Internet as a provider of cable television services. The key point of OTT is that the same set of services that was traditionally offered over a dedicated communication network can be offered over the Internet without other involvement of the ISP and the NP than transporting bits.

The major challenge for the ISP is smaller revenue because of competition from OTT services. This is because the price per bit for the telephone service has traditionally been orders of magnitude higher than the price per bit for Internet access. Hence, the ISP will face reduced revenue as consumers move from, for example, telephone service to OTT voice services since the price per bit that the ISP charges the OTT provider for network access is much lower than the price per bit that the ISP charges the consumer directly. For the consumer, OTT means significantly lower prices for digital services such as telephony and messaging. OTT is one step toward the convergence of services (see ▶ Chap. 3), in which traditional telephone service is replaced by VoIP and cable television services are replaced by video streaming.

Network access services are close to becoming *digital commodities*. This is because it is almost impossible to differentiate between the various network access services provided by different network access suppliers. In commodity markets, price is the most important differentiator between suppliers. This may also be one reason for the ongoing price war between suppliers of broadband access and mobile telephone services.

◘ Figure 17.8 extends ◘ Fig. 17.2 to include *device providers* (DP). Device providers are providers of user equipment such as smartphones, laptops, and

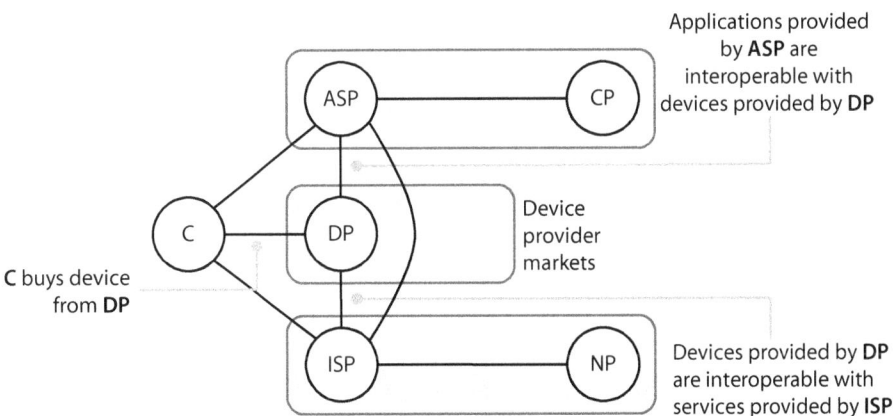

◘ **Fig. 17.8** Device providers in digital markets. (Authors' own figure)

personal computers. Production and trade of such devices are not part of the digital economy as defined in this book. However, they constitute an integral part of the digital service ecosystem because digital services must be accessed through some sort of device produced and marketed by device providers. A specific device is interoperable with both the access services provided by ISPs and the applications provided by ASPs. This condition may, however, be device specific. For example, apps available at Apple App Store are only available for devices provided by Apple. However, technologically speaking, full interoperability exists between network access, devices, and applications—any device can be connected to any network and run any application. This separation of technologies between ISP, device provider, and ASP is the basic concept of the layered Internet model described in ▶ Chap. 4.

17.5 Information Service Markets

Information services are jointly offered by the ASP and the content provider and are traded in an information service market (Linde & Stock, 2011). They include content and applications ranging from simple apps to complex software. Huge amounts of digital content and applications are available for consumers. ◘ Table 17.1 contains examples of information services and how they may be categorized.

Some of the services listed in ◘ Table 17.1 are available internationally, while others have a regional target. Since the marginal cost of digital services is zero, it is

◘ **Table 17.1** Examples of information services. (Authors' compilation)

Type of service	Examples of information service
Social media services	Facebook, LinkedIn, Twitter, QZone, VKontakte
Music streaming	Spotify, Apple Music, Google Play Music, Tidal
Video streaming	Netflix, HBO, Amazon Video, YouTube TV
Web browsers	Chrome, Safari, Internet Explorer, Firefox
Word-editing software	Microsoft Word, Google Docs, Pages
Internet telephony (VoIP)	Skype, Google Voice
Messaging	WhatsApp, WeChat, Messenger, SMS
Multiplayer online games	*World of Warcraft, Starcraft 2*
Travel and accommodation	TripAdvisor, Citymapper, Uber, Airbnb
Online payment	PayPal, Alipay, Google Pay, Apple Pay
Language	Google Translate, Duolingo
News	*NY Times*, Google News, Reddit

17.5 · Information Service Markets

simple to distribute them on the international marketplace. However, there may be several reasons why some of them are restricted to certain geographical areas, for example:
- Political regulations (e.g., Facebook is not allowed in China)
- Competition regulations (e.g., Uber is forbidden in several countries)
- Language (e.g., local newspapers)
- Local target (e.g., regional transportation apps)
- Infrastructure limitations (e.g., local network not supporting broadband access)
- Local information (e.g., road, traffic, and weather conditions)

In an article published in *Harvard Business Review* in 1998, Josef Pine and James Gilmore coined the term *experience economy* (Pine & Gilmore, 1998). Their argument is that people are willing to pay for the experience of being "engaged" in the product they buy. Several information services belong to the category of *experience goods*. Examples of experience goods are movies, interactive games, music, and newspaper articles. It is hard to assess the quality of an experience good in advance since it is difficult for an individual consumer to assess the quality of a specific music track or a movie before it is purchased. To give consumers some information about the digital good or service, the provider may have to give away samples of the product or present evaluations of the product by professional reviewers or by feedback from the public. Network access, on the other hand, is classified as a *search good* (Nelson, 1970). The most important characteristic of a search good is that the quality of the good can be assessed before it is purchased. Search goods are more subject to price wars and fierce competition than experience goods. Search goods are often commodity markets, while experience goods are markets with monopolistic competition; see ▶ Chap. 13.

> **Definition 17.4 Search Good and Experience Good**
> *Search good* is a good with attributes or qualities that can be evaluated before consumption. *Experience good* is good with attributes and qualities that can only be evaluated after consumption.

When content is produced in-house, as explained in ▶ Chap. 7, the content provider producing it is a professional company. One example is the film industry, which requires huge budgets and a professionalized mode of operation when making a movie. On the other hand, when content is produced by crowdsourcing or peer production, the content provider (CP) and the consumer (C) may be the same entity, called a *prosumer*.

> **Definition 17.5 Prosumer**
> Prosumer can be defined as "individuals who consume and produce value, either for self-consumption or consumption by others, and can receive implicit or explicit

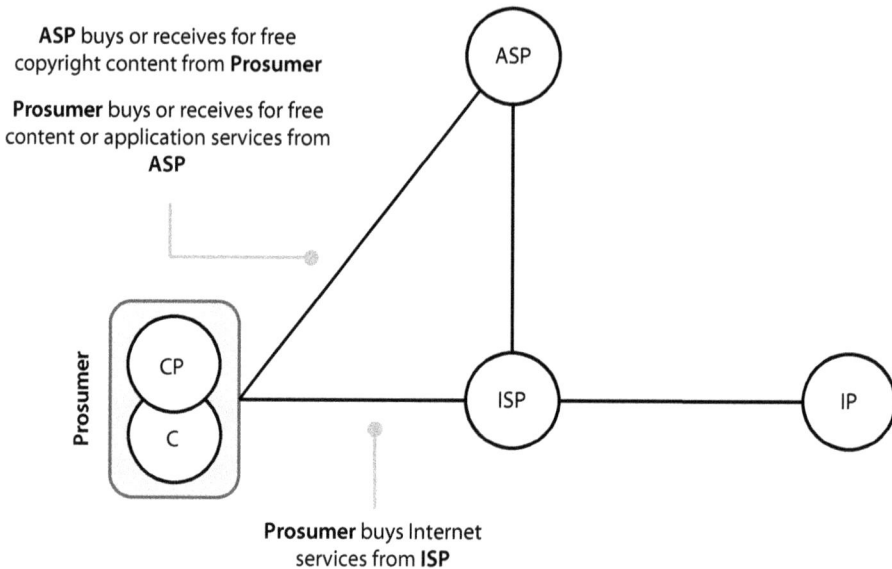

Fig. 17.9 Prosumers in digital markets. (Authors' own figure)

> incentives from organizations involved in the exchange" (Lang et al., 2020). In the digital economy, this definition may be limited to encompass organizations where individuals may both produce content for other individuals and consume content produced by other individuals.

This is illustrated in Fig. 17.9. There are several business models available for the ASP:
- The ASP may buy copyrighted content from the prosumer and sell it back to the prosumer.
- The prosumer may give content for free to the ASP, and the ASP may offer the content to the prosumer either for free or for a certain fee.
- The ASP may charge the prosumers for using the mediation service, either as producer, consumer, or both.

A prosumer may either only produce content, only consume content, or both. The ASP considers the groups of consumers and producers as a single stakeholder. YouTube is an example of a company connecting prosumers.

17.6 Conclusions

Digital markets can be categorized in several ways.
- E-commerce markets include all kinds of trading using the Internet for product search, purchasing, and payment. The good may be tangible or digital. In the

17.6 · Conclusions

latter case, the good is also delivered on the Internet. One basic requirement for a trade to be categorized as e-commerce is that the trade is associated by financial transactions. Examples are Amazon and Spotify.
- Network access markets are the commercial activities associated with network access and transfer of bits between users. The stakeholders include owners of infrastructures such as Internet routers, optical fiber networks, wireless access networks, and satellite networks. The concept also includes Internet service providers (ISP) offering the infrastructure services such as Internet access and 5G mobile services to the customers.
- Information service markets consist of the myriad of services offered by content providers and application service providers.

Moreover, the information service markets may also be categorized as:
- Over-the-top services where the provider of the service is bypassing traditional services offered on the network such as voice, television, and messaging by hiding them in unspecified Internet packets.
- Search goods where the attributes of the service are known before consumption.
- Experience goods where the attributes of the service are only known after consumption.
- Prosumer markets where the users are both producers and consumers of value.

❓ Questions
1. Amazon and Alibaba are two of the largest e-commerce companies in the world.
   (a) Are Amazon and Alibaba doing B2B, B2C, C2B, or C2C e-commerce?
   (b) How are Amazon and Alibaba handling online payments?
   (c) Have Amazon's and Alibaba's business operations influenced transaction costs?

2. Apple Pay is an online payment service.
   (a) Is Apple Pay an experience good or a search good?
   (b) Is Apple Pay an OTT service?

3. Why can we categorize the users of eBay, Twitter, Airbnb, and Wikipedia as prosumers?

✅ Answers
1. Amazon and Alibaba
   (a) Amazon is primarily a B2C and Alibaba is primarily a C2C. However, Amazon has also enabled C2C on its platforms.
   (b) Alibaba has its own payment system called Alipay. Amazon relies on external payment systems.
   (c) Both Amazon and Alibaba have contributed to reduced transaction costs in the digital economy. This is because they allow consumers to search for millions of products on their websites in a very efficient way compared to traditional retail businesses, e.g., by using keywords.

2. Apple Pay
    (a) Apple Pay is a search good: the attributes of the service are known before it is used.
    (b) Apple Pay is not an OTT service but offered in combination with other Internet services (e.g., e-commerce).
3. eBay offers a platform on which users may sell goods directly to other users. Users post messages on Twitter that is read and commented by other users. Airbnb mediates between users having assets for short-term rental (e.g., vacation homes) and other users in search for such assets. The users of Wikipedia are both producers and readers of the information on the encyclopedia. In all cases, the user may be both producer and consumer.

References

E-commerce in the United States, Statistics and Facts. *Statista*. July 7, 2020.
Global Mobile Commerce Forum: Inaugural plenary conference. November 12, 1997.
Lang, B., Dolan, R., Kemper, J., & Northey, G. (2020). Prosumers in time of crisis: Definition, archetypes and implications. *Journal of Service Management, 32*(2), 176–189.
Linde, F., & Stock, W. G. (2011). *Information markets. A strategic guideline for the I-commerce*. De Gruyter Saur.
Long, D. (2017, July 5). China's ecommerce market to pass $1.1tn in 2017. *The Drum*.
Nelson, P. (1970). Information and consumer behavior. *Journal of Political Economy, 78*(2), 311.
Pine, B. J., & Gilmore, J. (1998, July 1). Welcome to the experience economy. *Harvard Business Review*.
Popovic, A. (2019, August 21). *mCommerce: How mobile commerce is changing the way we do business*. Price2Spy.
Rhodes. (2017, September 22). UBER: Which countries have banned the controversial taxi app. *The Independent*.
The impact of Covid-19 on ecommerce. *Ecommerce News Europe*. January 15, 2021.

Further Reading

Laudon, K. C., & Traver, C. G. (2017). *E-commerce 2017: Business, technology, and society*. Pearson.

Digital Market Modeling

Contents

18.1 Introduction – 260

18.2 Bass Diffusion Model – 261

18.3 Model for Markets with Competition and Churning – 268

18.4 Models for Massive Multiplayer Online Games – 271

18.5 Analysis of Real Markets – 275

18.6 Conclusions – 277

References – 279

© The Author(s), under exclusive license to Springer Nature Switzerland AG 2021
H. Øverby, J. A. Audestad, *Introduction to Digital Economics*, Classroom Companion: Business,
https://doi.org/10.1007/978-3-030-78237-5_18

Chapter 18 · Digital Market Modeling

Learning Objectives

After completing this chapter, you should be able to:
- Identify the growth mechanisms of evolving markets.
- Set up departmental mathematical models for simple digital markets.
- Apply strategic issues such as latency, effects of churning, growth rate, and inflexion on the evolution of real markets.

18.1 Introduction

This chapter presents quantitative models for the temporal evolution of digital markets. The chapter requires some basic knowledge of elementary calculus such as ordinary differential equations and simple algebraic manipulations. Some of the mathematical derivations are placed in separate boxes to make the text more easily available also to those who are less skilled in calculus.

The objective is to uncover the dynamic behavior of markets that are common in the digital economy, for example, social media, interactive games, communication services, and sales of electronic gadgets. An evolving market is not in an equilibrium state, and standard supply-demand theories do not apply to these markets. Moreover, in several of these markets, the marginal cost and the price of products is zero (e.g., Facebook and Google Search) making supply-demand curves meaningless.

The purpose of this chapter is to show:
- How the markets for certain products (e.g., durables and certain digital services) evolve and mature as a function of time (▶ Sect. 18.2)
- Why competition may, in some cases, lead to winner-takes-all markets and, in other case, to stable markets shared by several suppliers (▶ Sect. 18.3)
- How markets like interactive games grow, mature, and die (▶ Sect. 18.4)

The temporal evolution of the market can, to a first approximation, be modeled using single first-order differential equations or coupled sets of such equations. For simplicity, all markets that are considered consist of a fixed number, N, of potential customers buying the good; that is, market variations owing to births and deaths processes are ignored. The equations then become simpler, and the solutions are easier to understand. The simplification does not alter the validity and generality of the conclusions.

In some markets, eventually all potential customers have purchased the good at some time, and no more sales take place. It is also assumed that there are no other saturation effects (e.g., insufficient supply) influencing the likelihood that a product is purchased. There are several examples of services that have evolved in this way—for example, mobile phone subscriptions and Internet access. In both cases, no significant saturation effects caused by overload in the technical infrastructure have been observed during the evolution of these networks. Similar observations are made regarding the evolution of several social media services—the providers of the

18.2 · Bass Diffusion Model

services seem to be able to put up enough capacity to avoid the saturation effects that moderate the evolution of the service.

We start with analyzing markets using the market diffusion equation developed by Frank Bass in 1969 (Bass, 1969). There are several reasons for this:
- The Bass diffusion model describes rather well the evolution of markets for durable commodity products where every household usually needs one item of each, for example, refrigerators, home freezers, stoves, and lawn mowers. The model is also valid for social media such as Facebook and Twitter and for subscription-based digital services such as Internet access, Spotify, and Netflix.
- The Bass diffusion model allows simple analytic solutions from which we may draw important conclusions concerning the temporal evolution of the market.
- The model can also be used in more complex cases such as competition and online games to describe processes such as customer churn and the rate by which customers are leaving the service.

18.2 Bass Diffusion Model

◘ Figure 18.1 shows a simple market model for durables (e.g., refrigerators and radios) or goods where only one unit of the good is needed (e.g., newspaper subscription). The model is called the Bass diffusion model. Examples of applications of the Bass diffusion model in the digital domain include smartphone subscriptions, Facebook accounts, and Twitter accounts. The container (or compartment) to the left in the figure represents individuals who have not yet purchased the good (potential customers). There are $N - B$ such individuals, in which N is the total population. The container (or compartment) to the right represents individuals

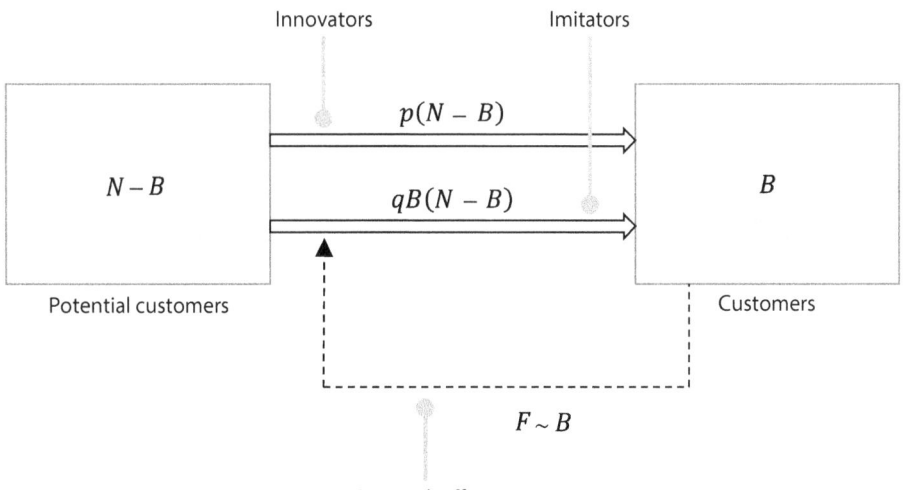

◘ Fig. 18.1 The Bass diffusion model. (Authors' own figure)

who have already purchased the good. There are B such customers. Note that the total population (potential adopters plus adopters) is assumed to be constant and equal to N and that anyone having bought the good keeps it indefinitely. This implies that birth or death processes are not included in the model. To be able to solve the equations using analytic tools, it is also assumed that all flow parameters are constants.

When individuals buy a good, they become customers and move from the *potential customers* container to the *customers* container. This is the basic dynamics of the model.

There are two flows of new buyers of the good:
- Flow of *innovators* consists of individuals who buy the good independently of who else has bought it. These are the *spontaneous buyers*—also referred to as *early adopters*. The strength of the flow is $p(N - B)$ in which the intensity by which an arbitrary individual will buy the good is p. The parameter p is called the *coefficient of innovation*.
- Flow of *imitators* consists of individuals who buy the good because others have bought it. These individuals are also called *late followers* (or just followers) or *stimulated buyers*. The strength of the flow is $qB(N - B)$ in which qB is the intensity by which an individual is stimulated into buying the good, expressing that the intensity by which the imitator will buy the good is proportional to the current number of customers. The parameter q is called the *coefficient of imitation*.

The model also contains a feedback loop representing the network effect. The strength of the feedback is proportional to the number of customers who have already bought the good. This is a network effect of the Metcalfe type; see ▶ Chap. 9. ◘ Table 18.1 summarizes the parameters used in the Bass diffusion model.

The total flow of customers at any instant of time, dB/dt, is equal to the sum of innovators and imitators buying the service at that instant of time. The differential equation for the market dynamics follows then directly from ◘ Fig. 18.1:

◘ **Table 18.1** Parameters in the Bass diffusion model. (Authors' compilation)

Parameter	Description
N	Total population
B	Individuals that have bought the product or are using the service at time t (i.e., the current customers)
p	Coefficient of innovation
q	Coefficient of imitation
t	Time

18.2 · Bass Diffusion Model

$$\frac{dB}{dt} = p(N-B) + qB(N-B) = (p+qB)(N-B).$$

This is the Bass diffusion equation. Note that the term $p + qB$ is the intensity by which an item is sold in the infinitesimal period dt. dB/dt is, therefore, the demand for the good at time t since the demand is, by definition, the same as items sold per unit of time. The Bass equation is solved in ▶ Box 18.1.

Box 18.1   Solution of the Bass Equation

The Bass equation is separable since $dB = (p + qB)(N - B)dt$, resulting in the following equation where the dependent variable B and the time variable t have been moved to each side of the equation:

$$\frac{dB}{(p+qB)(N-B)} = dt.$$

By simple algebraic manipulations we find:

$$\frac{p+qB}{N-B} = ce^{(p+qN)t},$$

in which c is the constant of integration. Observe that for $t = 0$, $B(0) = B_0$ (the initial condition), so by setting

Expanding the left-hand side of the equation and multiplying both sides by $p + qN$ results in:

$$\frac{qdB}{p+qB} + \frac{dB}{N-B} = (p+qN)dt.$$

Integrating both sides of this equation term by term gives:

$$\ln(p+qB) - \ln(N-B) = \ln c + (p+qN)t.$$

$t = 0$ and $B = B_0$ in the equation, the constant of integration is easily found:

$$c = \frac{p+qB_0}{N-B_0}.$$

Inserting this and solving for B finally results in the solution of the Bass equation:

$$B(t) = \frac{pN + qNB_0 - p(N-B_0)e^{-(p+qN)t}}{p+qB_0 + q(N-B_0)e^{-(p+qN)t}},$$

in which $B_0 = B(0)$ is the initial number of individuals possessing the good. These may be individuals who have attained the good as part of a marketing promotion, a product test, or together with a complementary product (e.g., the SMS attached to mobile phones). The significance of these customers is discussed in the main text.

● Figure 18.2 shows the solution of the Bass equation for a total population of $N = 10^6$ individuals, $B_0 = 10^4$ initial customers, the coefficient of innovation $p = 0.03$, and the coefficient of imitation $q = 3.8 \times 10^{-7}$. The values of p and q are based on the typical and average values found in the paper by Mahajan et al. (1995).

There are two special cases of the Bass equation:

- If $p = 0$, there are only imitators, and the solution of the Bass equation is reduced to the logistic distribution (see, e.g., the Wikipedia article for the definition of the logistic distribution):

$$B = \frac{NB_0}{B_0 + (N - B_0)e^{-qNt}}.$$

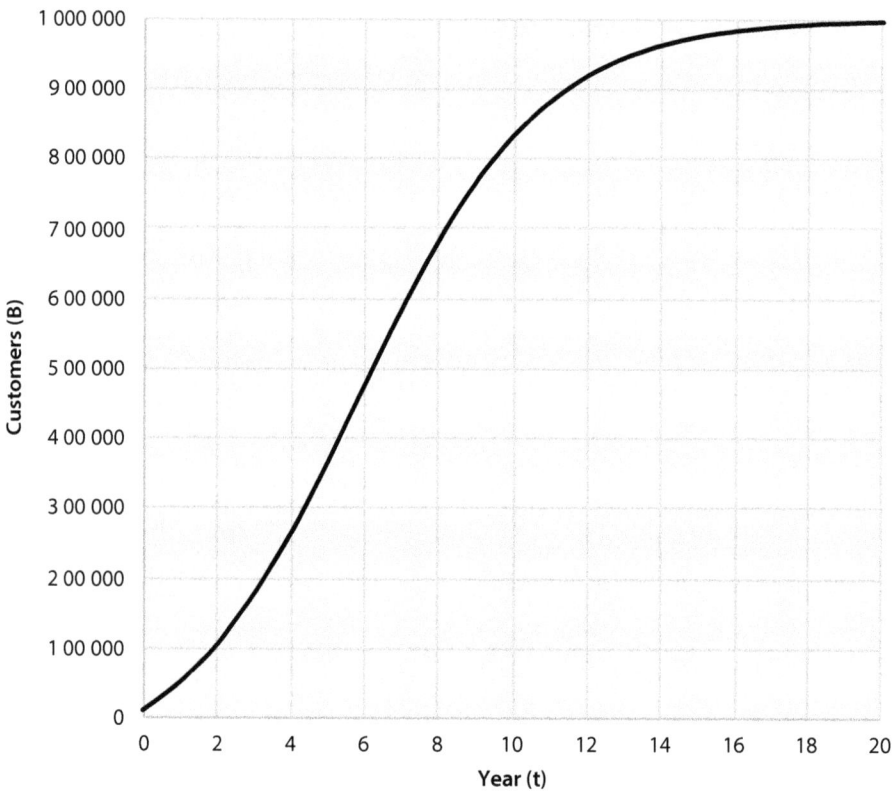

● **Fig. 18.2** Plot of the Bass diffusion model. (Authors' own figure)

18.2 · Bass Diffusion Model

- If $q = 0$, there are only innovators, and the solution of the Bass equation is reduced to the exponential distribution:

$$B = N - (N - B_0)e^{-pt}.$$

Note that if there are no innovators (early adopters) but only imitators (i.e., $p = 0$), the solution of the differential equation is $B = 0$ for all t if $B_0 = 0$; that is, no one will ever buy the product. Therefore, $B_0 > 0$ for a non-zero solution to exist if $p = 0$; that is, a customer base must exist before the sales begin. This requirement is not necessary for the case of only innovators. In this case, customers will buy the good even if there are no initial customers.

◻ Figure 18.3 shows the solution of the Bass equation for the two cases with only imitators ($p = 0$, $q = 3.8 \times 10^{-7}$) and only innovators ($p = 0.05$, $q = 0$). For both graphs, the total population is $N = 10^6$, and the initial number of customers is $B_0 = 10^4$.

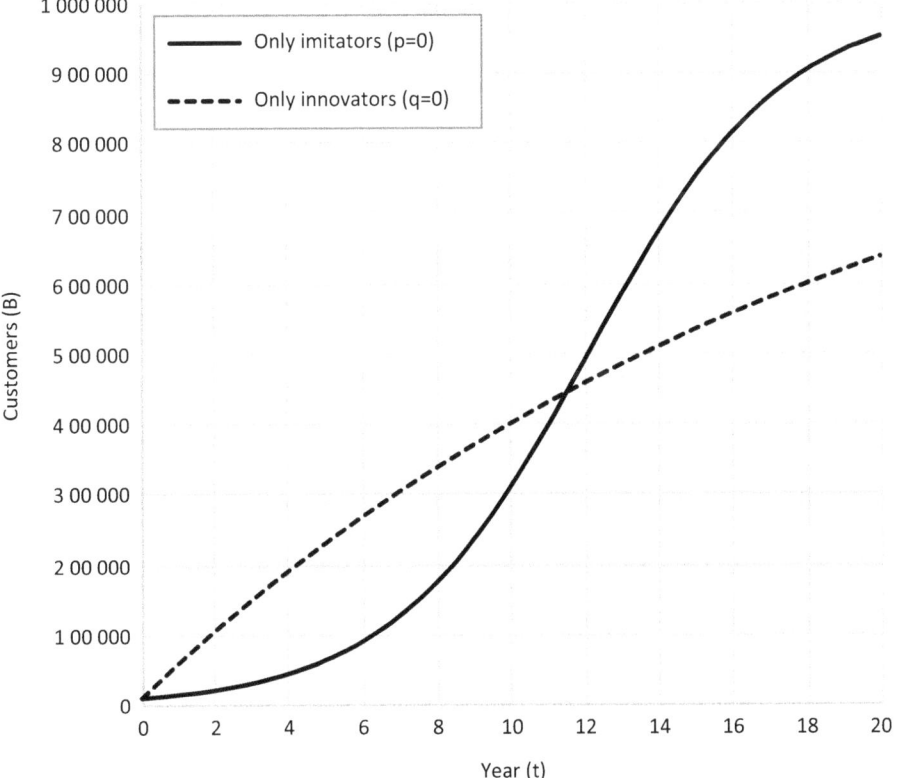

◻ **Fig. 18.3** The Bass diffusion model with only imitators and only innovators. (Authors' own figure)

The condition that the Bass equation produces an S-curve is that there is an *inflexion point* somewhere on the curve. An inflexion point is a point in which the tangent to the curve has a maximum (or minimum) value; that is, the increase in the growth rate changes from positive to negative (or vice versa). At this point, the second derivative of the curve is zero. How the inflexion point is found is shown in ► Box 18.2.

> **Box 18.2 Finding the Inflexion Point**
>
> The inflexion point is the point where the second derivative of the solution of the Bass equation vanishes, i.e., $d^2B/dt^2 = 0$. The second derivative of the solution to the Bass equation is:
>
> $$\frac{d^2B}{dt^2} = \frac{d}{dt}\frac{dB}{dt} = \frac{d}{dt}(p+qB)(N-B) = q\frac{dB}{dt}(N-B) - \frac{dB}{dt}(p+qB)$$
>
> The condition for the existence of an inflexion point is:
>
> $$\frac{d^2B}{dt^2} = q\frac{dB}{dt}(N-B) - \frac{dB}{dt}(p+qB) = 0.$$
>
> Since $dB/dt > 0$, this leads to the linear equation $q(N-B) - (p+qB) = 0$ with solution:
>
> $$B_{infl} = \frac{qN - p}{2q},$$
>
> in which B_{infl} is the value of B at the inflexion point. Observe that there is an inflexion point on the curve for $B \geq 0$ provided that $p < qN$. If this condition is not fulfilled, there is no inflexion point on the positive part of the curve.

One of the most important issues when introducing a new product is the time it takes until enough customers have purchased the good so that the business has become profitable. This may be called the *latency period* for market penetration. It is reasonable to define the latency period to be the time it takes to reach 10% of the full market size (T_{10}). For a market with only imitators ($p = 0$ in the Bass equation), we find by simple algebra that:

$$T_{10} \cong T_{50}\left[\frac{2.2}{\ln(B_0/N)} + 1\right],$$

in which T_{50} is the time it takes to reach 50% of the potential market. ◘ Table 18.2 shows the latency period for several values of B_0 (the number of customers that must be captured before the product is launched). In the table, the time to reach 50% of the market, T_{50}, is 5 years.

18.2 · Bass Diffusion Model

- **Table 18.2** Latency periods vs initial customer base. (Authors' compilation)

B_0/N	T_{10}/T_{50}	T_{10} for T_{50} = 5 years
0.001	0.67	3 years and 4 months
0.005	0.58	2 years and 11 months
0.01	0.52	2 years and 7 months
0.02	0.44	2 years and 2 months
0.04	0.31	1 year and 6 months

If T_{50} = 5 years and B_0/N = 0.001, the latency period is 3 years and 4 months. If B_0/N = 0.01, the latency period is still 2 years and 7 months. In markets without (or with very few) spontaneous buyers, the latency period is long, and the supplier may choose to terminate the service before the network effects become significant. This is the strategic dilemma in markets with strong network effects and, in which, there is a minor incentive for users to spontaneously join the service. The service may then be terminated before the market has started to mature. See also ▶ Chap. 9 where the problem of long latency period is discussed in the context of network effects.

If there are only innovators (i.e., q = 0) and B_0 = 0, the solution reduces to:

$$B(t) = N\left(1 - e^{-pt}\right).$$

In this case the latency period (T_{10}) is given by:

$$T_{10} = T_{50}\frac{\ln 2}{\ln 0.9} = 0.15 T_{50}.$$

For T_{50} = 5 years, the latency period is only 9 months. In the case with only innovators, the market increases linearly, $B(t) \approx pNt$, for small t. On the other hand, if there are only imitators, the market increases exponentially for small t, $B \approx B_0 e^{qNt}$. The importance of this observation is that initially (i.e., for small t) exponential growth is much slower than linear growth. This is the origin of long latency period in markets with only imitators.

On the other hand, observe that the time for the market to increase from 50% to 60% is only 6 months in the case of only imitators and B_0/N = 0.01, but more than four times as long without feedback (i.e., only innovators). The conclusions of this discussion are shown in ◘ Fig. 18.4 and summarized as follows:
- If all customers are innovators, then the latency period is short; however, the time to capture market shares above 50% is long.
- If all customers are imitators, the latency period is long; however, the time to capture market shares above 50% is short.

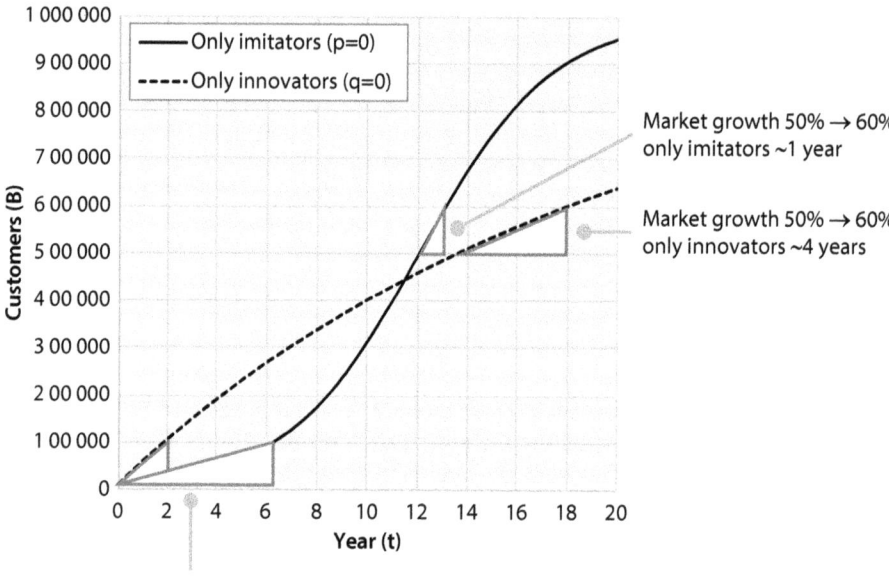

☐ **Fig. 18.4** Latency period in the Bass diffusion model. (Authors' own figure)

There are two strategic dilemmas in a market with only imitators:
- As previously discussed, the market will not start growing unless there are some initial customers. The problem for the supplier is, then, to establish an initial pool of customers so that the growth process will start.
- Even with an initial pool of customers, the growth rate may initially be so slow that the supplier will terminate the service before it takes off.

Facebook is an example of a service in which there are very few innovators, since the reason to use the service is to interact socially with other users; that is, $p \approx 0$ for Facebook. The service was launched at the campus of Harvard University, building up a small initial user group among students. It took about 5 years (from 2003 to 2008) before the market share really started to increase and Facebook started to become a dominating social networking service (Roberts, 2017). Other social networking services, such as LinkedIn, also grew slowly initially.

18.3 Model for Markets with Competition and Churning

☐ Figure 18.5 shows a model for the competition between two suppliers—Supplier 1 and Supplier 2—offering the same service; for example, mobile communications. The model consists of three customer states: potential customers, customers of Supplier 1, and customers of Supplier 2. Furthermore, the model consists of four flows:

18.3 · Model for Markets with Competition and Churning

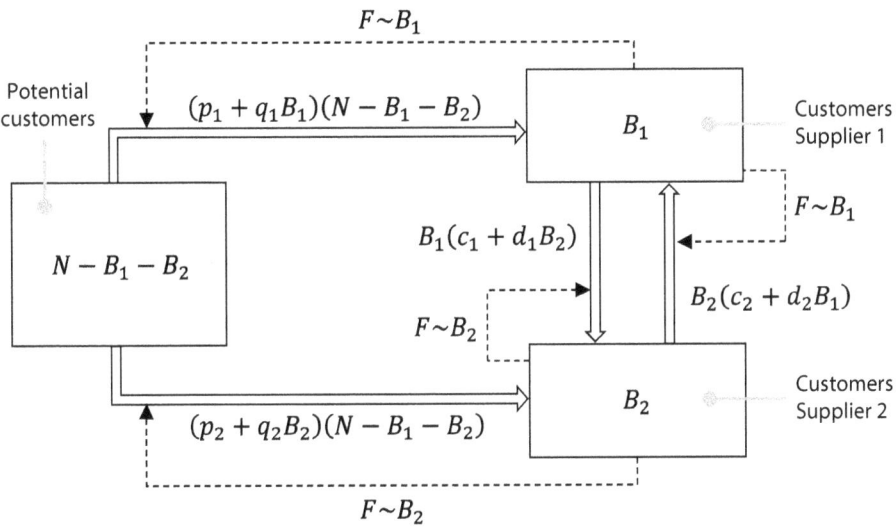

Fig. 18.5 Model of two competing suppliers with churning. (Authors' own figure)

- The flow of new customers from potential customers to Supplier 1.
- The flow of new customers from potential customers to Supplier 2.
- The flow of customers from Supplier 1 to Supplier 2.
- The flow of customers from Supplier 2 to Supplier 1.

The latter two flows are called *churning*. The model also includes four feedback loops as shown in the figure.

The rate of new customers choosing Supplier 1 is $(p_1 + q_1 B_1)(N - B_1 - B_2)$, and the rate of new customers choosing Supplier 2 is $(p_2 + q_2 B_2)(N - B_1 - B_2)$. Here, the Bass equation is used to express the dynamics of the flows.

The net number of customers churning from Supplier 2 to Supplier 1 is $C_{21} = B_2(c_2 + d_2 B_1) - B_1(c_1 + d_1 B_2)$. The first term is the rate at which Supplier 1 gains customers from Supplier 2, and the second term is the rate at which Supplier 1 loses customers to Supplier 2. The net number of customers churning to Supplier 2 is $C_{12} = -C_{21} = B_1(c_1 + d_1 B_2) - B_2(c_2 + d_2 B_1)$ since the churning process does not create new customers (the net result of the two churning flows must be zero). The parameters c_1 and c_2 are denoted *coefficients of spontaneous churning*, and the parameters d_1 and d_2 are denoted *coefficients of stimulated churning* (or imitated churning). Again, the Bass equation is applied to the churning flows. Imitated churning constitutes churners that switch suppliers because of the size of the competing supplier.

The dotted lines in the figure are the feedback loops representing the network effect that stimulates imitators into choosing a supplier or stimulates customers into churning to the other supplier.

Putting all this together results in the following coupled set of dynamic market equations:

$$\frac{dB_1}{dt} = (p_1 + q_1 B_1)(N - B_1 - B_2) - B_1(c_1 + d_1 B_2) + B_2(c_2 + d_2 B_1),$$

$$\frac{dB_2}{dt} = (p_2 + q_2 B_2)(N - B_1 - B_2) + B_1(c_1 + d_1 B_2) - B_2(c_2 + d_2 B_1)$$

There is little hope to solve these nonlinear differential equations analytically, except in a few special cases. However, we may still draw some important conclusions concerning the long-term evolution of the market without solving the set of differential equations as explained in ▶ Box 18.3.

> **Box 18.3 Market Stability and Churning**
>
> In the long run, all potential customers have become customers of either Supplier 1 or Supplier 2, and there are no more potential customers left. This is, for example, the case in the mobile phone market in several countries (this has nothing to do with the sales of mobile phones but with the total number of mobile subscriptions). This means that $B_1 + B_2 = N$. A steady state solution implies, moreover, that $dB_1/dt = dB_2/dt = 0$; that is, there is no net flow of customers in the steady state. In the steady state, there is, therefore, no net churning (i.e., $C_{12} = -C_{21} = 0$), which results in the solution of the quadratic equation $B_1(c_1 + d_1 B_2) = B_2(c_2 + d_2 B_1)$, in which $B_1 + B_2 = N$, for the final state of the market. This means that a potential customer has either become a subscriber of Supplier 1 or Supplier 2 and that the churning rates of the two suppliers are equal. The general solution is then:
>
> $$B_1 = \frac{c_1 + c_2 + (d_1 - d_2)N - \sqrt{(c_1 + c_2 + (d_1 - d_2)N)^2 - 4(d_1 - d_2)c_2 N}}{2(d_1 - d_2)}$$
>
> $$B_2 = N - B_1 = \frac{c_1 + c_2 + (d_2 - d_1)N - \sqrt{(c_1 + c_2 + (d_2 - d_1)N)^2 - 4(d_2 - d_1)c_1 N}}{2(d_2 - d_1)}.$$
>
> From these observations, we draw some important conclusions in the main text.

In the case of two suppliers, there are two special cases that can be observed in different markets:

- If there is only stimulated churning ($c_1 = c_2 = 0$) and d_1 and d_2 are independent of time, then the final state is $B_1 = 0$, $B_2 = N$ if $d_1 > d_2$, or $B_1 = N$, $B_2 = 0$ if $d_1 < d_2$. These are, then, winner-takes-all markets leading to de facto monopolies (e.g., Facebook vs Myspace or VHS vs Betamax).

18.4 · Models for Massive Multiplayer Online Games

- If there is only spontaneous churning ($d_1 = d_2 = 0$), then it follows most easily directly from the churning conditions (or from the above equations by letting $(d_1 - d_2) \to 0$) that the market ends up in the stable state with the following steady-state distribution of customers:

$$(B_1, B_2) = \left(\frac{c_2 N}{c_1 + c_2}, \frac{c_1 N}{c_1 + c_2} \right).$$

This case may apply to mobile communications where competitors have rather stable market shares over long periods of time. We see that this state depends only on the churning parameters and is independent on how the market grows before it is saturated. In this simple model, the spontaneous churning coefficients are treated as constants. However, in actual markets, they may be complex time-dependent functions of prices, service content, user experience, user preferences, and so on. The market shares will then become fluctuating functions of time which, in some cases, may lead to winner-takes-all markets, for example, if churning only takes place from one competitor to the other (e.g., if $c_1 = 0$, $c_2 > 0$, then $B_1 = N$ and $B_2 = 0$).

It is easy to extend the model to more than two competitors. If there is only spontaneous churning, it is feasible to find analytic expressions for the stable end state of the market for any number of competitors, though it is numerically cumbersome to calculate the exact values if there are more than three competitors. On the other hand, if there is only stimulated churning (and no spontaneous churning), then the market will eventually end up in a state in which one of the competitors has captured the whole market. This is also a winner-takes-all market.

Note that in these models, the assumption is that the average churning probability is constant. In real systems, this is not the case, and it is reasonable to assume that the churning probability is a complex, fluctuating function of time depending on parameters such as price, loyalty, technical quality, customer laziness, or other mechanisms which may motivate the user to churn or not to churn to another supplier. The motivation of this chapter is not to describe why users may churn but to show that churning may result in a number of final market states ranging from de facto monopolies to rather stable markets shared by two or more suppliers. The theory also shows that the long-term evolution is path dependent, where the path the market evolution will follow depends on all the parameters just mentioned (see also ▶ Chap. 11).

18.4 Models for Massive Multiplayer Online Games

◘ Figure 18.6 is a simple model for a massively multiplayer online game (MMOG) such as *World of Warcraft*. The model may also be used to analyze services in which the users may leave the service with a certain probability. Examples include social networking services and newspaper subscriptions. An individual or a player

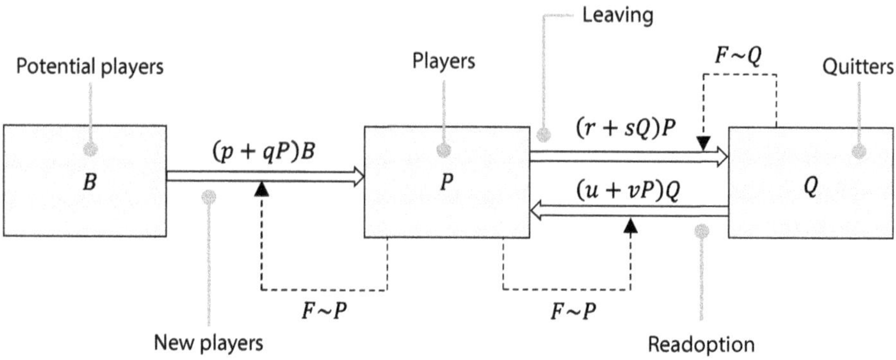

Fig. 18.6 Model of a massively multiplayer online game. (Authors' own figure)

may be in one of three possible states: *potential player* (B), *player* (P), or a player who has quit the game (*Quitter*) (Q).

There are three flows, in which it is assumed that the rate of each flow obeys the Bass equation:

- New players enter the game with rate (p + qP)B.
- Players leave the game with rate (r + sQ)P.
- Players rejoin the game with rate (u + vP)Q.

The dotted lines in the figure show the network effect. For simplicity, we will call this model the BPQ model (Øverby & Audestad, 2019).

The coupled set of differential equations is now:

$$\frac{dB}{dt} = -(p+qP)B,$$

$$\frac{dP}{dt} = (p+qP)B - (r+sQ)P + (u+vP)Q,$$

$$\frac{dQ}{dt} = (r+sQ)P - (u+vP)Q.$$

Adding the three equations results in $dB/dt + dP/dt + dQ/dt = 0$. This leads to the obvious conservation law $B + P + Q = N$, in which N is the total population of potential players. As usual, the model is simplified by assuming that N is constant (no birth or death processes). The number of independent differential equations is then reduced to two since the conservation equation can be used to eliminate one of them. These equations can then easily be transformed into a single, rather intractable, nonlinear second-order differential equation for P. There are a few cases in which analytic solutions can be found. However, we shall not pursue this here.

▪ Figure 18.7 is an example of a typical solution of the differential equations of the BPQ model. The differential equations were solved using numerical methods. The figure shows the share of the population that are *potential players* (B),

18.4 · Models for Massive Multiplayer Online Games

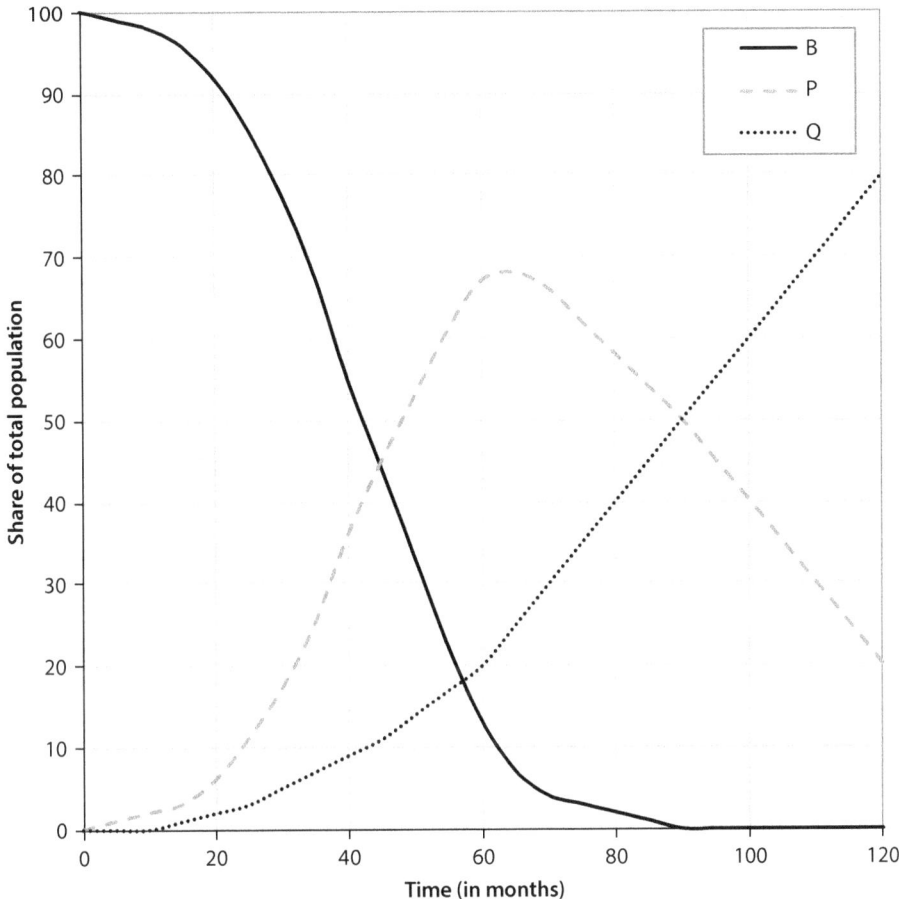

Fig. 18.7 Plot of the BPQ model. (Authors' own figure)

players (P), or *quitters* (Q) as a function of time. Observe that the sum of these categories of individuals is always 100%. At $t = 0$, there are only *potential players* and no *players* or *quitters* (i.e., $B = 100\%$ and $P = Q = 0\%$). As time increases, more and more *potential players* become *players*, who, after some time, leave the game and become *quitters*. However, *quitters* may rejoin the game and become *players* again. Eventually (in the figure, for $t > 90$), all individuals are either *players* or *quitters*.

From the form of the differential equations, important conclusions can be drawn without solving the equations:

- If there are no innovators among the potential players, the time it takes for the game to reach sufficient popularity may be long in the same way as in the Bass model with only imitators. The game may then be prematurely withdrawn from the market.
- To prolong the lifetime of the game, quitters must be stimulated to rejoin the game. This requires frequently updating of the game with interesting new features.

- Updating of the game may also stimulate current players to continue to play, thereby reducing the rate by which payers are leaving the game.

> **Box 18.4 The SIR Model**
>
> The simplest model of interactive games is similar to the model used in biological sciences to describe how epidemic diseases spread in a population, the SIR model (Murray, 2002).
>
> The SIR model consists of three groups of individuals: *Susceptible* (S), *Infected* (I) and *Recovered* (R). This corresponds to B, P, and Q, respectively, in the BPQ model. The flow of new infected individuals in the SIR model depends only on network effects—someone must infect you; the flow of recovered individuals does not depend on network effects—you recover independently of how anybody else recovers. The parameter β^{-1} denotes the time between contacts which is required for the transmission of the disease. The parameter γ^{-1} is the time it takes to recover from the disease. ◘ Figure 18.8 shows the SIR model. The resulting differential equations for the SIR model are:
>
> $$\frac{dS}{dt} = \beta SI,$$
>
> $$\frac{dI}{dt} = \beta SI - \gamma I$$
>
> $$\frac{dI}{dt} = \gamma I$$
>
> The set of differential equations is non-linear and does not have a closed-form solution; however, the solution is easily found by numerical integration. The most important conclusion is that, initially, the number of infected increases very slowly (as in the Bass model with only imitators) and then to increase very rapidly.
>
> The spread of the COVID-19 pandemic follows the simple SIR model. Countries have implemented several countermeasures to reduce the spread of the disease. The differential equation shows that this is achieved by reducing the term βSI. Examples of countermeasures that reduce this product are:
>
> - Increased social distance and hand washing reduces β.
> - Isolation of particularly vulnerable people, curfews, and prohibiting many people to assemble in places where social distance cannot be upheld reduces S.
> - Isolating infected and possibly infected people reduces I.
>
> The SIR model was published by A. G. McKendrick and W. O. Kermack in a series of papers in the period from 1927 to 1933. The SIR model is the basis for more advanced compartmental models in epidemiology, such as the SIS model, MSIR model, and the SEIR model. The major differences between these models are the number of compartments (user groups) and the interaction between them.
>
> Compartmental models have inspired academics to develop similar models for the evolution of digital goods and services in the digital economy—the Bass model, the model with competition and churning, and the

BPQ model are examples of such compartmental models in the digital economy. J. Cannarella and J. A. Spechler modified the SIR model by adding positive feedback to the recovery mechanism. They called the model the irSIR model, where "ir" stands for "infectious recovery," and used it to forecast the evolution of Facebook and Myspace (Cannarella & Spechler, 2014). The model fitted well with the evolution of Myspace but not for Facebook. The growth rate of Facebook had started to decline during 2013, and from this data, they predicted (in 2014) a rapid decline in Facebook users starting from 2017. The growth rate of Facebook regained its original speed in 2015, so the prediction was based on too little data. This is similar to the problem the health authorities have to predict the evolution of COVID-19.

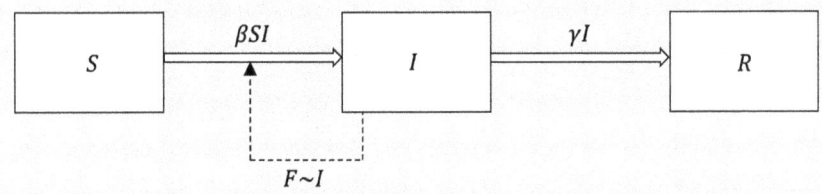

Fig. 18.8 The SIR model. (Authors' own figure)

18.5 Analysis of Real Markets

As shown, the temporal evolution of markets can be described mathematically using coupled sets of ordinary differential equations. In most cases, these equations cannot be solved using analytical methods. In the few cases in which analytical solutions can be found, it is necessary to treat all flow parameters as constants. Even the simple Bass equation cannot be solved analytically if the coefficients of innovation and imitation are functions of time.

Real markets are much more complicated than the three simple cases described in this chapter: system parameters are not constants but may be complex functions of time and the number of current customers; the model itself may be more complex containing additional customer states (or compartments) and flows; and there may be more complex feedbacks from the market regulating the flows between states. Such complex cases can be analyzed using *system dynamics*. The method is briefly outlined in ▶ Box 18.5. The interested reader is advised to consult the specialized literature on system dynamics (e.g., the two books listed below) to learn more about this important method for the analysis of complex systems.

Box 18.5 System Dynamic Models

System dynamics is based on essentially the same method as differential equations. However, instead of solving the equations using standard analytical or numerical methods, the equations are converted into a dynamic simulation model. The strength of system dynamic simulations is that the complete simulation model can be compiled into executable software programs directly from the graphical description of the model. There are several commercially available software packages for system dynamic modeling, all of them based on graphical description of the system. The task for the designer is then to develop the graphical model.

The method was developed by Jay Forester during the late 1950s (Forester, 1971). The first major application of the method was the project at MIT resulting in the book *The Limits to Growth* published in 1972 (Meadows et al., 1972).

The system dynamic model allows us to treat all system parameters as continuous or discrete functions of time and simulate cases that are far out-of-reach using differential equations. ◘ Figure 18.9 shows a system dynamic model of the Bass equation, demonstrating that the simulation model is identical to the differential equation in ▶ Sect. 18.1.

In system dynamics, the aggregates of people, things, or money are called *stocks*. In the Bass model, there are two stocks, *potential adopters* and *adopters*, and there is one flow from *potential adopters* to *adopters*. There are three functions:

- *Innovators* having a flow rate of $p(N - B)$. The function is realized by the multiplication operation × with inputs p and $N - B$.
- *Imitators* having a flow rate of $qB(N - B)$. The input to the multiplication function × is in this case q, $N - B$, and B.
- *New adopters* which is the sum of innovators and imitators; that is, the flow rate of new adopters is $(p + qB)(N - B)$.

Setting *adopters* equal to B, the flow of *new adopters* per unit of time equal to dB/dt, and *potential adopters* equal to $N - B$, the Bass equation of ▶ Sect. 18.1 is deduced. When the simulation starts, the stock of adopters may be empty or contain an initial number of adopters, B_0. The initial stock of potential adopters is, then, either N or $N - B_0$.

18.6 · Conclusions

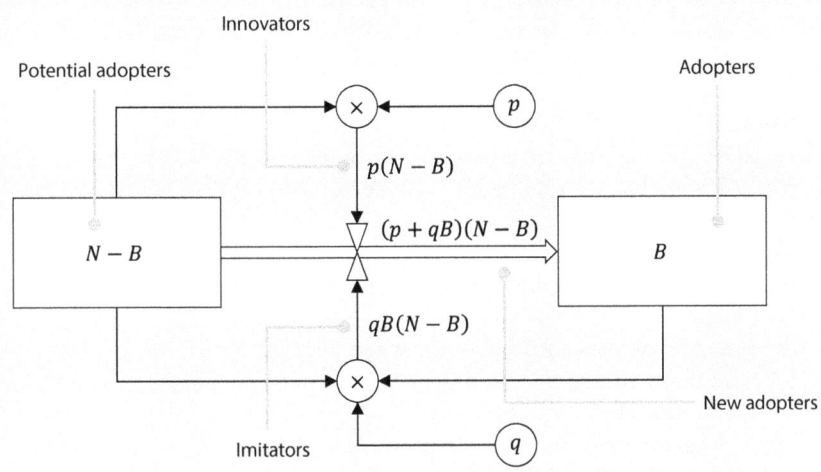

Fig. 18.9 System dynamic model for the Bass equation. (Authors' own figure)

18.6 Conclusions

This chapter shows how some important observations in the digital economy can be substantiated using simple mathematical tools.

The solution of the Bass equation pinpoints some strategic dilemmas:
- If all customers are innovators, then the latency period is short; however, the time to capture market shares above 50% is long. This implies that the total market is smaller than anticipated.
- If all customers are imitators, the latency period is long; however, the time to capture market shares above 50% is short. The product may then be prematurely withdrawn from the market.

The differential equations for markets with competitors show that if there is stimulated customer churning between the competitors, the market ends up as a de facto monopoly. Which competitor captures the whole market is arbitrary depending on events during the evolution of the market. The equation also shows that there are cases where the market is shared between several competitors. In these cases, the churning is spontaneous and independent of the market shares of the competitors.

The form of the differential equations for interactive online games shows that strategy to extend the lifetime of the game is to reduce the rate by which players leaves the game and increasing the rate by which earlier players rejoins the game. The strategy is then to identify how these rates can be manipulated, for example, by adding new features and improving other aspects of the game.

Finally, more complex markets can be analyzed using system dynamics. In these models, the market parameters can be constants, depend on time, be discrete, and so on.

❓ Questions

1. Consider the Bass equation and the two graphs in ▶ Fig. 18.3 ($B_0 = 10^4$, $N = 10^6$, $p = 0.05$, and $qN = 0.38$). Assume that the graphs represent customer adoption to a social media service.
   (a) How large is the initial market share (i.e., at time $t = 0$)?
   (b) Consider the case with only imitators ($p = 0$). What is this distribution called?
   (c) How can the Bass equation be expressed when $p = 0$?
   (d) How many customers have adopted the service at the inflexion point when $p = 0$? And when $p = 0.05$?
   (e) At what time does the inflexion point occur when $p = 0$?
   (f) What is the rate of new customers joining the service at the inflexion point when $p = 0$?

2. Consider the Bass equation when there are only innovators ($q = 0$).
   (a) What is the solution of the Bass equation for $q = 0$ and $B_0 > 0$?
   (b) Find the inflexion point in this case (if any).
   (c) Show that the market increases linearly for small t.

3. Consider two digital services satisfying the model for markets with competition and churning. Assume that $c1 = c2 \neq 0$ and $d_2 > d_1$. Which of the following best describes the market state in the long run: $B_1 = B_2$, $B_1 > B_2$, or $B_1 < B_2$? Explain why.

✅ Answers

1. Bass equation.
   (a) At time $t = 0$, the initial market share is $B_0/N = 10^4/10^6 = 1\%$.
   (b) The distribution is called the *logistic distribution*.
   (c) When $p = 0$, the solution of the Bass equation is:

   $$B(t) = \frac{NB_0}{B_0 + (N - B_0)e^{-qNt}},$$

   (d) The number of customers at the inflexion point for $p = 0$ is $B_{infl} = N/2 = 500{,}000$. When $p = 0.05$, the number is $B_{infl} = (qN - p)/2q = 434.211$.
   (e) Solving the Bass equation with $p = 0$ for t gives:

   $$t = \frac{1}{qN} \ln \frac{B(N - B_0)}{B_0(N - B)}.$$

   Inserting the value for B_{infl} and the other parameters, we find that the inflexion occurs at time $t = 12.09$.
   (f) The rate of new customers is $dB/dt = qB(N - B)$. When $B = B_{infl} = 500{,}000$, this gives $dB/dt = 3,8 \times 10^{-7} \times 500{,}000^2 = 95{,}000$ customers/year.

2. Bass equation for $q = 0$.
   (a) For $q = 0$, the solution of the Bass equation is $B(t) = N - (N - B_o)e^{-pt}$.
   (b) We easily find that $d^2B/dt^2 = -p^2(N - B_0)e^{-pt} < 0$ for all t. Therefore, there is no inflexion point in this case.
   (c) Expanding the equation for $B(t)$ as a series, and only keeping terms to the first order in t gives:

   $$B(t) = N - (N - B_0)(1 - pt) = B_0 + (n - B_0)pt.$$

   This is the equation for a straight line.

3. The correct answer is $B_1 > B_2$.

References

Bass, F. M. (1969). A new product growth model for consumer durables. *Management Science, 15*(5), 215–227.

Cannarella, J., & Spechler, J. A. (2014) Epidemiological modeling of online social network dynamics. *ArXiv* 1401.4208.

Forester, J. (1971). Counterintuitive behavior of social systems. *Theory and Decisions, 2*, 109–140.

Mahajan, V., Muller, E., & Bass, F. (1995). Diffusion of new products: Empirical generalizations and managerial uses. *Marketing Science, 14*(3), G79–G88.

Meadows, D. H., Meadows, D. L., Randers, J., & Behrens, W. (1972). *The limits to growth*. Potomac Associates – Universe Books.

Murray, J. D. (2002). *Mathematical biology. I: An introduction* (3rd ed.). Springer.

Øverby, H., & Audestad, J. A. (2019). Temporal market evolution of interactive games. SSRN.

Roberts, P. (2017). The most important Facebook statistics for 2017. *Our Social Times*, Cambridge.

Digital Business Models

Contents

19.1 Modeling Concepts – 282

19.2 The Business Model Canvas – 285

19.3 The Stakeholder Relationship Model – 288

19.4 Digital Business Models – 289

19.5 Conclusions – 301

References – 304

© The Author(s), under exclusive license to Springer Nature Switzerland AG 2021
H. Øverby, J. A. Audestad, *Introduction to Digital Economics*, Classroom Companion: Business,
https://doi.org/10.1007/978-3-030-78237-5_19

Learning Objectives

After completing this chapter, you should be able to:
- Use the business model canvas to model digital businesses.
- Use the stakeholder relationship model to model network effects in digital industries.
- Explain the business model of some popular digital services, including *World of Warcraft*, Spotify, Facebook, Wikipedia, and Airbnb.

19.1 Modeling Concepts

Business modeling as a tool for strategic business analysis was developed in the beginning of the twentieth century. One of the first business models was the "bait-and-hook" business model, in which a basic product is first offered for free or for a very low price, while necessary add-ons are sold for a high price. One example is the razor (bait) and blades (hook). Another example from the digital economy is the Adobe PDF software suite, in which the software needed to read PDFs is free (bait), while the software needed to generate a PDF is expensive (hook).

Leading developers of new business models in the twentieth century include companies such as Ford, Toyota, Wal-Mart, FedEx, and Dell. Dell revolutionized the way computers are sold to customers by bypassing retailers. Customers place the order directly with Dell who assembles the computer and ships it directly to the customer (just-in-time production). This business model was enabled and fueled by the mass adoption of the Internet. A common feature of these new business models is that they often exploited breakthroughs in novel technologies.

A business model describes how an organization (or company) creates, delivers, captures, and keeps value (Ovens, 2015). The model consists of items such as:
- How the organization earns money and controls expenditures
- Economic and organizational aspects of the organization
- Competition and market evolution
- Interrelationships between the organization and its customers, key partners, and other stakeholders

Business models are used as a strategic tool to identify key aspects of an organization's business operations, that is, the most important logics and operations that the organization relies on to earn money. The main purpose of a business model is to describe the current state of the organization. However, business models are also used as input to identify key strategic actions required for competitive evolution of the organization. The business model may be detailed and contain every aspect of the organization's business operation. It may also be used to analyze and describe only parts of an organization's business operations. Business models can be applied to all kinds of organizations.

19.1 · Modeling Concepts

Definition 19.1 Business Model
A business model describes how an organization creates, delivers, captures, and keeps value.

In the definition of business model, the concept of value appears. Value, in this context, is an abstract concept comprising more than just the monetary value of a product. Value might, for instance, comprise new features enabled by novel technologies, improved performance, exclusive design, and usability of the product. The core of a business model is the value that the organization creates. An organization can justify its existence by creating value, delivering value to customers, and supporting efficient mechanisms for gaining revenue from the value created. In addition to this, the organization must also defend this value from competing organizations. This may be called the *business process* as defined in ▶ Definition 19.2.

Definition 19.2 Business Process
The business process consists of the following elements:
- The organization *creates* value by solving problems or satisfying customer needs. A manufacturer of mobile phones may offer a low-cost mobile phone to people with slender means and expensive mobile phones with exclusive design and additional features to techno-freaks. Built on the same basic technology, the manufacturer may then satisfy several user segments at the same time.
- The organization *delivers* value to the customer through either physical or digital channels. Value delivery in this context refers to how the organization transfers the value created to the customer. An example of value delivery is to ship a purchased mobile phone to the customer via postal services. Another example is to update the phone by downloading new software.
- The organization *captures* value when its customers pay for the good or reward the organization by other means. The revenue covers costs and creates profit for the organization. An example of captured value is payment for the mobile phone and fees for using particular features such as apps.
- The organization *keeps* value by, for example, improving the design and functionality of the product and by mechanisms protecting against competition. Protection mechanisms are lock-in of customers to products or services that are difficult to copy, protecting the product by copyrights and patents, or selling it for prices that cannot be matched by competitors.

A digital business model is a business model applied to digital goods or services. Digital business models are facilitated by the widespread use of the Internet, mobile technologies, smartphones, and fast and small computers. As digital technologies mature and become adopted by the population, novel business models that build on these technologies are created; for example, a completely new market for app design emerged after the 4G mobile technology was introduced in 2010. This may lead to market disruption where new business models may replace existing ones or create entirely new markets (Christensen, 1997). One example is the app market just mentioned. Another example is the music industry which has been radically changed after the introduction of small and powerful music devices (e.g., the iPod) and online streaming services (e.g., Spotify).

> ▶ **Example 19.1 Funcom's Business Model**
> Funcom is a Norwegian company developing video games, known for titles such as *Anarchy Online* (2001), *Age of Conan* (2008), and *The Secret World* (2012). At its peak in 2008, Funcom had over 680 employees in several countries. The company focused on developing big games with large budgets, thereby competing with successful and market-leading games such as Blizzard's *World of Warcraft*.
>
> The year 2012 was critical for Funcom. The company launched the game *The Secret World* with little financial success. Funcom had to cut its staff by several hundred people. *The Secret World* did not attract as many players as expected. One of the most important reasons for this was the choice of business model. *The Secret World* was initially using a subscription-based business model. This was, in part, inspired by the success of the business model of Blizzard's *World of Warcraft*. Blizzard had already used the subscription-based business model successfully from the launch of *World of Warcraft* in 2004. However, in 2012, many computer gamers switched to a free-based business model used on most games available on social media networks such as Facebook. Users did not accept to pay a monthly fee for playing a game anymore. In the end, Funcom had to change the business model on *The Secret World* from subscription-based to buy-to-play to align with market and user trends. ◀

Recent years have witnessed an increased complexity of business model designs. This is primarily due to globalization and widespread competition, more complex and refined technologies, extensive use of ICT, and more complex organizations. A digital company need not own the goods they are selling as exemplified by the business models of eBay, Airbnb, and Uber. The business model of these companies is to offer a platform for mediation between buyers and sellers of tangible or intangible goods—eBay does not own any of the physical goods they are selling even though millions of items are sold through eBay every year. Airbnb is the world's largest hospitality service without owning any hotels or property. Uber provides ridesharing services without owning any cars.

The business of connecting customers or different user groups is perhaps the most important contribution of ICT in business modeling. This has similarities to the transition from business models for value chains to business models for value networks. While the best way to model companies in the industrial economy is the value chain, the best way to model companies in the digital economy is the value network (see ▶ Chap. 8). The business model of a company may also need revision and updating over time and must sometimes be completely rewritten due to changes in customer behavior, social trends, economic boundary conditions, and technological evolution. Failure to update business models may result in reduced profits and, eventually, bankruptcy.

19.2 The Business Model Canvas

Alexander Osterwalder proposed the business model ontology as part of his Ph.D. thesis in 2005. Later, this business model ontology was refined to become the business model canvas (BMC) (Osterwalder & Pigneur, 2010). The BMC is a framework for describing business models. It can be applied to all kind of businesses, including digital businesses. The BMC is based on describing nine central building blocks of a business and modeling the relationships between these building blocks. ◘ Figure 19.1 shows an outline of the BMC and how the BMC is visualized in this book. The different building blocks in the BMC are described in ◘ Table 19.1. The BMC has been applied to several digital businesses to uncover business operations and relationships between stakeholders. In addition to the BMC, there are several other frameworks for describing businesses. These frameworks focus on slightly different aspects of the business operations of a company; however, they mostly agree on the core concepts of the business model.

The nine building blocks of the BMC can be divided into three groups: value proposition, value turnover, and value generation.

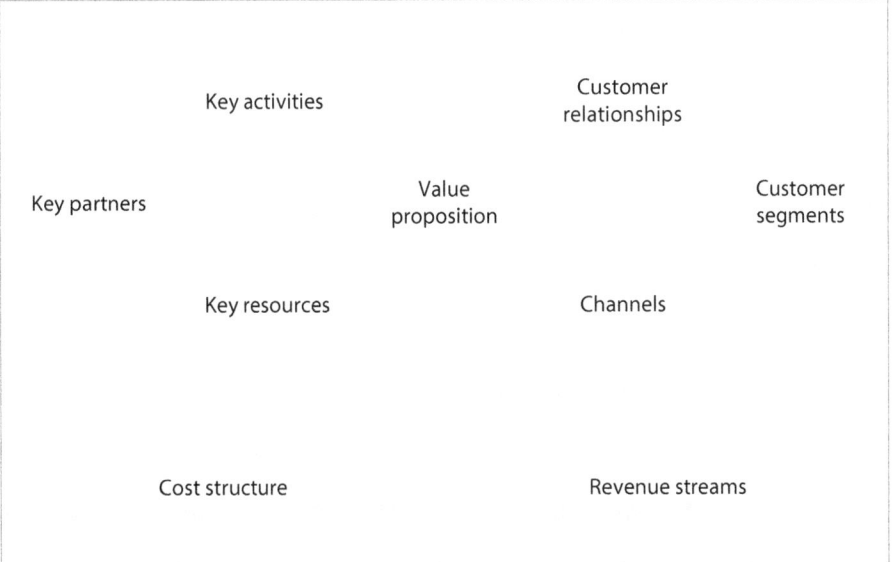

◘ Fig. 19.1 The business model canvas. (Authors' own figure)

Table 19.1 The nine building blocks of the BMC. (Authors' compilation)

Building block	Description
Value proposition	Describes the values and benefits created by the organization that are offered to one or more customer segments. The value proposition may comprise one or several different propositions targeting different customer segments. The value proposition describes the goods and services that the organization produces and delivers to customers, as well as the benefits that customers get by buying them
Customer segments	Identifies one or several customer segments targeted by the organization's value proposition. Different customer segments may have different roles in the BMC
Channels	Describes how the value proposition is transferred to the customer segments
Customer relationships	Defines the organization's relationship with the customer segments
Key activities	Describes the key activities needed to create and offer the value proposition
Key resources	Classifies the key resources needed to support the key activities and to create and offer the value proposition to the customer segments
Key partners	Identifies the key partners required for creating and offering the value proposition to the customer segments
Cost structure	Identifies the elements that contribute to the cost of the organization, including the cost of the various key activities
Revenue streams	Describes how the different customer segments contribute to the organization's income

Value proposition is the core building block of the BMC. The advantages of well-defined value propositions are:
- Upholding a clear focus on the fundamental activities of the business
- Identifying and maintaining any core competencies that the company may possess
- Precise targeting of the production toward products that the users will have and, thereby, avoiding production of goods that nobody will buy
- Willingness to change direction as processes, technologies, and products are substituted by new ones
- Willingness to change direction based on feedback from the users as the market evolves
- Effective marketing that focuses on user needs and user satisfaction
- Creating customer confidence in the product
- Understanding how and why the product creates value for the users

Value turnover includes four building blocks: customer segments, channels, customer relationships, and revenue stream. These building blocks describe how the

19.2 · The Business Model Canvas

organization disseminates its value proposition to the customers and how the customers generate revenues for the company.

Value generation includes the building blocks of key partners, key activities, key resources, and cost structures. More specifically, it describes what is needed in terms of resources, activities, and partners to create the value proposition and the costs associated with these activities. Value generation should also specify—either directly or indirectly—the value model (see ▶ Chap. 8) used by the company and whether the platform is single-sided or multisided (▶ Chap. 10).

The BMC of specific organizations is a thorough description of each of the nine building blocks and the relationships between them. ◘ Figure 19.2 shows an example of these relationships.

The steps in the analysis are as follows (the numbered list refers to the numbers in ◘ Fig. 19.2):

1. The analysis starts with defining the set of value propositions the organization delivers to the customers. This includes the goods and services that the organization delivers and the value and benefits they may have for the customers.
2. Identify the various customer segments and the value proposition each segment receives.
3. Describe how the product is provided to the identified customer segments through specific channels, for example, over the Internet or by postal services.
4. Describe how customers directly and indirectly generate the revenue stream for the organization, also including customers or users receiving the product for free (i.e., those with zero average return per user (zero ARPU)) because their contribution may be significant through indirect revenue channels.
5. Identify the relationships between the organization and the customers.

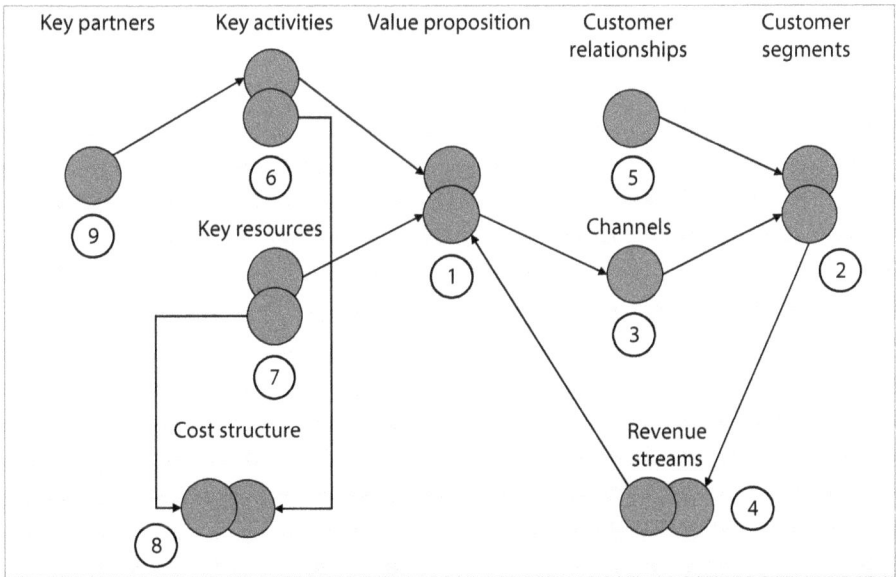

◘ Fig. 19.2 Relationships between the building blocks in the BMC. (Authors' own figure)

6. Identify the set of key activities that are required to create and support one or several value propositions.
7. Identify the key resources required for these activities and for other purposes.
8. Determine the costs associated with key activities and key resources and the overall cost structure of the organization.
9. Identify strategic relationships with one or several key partners to support or contribute to the value proposition, key activities, and key resources.

The BMC is used to model high-level abstractions of an organization's business operations. For two different organizations doing business in the same business domain, there might be small differences in the resulting BMC. However, even a small difference in the BMC of two organizations—for example, if one of them is using the core competencies in a smarter way—may render the business operations of the two organizations radically different. If the BMCs of the two organizations are identical, there is a motive for the organizations to reconsider the BMC to create significant differences in their business operations to distinguish it from that of the competitors.

To gain a strategic advantage, it is often enough to focus on one specific building block in the BMC. It is seldom necessary to redesign the business model completely to differentiate itself from the competitors. This may be a critical issue if the value proposition offered by a company is a commodity. In that case, price may be the only parameter that distinguishes the competitors.

Successful business models may change over time—what turned out to be a successful business model 5 years ago may not be a successful business model today. The reasons may be technological development, altered competition arena, new user demands, and different market behavior. Technological developments may render a business model obsolete.

19.3 The Stakeholder Relationship Model

The relationships between an organization and its stakeholders are important aspects of its business operations. The stakeholder relationship model (SRM) identifies key stakeholders engaged in the organization's business model and the interactions that the organization has with these stakeholders. Stakeholders in the SRM are the organization itself, customer segments, and key partners. The customers and the key partners are identified and described in the BMC as explained above. Relationships defined in the SRM can, for instance, be exchange of assets (e.g., services, value, or money), formal agreements, network effects, or other dependencies between the stakeholders. ◐ Figure 19.3 shows the notations used to visually model the SRM.

One key relationship between stakeholders is network effects (see ▶ Chap. 9). Network effects can either be positive or negative. The SRM models three different kinds of network effects between two stakeholders, A and B: (+/+), (−/−), and (+/−). The (+/+) network effect means that stakeholder A induces a positive network effect on stakeholder B and vice versa. Users in a telephone network have,

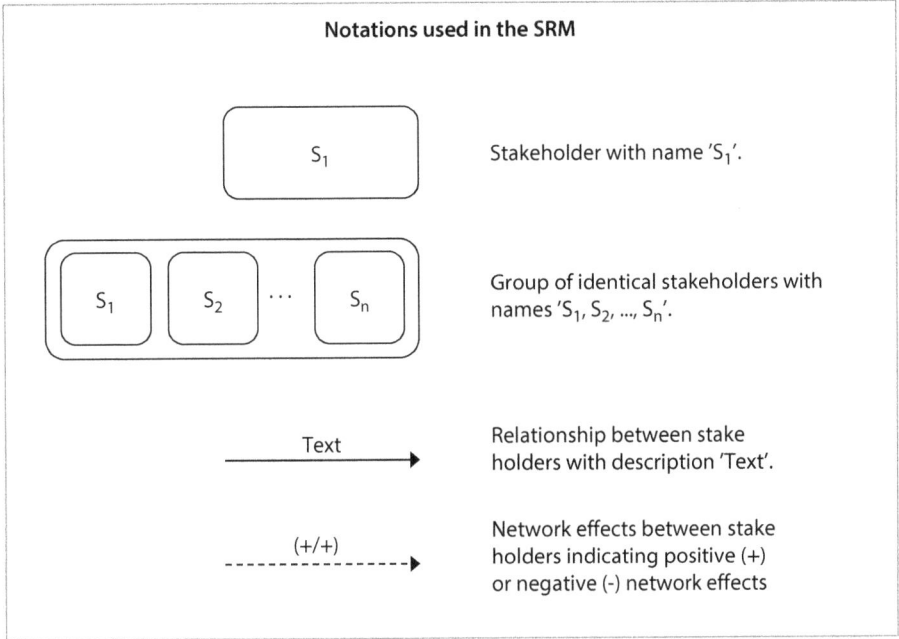

● Fig. 19.3 Notations used in the stakeholder relationship model. (Authors' own figure)

for example, a positive network effect on the other users in the network. The (−/−) network effect implies that stakeholder A has a negative network effect on stakeholder B and vice versa. One example is highway traffic in which each car has a negative network effect on other cars on the same road because of potential traffic congestion and increased probability of accidents. The (+/−) network effect means that stakeholder A has a positive effect on stakeholder B, but stakeholder B has a negative effect on stakeholder A. One example is commercials on television: the number of viewers has a positive network effect on advertisers that want a large audience for the commercials, while advertisements interrupting the flow of the program have a negative network effect on the viewers.

The SRM supplements the BMC by visualizing the relationships between the organization and other stakeholders. One important purpose of the SRM, especially for businesses in the digital economy, is that it illustrates the network effects that may modify the competitive strength of the organization. Sometimes, these network effects depend on each other and induce positive feedback that adds to the complexity of the business model.

19.4 Digital Business Models

In a digital business model, the value proposition is related to a digital good or service. Typical examples include the business models of Facebook, Spotify, Twitter, Wikipedia, Microsoft Windows, and Skype. The definition also includes the business models of sharing services—such as Uber and Airbnb—since the platform that enables mediation between buyers and sellers is digital. Platforms used for the sale of tangible goods—such as Amazon and eBay—are also examples of digital business models.

Every digital good or service is associated with a unique business model. For multisided platforms, for example, Facebook, it may sometimes be convenient to specify more than one business model. Facebook may have one business model for attaching users and another business model for capturing advertisers and other stakeholders buying access to data Facebook collects about the users. In this case, there is a strong relationship between the models because of strong cross-side network effects.

> **Definition 19.3 Digital Business Model**
> In a digital business model, the value proposition is a digital good or service.

▶ Case studies 19.1, 19.2, 19.3, 19.4, and 19.5 present five examples of digital business models that have had a substantial impact on the evolution of the digital economy: *World of Warcraft*, Spotify, Facebook, Wikipedia, and Airbnb. These examples represent different types of business models since they exploit the various fundamental properties of the digital economy differently. ◘ Table 19.2 summarizes the business models according to type and the most fundamental properties exploited by the particular digital service. Note that the business models presented in the case studies do not represent an exhaustive list of all business models available for digital services.

◘ **Table 19.2** List of presented business models. (Authors' compilation)

Digital service	Type of business model	Payment method	Fundamental properties exploited
World of Warcraft	Subscription	All users pay a fee for using the service	Zero marginal cost, network effects
Spotify	Freemium	Some users get the service for free. Other users pay for using the service	Long tail, network effects
Facebook	Ad-based free	The social network service is free. Advertisers pay for user-targeted ads	MSP, zero ARPU, zero marginal cost, network effects
Wikipedia	Commons-based peer production	No fees for readers and authors. Revenues based on donations	Public good, CBPP, MSP, zero ARPU, zero marginal cost
Airbnb	Multisided digital mediation platform supporting non-digital service	Users pay for the mediation services provided by the platform	MSP, network effects

19.4 · Digital Business Models

Case Study 19.1 World of Warcraft

Blizzard's online game, *World of Warcraft* (WoW), is an example of a digital service based on the *subscription business model*. Here, customers (or subscribers) pay a periodic (e.g., monthly or yearly) fee for accessing the service. Without subscription, customers are not allowed to access the service. If a customer terminates the subscription, the customer also loses access to the service.

WoW is a massively multiplayer online game (MMOG) released in 2004. The game had over 12 million concurrent gamers (subscribers) at its peak in 2010. WoW features a persistent 3D world, where gamers can interact, solve quests, and perform tasks in collaboration with other gamers. New content and upgrades are continuously added to the game by Blizzard's team of game developers. Blizzard offers access to several servers—each featuring a persistent world—to ensure load balancing and optimal performance of the game. The persistent worlds are divided into several geographical regions.

The BMC and the SRM of WoW are outlined in ◘ Figs. 19.4 and 19.5, respectively. The value proposition of WoW consists of giving gamers access to the game and the persistent world's content (1). The only defined customer segment is gamers (2). The gamers pay monthly subscription fees to access the game in addition to purchasing the game itself. Both the subscription and the game purchase are done via Blizzard's battle.net website. The game can also be purchased at a physical retail store. The main source of income from the game is monthly subscriptions, which are proportional to the number of active gamers (3). Another source of income is the product sales from the WoW game itself.

The key activities needed to offer WoW is creation of content and game development. These activities are the

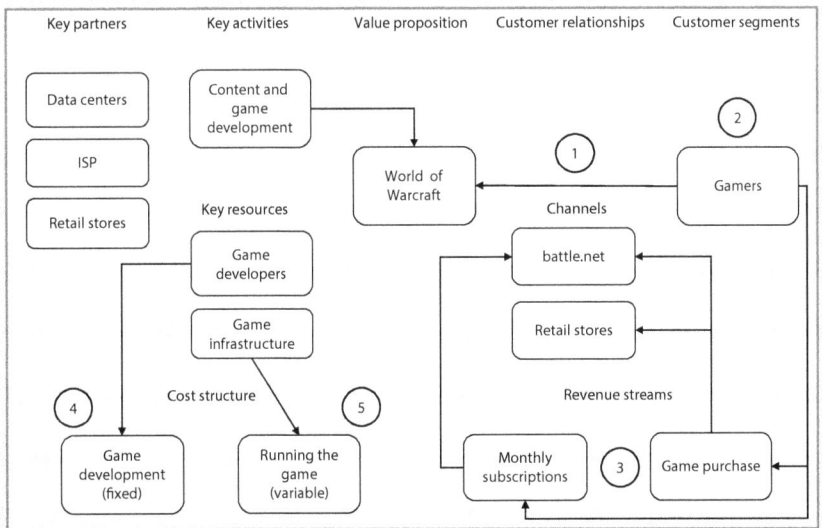

◘ **Fig. 19.4** *World of Warcraft* modeled using the BMC. (Authors' own figure)

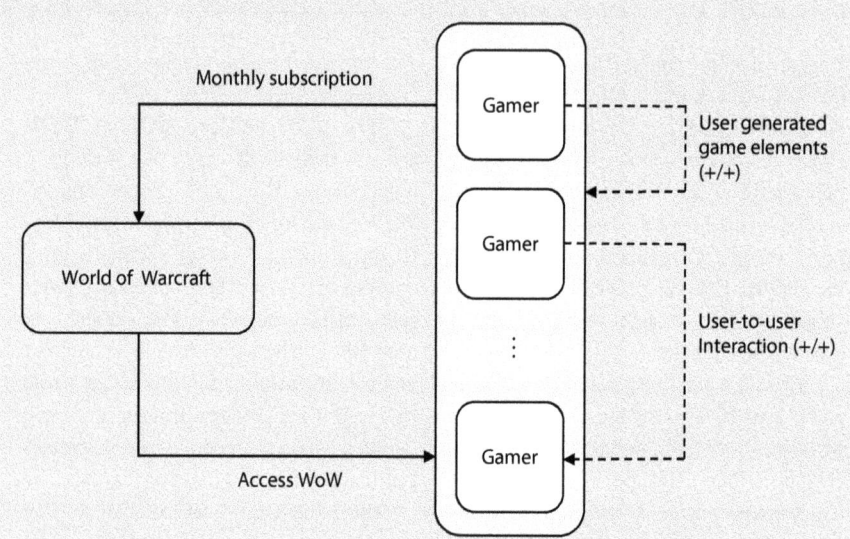

Fig. 19.5 *World of Warcraft* modeled using the SRM. (Authors' own figure)

core activities for Blizzard's own development team and are essential for the value proposition. In other words, the key resources are the game developers themselves. In addition, Blizzard needs an infrastructure of game servers to run the game. Both the game developers and the server infrastructure are significant elements contributing to the total cost of the company. Expenses related to developing the game are, to a large degree, fixed and independent of the number of gamers (4). Expenses related to the game infrastructure are partly dependent on the number of gamers (5). The key partners are data centers running persistent WoW worlds, ISPs providing high-speed worldwide Internet access, and retail stores promoting and selling the game.

Gamers exhibit positive direct same-side network effects on other gamers—or, at least, on other gamers on the same server—as shown in **Fig. 19.5. Gamers can come together in teams—or "clans"—to perform quests and tasks together, thereby increasing the gaming experience. Gamers also provide in-game items and content that other gamers may use. WoW Auction House is an example of a place where gamers can sell and buy items found during the game.

Key strategies for WoW are to acquire and retain customers who will pay monthly subscriptions. This can be done by aggressive marketing, offering a superior product, or exploiting the benefits of network effects. WoW has exploited all these strategies. WoW is the most successful MMOG developed so far, at least from a financial point of view. Due to its success and impact in the gaming industry, WoW has been a trendsetter of business models for online video games.

Case Study 19.2 Spotify

Spotify is an example of a digital service that uses the *freemium business model*. Here, the digital service is offered to two different consumer segments: One segment gets the service for free, while the other segment pays for the service. The consumer segment that gets the service for free is offered a simple—or "stripped down"—version of the service. The consumer segment paying for the service is offered access to all features of the service. Both consumer segments are important in the business model since there are positive network effects between them (Anderson, 2009). Spotify offers a music streaming service either for free or for a monthly subscription fee. The users receiving the service for free must listen to or view advertisements, while those paying a subscription fee can listen to music without interruptions.

Spotify's business operation is modeled using the BMC and the SRM as shown in ◘ Figs. 19.6 and 19.7, respectively. Spotify has two value propositions (1): one for music streaming services and one for advertisements. The subset of listeners paying for the service contributes to the revenue of Spotify (2). This corresponds to about 90% of the revenue (2017) (Spotify's revenues from 2012 to 2019, by segment. *Statista*.). The other source of revenue—advertisements—constituted about 10% of the income (2017). Key activities include software development and content management. Software development includes expanding, maintaining, and upgrading software and infrastructure of servers and databases. Content management is performed in close collaboration with the copyright owners (the music industry). A key activity is to acquire the rights to offer licensed music to the consumers (3). For these rights, Spotify must pay royalties to copyright owners.

The two segments of paying and non-paying listeners induce positive

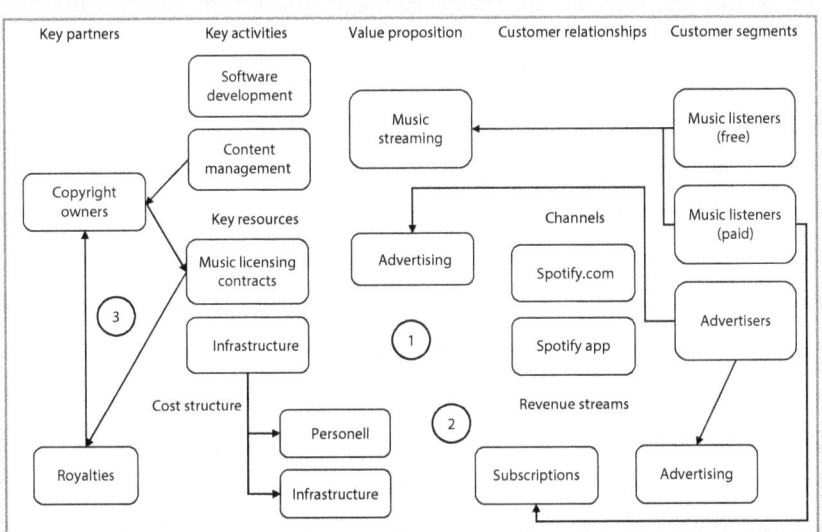

◘ **Fig. 19.6** Spotify modeled using the BMC. (Authors' own figure)

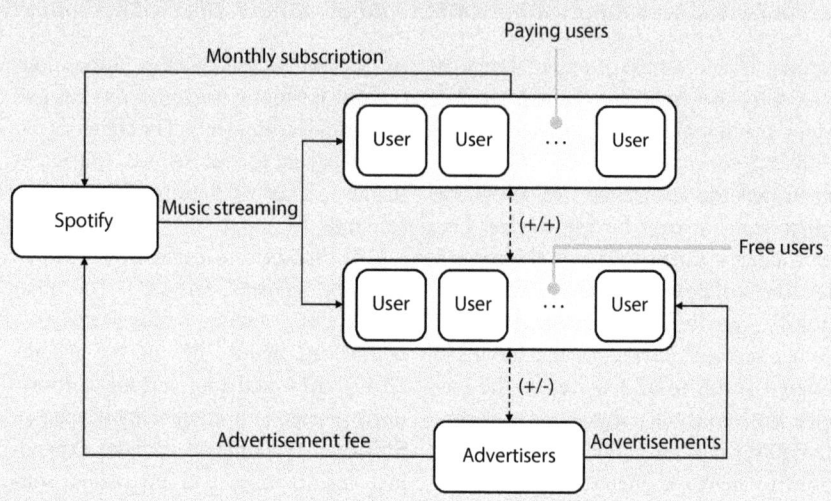

● **Fig. 19.7** Spotify modeled using the SRM. (Authors' own figure)

network effects on each other as shown in ● Fig. 19.7: getting more free music listeners also increases the value for those who pay for the service. This is so because a larger user base means that Spotify can negotiate better deals with the music industry. More importantly, with a large user base, Spotify will be in a stronger position when competing with other music streaming services. Users can also exchange playlists with one another.

The number of non-paying users induces positive indirect network effects on the advertisers since more users means a potentially larger audience for the advertisements. On the other hand, advertisements—or rather the amount of advertisements—induce negative indirect network effects on the users. This is because advertisements are, for most people, an annoyance and disruptions from using the digital service.

Spotify's business model has had an effect on how people pay for content on the Internet. It has also changed the size and operations of the online content piracy industry.

Key strategies of Spotify—operating under the freemium business model—are to minimize costs related to marketing, customer acquisition, and customer care because most of Spotify's customers are non-paying customers generating only a small income per customer. The foremost challenge for Spotify is to acquire and keep customers and to communicate with them for the lowest cost possible.

19.4 · Digital Business Models

Case Study 19.3 Facebook

Facebook offers a social networking service in which users can interact, socialize, share pictures and videos, play games, and use other professional content. Facebook uses the *ad-based free business model*. Here, users have free access to the digital service but must give away control of personal data to Facebook and accept that they will be exposed to advertisements. Revenue is generated by selling targeted advertisement space based on data collected about the users. Unlike the freemium business model, all users have access to a complete and full version of the digital service. Facebook is the world's biggest social network service with more than two billion monthly active users. Its international impact has influenced business models worldwide in several other business sectors, as well as motivated how people organize their social lives and spend time on the Internet. Facebook is modeled using the BMC and the SRM in ◘ Figs. 19.8 and 19.9, respectively.

Facebook offers three value propositions to three different customer segments (1): users involved in social interactions, advertisers, and third-party content developers. Revenue is generated from advertisements and service fees from third-party content developers (2). About 90% of Facebook's revenue is from advertisements. Due to the large number of users, it is not possible to establish a personalized customer relationship with every user. Instead, Facebook relies on automated messages to nurture relationships with the user segment. All customer segments access the value proposition through the Facebook web page (► facebook.com) or the Facebook app (3).

Key activities are the software development of ► facebook.com and the Facebook app (4). Key resources are

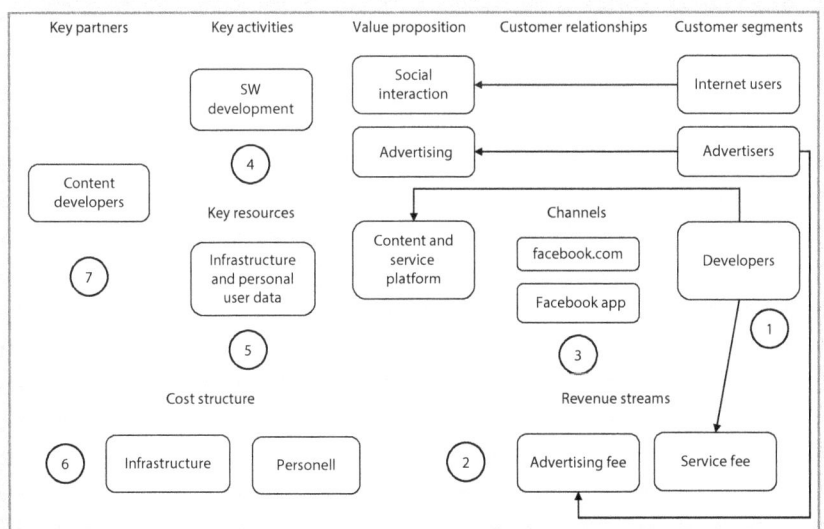

◘ **Fig. 19.8** Facebook modeled using the BMC. (Authors' own figure)

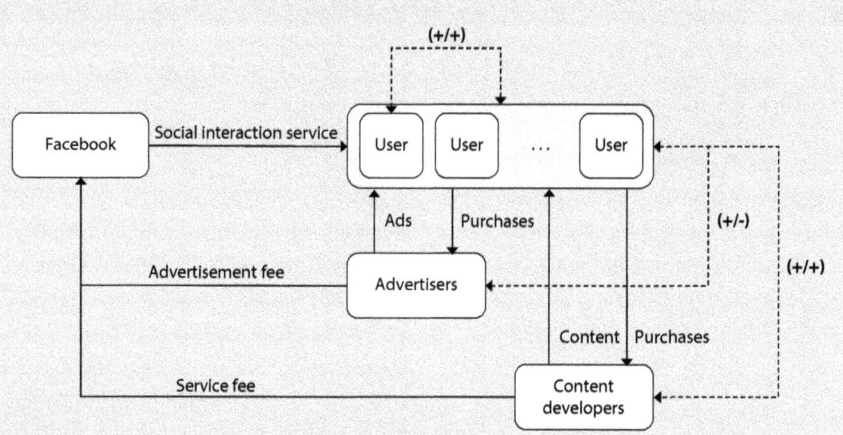

● Fig. 19.9 Facebook modeled using the SRM. (Authors' own figure)

the infrastructure hosting the Facebook service and the facilities storing and analyzing personal and behavioral data collected about the users (5). The stored user data is crucial for the business operations since it is used to provide user-targeted advertisement space to marketers. This data may also be sold to third parties for production of statistics and other materials based on user behavior, for example, political preferences, personality type, personal economy, and attitudes. Trade and storage of such data was the key issue in the Cambridge Analytica event in 2018 (Facebook value drops by $37bn amid privacy backlash, 2018).

The major costs include salaries for software developers, service management, and data storage and analysis (6). Key partners are third-party content developers (7) who offer content (e.g., games) directly to Facebook users.

As seen in ● Fig. 19.9, there are strong positive direct same-side network effects in the user segment since gaining new users implies that there are more opportunities for communication and interaction in the social network. Content developers exhibit positive direct network effects on users since gaining more users creates a bigger market for content, while attaching more content providers means that there is more available content for the users. Advertisements, on the other hand, may have a negative network effect on the users. For most users, advertisements are disturbing and annoying and reduce the pleasure of social networking.

Finally, observe that Facebook offers the social interaction service for free. Hence, the business model of Facebook is based on a model where the average return per user (ARPU) is zero.

19.4 · Digital Business Models

Case Study 19.4 Wikipedia

Wikipedia offers an online encyclopedia in several languages via its website ▶ wikipedia.org and the Wikipedia app for mobile devices. The content of Wikipedia is created by thousands of contributors. These contributors write new content on Wikipedia and edit, correct, update, and quality-check content from other authors. Wikipedia is used by millions of readers from all over the world.

Wikipedia is an example of the *commons-based peer production (CBPP) business model*. In CCBP, as explained in ▶ Chap. 7, the value proposition is not produced by a firm but by a potentially large number of people who, in a collaborative way, contribute to the development of the service, normally, not receiving any financial reward for their contribution. The reward may be in the form of recognition, respect, or the satisfaction of having contributed to the evolution of the content. CBPP requires effective mechanisms to ensure collaboration between peers across distance, cultures, and timespans since the collaborators may come from all over the world. Recovering the costs of running and developing the service depends on donations and public or private funding. The benefactors providing these donations do not gain any direct revenue from the digital service receiving the donations.

Wikipedia is modeled using the BMC in ◘ Fig. 19.10. The value proposition is access to the online encyclopedia (1). Wikipedia is available for free to users (readers) on ▶ wikipedia.org and the Wikipedia app (2). Hence, it is considered to be a public good. Wikipedia is created by many writers who edit, create, and manage Wikipedia articles through an online editing service (3). Key partners are the benefactors who provide all the revenue needed to run Wikipedia (4). Even

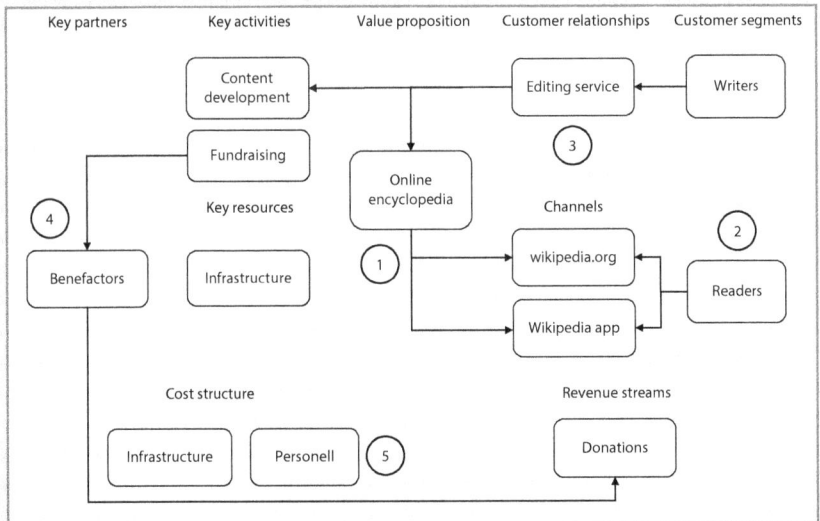

◘ Fig. 19.10 Wikipedia modeled using the BMC. (Authors' own figure)

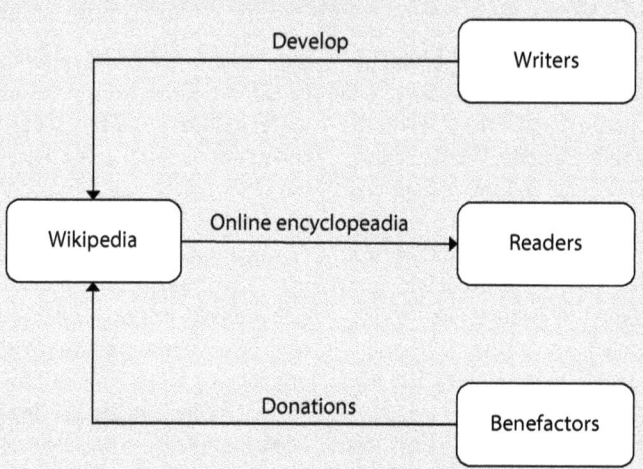

Fig. 19.11 Wikipedia modeled using the SRM. (Authors' own figure)

though the content of Wikipedia is created without any financial costs, there are costs of running the servers and for covering the salaries of Wikipedia's employees (5). Wikipedia is owned by the nonprofit organization, Wikimedia Foundation.

The SRM of Wikipedia is shown in Fig. 19.11. There are three stakeholders: benefactors, writers, and readers. All three stakeholders have a relationship to Wikipedia—the writers develop Wikipedia, the readers use Wikipedia, and the benefactors fund Wikipedia. There are no relationships between these stakeholders because:

- The authors are anonymous.
- Usually, several authors contribute to each article.
- The readers may also take the role of watchdogs monitoring the quality of the content and, if necessary, correct it.
- The benefactors contribute because of the quality and correctness of the encyclopedia and the importance the encyclopedia has on society at large.

Wikipedia is an example of a large digital service without any form of relationships between the stakeholders. Hence, there are no significant network effects associated with the various actors in the business model.

The two main strategies of Wikipedia are to (1) develop and maintain a platform that encourages writers to create and edit content and (2) to ensure that the content is relevant, correct, and important.

19.4 · Digital Business Models

Case Study 19.5 Airbnb

Airbnb is an example of an organization using the *multisided platform business model* (see ▶ Chap. 10). Airbnb offers a website and a mobile app in which people may lease or rent houses, apartments, or single rooms for shorter or longer stays. They have also recently entered other businesses such as restaurant booking, concert booking, and videos promoting different places around the world. Hosts announce the availability of properties for rent on the Airbnb website or app, often supplemented with photos, videos, and describing text. Payment is done via the Airbnb website or app using the Airbnb payment service. The host and guest arrange practical details regarding the rental without involving Airbnb directly.

In this business model, the organization (Airbnb) offers a platform for mediating between and connecting users belonging to different groups (hosts and guests). Unlike the ad-based business model, the multisided platform business model does not use ads to generate revenue but instead receives revenue from transaction fees levied when users exercise the services offered by the platform. In the platform business model, the matching of users is often motivated by the exchange of personal services (e.g., Airbnb and Uber) or tangible goods (e.g., eBay). There are several variations of the multisided platform business model; however, the key idea is that a platform is employed for connecting different user groups. The BMC the SRM of Airbnb is illustrated in ◘ Figs. 19.12 and 19.13, respectively.

The main value proposition (1) of Airbnb is to offer a mediation service between the two customer segments hosts and guests (2). This is done on the website ▶ airbnb.com or the Airbnb mobile app (3), in which the guest must

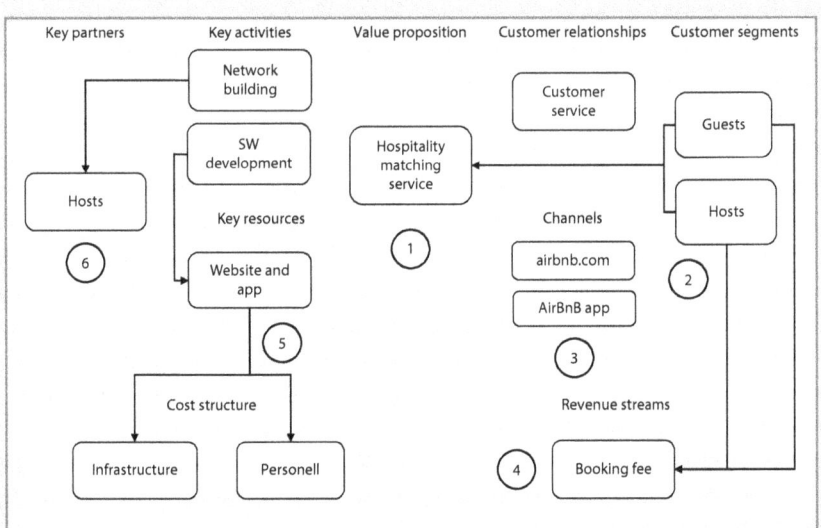

◘ **Fig. 19.12** Airbnb modeled using the BMC. (Authors' own figure)

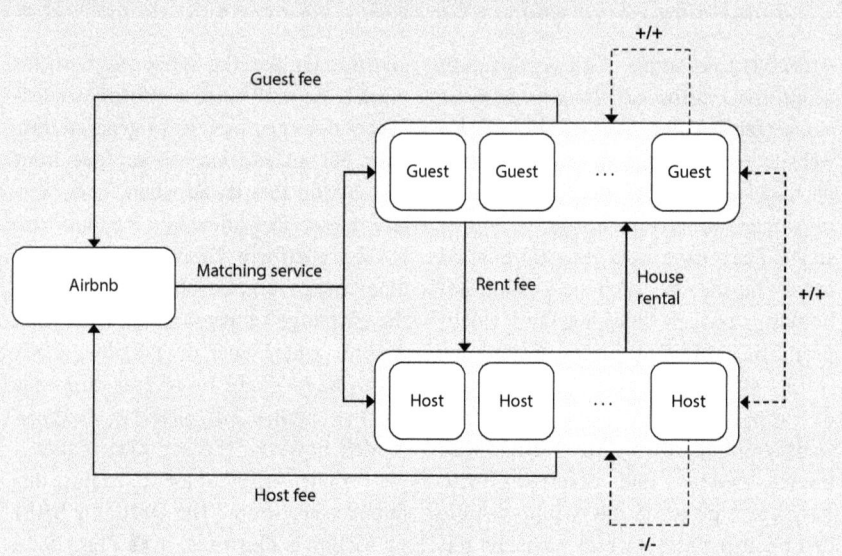

Fig. 19.13 Airbnb modeled using the SRM. (Authors' own figure)

provide a valid name, email address, telephone number, photo, and payment information. Airbnb gets its revenue from a booking fee paid by both the guest and the host (4). Key resources are the website ▶ airbnb.com and the mobile app (5). These sites must be user-friendly for both hosts and guests, have high availability, and offer a high-quality service. Key partners are people owning properties for lease (the hosts) (6). Hence, hosts are both a key partner and a customer segment for Airbnb. This is because hosts provide the content of the Airbnb site (properties for rent), while at the same time, they contribute to revenues when a guest books the host's property for rent. A key activity is network-building to build up a large base of available hosts.

The business model contains positive indirect network effects between guests as seen in ◘ Fig. 19.13. Guests leave comments that other guests may review before booking a property. There are also positive direct network effects between guests and hosts—having more hosts means there are more choices available for the guests and more guests implies a higher likelihood of bookings. There are negative network effects between hosts since hosts compete for the same guests. However, note that the network effects have local significance only: available properties in Bangkok do not induce positive network effects on users who are looking for a house in Paris.

A key strategy for Airbnb is to ensure a healthy supply of property in the areas Airbnb operates and to promote these properties to attract enough guests. Another important aspect is to ensure that guests trust the bookings made through Airbnb. For this purpose, Airbnb offers a review system for both hosts and guests that may be used to rise the quality of the services offered by Airbnb.

19.5 Conclusions

Business models are developed to identify key aspects of an organization's business operations. The models are used both to describe the current state of the organization and to identify key strategic actions required for taking the organization into the future. In other words, the purpose of the model is to identify the current market position of the organization, estimate how the market and the technology will evolve, and on this basis, develop strategies for future market positioning and revenue generation.

The business model canvas developed by Osterwalder is a simple and effective tool to develop and analyze business models for enterprises in the digital economy. These enterprises are often multisided platforms where each business sector supported by the platform is based on entirely different value proposition, production, cost, and revenue models. The stakeholder relationship model supplements the business model by identifying the type of relationship that exists between the stakeholders and the impact these relationships have on the business model. The principles have been illustrated for five enterprises with entirely different underlying value proposition models.

? Questions
1. Massive Open Online Course (MOOC) was envisioned to disrupt the educational sector by offering virtually free and ubiquitous teaching online.
   (a) Would you categorize MOOC as either a sustainable innovation or a disruptive innovation?
   (b) Design the business model of a company offering an MOOC (e.g., Coursera) using the business model canvas.

2. Popcorn Time (now terminated by regulations) and Netflix were two digital services with similar value propositions.
   (a) Use the BMC and the SRM to design the business model for Popcorn Time and Netflix.
   (b) What are the major differences in the resulting business models?
   (c) What is the major technological difference between Popcorn Time and Netflix?

3. Search the web and find answers to the following questions concerning Spotify:
   (a) How many of Spotify's users subscribe to its premium service?
   (b) What is the largest cost of running Spotify?
   (c) Does Spotify generate profits?
   (d) Which companies are Spotify's main competitors?
   (e) What is Spotify's market share in the music streaming industry?
   (f) Based on your answers, identify the major strategic challenge for Spotify?

4. Wikipedia
   (a) Why does Wikipedia rely on donations and not advertisements to provide revenue for its business operations?
   (b) Is it possible for Wikipedia to use the subscription-based business model?

✓ Answers

1. MOOC (see Wikipedia article)
   (a) Currently, MOOC looks more like a sustainable innovation than a disruptive innovation. This is because it has not changed the performance metrics or value chain in the education business. It is a sustainable innovation because it has added to the current selection of teaching methods that teachers may employ. However, MOOC has the potential to become a disruptive innovation in the future. However, predicting such an event is speculative at best.
   (b) A company offering an MOOC is a value network and an MSP. It connects two user groups: teachers and students. A key insight in the business model of an MOOC is that the teacher user group is producing the key resource of the MOOC—the teaching material. Another insight is related to the revenue stream. Should MOOC be free of charge or should there be a fee for the students? If there is a fee, how should this fee be distributed between the provider of the MOOC and the teachers? (◘ Fig. 19.14)

2. Popcorn Time and Netflix
   (a) Popcorn Time and Netflix are both providers of online streaming media (e.g., video, series, and movies). The BMCs are as shown in ◘ Figs. 19.15 and 19.16.
   (b) The major business difference is that Popcorn Time is free and has a disputed legality, as users uploading and distributing content in many cases (but not all) do not have the copyright owners' permission. Netflix, however, is a paid service and legal, as Netflix has bought copyright content in addition to producing its own content.

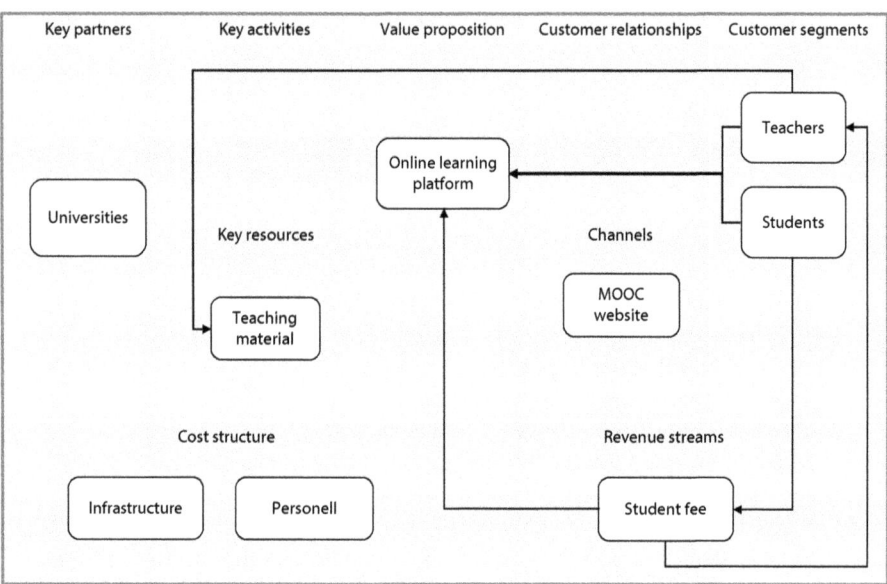

◘ **Fig. 19.14** MOOC modeled using the BMC

19.5 · Conclusions

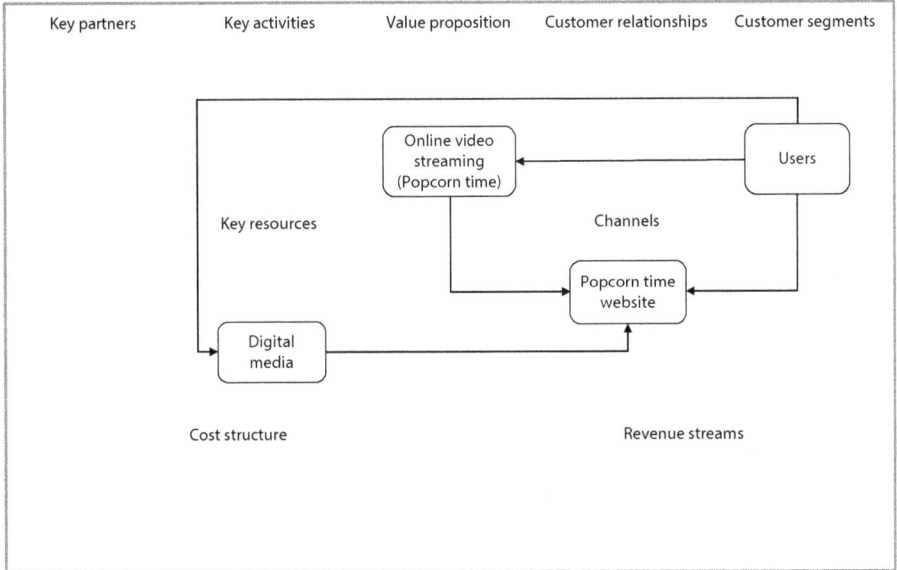

■ **Fig. 19.15** Popcorn Time modeled using the BMC

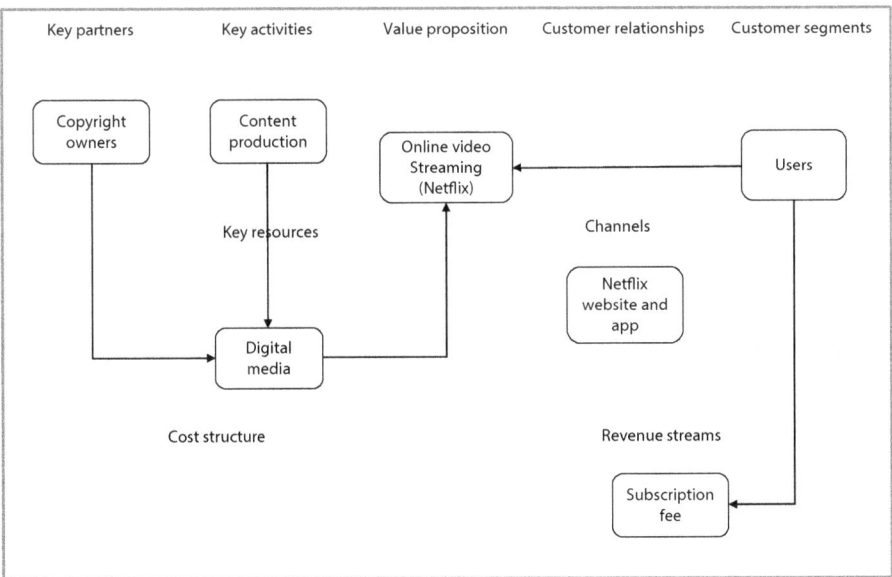

■ **Fig. 19.16** Netflix modeled using the BMC

(c) The major technological difference between Popcorn Time and Netflix is that the former is based on a peer-to-peer architecture, while the latter is based on a server-client architecture. On Popcorn Time, content is streamed from a network of users (BitTorrent technology). On Netflix, content is streamed from a server owned by Netflix. This results in strong network effects between users of Popcorn Time and non-existing network effects between users of Netflix.

3. Data for Spotify December 2020 retrieved from Spotify's homepage, Statista, and Wikipedia:
   (a) 155 million premium users.
   (b) Major costs are licenses to the music industry.
   (c) No—losses were 186 million euros in 2019.
   (d) The three biggest competitors are Apple Music, Amazon Music, and TenCent.
   (e) The market share was 32%.
   (f) The major challenge is how to become profitable.

4. Wikipedia article about Wikipedia:
   (a) Wikipedia believes that ads are annoying and distracting for the users, will influence the neutrality and threaten the credibility of the content, and may generate conflicts of interest between stakeholders that lead to censorship of the content.
   (b) Currently, Wikipedia cannot use the subscription-based business model. This is because Wikipedia uses the GNU Free Documentation License.

References

Anderson, C. (2009). *Free: The future of a radical Price*. Hyperion.
Christensen, C. (1997). *The innovator's dilemma: When new technologies cause great firms to fail*. Harvard Business Scholl Press.
Facebook value drops by $37bn amid privacy backlash. *BBC News*. March 19, 2018.
Osterwalder, A., & Pigneur, Y. (2010). *Business model generation: A handbook for visionaries, game changers, and challengers*. Wiley.
Ovens. (2015, January). What is a business model? *Harvard Business Review*.

Further Reading

Anderson, C. (2009). *Free: The past and future of a radical Price*. Hyperion.
Granstrand, O. (2016). *Industrial innovation economics and intellectual property*. Svenska Kulturkompaniet.
Osterwalder, A. (2010). *Business model generation*. Wiley.

Big Data Economics

Contents

20.1 Zettabyte Era – 307
20.1.1 Generation – 307
20.1.2 Processing – 307
20.1.3 Distribution – 308
20.1.4 Storage – 309

20.2 Characteristics of Big Data – 312

20.3 Use of Big Data – 314
20.3.1 Marketing – 314
20.3.2 Health Care – 314
20.3.3 Algorithmic Financial Trading – 314
20.3.4 Government and Public Services – 315
20.3.5 Insurance – 315
20.3.6 Retailers – 315
20.3.7 Data Brokers – 315
20.3.8 Electronic Media – 315
20.3.9 Science – 315
20.3.10 Data Illiteracy – 316

© The Author(s), under exclusive license to Springer Nature Switzerland AG 2021
H. Øverby, J. A. Audestad, *Introduction to Digital Economics*, Classroom Companion: Business,
https://doi.org/10.1007/978-3-030-78237-5_20

20.4	**Abuse of Big Data – 317**	
20.4.1	Clandestine Operations – 318	
20.4.2	Social Control – 319	
20.4.3	Tracking People – 320	
20.4.4	Violation of Personal Integrity – 320	
20.5	**Conclusions – 320**	
	References – 322	

20

20.1 · Zettabyte Era

> **Learning Objectives**
> After completing this chapter, you should be able to:
> — Understand the basic concepts related to big data.
> — Identify business opportunities offered by the big data technology.
> — Explain how big data can be abused.

20.1 Zettabyte Era

Generation, processing, distribution, and storage of data have undergone major transformations during the last 30 years (Hilbert & López, 2011; Cisco Annual Internet Report (2018–2023) White Paper. Published March 9, 2020) (the data below are based on raw data from these two sources).

20.1.1 Generation

In 1993, only 3% of all data stored was digital; the rest was stored on analog media such as books, cassettes, and video tapes. In 2007, this number had increased to 84%. Today, almost all data is available in a digital format. The main reasons are that most of the analog data from earlier times has been converted to digital data and, more important, that almost all data generated after 1990 has been produced directly in a digital format. The evolution is shown in ◘ Fig. 20.1. The total amount of annually generated data is shown in ◘ Fig. 20.2. The amount of data generated in 2019 is estimated to be 43 zettabytes, and it is predicted that this number will increase to 175 zettabytes in 2025 if the amount of data produced continues to increase by 23% per year. One zettabyte is one trillion gigabytes or 10^{21} bytes. Data is generated by four major sources: imaging (e.g., medical imaging and surveillance cameras), entertainment (e.g., television and radio shows, videos, podcasts, social media, and video games), manufacturing and administration (e.g., automation, Internet of Things, and word processing), and voice (mobile phones and VoIP). Not all this information is stored; for example, most telephone conversations are not stored (Reinsel et al., 2018).

20.1.2 Processing

The doubling time for the processing capacity in terms of instructions processed per second (IPS) is estimated to be 1 year and 2 months for general purpose computers and 10 months for application-specific computers (e.g., supercomputers). The processing capacity cannot be determined exactly since it is a complex function of variables such as memory capacity and organization, clock rate, program-

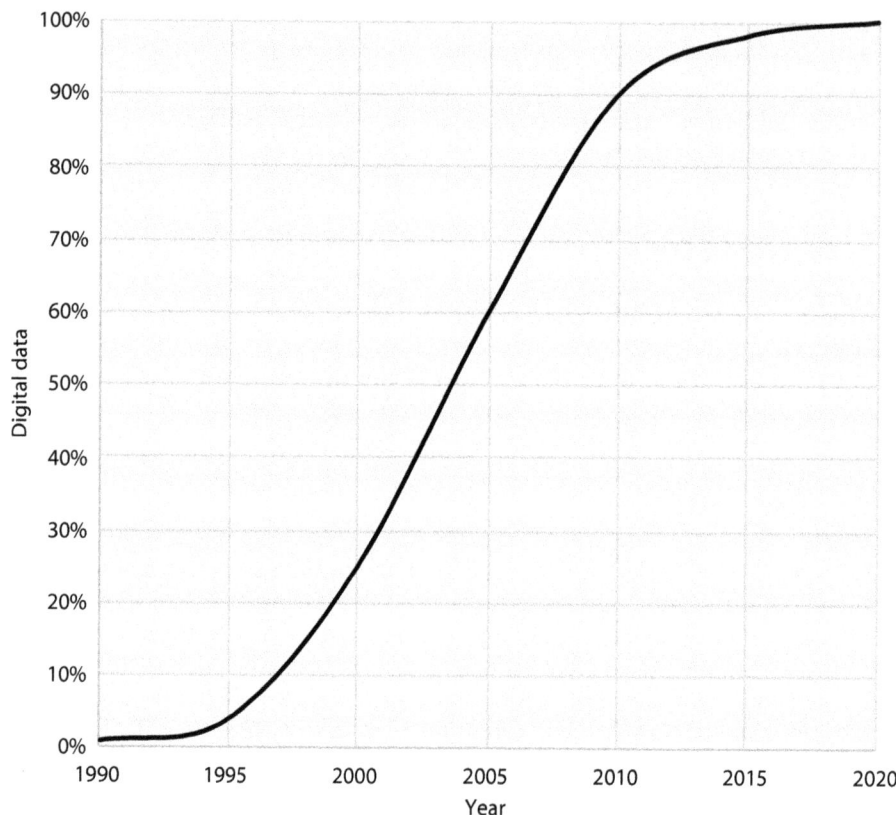

Fig. 20.1 Percentage digitally stored data. (Authors' own figure)

ming language, computer architecture, and operating system. The above numbers are therefore crude estimates of the doubling time for the processing capacity.

20.1.3 Distribution

In 1993, more than 30% of the telecommunications networks and almost all broadcast networks were still analog even though the digitization of these networks started 20 years earlier. In 2020, the digitization is complete, and all information sent over the telecommunications networks is digital. Since 2000, the Internet has become the dominant carrier of information. The doubling time for the capacity of the Internet has been 1 year and 8 months during the last 20 years as shown in ■ Fig. 20.3. In 2016, one zettabyte of data was transmitted over the Internet. The largest contributor to the traffic growth is video streaming.

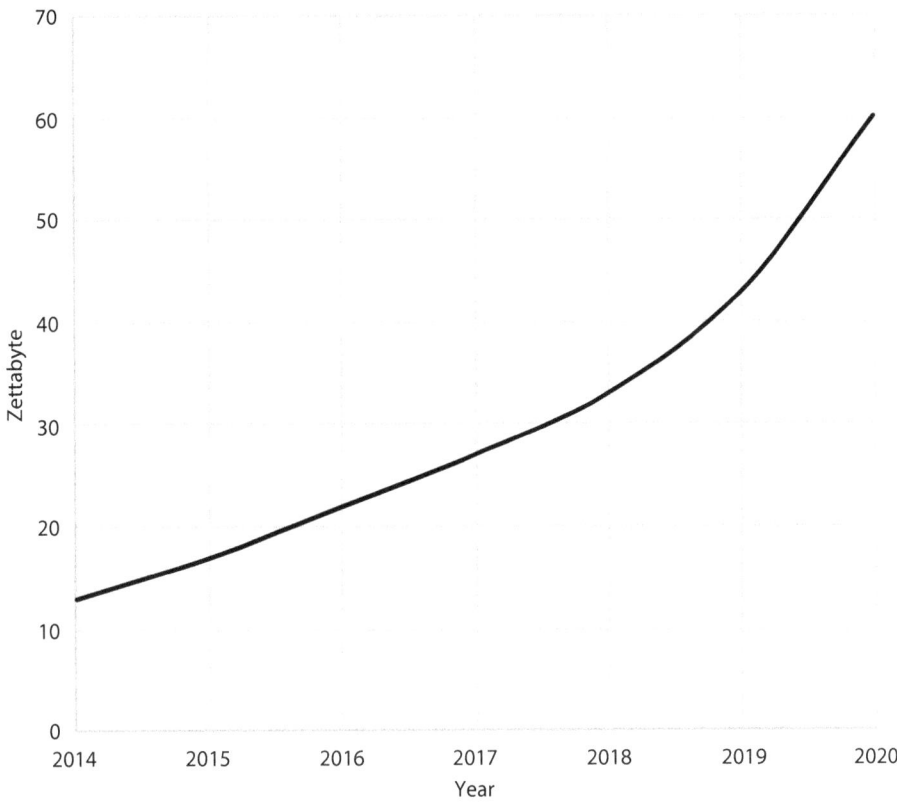

● Fig. 20.2 Annually generated data. (Authors' own figure)

20.1.4 Storage

The amount of stored data has increased by about 30% per year. This corresponds to a doubling time of about 2 years and 4 months. The amount of data stored surpassed one zettabyte in 2012 and is estimated to reach almost 20 zettabytes in 2020.

During the last 10 years, the amount of data generated, stored, and distributed has surpassed one zettabyte (10^{21} bytes), and computer science has entered a new historic period, the *Zettabyte Era*.

The Zettabyte Era has laid the basis for the *big data technology*—the systematic analysis of huge data sets, usually too large and unstructured to be handled by traditional methods. This may be viewed as a possible, though vague, definition of big data technology. Big data economics may, in a similar vein, be defined as follows.

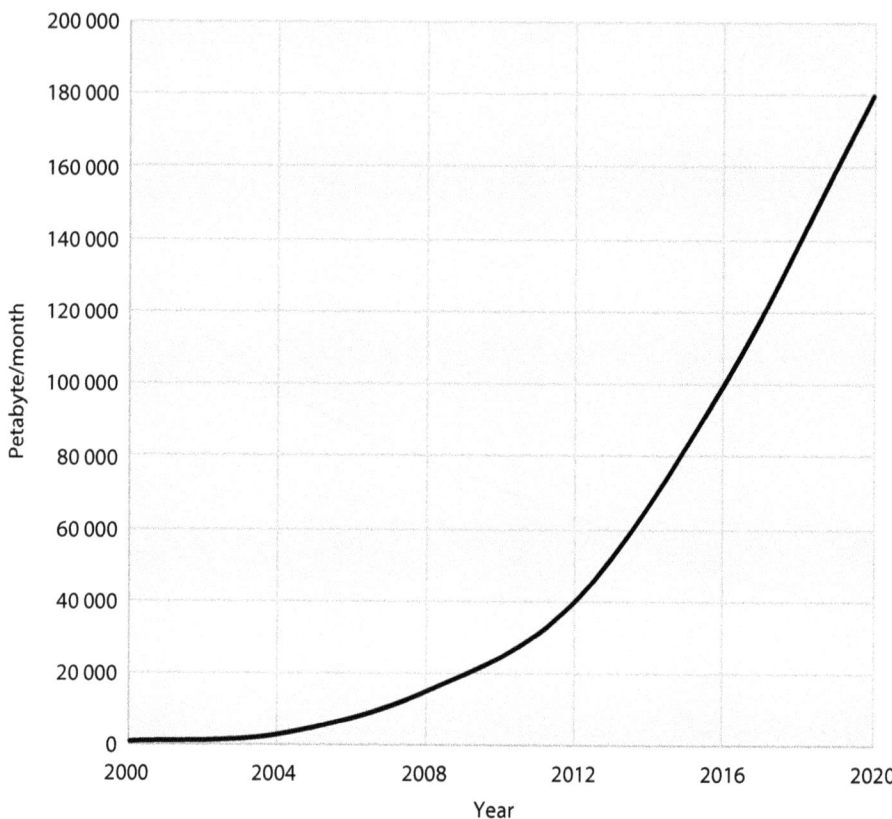

☐ **Fig. 20.3** Capacity of the Internet. (Authors' own figure)

> **Definition 20.1 Big Data Economics**
> Big data economics is the study of how big data can be turned into economic value, where the key value proposition is systematic processing of digital data to detect hidden information that can be used for business purposes.

Big data usually refers to advanced data analysis methods to determine user behavior, to uncover patterns in large data sets, and to extract particular information from unstructured data. The term does not refer to the size of the data set itself since even large data sets may contain information that can be extracted by simple methods (e.g., identities and addresses of persons stored in national registers). On the other hand, the data set must be large in order to contain information that is hidden by structural complexity and, therefore, requires big data analysis techniques to be uncovered. ▶ Box 20.1 lists some of these technologies.

Box 20.1 Artificial Intelligence, Machine Learning, Expert Systems, and Data Mining

Big data analytics often requires complex computational methods and draws on methods developed in other fields of computer science.

Artificial intelligence (AI) is "defined as a system's ability to correctly interpret external data, to learn from such data, and to use those learnings to achieve specific goals and tasks through flexible adaptation" (Kaplan & Haenline, 2019). Big data analysis is not a subfield of AI but may apply methods and tools developed for AI, for example, advanced search algorithms to identify hidden information, image analysis for face recognition, learning algorithms predicting customer behavior that can be used for targeting advertisements and individual pricing, trading algorithms for the stock market, trend predictions, and several other technologies.

Machine learning uses computer algorithms that are automatically updated and modified as new information and experience is gathered about the family of problems to be solved. Machine learning is an efficient method in cases where the algorithms are too complex or infeasible for standard algorithm design, for example, for spam filters for emails and navigators for trucks in automated warehouses.

Expert systems consist of a knowledge base and a set of inference algorithms. The knowledge base is continuously updated by external input and by internal machine learning algorithms where results of earlier predictions are fed back to the knowledge base. The inference algorithms consist of if-then rules to estimate the consequences of a decision (scenario analysis and decisions under uncertainty). Expert system technology may be used to manage business operations and customer relations.

Data mining refers to large-scale data analysis methods to discover patterns and dependencies in complex data sets, in particular, unknown patterns and dependencies. Among the methods used are AI, machine learning, statistics, mathematical inference, and database management. One particularly challenging problem in statistical analysis of complex data sets is *causality*. The purpose of causality analysis is threefold (Pearl, 2009):

- To determine if two variables actually depend on each other and, if so, to determine which of them is the cause and which is the effect
- To determine if two independent variables are correlated because there is a common cause that the two variables are correlated
- To determine if the variables are independent and the correlation between them is accidental

To make things even worse, correlation implies that the two variables are *linearly* related. If this is not the case, the variables may by strongly related, but the correlation between them is zero; for example, if one of the variables increases as the square of the other variable, then the variable are strongly related but the correlation between them is zero!

20.2 Characteristics of Big Data

Big data are defined by the following characteristics (see ◘ Fig. 20.4) referred to as *the four* Vs:
- *Volume*, referring to the amount of digital data available for analysis.
- *Variety*, referring to the richness of data categories. During the Zettabyte Era, stored data has evolved from being mainly structured data—data that is organized and adheres to a specific format—to unstructured data such as fusion of text, location data, video, images, and social media activity. Such complex data structures cannot be processed or analyzed by simple analytical tools.
- *Velocity*, referring to the speed by which data is generated and processed. Big data is usually produced in continuous processes. Some of this data is captured, processed, and published in real time.

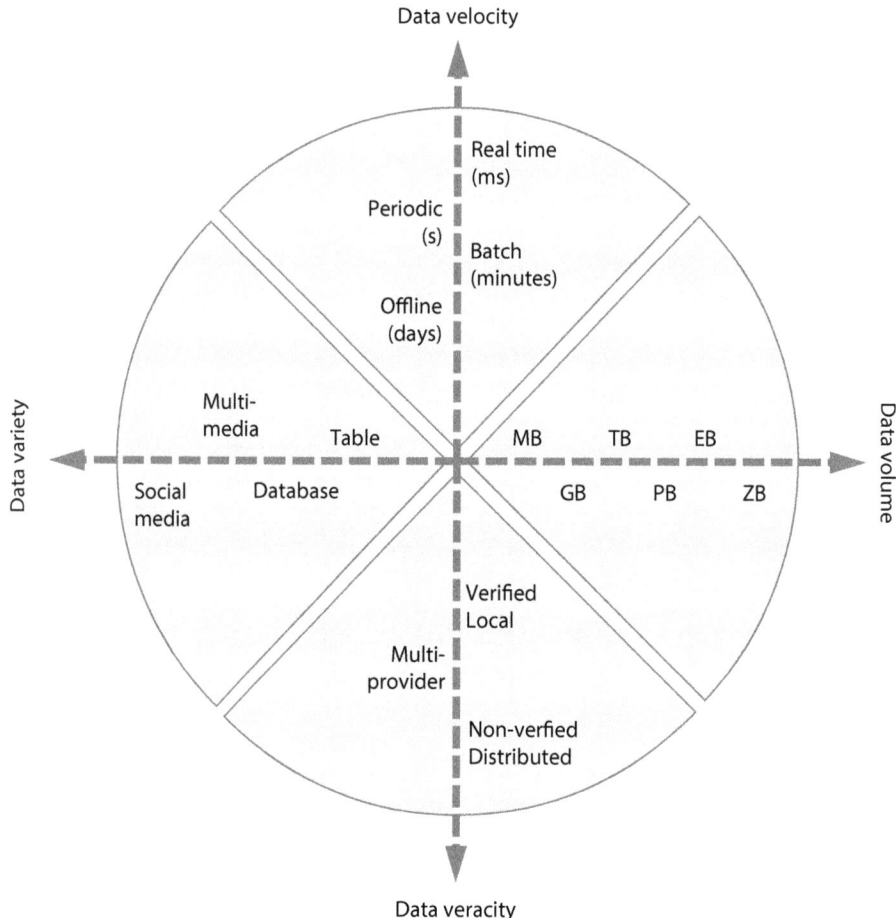

◘ Fig. 20.4 Growth in key characteristics of big data. (Authors' own figure)

- *Veracity*, referring to the exactness of the data. The accuracy of the data analysis depends on biases, noise, inaccuracies, and irregularities in the data set. Insofar as possible, the data analysis should take such anomalies into account and estimate the validity of the result of the analysis.

The huge volumes of data are generated by both people and machines. Data produced by people include photos, text, videos, movies, music, professional content, video conferencing, and chat logs. Data produced by machines (M2M) include sensor data (e.g., measurement of environmental data, health monitoring, and intelligent traffic management), medical images (in particular MRI), videos from surveillance cameras, and system updates and configurations. The annual compound growth rates for the various segments of M2M communication are expected to be between 10% and 50% from 2018 to 2023 (Holst, 2018).

Big data analytics includes tools and techniques to convert vast amounts of raw data into meaningful information that can be used as tradable goods or for optimization or personalization of services offered to users and customers. The input to the big data analytics algorithms is the vast amount of digital data that is collected about users, processes, and events. The output is information used in marketing, business planning, behavioral control, trend analysis, and statistics. Unstructured data turned into meaningful information is the basis for the value propositions of the big data services.

An example of a computer facility designed for big data storage and processing is shown in ▶ Box 20.2.

Box 20.2   The Lefdal Mine Datacenter

Handling the enormous amount of data generated in the Zettabyte Era requires huge installations of processors, storage devices, and communication equipment, sometimes covering several football fields. These datacenters consume massive amounts of electricity, especially for cooling of equipment to avoid overheating. Public awareness, environmental impact, cost efficiency, and social policies require that such datacenters operate with high energy efficiency and at the lowest cost possible.

The Lefdal Mine Datacenter is a company offering storage capacity and space for installation of data equipment in an abandoned mine deep into the mountains in the western part of Norway. The mine offers a cool environment reducing the requirement for artificial cooling. Additional cooling is supplied by cold seawater from the fjord nearby. Moreover, the center is powered only by renewable hydroelectric power from the Norwegian power grid. Lefdal Mine Datacenter claims to be the "greenest" datacenter in Europe (Homepage Lefdal Mine Datacenter).

High-speed Internet communication with mainland Europe and the UK is by fiber cables from the Norwegian coast to the UK and the Netherlands.

The Lefdal Mine Datacenter is not the only cave or mine that has been used as datacenter. Similar centers exist in, for example, Finland (Sverdlik, 2015) and the USA (Abandoned mines have a future as data centres, 2014).

20.3 Use of Big Data

Data abundance refers to the huge amount of data available today. Data has become abundant and widespread to such a degree that it opens up for completely new ways of doing business, including development of new products, building up markets for these products, and finding new ways to earn money. Several enterprises and organizations must realize that their business models must be organized in radically new ways to keep up with the evolution. Data management and analytics have also become completely new industries, offering huge computer resources for data management and specialized expertise in big data technologies.

Some of the new opportunities offered by big data are described next. In ▶ Sect. 20.4, we will come back to questions concerning ethics, governmental control, and violation of personal integrity and privacy.

20.3.1 Marketing

Marketing and advertising are among the biggest applications of big data. By sifting through the enormous amounts of information users place on social media, inspecting how mobile apps are used, monitoring web search, and recording bank card transactions, patterns may be found that can be used in targeted and personalized marketing or to promote sales in new ways.

20.3.2 Health Care

The most important application of big data in health care is computer-aided diagnostics. This includes analysis of enormous data sets to match symptoms with possible diseases and for interpretation of X-ray, MR, and ultrasound images. Big data analytics is also important in medical research to handle complex and enormous data sets generated in research projects and for meta-analysis where data and results from several independent studies are combined.

20.3.3 Algorithmic Financial Trading

Value and availability of stocks and securities in the stock market and currency exchange rates in the foreign exchange market (FOREX) fluctuate so rapidly that human traders are not able to follow them in real time. On the other hand, traders may earn much money from these markets if they are able to react to the fluctuations rather than to time averages. Algorithmic trading is based on fast computer algorithms that can react to changes in the market in microseconds and sell or buy stocks or currencies at optimal instances. The technology requires algorithms that can sift through large amounts of data and make trading decisions within microseconds based on patterns in these data.

20.3.4 Government and Public Services

Governments may use big data to prepare more extensive national statistics by combining information from public and private databases. Big data may also be used to monitor and improve public services. Fingerprints, retina scans, face recognition data, DNA profiles, and other biometric data of own inhabitants and foreigners visiting the country are also stored. These and other data may be used by governments for social control of the population and monitor or expel unwanted visitors.

20.3.5 Insurance

The insurance industry uses big data to predict variations in life expectancy, health costs, and cost of natural disasters and personal accidents using information from public and private databases.

20.3.6 Retailers

Big department stores collect enormous amounts of data about their customers. If goods are paid by cash, the customer is anonymous but not if bank and membership cards are used. In the latter case, the retailer may use the information for personalized marketing. The retailers also use the information for logistics and other administrative purposes.

20.3.7 Data Brokers

Data brokers (or information broker) receive or buy information from various suppliers, for example, social networks, retailers, influencers, app owners, and so on. This may be unprocessed raw data or data that has been processed to some degree. The data broker may then process the data further and sell processed data to other organizations on demand or in the open market.

20.3.8 Electronic Media

Social media, newspapers, journals, and the TV industry use data they collect about the customers to produce targeted advertisements, editorials, and articles. They may also use the data to detect changes in user behavior, increase customer loyalty, and prevent churning. They may also sell this information to marketers (see above).

20.3.9 Science

Big data analytics is a key feature of several of the world's largest scientific experiments, for example, the Large Hadron Collider at CERN in Geneva, Switzerland, correlated gravity wave detectors in the USA, Japan, and Italy, neutrino detectors, and big arrays of astronomical radio telescopes. In all these cases, the problem is to sift through enormous amounts of data to detect rare events that may predict new physics and provide knew knowledge in the fields of astronomy and cosmology. Big data is also used in sport sciences to determine the effect of training, diet, and body functions measured by sensors in or attached to the body.

20.3.10 Data Illiteracy

Big data analytics and artificial intelligence are highly specialized disciplines taught in advanced courses at several universities. Both fields require insight into highly specialized technologies and advanced mathematical methods. The technology and its applications are not taught at business schools. One concern is, therefore, that the benefits of big data technologies often are neglected by the management because of data illiteracy.

An example of how big data can be exploited to create several new business opportunities for a media company is described in ▶ Box 20.3.

Box 20.3   Netflix and Big Data

Big data is an essential commodity for Netflix in its business operations. Netflix gathers and stores data from its over 180 million users and uses this data to discover user behavior and viewer patterns. The data collected is detailed and creates a comprehensive profile of the subscribers, for example, the time it takes the user to finish viewing a movie or a show, devices used to view the show, pauses taken during the show and whether the viewer continues to watch the show after the pause, and which days of the week and time of the day the user is active.

Netflix uses big data analytics to process this data and turn it into useful information. The information is used to recommend movies and TV shows to the users, matching their preferences as accurately as possible. Over 75% of movies and TV shows the user watches are based on recommendations by Netflix. Netflix also uses the information to decide which new content to produce. Observing that exceptionally many customers are viewing a particular series may result in the production of new series in the same genre.

Netflix also uses this information for marketing purposes, e.g., by attaching different marketing trailers to the film or the show that are tailored to match the interests of different user groups.

The recommendation algorithm used by Netflix does not require any direct input from the subscribers. It is only based on information collected from the Netflix servers. The economic value of recommendation algorithms must not be underestimated. They may reduce customer churn, increase the value of Netflix as a marketing arena, and boost user satisfaction. Netflix may be regarded both as a data analytics company and as a media company (Sivasubramian, 2020).

One problem associated with big data is lack of knowledge about how the data can be used in decision-making. Many decision makers and managers lack data literacy and do not understand how the enormous amount of data the firm is collecting about itself and its customers can be used to improve the business. Big data analytics is so new and complicated that it is not taught in management courses and at business schools. Investments in big data may then be useless if the management does not understand how to use these data in decision-making. On the other hand, the output from a big data analysis may be flawed or irrelevant so that decision making cannot be based on the data only; the decision maker must also use other knowledge and guts feelings as a supplement to avoid fatal mistakes (Vigen, 2015). One particularly important observation is that in huge data sets spanning over several categories of observed data, it is likely to find coincidentally correlated data. Obviously, this may lead to wrong and, sometimes, disastrously conclusions. An eye opening and amusing account of such coincidences is found in (Shah et al., 2012).

Decision making was easier before the Zettabyte Era because the business processes then depended only on simple and easily comprehensible data structures.

20.4 Abuse of Big Data

Big data often uses personal data. Because personal data may be sensitive and contain private information that the subject do not want to share, there are several legal frameworks that big data systems need to adhere to. One such legal framework is the European General Data Protection Regulation (GDPR), which came into force in the European Union and the EEC in 2018. Other countries, including several US states and many Asian countries, have lately adopted similar laws. Such regulations limit the amount of personal data that may be harvested. On the one hand, this in turn limits the value of big data, since some useful data may not be collected due to legal issues.

United Nations Declaration of Human Rights Article 12 states: "No one shall be subjected to arbitrary interference with his privacy, family, home or correspondence, nor to attacks upon his honor and reputation. Everyone has the right to the protection of the law against such interference or attacks." One of the key problems of big data is that it so easy to violate this rule and so difficult to prosecute those who do so. One particular problem is that the technology advanced very rapidly, while the production of new laws protecting the users progresses very slowly. Ownership of personal data is in itself a political question. In China, the government claims that it owns all data about the inhabitants.

Despite these regulations and legislations, personal data is used for purposes that may be unethical or against the interests of the majority of the population.

Some examples of misuse of big data are presented next.

20.4.1 Clandestine Operations

Big data is used by intelligence and security agencies for collection and analysis of clandestine information. One example is the NSA-led PRISM program, where the US government collects data from various Internet service providers in the USA and by intercepting all Internet traffic into the USA. A large part of the world's Internet traffic passes through the USA and is, therefore, the best source there is for collection of clandestine information. Close cooperation with the Government Communications Headquarters (GCHQ) in the UK also provides them with clandestine information that GCHQ collect by intercepting Internet traffic into the UK. The program is secret, but the existence of it was leaked by Edward Snowden in 2013 and published in *The Washington Post* and *The Guardian*.

Most of the large companies in the digital economy have provided input to the program, including Microsoft, Google, Facebook, Apple, and YouTube, just to mention some of the biggest contributors.

Another related interception program is he ECHELON project operated by the USA, the UK, Canada, Australia, and New Zealand for interception of satellite traffic, telephone traffic, and the Internet (Gerhard, 2001). Its existence was disclosed by *The Guardian* in 2001: "What is Echelon? A global network of electronic spy stations that can eavesdrop on telephones, faxes and computers. It can even track bank accounts. ... Officially, however, Echelon doesn't exist. Although evidence of Echelon has been growing since the mid-1990s, America flatly denies that it exists, while the UK government's responses to questions about the system are evasive" (Perrone, 2001).

The biggest problem that programs like PRISM and ECHELON generate is that they are not under democratic control and can be misused by the government to control and manipulate the population. There are two major types of information that is intercepted and stored: the content of messages and conversations and the metadata associated with the messages. These concepts are explained in ▶ Box 20.4.

Box 20.4 Metadata, Content, and Privacy

Three concepts that are important in the context of data protection are *metadata*, *content*, and *privacy*. In clandestine data collection, the purpose is to find out as much as possible about the message that is intercepted. This includes not only access to the plaintext data contained in the body of the message but also harvesting as much metadata about the data traffic as possible.

Metadata (or "data about the data") includes identities of the sender/origin and the receiver/destination, URLs identifying the type of content, type of message (WWW message, email, file transfer, VoIP, streaming service, etc.), protocol details (IP, UDP, TCP, and tunneling headers, service initiation protocols, encryption method, etc.), length of the message, and the time the message was sent or intercepted. Even if the content of data cannot be read, the metadata may provide the secret services with information from which

20.4 · Abuse of Big Data

they may infer political, criminal, or other activities by using artificial intelligence or big data algorithms for discovering patterns in the data steam.

Content is the information contained in the data field of the message, for example, the text in an email, bank account details and the amount transferred in a bank transaction, search words in a web search, and the content of a file.

Privacy is the act of hiding the information. This includes encryption of information stored on hard discs and information sent over the Internet. The most common encryption method used to hide the content of Internet messages is Transport Layer Security (TLS) encrypting the body of the message (e.g., the https protocol used for protection of web messages). Better protection is provided by IPsec used in Private Virtual Networks supporting secured communications within and between geographically distributed organizations. Metadata such as addresses and protocol types are not protected by these methods.

Addresses may be kept secret by using the onion router (Tor) where the address of the sender is anonymized. This reduces the value of the metadata collected from such messages because it is not possible to correlate sender and receiver of the messages. Tor is also used in the dark web together with encryption to hide information and make transactions untraceable. The dark web is used by terrorists, criminals, and hackers and for other illegal purposes, as well as for legal purposes such as protection against industrial espionage. If it is observed that frequent interactions take place between two companies during a short period, a competitor may conclude that a new business relationship (e.g., a merger) is planned.

Note that information may be sent in plaintext in local networks and only be encrypted when sent on the open Internet, so that tapping the information is still possible. This possibility is sometimes used (or misused) by the management of some firms to control that the staff is not using the Internet for private purposes.

20.4.2 Social Control

China's social credit system is a governmental application of big data. The Chinese government gathers information about its inhabitants using a vast number of surveillance cameras, information retrieved from online Internet activity, and financial transactions. The data is used to calculate a credit score ranging from 0 to 1000 for every Chinese individual. This score is used to determine whether an individual will get access to particular services, worthy of getting loans, or enjoy particular benefits. It is also used for punishment such as exclusion from high prestige work, only getting slow internet access, exclusion from certain schools, travel restrictions, or included in public blacklists. The system is designed to promote "good" behavior in the population.

20.4.3 Tracking People

Several companies have developed camera surveillance systems for real-time face recognition (See for example the homepage of Innovatrics). The technology is common in China where surveillance cameras on streets, railway stations, airports, shops, and many other sites are used together with face recognition algorithms to identify people (A lawsuit against face scans in China could have big consequences, 2019). This is part of the social credit system described above.

Several mobile apps include GPS location data in the messages they send to the server. To meet regulatory requirements, these data are not coupled to the identity of the mobile user and are therefore claimed to be anonymized. Tamoco is a UK-based company buying location information from app owners and reselling it to customers (See the official homepage of Tamoco). Coca Cola, Uber, and Nestlé are among their customers. This allows the customer to follow the movements of a particular mobile phone without knowing the identity of the user of the phone. May 9, 2020, the Norwegian Broadcasting Corporation showed how easy it is to use the anonymized data from Tamoco to identify a person: determine where the mobile is usually located during the night and during the day, and the owner is easily identified (▶ https://www.nrk.no/norge/xl/avslort-av-mobilen-1.14911685).

20.4.4 Violation of Personal Integrity

The users of social media and other services offered over the Internet usually do not know what data the provider of the service collects about them and for what purposes the provider is using this information. Most of the revenues of the application service providers are, in fact, generated by the information the provider has been able to collect about their customers. One particular problem is that if the user does not allow that data is collected and used for other commercial purposes, they will be denied receiving the service. One case where regulations help is the use of cookies. The service provider must show the content even if you do not accept the use of cookies, though there are still providers who deny access if you do not return the cookie, let you only view part of the content, or do not remove the text of the request so that it masks three quarter of the screen making it difficult to read the content.

One of the most quoted examples of misuse of personal data is the Cambridge Analytica scandal in 2018, where Cambridge Analytica collected information from Facebook which they attempted to sell to the Republican presidential campaign.

20.5 Conclusions

Nobel Laureate Ronald Coase once said: "if you torture the data long enough, it will confess to anything" (Wiktionary). This is indeed a truism for big data analytics. Treated without caution and skepticism, big data analytics may lead to wrong—

20.5 · Conclusions

and sometimes disastrous—decisions. Handled with care and expertise, big data is a formidable competitive tool in the digital economy improving customer satisfaction and perfecting sales and marketing operations by precisely targeted information bulletins and ads.

The challenge is that the firm must possess deep knowledge in advanced data management tools such as artificial intelligence, machine learning, expert systems, and data mining. The result may be that the company is not able to discover and utilize the huge amount of data it may possess about its business operations and customers.

Big data offers big opportunities in several sectors, for example, in health care, marketing, digital service provision, statistics, and management of public services. Large amount of data about people is collected by government bodies, both public and clandestine, by intercepting Internet traffic; receiving data captured by social media providers, telecommunications operators, and application providers; storing information received from surveillance cameras; and storing biometric information about inhabitants and visitors. This information is used for crime prevention, criminal investigation, and antiterrorism. The same data may be misused for social control of the population and for identifying, tracking, and harassing dissidents and political opponents.

❓ Questions
1. Is causation and correlation the same thing? Explain.
2. From which sources do data brokers collect information? Hint: see, for example, *ProPublica* (Everything We Know About What Data Brokers Know About You) and *Clearcode* (What Is a Data Broker and How Does It Work?).

✅ Answers
1. No. That two events are causally related means that one event is caused by the other event. That two events are correlated means that a linear statistical relationship exists between them (e.g., both increase at statistically proportionate rates—or one increases, while the other decreases at a proportionate rate). The events may be correlated because the events are causally related, both are caused by a third event and not causally related themselves, or they are entirely unrelated but varies in the same way (spurious correlation). If the relationship between two variables is nonlinear, then the correlation between them is zero so that causation does not imply correlation.
2. The data brokers may buy or retrieve information from several resources, for example:
   - Publicly available information (e.g., birth certificates, criminal registers, taxation registers)
   - Webpages mentioning the person
   - Loyalty cards for shops, hotels, etc.
   - Membership lists of organizations
   - App owners
   - Dealers of products that can be connected to data about the customer (e.g., car dealers and realtors)

- Media providers
- Search engines
- Telecommunications operators
- Other data brokers

References

A lawsuit against face scans in China could have big consequences. *The Economist*, November 9, 2019.

Abandoned mines have a future as data centres. *Aggregate Research*, September 18, 2014.

For the story in Norwegian, follow the link https://www.nrk.no/norge/xl/avslort-av-mobilen-1.14911685

Gerhard, S. (2001). On the existence of a global system for the interception of private and commercial communications (ECHELON interception system) (2001/2098(INI)).

Hilbert, M., & López, P. (2011). The World's technological capacity to store, communicate, and compute information. *Science, 332*(60), 60–65.

Holst, A. (2018, October 17). M2M (machine-to-machine) – Statistics & Facts. *Statista*.

Kaplan, A., & Haenline, M. (2019). Siri, Siri, in my hand: Who's the fairest in the land? On the interpretations, illustrations, and implications of artificial intelligence. *Business Horizons, 62*(1), 15–25.

Pearl, J. (2009). Causal inference in statistics: An overview. *Statistic Survey, 3*.

Perrone, J.. (2001, May 29). The Echelon spy system. *The Guardian*.

Reinsel, D., Gantz, J., & Rydning, J. (2018). *The digitization of the world: From edge to core*. International Data Corporation.

Shah, S., Horne, A., & Campellá, J. (2012). Good data won't guarantee good decisions. *Harvard Business Review*.

Sivasubramian, B. (2020, August 7). How Netflix became $100 billion company using data science. *Analytics Vidhya*.

Sverdlik, Y.. (2015, July 1). *Start-up to build underground data Center in Finland*. Data Center World.

Vigen, T. (2015). *Spurious correlations*. Hachetts Books.

Further Reading

Ford, M. (2017). *The rise of the robots*. Oneworld Publications.

Net Neutrality

Contents

21.1 Basic Net Neutrality – 324

21.2 5G and Net Neutrality – 326

21.3 Device and Search Neutrality – 328

21.4 Business Implications of Net Neutrality – 329

21.5 Zero-Rating – 331

21.6 Conclusions – 332

References – 333

© The Author(s), under exclusive license to Springer Nature Switzerland AG 2021
H. Øverby, J. A. Audestad, *Introduction to Digital Economics*, Classroom Companion: Business,
https://doi.org/10.1007/978-3-030-78237-5_21

Learning Objectives

After completing this chapter, you should be able to:
- Explain why net neutrality implies that ISPs must treat all communication on the Internet equally and without any kind of discrimination.
- Explain how net neutrality promotes innovation, prompts competition, and supports free exchange of information on the Internet.
- Identify reasons why strict adherence to net neutrality is not desirable in certain cases, for example, to support streaming services and real-time online gaming, and discuss the implications this may have on resource sharing and network performance.

21.1 Basic Net Neutrality

> **Definition 21.1 Net Neutrality**
> *Net neutrality* is the principle that all communication on the Internet shall be treated equally and without any form of discrimination by the Internet service providers (ISPs).

With net neutrality in force, there shall be no discrimination of the transmission of data based on the identity of the sending or the receiving users, the content of the data, or the associated application. This means that data packets transmitted on the Internet should be subject to the best-effort paradigm and handled on a first-come-first-served basis. This also means that the ISPs cannot perform any kind of blocking of applications, data rate throttling of specific applications, or any differentiated treatment of data packets based on the identity of the sender or the receiver of the data packets. With full net neutrality in force, even advanced network management to support service quality is forbidden; for example, schemes that give different treatments to voice communication compared to other Internet traffic. ▶ Section 21.2 discusses why 4G and 5G mobile networks are an exception to the strict rule of net neutrality.

Net neutrality is an important part of the *Open Internet Rule*, in which the Internet shall be open and accessible for everybody without any kind of discrimination. Moreover, under the Open Internet Rule, any consumer's access to or usage of the Internet should not be driven by financial motivations of the ISPs. Net neutrality effectively reduces the ISPs to a carrier of bits between senders and receivers. Any involvement of the ISP in higher layer functionalities or other services is in general not compatible with net neutrality (Murray, 2016).

The term net neutrality was coined by Professor Tim Wu in his paper *Network Neutrality, Broadband Discrimination* (2003) (Wu, 2003) and has been the target of much political debate since then. The main issue is whether or not the principle of net neutrality shall be enforced on the Internet.

21.1 · Basic Net Neutrality

Proponents of net neutrality claim that equal treatment of all services will foster innovation on the Internet—for example, development of new apps and services—and safeguard a democratic platform in which all information is treated equally. If net neutrality is not enforced, ISPs may offer fast lanes to established and dominating application service providers (ASPs) for an extra fee, an action which will strengthen the dominance of certain ASPs. ISPs may also block or throttle Internet speeds for ASPs competing with the ISP's own services, for example, an ISP offering traditional voice communication in competition with Skype throttles the Internet speed of Skype to gain competitive advantage.

Net neutrality is also required to ensure that the Internet remains a democratic platform. This is so because, without net neutrality in force, ISPs may block content for some reason, for example, political motives violating free speech and democracy. Net neutrality is thus not only a technical or economic issue but a central point concerning human rights and the evolution of democratic and political standards.

Opponents of net neutrality claim that net neutrality will reduce incentives of the ISPs to invest in the network and thus slow down further Internet adoption and technological progress and innovation. The ISPs claim that it will be hard for the ISPs to get sufficient returns on infrastructure investments if they cannot charge large application service providers—such as YouTube and Netflix—extra for their enormous usage of the network. Therefore, it is not surprising that the main stakeholders that favor net neutrality include ASPs such as Facebook, Netflix, and Microsoft, while the stakeholders opposing net neutrality include mostly ISPs.

Many countries have passed legislations on net neutrality. Among them, Chile was the first country to pass full net neutrality legislation in 2010. As a consequence of this law, zero-rated applications (see ▶ Sect. 21.5)—including Facebook Zero—are no longer available in Chile. In the USA, net neutrality has been a source of conflict since the 1990s. The Federal Communication Commission (FCC) published in 2010 a set of six net neutrality principles to govern the providers of Internet access (i.e., ISPs) (Preseving the Open Internet, 2010). After that, net neutrality in the USA has been subject of political debate several times. In 2017, President Donald Trump and the FCC reversed the rules, and the USA (except California) is still (by March 2021) without regulations concerning net neutrality (Kastrenakes, 2017; Kelly, 2019).

Six principles are termed the FCC Open Internet Order. Though they may no longer be in force in the USA, they are probably the most concise definition of net neutrality that exists:

1. *Transparency*: Consumers and innovators have a right to know the basic performance characteristics of their Internet access and how their network is being managed.
2. *No blocking*: Consumers and innovators have a right to send and receive lawful traffic, to go where they want, to say what they want, to experiment with ideas—commercial and social—and use the devices of their choice. The rules thus prohibit the blocking of lawful content, apps, services, and the connection of devices to the network.

3. *Level playing field*: Consumers and innovators have a right to a level playing field. No central authority, public or private, should have the power to pick winners and losers on the Internet.
4. *Network management*: Broadband providers need meaningful flexibility to manage their networks to deal with congestion, security, and other issues.
5. *Mobile*: The principle of Internet openness applies to mobile broadband.
6. *Vigilance*: Promptly enforcing the rules to be adopted and vigilance in monitoring developments in areas such as mobile and the market for specialized services, which may affect Internet openness.

In the EU, net neutrality is laid down by article 3 of EU regulation 2015/2120: *safeguarding of open Internet access* (Regulation (EU) 2015/2120 of the European Parliament and of the Council, 2015). This regulation is a part of the union's Digital Single Market policy and was announced in 2015. The law broadly ensures net neutrality in the EU/EEA zones. However, countries within the union may specify stricter net neutrality rules than those in the EU regulation. This is done in the Netherlands and in Slovenia. The EU regulation on net neutrality has been criticized for being vague and open up for prioritization of "specialized services" such as remote surgery and driverless cars. Such prioritization is in violation of the principles of net neutrality as differentiated treatment of data packets in the network is needed to improve the quality and precision of such services. Another criticism of the EU regulation is that it opens up for zero-rated applications.

China, on the other hand, has not enforced net neutrality. On the contrary, China blocks or restricts certain services, for instance, Facebook, within China for political reasons.

Mobile systems represent a particular problem concerning net neutrality as explained next.

21.2 5G and Net Neutrality

5G systems may violate some of the net neutrality principles. The 5G technology is an extension of the Internet to mobile devices. For technical reasons (e.g., bandwidth efficiency, dynamic bitrate allocation, and forward error correction to reduce packer-loss rate), the mobile network provider must know more about the type of signal to set up a connection between the mobile user and the network. For this purpose, some degree of signaling identifying the service is required over the interface and in the mobile network. This is called the IP multimedia subsystem (IMS). In addition, the provider may offer different priorities and meet certain latency requirements for different services as shown in ◘ Table 21.1. Technically, this is referred to as quality of service (QoS) management. In principle, QoS management makes it possible for the mobile provider to charge different services differently and to offer different user experience depending on the type of service. This may

21.2 · 5G and Net Neutrality

Table 21.1 QoS parameters for 5G mobile networks

Service class	Resource type	Priority	Packet delay (latency) (ms)	Packet loss rate[a]	Example services
1	GBR[b]	2	100	10^{-2}	Telephony
2	GBR	4	150	10^{-3}	Person-to-person video (video telephony)
3	GBR	5	300	10^{-4}	Real-time TV quality video stream
4	GBR	3	50	10^{-3}	Real-time interactive games
5	Non-GBR	1	100	10^{-4}	IMS[c] signaling
6	Non-GBR	6	100	10^{-3}	Simple interactive games and live streaming (video, podcast)
7	Non-GBR	7	300	10^{-4}	Common Internet services (WWW, e-mail, over-the-top services, etc.) and SMS

Authors' compilation, based on data from 3GPP Specification TS 23.501. System architecture for the 5G system. Section 5.7

[a] A loss rate of 10^{-2} means that at most one out of 100 packets is allowed to be lost on average
[b] GBR = minimum guaranteed bitrate on the radio interface
[c] IMS = IP multimedia subsystem (signaling and packet-transfer management)

infringe with the net neutrality principle. It is then up to national regulations and market supervision to ensure that net neutrality is not violated.

3GPP defines four QoS parameters for 5G systems resulting in seven service classes as shown in the table.

— *Minimum guaranteed bit rate.* Some services such as telephony, real-time video, and real-time gaming require a minimum guaranteed bit rate, while services such as web-browsing services and buffered video-streaming services require no such guarantee. Telephony and real-time video require a minimum guaranteed bitrate because speech samples and video pixels are generated at a fixed rate at the encoder and the signal must be fed to the decoder at the same speed for proper decoding.

— *Priority* has to do with the priority given to packets queuing up at buffers. A packet with priority 1 will be put in the front of the queue but after priority 1 packets that are already queued up. Equivalent rules apply to the other priorities. Generally, real-time services such as telephony, signaling, and real-time gaming should be handled first, while packets belonging to a web-browsing service may wait.

- *Packet delay* has to do with latency. For some services latency is critical such as for real-time gaming, while for buffered streaming services and web browsing, latency is not critical. For other services such as telephony, latency is a problem. The roundtrip delay (i.e., the time from one party finishes speaking to the earliest time the reply can be received from the opposite party) should preferably be less than 300 milliseconds. For communication over geostationary satellites, the roundtrip delay is about 500 milliseconds. At this delay, it starts getting difficult to maintain a fluent conversation without interruptions. For two satellite hops in tandem, the roundtrip delay is 1 second. In that case, fluent conversation is difficult.
- *Packet loss* should usually be kept low for data services. On the other hand, voice and video services may tolerate much higher packet loss probability than, for example, downloading of a web page. This is so because a lost speech sample or video pixel may be replaced by the previous sample or pixel without being noticed by the listener or viewer. A lost packet containing part of a web file may make the file unreadable.

Note that it is not possible to distinguish between traditional Internet services (web search, e-mail, over-the-top services (e.g., Skype), Facebook, Twitter, YouTube, and so on) since all of them belongs to the same service class (class 7), so that the original idea of net neutrality is not violated by 5G. 5G illustrates that full net neutrality may not always be possible for technical reasons. In general, high-quality VoIP, real-time video streaming, and real-time interactive games offered over fixed Internet interfaces will also require QoS management similar to 5G. The net neutrality regulations in the USA and EU open up for this possibility.

21.3 Device and Search Neutrality

Two terms related to net neutrality are device neutrality and search neutrality.

> **Definition 21.2 Device Neutrality**
> *Device neutrality* means that any application should be able to run on any device and that it is possible to connect the device to the network of any ISP without differentiation of price or quality.

The standardization of the technical infrastructure of ICT supports these requirements.

> **Definition 21.3 Search Neutrality**
> *Search neutrality* means that search engines shall return unbiased results to the user and be optimized to provide the most relevant results based solely on the search keywords provided by the user.

Hence, commercial interests such as promotion of paid services or services owned by the company offering the search engine should not be a parameter in the algorithm calculating the results of the search. Device and search neutrality have a less—if any—legal basis compared to net neutrality. However, there have been legal cases where companies—most notably Google—have been fined for breaching search neutrality.

Google was accused of favoring services from their own ecosystem. For this practice, Google was fined €2.42 billion in 2017 by the European Commission (Vincent, 2017). More specifically, Google was fined for manipulating the search results in Google Search to favor results from Google Shopping—a Google service that allows users to search for products on e-commerce websites. Competing price comparison services were—according to the judgment—intentionally put far down on the list of Google Search results in such a way that consumers often ignored these results. This is a clear violation of search neutrality since Google used its monopoly dominance in the search market to favor its own products (Google has over 90% market share in the search market in Europe). Google has appealed the decision. Andrew Odlyzko predicts that device and search neutrality may become "hot topics" in the future representing "the next step" in regulating the Internet (Odlyzko, 2009). The legal case of *EU* vs. *Google Shopping* may mark the start of recognizing the importance of search neutrality.

To make the discussion of search neutrality less clear, it should be noted that search engines are standard devices in newspaper databases, product catalogs, address lists, and social media. For some of these, research neutrality is irrelevant but not for all of them. Both Amazon and Facebook are accused for strongly biased search (Shavins, 2014). Publishers may pay Amazon to get a higher rank in their bestselling lists and to include their books among search results. Facebook is accused to filter news to match user "preferences" based on previous behavior of the users.

21.4 Business Implications of Net Neutrality

The business implications of net neutrality are significant. With net neutrality in force, ISPs cannot discriminate data from over-the-top (OTT) providers—e.g., Netflix, Skype, and WhatsApp—to curb competition with their own equivalent services. Net neutrality works as a barrier and strengthen the division between the business domains of the ISP and the ASP. The ISP has less—if any—opportunities to enter the business domain of the ASP if net neutrality is enforced. For reasons explained in ▶ Chap. 4, full net neutrality divides the business domains of the ISP and the ASP in such a way that the ISP becomes the transporter of bits—a commodity—and the ASP becomes the provider of the services that uses these bits in its service design. This means that the ASP builds its business on the bit-transportation capabilities provided by the ISP and no other features of the network. Therefore, net neutrality has consequences for the business of the ISP since the ISP is reduced to a commodity and cannot enter the—sometimes lucrative—business domain of the ASP. This is one of the reasons why many major ISPs oppose net neutrality. The 5G technology and other broadband Internet access technologies may alter this picture as described in ▶ Sect. 21.2.

The ASP may sometimes be willing to pay the ISP extra for caching parts of their content material closer to the consumer. This may be regarded as advanced network management to increase the quality of the ASP service. In this case, certain types of traffic are given priority over other types of traffic but without discriminating traffic belonging to the same type of service. This can be seen as a "mild" violation of net neutrality. 5G mobile systems are planned to exploit these capabilities to reduce latency and traffic load in Internet of Things applications by providing storage and processing capabilities at the radio interface (edge computing) (Shaw, 2019).

The Internet was originally designed as a "dumb pipe" or "dumb network" only capable of forwarding IP packets. David Isenberg denoted the Internet the "stupid network" interconnecting intelligent terminals in contrast to the "intelligent network" interconnecting stupid terminals in the telephone network (Isenberg, 1997). There is no "intelligence" or functionalities built into the IP network apart from those required for routing IP packets hop-by-hop from the sender to the receiver. Management and control functionalities are limited to keeping updated routing tables in the IP routers. If required by the user application, reliable end-to-end communication is ensured by the end-to-end protocol Transmission Control Protocol (TCP); if end-to-end reliability is not required, the simpler User Datagram Protocol (UDP) is used. These protocols contain an address called port number identifying the software the receiver must instantiate in order to interpret the information content of the packet. Sometimes the port number is unique for a certain service. However, in most cases, knowing the port number is not enough information to distinguish between various services. To do so, deeper analysis of the content of the packets is required. Differentiated treatment of Internet traffic will require some form of deep packet inspection; see ▶ Box 21.1.

Box 21.1 Deep Packet Inspection

Deep packet inspection (DPI) implies, as a minimum, that the network provider reads the UDP/TCP headers to obtain the port numbers to identify the type of protocol being used (shallow DPI) and, if possible, analyzes the actual information in the packet itself (proper DPI).

Sometimes shallow DPI is enough for special treatment of the packet; in other cases, for example, distinguishing between different services using the World Wide Web, deeper analysis is required. Information obtained in this way, together with the addresses of the sender and the receiver, is used to differentiate the traffic; that is, decide how the packets shall be treated in the router queues (e.g., be given priority, throttled, or blocked). Proper DPI is not possible for applications using Transport Layer Security (TLS) such as https since information beyond the port numbers is encrypted and cannot be decoded by the inspector of the packet unless the encryption key has been compromised or provided voluntarily or by law to the authority inspecting the packets. DPI is also impossible for packets sent over virtual private networks (VPN) because these networks are usually protected using the strong IPsec encryption protocol and tunneling techniques where even the addresses of the sender and receiver are hidden so that there is no information available for discriminating the traffic.

DPI is used within local networks both at the sending and receiving end (e.g., in stateful firewalls and for e-mail filtering) to detect illegal operations, intrusion attempts, spam, and malware and to prevent sending of protected information into the open Internet.

21.5 Zero-Rating

Some ISPs, in collaboration with selected ASPs—such as Wikipedia and Facebook—offer *zero-rated access* to the Internet. This means that consumers get free Internet access, but then only for accessing selected applications or services. Put in another way, unlimited data volumes are provided for a specific application to users opting for zero-rating access. This practice is in conflict with the current strict definitions of net neutrality since it differentiates Internet access based on application—one service can be accessed for free, while another competing service requires paid access or are not accessible at all.

One example of zero-rating is Wikipedia Zero offering free access to Wikipedia on mobile devices in some countries in collaboration with selected ISPs (Russell, 2013). The program was launched in 2012 and provided free access to over 800 million people, mostly in developing countries. After receiving criticism for net neutrality violation, Wikipedia Zero discontinued the program in 2018. In some of the areas where Wikipedia Zero was deployed, it was, in fact, the only choice for many people to access the Internet. In these countries, Wikipedia Zero became synonymous to the Internet. In lack of popular services such as YouTube—which was only available to those with a regular mobile data subscription—copyrighted material started to be spread via Wikipedia. This material was mostly removed by Wikipedia editors; however, it also meant that these editors collectively became a central force in deciding what should be available on the Internet through Wikipedia Zero.

Another example of zero-rating is Facebook Zero, a program providing free access to Facebook. Launched in 2010, it currently provides free access to Facebook in collaboration with selected ISPs in more than 30 countries, both developed and developing countries. In Nigeria, Indonesia, India, and Brazil, where the Facebook Zero program is available, more than 50% of the people believe "Facebook is the Internet" (Mirani, 2015). Compared to Wikipedia Zero, Facebook Zero is more questionable from a net neutrality viewpoint. This is because Facebook is a commercial service and not a nonprofit service like Wikipedia. Providing free access to Facebook changes the competition in the social media market and may further increase Facebook's dominating position in this market.

Twitter has also initiated a zero-rating program—Twitter Zero—which is available for subscribers of selected ISPs in more than six countries.

Zero-rating gives the ISPs the power to select winners in the digital markets motivated by how much they are willing to pay for zero-rating access of their service. Even though zero-rating means free services for the users, the cost of providing this service is in many cases paid by the ASP. Consumers, when everything else is equal, prefer services that have zero-rated access compared to paid access. Therefore, starting a zero-rating program for a service may be a way to circumvent competition, thereby creating a virtual monopoly for this service.

One issue concerning zero-rated content is that ASPs may offer access to their websites or services for free also in cases where these services are not the best services for the consumers. For instance, a bank with high interest rates for loans may pay an ISP to offer free access to its website to attract customers. This will have an undesirable effect on the free market for loans. A particularly vulnerable target group for such practices is poor people with few other opportunities to access the Internet than through a zero-rated service.

21.6 Conclusions

Net neutrality has transformed the Internet into a formidable arena for innovation of new services and applications. The technology has also created entirely new business concepts. This includes concepts such as sharing economies, social media, e-commerce, streaming of music and films, multiplayer online games, distance learning, telemedicine, and much more. The main reasons have been that:

- The extremely simple Internet technology itself does not discriminate between the different content the data packets may contain—the Internet itself is completely neutral.
- The evolution of the information and communication technology is characterized by steady progression toward higher data rates, wider range of mobile applications, more storage capacity, and increased processing speed. Hence, the arena for experimentation and innovation is expanding, steadily allowing new opportunities to be explored.
- The Internet protocol is such that the ISPs, in most cases, cannot identify the type of content the data packets contain and for what purpose they are sent. In democracies, regulations also oblige them to treat all users equally. The same applies to services except in cases where differentiation is necessary for technical reasons, e.g., real-time streaming versus downloading of webpages. This also leads to flat price structures independent of application and, to a large extent, also to the volume of data exchanged.

Net neutrality obviously restricts the business opportunities of the ISP. Therefore, the strongest opponents against net neutrality are the ISPs. They claim, among others, that net neutrality reduces the willingness to invest in advanced fiber-optic technologies and broadband networks. Proponents argue that this is, by fare, counterweighted by innovations in new technologies and applications. The proponents include application service providers, content providers, research communities, and consumer organizations.

Questions
1. What are the effects of strict net neutrality on picture and sound reproduction on video conferencing?
2. Why is it possible for operators of 5G mobile network to levy different charges for the telephone service and data communication?
3. Does the Apple ecosystem—iPhone and App Store—constitute a violation of device neutrality?

Answers
1. With strict net neutrality, packets are handled by network routers using the first-in-first-served principle. This means that a packet received at the router is queued until all earlier packets in the queue have been forwarded. Moreover, packets belonging to the same service may be forwarded on different routes with different propagation delay. This results in unpredictable variation in the time adjacent packets are received by the decoder. Real-time video, music, and voice are extremely sensitive to this type of jitter that, in the worst case, may distort the picture or garble the speech.
2. When accessing the network, the mobile terminal indicates the type of services, e.g., telephone call, data call, or one of several other categories. This information is required by the network to allocate bandwidth (e.g., narrowband for telephony, wideband for video streaming) and to indicate how the call shall be handled by the network (real-time priority, minimum required bandwidth, no restriction). The mobile ISP then knows the category of service the user wishes and may, therefore, levy different charges for different service categories. This is violation of net neutrality necessary for technical reasons (for efficient usage of frequency recourses and for guaranteeing a minimum quality of service).
3. Yes. This is because apps that run on the iPhone can only be downloaded from the App Store. Apps not available on the App Store cannot be run on the iPhone. Furthermore, apps on the App Store cannot be downloaded on devices other than the iPhone.

References

Isenberg, D. (1997, August). Rise of the Stupid Network: Why the Intelligent Network was once a good idea, but isn't anymore. One telephone company nerd's odd perspective on the changing value proposition. *Computer Technology*.

Kastrenakes, J. (2017, December 14). The FCC just killed net neutrality. *The Verge*.

Kelly, M. (2019, May 6). Democrats push new bill to write net neutrality into law, but can it pass? *The Verge*.

Mirani, L. (2015, February 9). Millions of Facebook users have no idea they're using the Internet. *Quartz*.

Murray, A. (2016). *Information technology law: The law and society*. Oxford University Press.

Odlyzko, A. (2009). Network neutrality, search neutrality, and the never-ending conflict between efficiency and fairness in markets. *Review of Network Economics, 8*(1), 40–60.

Preseving the Open Internet. (2010, December 21). *Broadband industry practises. Report and order.* Federal Communication Commission.

Regulation (EU) 2015/2120 of the European Parliament and of the Council. November 25, 2015.

Russell, B. (2013, February 21). Wikipedia zero wants to bring Wikipedia to mobile users without a data plan. *TechnoBuffalo*.

Shavins, N. (2014, July 2). Are Google and Amazon the next treat to net neutrality? *Forbes*.

Shaw, K. (2019, November 13). What is edge computing and why it matters. *Network World*.

Vincent, J. (2017, June 27). Google fined a record €2.4 billion by the EU for manipulating search results. *The Verge*.

Wu, T. (2003). Network neutrality, broadband discrimination. *Journal of Telecommunications and High Technology Law, 2*, 141–179.

Digital Regulation

Contents

22.1 Introduction – 336

22.2 Mobile Network Regulations – 337
22.2.1 Fair Competition – 337
22.2.2 Denial of Interconnection – 338
22.2.3 Excessive Pricing – 338
22.2.4 Cross-Subsidizing – 338
22.2.5 Price Discrimination – 339
22.2.6 Lock-In of Customers – 339
22.2.7 Non-Price Discrimination – 339

22.3 Internet Regulations – 340

22.4 Lessig's Four Modalities – 342

22.5 Conclusions – 343

References – 345

© The Author(s), under exclusive license to Springer Nature Switzerland AG 2021
H. Øverby, J. A. Audestad, *Introduction to Digital Economics*, Classroom Companion: Business,
https://doi.org/10.1007/978-3-030-78237-5_22

Learning Objectives

After completing this chapter, you should be able to:
- Explain why and how mobile communication is regulated.
- Discuss the complexity of regulating the Internet not only because of its inherent complexity but also because there is an ongoing conflict between opponents and proponents of net neutrality and the need to regulate the network.
- Discuss why legislation is not the only way to regulate the market but that the market itself, the technology, and the public also contribute to such regulation.

22.1 Introduction

Since the early 1980s, competition has gradually been introduced in the telecommunications market, first in the UK in 1982 for regulating the market for cellular mobile communications. In the rest of Europe, mobile communications were opened for competition in 1992. In 1998, all telecommunications in Europe were de-monopolized and opened for general competition. This development and the extensive use of the Internet have generated a demand for regulating the telecommunications market to make it a level playing field.

Market regulation for ICT can be defined as follows. (Note that this definition is not essentially different from the regulation of other markets.)

> **Definition**
> Regulation of the ICT market is the intervention of governmental, legal, social, economic, or technological authorities, by rules or procedures, to restrict the freedom of operations for market participants (in particular, mobile operators, Internet service providers, and application service providers) and to target the evolution of the market.

There are several motives for regulation:
- To avoid market failure such as formation of monopolies
- To foster fair competition
- To secure that the users have correct and adequate information about the market
- To ensure affordable access to the ICT infrastructure, thereby satisfying collective needs of the public
- To protect individuals against unethical business conduct and abuse of personal data
- To promote professional and ethical conduct of market participants
- To stimulate peer-based service innovation and development of new technologies

The regulations apply to fixed and mobile network operators, user access providers, Internet service providers, application service provides, and content providers. This chapter examines more deeply the regulation of mobile communications and the Internet. These are regulations by law. ▶ Section 22.4 reviews how social norms, the marketplace itself, and technology also contribute to regulate the market.

22.2 Mobile Network Regulations

The most comprehensive overview of regulations of the ICT market is the *Telecommunications Regulation Handbook* (Black & Srivastava, 2011). This section and the next are based on this source and rules applied by the Norwegian Communications Authority (Nkom) (Nkom, 2017).

The main motive for regulating the mobile market is to build the foundation for a competitive market—or in other words, to avoid market dominance by one operator and to stimulate new operators to enter the market. To achieve this, a large number of market attributes have to be regulated and monitored.

22.2.1 Fair Competition

When Europe opened for full competition of mobile communication in 1992, one of the first company in each European country to established itself as mobile network operator (MNO) was the operator owning the entire telecommunications infrastructure of that country—the government-owned de facto monopoly (also called the *incumbent*). The incumbent had thus an enormous initial market power. To reduce the market power of the incumbent as MNO, the authorities required the MNO to commercially separate from the other business areas of the incumbent and that the conditions for interconnecting to the fixed network and for the use of infrastructure components (e.g., to connect base stations and exchanges) owned by the incumbent to be the same for all MNOs, including its own MNO.

The MNO must have access to exclusive slots in the radio-frequency spectrum. The amount of spectrum allocated for mobile communications is scarce, and there is room for only a few MNOs in the same region. Fair competition for frequency resources is achieved by dividing the spectrum into slots and then auctioning each slot to existing or new operators. This allowed only a few operators in each country. To increase competition, the market was also opened up for resellers and mobile virtual network operators (MVNOs). Resellers buy bulk traffic capacity from MNOs and resell it under their own brand to the customers. MVNOs own some network infrastructure but buy access to the wireless infrastructure from MNOs. Resellers and MVNOs need no frequency licenses to operate. The regulation authority enforces competition rules and supervises that resellers and MVNOs meet fair competition in the mobile market. See also ▶ Chap. 5 for more about resellers and MVNOs.

The mobile market is an oligopoly with just a few MNOs in each country. Some of these MNOs may have market power big enough to take actions that alter competition or establish new market rules. These are referred to as *dominating MNOs*.

There may be several dominating MNOs in a country with approximately equal market shares. The main objective of market regulation is then to hinder that dominating MNOs can misuse their market power to drive competitors out of the market, hinder new entrants to enter the market, or unduly exploit the customers by overcharging. The following is a list of competition problems that may arise in the mobile market and must be mitigated by market regulations.

22.2.2 Denial of Interconnection

MNOs are value networks (see ▶ Chap. 8 for definition) that benefit from interconnecting with other national or international MNOs and fixed networks to make their network of relationships between users as big as possible. Full interconnectivity in the international telephone network is governed by rules set up by the International Telecommunications Union and universally endorsed by the member countries. These requirements apply to both fixed and mobile telephone networks.

However, an MNO with dominating market power may squeeze new entrants out of the market by denying them interconnection or call termination. This means that users of the new entrant cannot call users of the MNO and, thereby, reducing the value of the new entrant dramatically. This conduct is also referred to as *denial of traffic termination*. One of the responsibilities of the regulator is to supervise that such actions do not take place.

22.2.3 Excessive Pricing

The terminating MNO is in a monopoly situation since this is the only network in which a particular call can end up (i.e., where the called user lives or are temporarily located). This allows the terminating network to decide the price for connecting the called user, a price the calling network (and the user) must accept. If the price claim is not accepted, the call is rejected by the terminating MNO. The terminating MNO may then be tempted to levy excessive charges. To avoid such behavior, the regulator may set a price cap for call termination, making the prices more predictable for the user. However, lower bilateral termination prices may be negotiated between MNOs to support roaming users.

In EEA, excessive pricing is avoided by the price cap method; that is, the termination price of all MNOs in the EEA region must be equal to or lower than the price cap set by the national regulator. Outside the EEA, there are several countries in which the termination price is not regulated and can be set independently by the termination MNO.

22.2.4 Cross-Subsidizing

Cross-subsidizing means to charge excessive prices for one service (the subsidizing service) and to use the additional earnings to reduce the charges for another service (the subsidized service). The major source for cross-subsidizing in the telecommunications market is high termination charges. These earnings may be used to subsidize another service and thereby obtain competitive advantages for that service.

Cross-subsidizing may, to a large extent, be avoided by price-cap regulation of call termination charges as explained above. Cross-subsidizing between fixed and mobile network operation is avoided by requiring that the subsidiaries offering fixed and mobile services are commercially separated.

22.2.5 Price Discrimination

The terminating MNO may charge lower termination charges for calls from MNOs belonging to the same group (e.g., a subsidiary in another country) and from other MNOs with which the terminating MNO has particular agreements (e.g., bilateral roaming agreements). Such practice may upset competition and should be avoided by regulations.

Price discrimination may also be used for cross-subsidizing by charging low termination charges from own subsidiaries and high charges from other MNOs.

22.2.6 Lock-In of Customers

Customers may be locked in by contractually binding the customer for a period of time and to enforce economic penalties if the customer leaves the provider before the end of the contractual period. This may be done by offering cheap mobile phones to customers who accepts the contract and mobile phones for market price for those who do not. Another method is SIM lock where the mobile phone will not accept a SIM from a competing MNO until the lock has been removed or after a certain time. In some countries, these activities are illegal, while they may be allowed to a certain extent in other countries.

22.2.7 Non-Price Discrimination

There are also several factors other than price that may twist competition in an undesirable direction. Examples are:
- Dragging out interconnection negotiations, thereby slowing down the market growth of the competitor
- Deliver insufficient interconnection specifications, also slowing down competition or making interconnection more expensive for the competitor
- Deliver stripped down functionality, thereby disallowing the competitor access to some interconnection services
- Reduced quality of technical interfaces (e.g., throttled data rate, slow connection establishment, long latency, and so on)
- Unwarranted requirements (e.g., liabilities in case of network failures)

Negotiating the interface between MVNOs and MNOs is particularly complicated because it includes both commercial and technical aspects that are much knottier than the interconnection of ordinary MNOs (Audestad & Gaivoronski, 2001).

22.3 Internet Regulations

Internet played no role in the de-monopolization of telecommunications. During the 1980s, the Internet grew in size to interconnect universities, laboratories, and innovative industries for exchange of emails, ideas, documents, and other information. The Internet was more or less a research network not recognized by telecommunications operators, except that they provided backbone connections between routers at universities and laboratories, thereby building up a global data network without central governance. At the same time, the telecommunications monopolies developed their own standards for data communications: an inflexible and short-lived circuit switched data network based on the same technology as the telephone network and a packet switched data network (the X.25 network) less flexible and more expensive to build than the Internet. The telecommunications operators levied charges for the use of these networks (e.g., a fixed price per data packet sent) to regain investments, cover operational costs, and increase their revenues. The use of these networks never gained momentum since the need for data communications outside the research community was almost absent at that time and the Internet offered the type and volume of data communications academia needed free of charge.

In the mid-1990s, the general public discovered that the World Wide Web offered them opportunities that had never existed before, for example, access to electronic newspapers, public information, and entertainment. Moreover, people could access this information from anywhere and at any time, thereby offering them a new freedom of choice. The World Wide Web was designed for implementation on the Internet, and in order to meet the new demands from the users, the telecommunications operators also started building their own fragments of the Internet to offer web browsing services. This replaced the need for other data networks, and the Internet soon became the only data network interconnecting users worldwide. As a consequence, the telecommunications operators could no longer levy charges for use of the Internet in the same way as in the telephone network.

When the 3G mobile network was introduced in 2000, the application of Internet services on mobile phones made a substantial jump. International telecommunications agreements included the telephone network but not the Internet. This had one particular effect on prices while roaming to another country. While the roaming prices for telephony where regulated and agreed upon by the mobile operators, they could levy any price for data calls to and from users roaming from another country. In several countries, the price roaming users had to pay for data calls was excessive. Moreover, some mobile networks generated data traffic to roaming mobile terminals such as unnecessary updating and messages. The user had no control over this traffic but had, nevertheless, to pay for it. For this reason, the mobile phone allows the user to disconnect data calls while roaming into another country while maintain roaming for telephone calls and SMS. In 2017, the EEA forbid member states to continue this practice: data calls should be handled in the same way as telephone calls and SMS while roaming in the EEA. The home network of the mobile user should inform the user that the mobile had roamed into a safe network and warn the user if the phone had roamed to a network where data roaming prices may not be regulated.

The increased popularity of the Internet in the 1990s triggered the rise of the *cyberlibertarian* movement (Borsook, 2001). The cyberlibertarian's main opinion is that the Internet should not be regulated by international, regional, or national laws. They claim that the Internet—or cyberspace—does not follow national borders. Data packets are often routed over several countries and legal jurisdictions from the sender to the receiver. Data from a single transaction could even take different paths in the network crossing different national borders. The legislation of a single nation can, therefore, not be applied to the Internet. The Internet user, including ASPs and content providers, could then exploit regulation arbitrage, meaning that the laws of the country with the most liberal laws and regulations would be used, for example, by placing the servers supporting the service in low-tax countries.

The cyberlibertarians argue that the Internet should be allowed to govern itself, democratically, and without any central control.

As a response to the cyberlibertarian movement the *cyber-paternalists* came on to the scene. They claimed—contrary to the cyberlibertarians—that the Internet should indeed be regulated to function properly. Even though cyberspace invisibly crosses national borders, cyberspace is built up of equipment—routers, switches, terminals, mobile stations, fiber-optic cables—owned and used by people or companies under the jurisdiction of the legal framework of a country. The question raised by the cyber-paternalists is not whether cyberspace should be regulated or not, but rather whether such regulations could be done by applying existing laws or by developing new laws and rules particularly for the cyberspace.

Today, most academics and decisions makers agree that the Internet both can and should be regulated. Indeed, legal frameworks of many countries have been or are about to be updated because of the widespread use of the Internet and other related information technologies. One major reason for regulating the Internet is to prevent market dominance. Because of strong network effects and that the marginal cost associated with many digital goods is zero, several markets in the digital economy will be dominated by de facto monopolies if regulations are absent.

One example of a de facto monopoly is Facebook. The market of Facebook is not regulated and, therefore, prone to market failure. Dominating network effects and path dependence have turned Facebook into a de facto monopoly as we have deliberated several times in this book (▶ Chaps. 9, 11, and 13). Moreover, the product Facebook offers the users has zero marginal cost and is provided to the users for free. The question is whether markets subject to such conditions can be regulated at all. One concern is that if Facebook is split into two competing companies (antitrust regulation), the market evolution will most likely follow a path where one of them ends up as a new monopoly, while the other will disappear from the market. In ▶ Chap. 11, a simple mathematical model shows that this evolution is indeed possible and quite likely.

Other areas of regulation on the Internet are to protect consumer privacy, to ensure that telecom operators pay for their use of public goods (e.g., frequencies), and to stop piracy and illegal distribution of content on the Internet. In general, an increasing number of regulations of the Internet have been put in force during the past decade. These include:
- The General Data Privacy Regulation of EU (General Data Privacy Regulation, 2018).
- Net neutrality as described in ▶ Chap. 21 is by far the most important regulation on the Internet limiting the power Internet service providers have on the evolution of the applications and service provisions of the network.

22.4 Lessig's Four Modalities

Regulating the Internet may not only be done by laws and legal frameworks. The *pathetic dot theory* developed by Lawrence Lessig (Lessig, 1997) defines four modalities of regulation, as illustrated in ◘ Fig. 22.1:
- Legal: How the legal framework in a jurisdiction is used to regulate
- Market: How trade, markets, and economic factors are used to regulate
- Technology: How the technology is used to regulate
- Society: How norms and societal factors are used to regulate

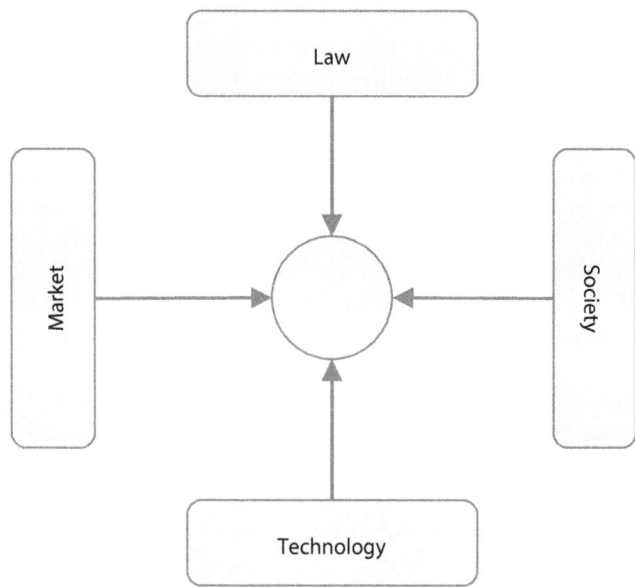

◘ Fig. 22.1 Lessig's four modalities of regulation. (Authors' own figure)

Regulating the digital economy—or a specific sector, domain, or market in the digital economy—can be achieved by using a combination of the four modalities. The principle is shown in ▶ Example 22.1 using the music industry as example.

> ▶ **Example 22.1 The Four Modalities Applied to the Music Industry**
> The regulation of music piracy is used as an example. One key problem in this industry is the violation of copyright and illegal downloading and spreading of music on the Internet. Such actions were made possible by the ubiquitous use of the Internet combined with applications or websites such as Napster and ▶ MP3.com. This was a major issue in the 2000s and still is, however, with less intensity today since a combination of the modalities described above has been employed to regulate the issue.
> **Regulation by Legal Measures:** In many countries, downloading copyrighted material is illegal by law. People downloading and sharing such material may be prosecuted and punished according to the laws in their jurisdiction. This is an example of *legal measures* in Lessig's model to regulate software piracy.
> **Regulation by Market:** In the 2000s, new services offering access to copyrighted media were launched—Spotify, iTunes, and Tidal. These services created a market for legal access to music and contributed to regulating the market. This is an example of *regulation by market*.
> **Regulation by Technology:** The 2000s also saw the emergence of technological copyright protection of music and other media by which copying a specific CD or DVD was not possible. This is the use of *technological measures* to regulate piracy.
> **Regulation by Society:** The last of Lessig's modalities—*society*—is about societal actions to regulate piracy. In spite of the laws passed to regulate piracy, people still in huge numbers continued to download and spread copyrighted material illegally. This was because the general opinion of the public was not to view free music downloading as a crime that should be punished. Campaigns comparing stealing music and stealing cars as the same thing did not have any lasting effect on the public. In many people's opinion, digital goods are different from physical goods since digital goods are non-rival, while physical goods are rival by nature: stealing a non-rival good is not the same as stealing a physical thing from someone. In this case, public opinion is a weak regulating force. ◀

The main point is that regulating the digital economy can be achieved not only by law but also by markets, business models, economic incentives, technology, design, and societal campaigns. These forces—or modalities as Lessig termed them—work together and influence one another. How well a specific service or part of the digital economy is regulated is the sum of all these effects and their interactions.

22.5 Conclusions

Several sectors of the digital economy must be regulated to avoid market failure and to create a level playing field for all providers of technology, services, applications, and content. Regulations also protect the users against access discrimination and protect them against excessive pricing and misuse of information about the users and their preferences, habits, and other personality traits. Some of these sectors may be difficult to regulate, for example, protection against formation of monopolies in the application and content provider sector and the use or misuse of personal information for commercial purposes.

Two of the most important sectors that need regulation are mobile communications and the Internet. The fixed network is also regulated, but this regulation is less and less important as telecommunications now converges rapidly toward a mobile Internet as explained in ▶ Chap. 3. These are regulations by law that are governed and supervised by public authorities. In addition, the market may also be regulated by the market itself, by means of technology, and by public opinion and ethics (the pathetic dot theory).

It is particularly difficult to regulate the Internet. The reason is, as explained in ▶ Chap. 4, that the Internet is divided into two commercially independent domains: Internet service providers in charge of transporting bits and application and content providers creating, storing, and disseminating information and services.

One important field of regulation is net neutrality, shaping the Internet into an open and unrestricted laboratory for innovation and exploitation of new ideas. In some countries, there are strong forces working against net neutrality and for an Internet where the Internet service providers alone determine the conditions for using the Internet. This development may hamper the evolution that have, during less than two decades, created several millions of new applications on the Internet.

❓ Questions

1. Is there a link between human rights and net neutrality?
2. What are the incentives for self-regulation in the mobile market based on Lessig's theory?

✅ Answers

1. Net neutrality is not stated as an explicit human right but is regarded as a must for the implementation of rights such "freedom of speech." The weaker requirement "right to Internet access" is a non-binding resolution of the United Nations Human Rights Council.
2. Incentives:
   (a) Law: penalties for not obeying national regulation legislation.
   (b) Market: the most important motive is to make the total market pie as large as possible by accurately designing the system in accordance with a common standard. This also maximizes the market for each operator both with regard to own customers and visiting customers (roaming). The marketplace then becomes a common in which providers can compete on price and customer care to attract and keep customers.
   (c) Technology: the cost of development of the technology is reduced for each operator if they collaborate to develop a common standard. If there are more than one incompatible standard, then a standards war is likely, and, in the long run, one of the standards will win the war. Building backward compatibility into the technology both in the mobile phones and the network ensures a smooth evolution of the technology.
   (d) Society: Word of mouth may increase the business of the MNO that offer the best and cheapest service.

References

Audestad, J. A., & Gaivoronski, A. (2001). Option pricing of mobile virtual network operators. *Telektronikk*, No. 4.

Black, C., & Srivastava, L. (Eds.). (2011). *Telecommunications regulation handbook* (Tenth Anniversary ed.). The International Bank for Reconstruction and Development / The World Bank, InfoDev, and The International Telecommunication Union.

Borsook, P. (2001). Cyberselfish: Revers, guilders, cyberpunks, and other silicon valley lifeforms. *Yale Journal of Law and Technology, 3*.

Decisions on designation of providers with significant market power and imposition of specific obligations in the markets for wholesale voice call termination on individual mobile networks (Market 2). Norwegian Communications Authorities (Nkom). 2017.

General Data Privacy Regulation. (2018). Intersoft consulting.

Lessig, L. (1997). *Code and other laws of cyberspace*. Basic Books.

Service Part

Index – 349

© The Editor(s) (if applicable) and The Author(s), under exclusive
license to Springer Nature Switzerland AG 2021
H. Øverby, J. A. Audestad, *Introduction to Digital Economics*,
Classroom Companion: Business,
https://doi.org/10.1007/978-3-030-78237-5

Index

A

Access economy 13, 250
Acquisition 212, 294
Ad-based free 295, 299
Adobe PDF 282
Advertisement 79, 106, 110, 172, 248, 295
Age of Conan 284
Airbnb 5, 13, 24, 25, 58, 74, 93, 112, 131, 151, 152, 235, 240, 250, 251, 254, 284, 290, 299–300
Albert, Réka 239
Alibaba 7, 85, 249, 257
Alipay 254, 257
Alphabet 6
Amazon 7, 49, 76, 78, 85, 110, 112, 160, 232–237, 247, 249, 254, 257, 290
Anarchy Online 284
Anderson, Chris 232, 233
Android 24, 25, 79, 101, 249
Anything-as-a-Service 75, 76
Apple 6, 7, 22, 24, 25, 86, 87, 118, 120, 211, 249, 254, 257
– App Store 24, 254
– Apple II 22
– iTunes 247
– Pages 254
– Pay 249, 254, 257
Application Service Provider 48, 52–54, 118, 245, 252–254, 256
Apps 2, 3, 9, 11, 18, 25, 52, 54, 57, 74, 78, 115, 136, 249, 254, 255
ARPANET 21
Assets 136, 209, 251
Attention economy 13

B

Baidu 199
Barabási, Albert-László 239
Bardeen, John 19
Bass diffusion model 57, 261–269, 272, 276, 278, 286, 290, 327
Bass, Frank 132, 140, 261
BBC 35

Benefactors 82, 138, 297, 298
Betamax 169, 199
Big Data 10, 13
Bing 199
Bitcoin 5, 24, 26, 87, 88, 249, 290
Blizzard 284, 291, 292
Blockchain 5, 26
Bluetooth 24, 25
Brattain, Walter 19
Broadcast network 34, 137, 138
Bundling 85, 86
Business model 2, 5, 13, 50, 79, 85, 86, 116, 138, 150, 248, 251, 282–285, 288–302, 304
Business Model Canvas 285–289, 291, 293, 295, 297, 299, 301
Business-to-Business (B2B) 249, 257
Business-to-Consumer (B2C) 249, 257

C

CAESAR 97
Cambridge Analytica 5, 296
Churning 179, 269–271, 274, 278
Cloud
– computing 3, 52
– storage 3, 6, 49, 88, 245
Commodities 84, 85, 253
Commodore PET 22
Common-pool resources 80
Commons-based peer production 93, 94, 97, 100, 290, 297
Compact disc (CD) 2, 87, 88
Complement 12
Complexity economics 50
Consumer adoption 50, 56
Consumer-to-business (C2B) 250, 257
Content provider 245, 255
Convergence 18, 42, 53, 54, 253
Cooperation 68, 77, 118, 119
– horizontal 116, 119
– vertical 116, 118, 120
Coopetition 116, 118, 119
Core competencies 286, 288
Cost structure 287
Crowdsourcing 13, 93, 97, 98, 102, 250, 255

Cryptocurrencies 3, 5, 26, 88, 249
- Bitcoin 5, 24, 26, 87, 88, 249, 290
- Ethereum 5, 26, 249
- IOTA 26
- Litecoin 5, 26
- Ripple 5, 26, 249
Customer relationships 286
Customer segments 286–288, 295, 299
Consumer-to-Business (C2B) 250, 257
Consumer-to-Consumer (C2C) 249, 250, 257

D

Data
- analog 10
- digital 9–11, 34
Dell 249, 282
Device provider (DP) 253
Differential equations 260, 272, 274, 276
Digital
- economy 2–8, 12, 13, 19, 22, 24, 25, 47–50, 53, 56, 57, 83, 84, 86–88, 104, 106, 111, 112, 114, 116, 150, 200, 208, 211, 214, 251, 254, 257, 274, 282, 284, 289, 290
- economy ecosystem 47–50, 56, 57
- goods and services 2, 5–7, 11–13, 18, 22, 25, 47–49, 53, 54, 56, 57, 74–76, 80, 83–88, 93, 94, 97, 102, 106, 111, 112, 116, 124, 130–132, 134–136, 138, 139, 141, 145, 151, 179, 180, 200, 239, 244–248, 250, 251, 253, 254, 261, 274, 278, 290, 291, 293–295, 297, 298, 301
- market 13, 48, 51, 85, 112, 116, 119, 232, 244–246, 248, 253, 256, 260
- photography 7
Digital audio broadcasting (DAB) 9, 35, 182
Digitization 8, 11
Dropbox 24, 74, 76, 245
Dunbar, Robin 126
DVD 88, 115
DVORAK 187, 188

E

E-banking 2, 77
eBay 7, 53, 85, 145, 146, 150, 151, 158, 160, 211, 235, 247, 249, 290, 299
E-commerce 5, 7, 49, 78, 112, 235, 245, 247, 249, 250, 257
EDGE 23
E-mail 6, 22, 75, 88
Erdös-Rényi (ER) graph 140
Ethereum 5, 26, 249
European Union 65
Experience economy 255
Exponential growth 267

F

Facebook 5, 6, 10, 11, 24, 57, 68, 75, 79, 83–85, 88, 93, 110, 112, 113, 125–127, 131, 132, 134, 136, 139, 144, 145, 150, 151, 173, 186, 198, 199, 211, 212, 245, 248, 254, 255, 261, 268, 275, 284, 289, 290, 295–296, 331
Firefox 199, 254
5G 4, 23–25
4G 4, 24, 25, 77, 87, 93, 182
Freemium 293–295
Funcom 284

G

Global system for mobile communications (GSM) 4, 23–25, 65, 77, 93, 182, 183
Goods
- club 80
- non-excludable 80–82
- non-rival 80–82
- private 80
- public 80, 82, 297
- rival 80, 83
- search 255, 257, 258
Google 6–8, 10, 24, 39, 53, 68, 76, 79, 83, 85, 88, 110, 112, 118, 135, 138, 145, 146, 150, 199, 211, 212, 215, 245, 249, 254
- Chrome 199
- Docs 6, 254
- Drive 6, 245
- Gmail 6, 81, 145, 146
- Google+ 88
- Hangouts 6, 39, 53
- News 254
- Pixel 118
- Play 24, 76, 254
- Voice 254
GPRS 23
Grameen Bank 235
Grand Theft Auto V 78
Groupon 249

H

HBO 2, 35, 87, 88, 245, 254
Hypertext Markup Language (HTML) 20, 88
Hypertext Transfer Protocol (HTTP) 20, 24, 88, 94

I

Imitators 132, 133, 262, 264, 265, 267–269, 276–278
Inflexion point 266, 278

Information and communication technology
  (ICT) 2, 3, 5, 7–10, 18, 20, 22, 24, 25, 42,
  47–49, 51, 62, 76, 198, 211, 244–246, 251,
  252, 284
– infrastructure 8–10, 22, 42, 48, 63, 244–246,
  251, 252
Information economy 13
Infrastructure provider 245, 251
In-house production 94, 102, 251
Innovation 2, 7, 18, 50, 107, 262, 264, 301
  , 302, 325
– disruptive 7
Innovators 132–134, 262, 265, 267, 268,
  276–278
Instagram 10, 144
Integration, vertical 6, 212, 213
Intel 19, 22, 115
Internet 2–6, 9–11, 13, 18, 20, 22–25, 35, 43, 47,
  48, 51–54, 57, 68, 74–77, 81, 82, 84, 86–88,
  94, 97, 101, 110, 113–116, 120, 233, 235,
  239–241, 244–247, 251–254, 260, 261, 282,
  283, 287, 292, 294, 295, 324, 331
– banking 76
– economy 13
– of Things 3, 4, 10, 23
– protocol 6, 21, 22, 24, 52, 53, 93, 182, 246,
  251–253
– routers 239, 240, 246, 251
Internet Engineering Task Force (IETF) 94
Internet Service Provider 48, 52–54, 118, 120,
  198, 245–247, 251–254
IOTA 26
iPhone 24, 74, 78, 87, 88, 118, 120
iPod 284

K

Key activities 286–288, 291
Key partners 282, 286–288, 292
Key resources 286, 287, 292
Kickstarter 99
Klarna 249
Kodak 7

L

Latency time 134, 266, 267, 277
Layered Internet model 51, 116, 254
Layering 22
Lilienfeld, Julius Edgar 19
Linear growth 267
LinkedIn 211, 254, 268
Linux 94, 101
Litecoin 5, 26

Lock-in 68, 113, 179, 181–183, 187, 188, 199, 283
Long tail 5, 232–237, 239, 240

M

Machine learning 25
Marginal cost 74, 78, 79, 83, 86, 87, 105, 106,
  110, 111, 232, 290
Market adoption 57
Market capitalization 6, 83, 110, 136, 249
Massive multiplayer online game 141, 271, 291,
  292
Massive open online course 301, 302
MasterCard 88, 112, 151, 152, 249
Merger 142, 145, 209
Mergers & acquisitions (M&A) 209, 211, 212,
  214
Messenger 118, 254
Metcalfe, Robert 139
Microsoft 22, 53, 74, 85, 88, 98, 115, 181, 183,
  211, 254, 289
– Internet Explorer 21, 87, 88, 254
– OneNote 85
– Outlook 85
– PowerPoint 85, 183
– Word 74, 254
Microsoft Disk Operating System
  (MS-DOS) 22
Minecraft 78
Monopoly 18, 62, 88, 131, 186, 199, 214
Mosaic 20
Multimedia Messaging Service 251
Multi-sided platform 5, 84, 104, 110, 150–152,
  154, 159–162, 232, 250, 290, 299, 302
Myspace 112, 127, 173, 199

N

Nakamoto, Satoshi 5
Negative feedback 130, 166
Net neutrality 53, 54, 324, 329
Netflix 2, 24, 35, 68, 81–83, 98, 138, 145, 146,
  245, 247, 249, 253, 254, 261, 301, 302, 325
Netscape 21, 88
Network effects 6, 12, 13, 57, 68, 84, 110, 112,
  113, 124, 125, 129–132, 134–136, 140, 144,
  154, 158, 162, 169, 172, 187, 199, 200, 214,
  267, 274, 288–290, 292, 294, 298, 300, 304
– cross-side 135, 136, 152, 158, 161
– direct 134, 135, 296, 300
– indirect 135, 154, 162, 294, 300
– negative 130, 138, 300
– positive 130, 208, 293, 294, 300
– same-side 144, 292, 296

Network laws 136, 139, 142
New York Times 87, 151, 245
Nobel Prize 19
Nordic Mobile Telephone 23, 64
NSFNET 22

O

Odlyzko, Andrew 140
Online banking 76, 245
Open source software 93
Optical fibers 22, 246, 251
Organic growth 208
Osterwalder, Alexander 285
Over-the-top services 53, 54, 252, 253, 257, 258, 329

P

Packet switching 21, 22
Panasonic 169
Path dependence 173, 187
PayPal 249, 254
Personal computer (PC) 9, 22, 88
Popcorn Time 138, 301, 302
Porter, Michael 105
Positive feedback 129, 130, 169, 173, 174, 208, 289
Postmates 161
Prosumer 255

Q

QWERTY 187, 188

R

Recommendation systems 135
Reddit 254
Riemann zeta function 237
Ripple 5, 26, 249

S

Safari 254
Samsung Galaxy 118
Sarnoff, David 138
Satellite networks 10, 34, 35, 251
Saturation 130, 134, 260
S-curve 266
The Secret World 284
Service level agreement 246, 247

Sharing economy 3, 5, 13, 24, 58, 135, 250, 251, 290
Shockley, William 19
Short Message Service 4, 77, 118, 245, 251, 253, 263
Simple Mail Transfer Protocol 22, 88
Six degrees of separation 125, 141
Skype 24, 53–54, 115, 118, 131, 211, 253, 254, 289
Smartphones 2–5, 9, 11, 18, 19, 22, 24, 47, 57, 76, 78, 114, 115, 136, 144, 187, 251, 253, 283
Snapchat 10, 24, 144, 145
Social media 5, 18, 24, 88, 109, 110, 113, 127, 132, 134–136, 139, 140, 144, 145, 199, 245, 260, 261, 278, 284
Social network service 110, 132–134, 295
SONY 169
Spotify 2, 24, 49, 74, 75, 81, 234, 245, 247, 254, 261, 284, 289, 290, 293–294, 301
Stakeholder Relationship Model 136, 288–289, 291–296, 298–301
Standards 25, 85, 88, 93, 98, 118, 169, 182, 199
Star Wars The Old Republic 78
Starcraft 2 254
Stream Control Transmission Protocol 52
Subscription 53, 81, 85, 87, 88, 138, 160, 180, 291, 293
Substitute 114
Switching costs 179–181, 187

T

Telecommunications 19, 34, 181
– industry 62
– service 35, 63, 65, 160
Telenor 118
Telia 118
3G 23–25, 77, 93, 182
Tidal 245, 254
Toshiba T1100 22
Tragedy of the commons 82
Transaction cost 77, 85, 87, 88, 257
Transistor 18, 19, 22
Transmission Control Protocol (TCP) 21, 22, 24, 52, 93, 94, 141
Tulip mania 27
Twitter 24, 83, 88, 110, 120, 131, 132, 134, 139, 145, 146, 198, 245, 254, 261, 289

U

Uber 13, 24, 25, 57, 58, 131, 151, 152, 160, 235, 250, 251, 254, 255, 284, 290, 299
Uniform Resource Locator (URL) 20, 88

United Nations (UN) 5
User Datagram Protocol (UDP) 52, 141

V

Value 6, 8, 12, 13, 47, 49, 53, 54, 68, 74, 75, 86, 104, 105, 107–111, 114, 120, 124, 125, 127, 132, 135–145, 150–152, 160, 162, 200, 211, 212, 237, 239, 250, 266, 282–295, 297, 299, 301, 302
- chain 104–106, 111, 114, 120, 284, 302
- generation 285
- network 54, 104, 108–111, 120, 151, 160, 250, 284, 302
- proposition 47, 75, 286–293, 295, 297, 299, 301
- shop 104, 107, 120

Video cassette recorder (VCR) 169, 199
Video home system 169, 199
Virtual network operator 68, 198, 252
- mobile 71
Virtualization 52
Voice-over-IP 86, 253, 254
Vortex 76

W

WeChat 118, 253, 254
WhatsApp 118, 211, 212, 254
WiFi 24, 25, 86–88, 93, 251
Wikimedia Foundation 298
Wikipedia 24, 74, 81, 82, 94, 138, 145, 146, 235, 245, 289, 290, 297–298, 301, 304, 331
World of Warcraft 13, 82, 131, 145, 146, 254, 271, 284, 290–292
World Wide Web (WWW) 19, 20, 24, 51, 93, 245

Y

YouTube 10, 24, 131, 132, 145, 146, 187, 198, 211, 254, 325

Z

Zero ARPU 83, 290, 296
Zero marginal cost 13, 54, 74, 78, 83, 84, 86, 106, 110, 232, 234, 254, 290
Zipf's law 236, 237

GPSR Compliance

The European Union's (EU) General Product Safety Regulation (GPSR) is a set of rules that requires consumer products to be safe and our obligations to ensure this.

If you have any concerns about our products, you can contact us on

ProductSafety@springernature.com

In case Publisher is established outside the EU, the EU authorized representative is:

Springer Nature Customer Service Center GmbH
Europaplatz 3
69115 Heidelberg, Germany

www.ingramcontent.com/pod-product-compliance
Ingram Content Group UK Ltd.
Pitfield, Milton Keynes, MK11 3LW, UK
UKHW022152230426